Political Bodies

The Bucknell Studies in Latin American Literature and Theory
Series Editor: Aníbal González, Pennsylvania State University

The literature of Latin America, with its intensely critical, self-questioning, and experimental impulses, is currently one of the most influential in the world. In its earlier phases, this literary tradition produced major writers, such as Bartolomé de las Casas, Bernal Díaz del Castillo, the Inca Garcilaso, Sor Juana Inés de la Cruz, Andrés Bello, Gertrudis Gómez de Avellaneda, Domingo F. Sarmiento, José Martí, and Rubén Darío. More recently, writers from the U.S. to China, from Britain to Africa and India, and of course from the Iberian Peninsula, have felt the impact of the fiction and the poetry of such contemporary Latin American writers as Borges, Cortázar, García Márquez, Guimarães Rosa, Lezama Lima, Neruda, Vargas Llosa, Paz, Poniatowska, and Lispector, among many others. Dealing with far-reaching questions of history and modernity, language and selfhood, and power and ethics, Latin American literature sheds light on the many-faceted nature of Latin American life, as well as on the human condition as a whole.

The aim of this series of books is to provide a forum for the best criticism on Latin American literature in a wide range of critical approaches, with an emphasis on works that productively combine scholarship with theory. Acknowledging the historical links and cultural affinities between Latin American and Iberian literatures, the series welcomes consideration of Spanish and Portuguese texts and topics, while also providing a space of convergence for scholars working in Romance studies, comparative literature, cultural studies, and literary theory.

Titles in Series

César Augusto Salgado, *From Modernism to Neobaroque: Joyce and Lezama Lima*

Robert Ignacio Díaz, *Unhomely Rooms: Foreign Tongues and Spanish American Literature*

Mario Santana, *Foreigners in the Homeland: The Latin American New Novel in Spain, 1962–1974*

Ronald J. Friis, *José Emilio Pacheco and the Poets of the Shadows*

Robert T. Conn, *The Politics of Philology: Alfonso Reyes and the Invention of the Latin American Literary Tradition*

Andrew Bush, *The Routes of Modernity: Spanish American Poetry from the Early Eighteenth to the Mid-Nineteenth Century*

Santa Arias and Mariselle Meléndez, *Mapping Colonial Spanish America: Places and Commonplaces of Identity, Culture, and Experience*

Alice A. Nelson, *Political Bodies: Gender, History, and the Struggle for Narrative Power in Recent Chilean Literature*

Julia Kushigan, *Reconstructing Childhood: Strategies of Reading for Culture and Gender in the Spanish American Bildungsroman*

Political Bodies

Gender, History,
and the Struggle
for Narrative Power
in Recent Chilean Literature

Alice A. Nelson

Lewisburg
Bucknell University Press
London: Associated University Presses

© 2002 Alice A. Nelson

All rights reserved. Authorization to photocopy items for internal or personal use, or the internal or personal use of specific clients, is granted by the copyright owner, provided that a base fee of $10.00, plus eight cents per page, per copy is paid directly to the Copyright Clearance Center, 222 Rosewood Dr., Danvers, Massachusetts 01923. [0-8387-5503-8/02 $10.00 + 8¢ pp, pc.]

Associated University Presses
2010 Eastpark Boulevard
Cranbury, NJ 08512

Associated University Presses
16 Barter Street
London WC1A 2AH, England

Associated University Presses
P.O. Box 338, Port Credit
Mississauga, Ontario
Canada L5G 4L8

The paper used in this publication meets the requirements of the American National Standard for Permanence of Paper for Printed Library Materials Z39.48-1984.

Library of Congress Cataloging-in-Publication Data

Nelson, Alice A., 1964–
    Political bodies : gender, history, and the struggle for narrative power in recent Chilean literature / Alice A. Nelson.
       p. cm. — (The Bucknell studies in Latin American literature and theory)
    Includes bibliographical references and index.
    ISBN 0-8387-5503-8 (alk. paper)
    1. Chilean literature—20th century—History and criticism. 2. Politics in literature. 3. Politics and literature—Chile. 4. Chile—History—Coup d'état, 1973—Literature and the coup. I. Title. II. Series.

PQ7955 .N45 2002
860.9'358—dc21

2002018431

PRINTED IN THE UNITED STATES OF AMERICA

For Pat

Contents

Prologue	9
Acknowledgments	13
Note on Translations	17
1. Introduction	21
2. The Disappeared Body and the Exiled Voice: Displacement and the Struggle for Narrative Power	49
3. The Hungry Body and Patchwork Histories	82
4. Erotic Desire and Bodily Violence	116
5. The Social Body and the Rebirth of History	148
6. Of Bodiless Spirits and the Transition to Democracy	193
7. Epilogue	220
Notes	235
Bibliography	275
Index	292

Prologue

The Pinochet dictatorship indelibly marked every aspect of Chilean society in ways we have only begun to understand today, nearly thirty years after its violent inception with the 11 September 1973 coup d'état, and well over a decade after Pinochet's defeat in the 1988 plebiscite. For many, the Pinochet years have come to signify one of the most painful periods in the country's history. The regime's systematic campaign of terror—including disappearances, torture, exile, and intimidation—designed to eliminate the political left, held devastating consequences for an untold number of people. The period also marked the inauguration of Chile's radical neoliberal economic experiment, whose ostensible success augured an entire wave of IMF and World Bank "structural adjustment" packages throughout Latin America and the world. Coupled with political authoritarianism, economic neoliberalism virtually guaranteed rewards for the elite, and ensured that those most harmed by its neo-Darwinian market-based principles would stay "safely" on the margins of the dominant social order.

But perhaps the most subtle and disturbing lessons of the Pinochet years have only more fully emerged since Chile's return to democracy, revealing the multiple internalized forms of authoritarianism still embedded deeply within the social fabric of the country. While the octogenarian former dictator may never have to stand trial in Chile, it is clear that his legacy has far transcended the materiality of his own body. Some Chileans speak of "pinochetismo sin Pinochet," authoritarianism without the dictator himself, as having characterized the first several years of the democratic transition. I take this to include phenomena as diverse as the silences created by the nature of "kid-glove" consensus and reconciliation during the first two governments of the center-left Concertación; the constitutional and legal mechanisms that institutionalized military impunity and the right's disproportionate political influence; the seeming triumph of individualism and consumer culture in the country at large; and a marked fatigue or cynicism toward politics and historical memory, variously expressed across generational, class, and political differences. The collective will to move beyond, or even to forget, the pain of *pinochetismo* in its many forms—which Tomás Moulian has called "el blanqueo" or "whitewashing" of Chile[1]— seems both symptomatic of, and a natural reaction to, the two decades of resistance and compromise involved in reestablishing democracy at all. It is ironically fitting, however, that Pinochet's 503 days of house arrest in London in 1998–99, followed by his return to Chile, loss of immunity, and house arrest there, have provided a powerful catalyst for Chileans to begin to address the limited scope and character that their democracy has taken since 1989.[2]

At the same time that the Pinochet years were among the country's most overtly repressive, however, they were also a time of enormous resilience and creativity exercised by those most threatened by the regime itself. Groups organized around human rights or subsistence issues, many of them initiated by working-class women, resisted the regime's efforts to eliminate entire sectors of the population from the dominant (military, masculinist) national narrative. They insistently embodied alternative values, and told a different story, in cultural forms ranging from *arpilleras* to the *cueca sola*. During the late 1970s and early 1980s, middle-class women joined these working-class women in the creation of an allied feminist movement, which in turn became visible among the variously (re)composed sectors of the opposition during the National Protests of 1983–84. Although fragmentation and disunity characterize many of these groups today—indeed, the emergent sectors of resistance under Pinochet have become, for a variety of reasons, the mostly hidden sectors of the institutional democracy—it is important to remember that this slowly growing network of "new social movements"[3] during the 1970s and 1980s in effect paved the way for Chileans to vote the dictator out of office in 1988.

In the context in which the future of Chile was being contested and radically reconceived within these new social movements, those literary authors most attuned to the opposition began to respond to the challenge and vitality of these sectors within their work. Such writers began to produce an extraordinary new literature, urgently waging what Jean Franco has termed "struggles for interpretive power."[4] Although many extant systems of representation had been overtly appropriated by the regime, these writers attempted, like the social movements themselves, to tell another story—to contest and rewrite local history—in such a way as to imagine a future without Pinochet. This book explores that literature within the complex historical and social conditions of its production. I have chosen not to restrict myself to those generations that began to write for the first time during the 1980s or the 1990s, authors of the so-called "nueva narrativa chilena" [new Chilean narrative].[5] Instead, I have found it more interesting to look at the ways in which progressive writers of older and younger generations responded to the challenges posed by the resistance culture after 1973. By no means did all writers respond, but among those who did, how did the postcoup years move them?

I have chosen to focus, then, on works by five authors: Ariel Dorfman, David Benavente and the Taller de Investigación Teatral [Investigative Theater Workshop], Pía Barros, Diamela Eltit, and Isabel Allende. I have selected this group to include members of the two literary generations most immediately marked by the Popular Unity experience and by the coup, writers working inside and outside the country, men and women sharing feminist-oriented concerns with social structures of power (including gender, class, and language itself), while also displaying significant aesthetic differences. Perhaps most crucially, I chose these five writers because they illustrate particularly well issues concerning the body as a real and symbolic terrain for contesting and rewriting the national narrative in the postcoup years. In this regard, their work breaks down the text/context distinction, joining with a range of alternative cultural forms (e.g., *arpilleras*, poetry, performance, demonstrations) developed by excluded communities to reaffirm their capacity to speak for themselves, to participate in the real and symbolic life of the nation. At the same time, my choice of these particular writers is somewhat arbitrary (as I could have achieved a similar balance with different authors and forms), and like any such decisions, ultimately circumscribes the kinds of conclusions available through analysis. Nevertheless, my hope is that the reader will find that the vision that these authors' works have allowed me to develop, while of course partial and incomplete, is suggestive of several salient dilemmas posed by postcoup culture overall. My intention is not to romanticize a moment in Chilean history or culture, but to understand its complex relevance for Chile today.

In the following pages, my hypothesis is that the cultural forms of resistance produced during the Pinochet years contained the seeds of what was to come: the achievements, and especially the shortcomings, of the democratic transition itself. The failings of these five authors—despite extraordinary efforts—to narrate a different future in a sense anticipated the failings of the Chilean opposition, from the late 1980s through the present Concertación. By focusing outside the cupolas of power in the legislative or executive branches of government, by looking instead to the stories Chileans have "told themselves about themselves" (the phrase is Clifford Geertz's),[6] I hope to illuminate precisely those aspects of Chilean resistance culture most resolutely forgotten during the first decade of the democratic transition. This, then, is an act of counter-memory, written in support of those who seek to demythologize the legacy of the postcoup years and to build a more progressive Chilean society into the twenty-first century.

Acknowledgments

There are several people and institutions to whom I owe special thanks for their assistance and encouragement during my completion of this project. I wish to thank the Tinker Foundation, the Andrew W. Mellon Foundation, and Duke University for funding various parts of my research and writing from 1989-1992, and The Evergreen State College for research and travel funds granted between 1995 and 1999. I owe thanks to those who graciously granted interviews, and in some instances access to private resources, during my research in Chile: the late Mariano Aguirre, Eugenio Ahumada, Pía Barros, David Benavente, Soledad Bianchi, Poli Délano, Erwin Díaz, Ariel Dorfman, Diamela Eltit, Alejandra Farías, Mónica González, Olga Grau, Carlos Mellado, Raquel Olea, Margarita Pisano, Nadia Prado, María Antonieta Saa, Adriana Santa Cruz, Coti Silva, Antonio Skármeta, Malú Urriola, the late Mercedes Valdivieso, José Zalaquett, and Raúl Zurita; members of the Agrupación de Familiares de Detenidos-Desaparecidos [Association of Family Members of the Detained-Disappeared], the Vicaría de la Solidaridad [Vicariate of Solidarity], and Compartiendo la Mesa [Sharing the Table], an organization supporting soup kitchens; the Taller "Los Almendros" and Taller "Sector Sur" (both artisans' workshops producing *arpilleras*); the literary workshops at Ergo Sum (with Pía Barros), at the Sociedad de Escritores de Chile [Chilean Writers' Society] with Edmundo Herrera, and in the shantytown Lo Hermida (with Pedro Araucana); and the group Lectura de Mujeres [Women's Reading Group] at La Morada.

Many thanks to those who granted permission to quote extensively from their work, particularly: Pía Barros (from *Miedos transitorios [de a uno, de a dos, de a todos]* [Santiago: Ergo Sum 1986], *A horcajadas,* introduction by Juan Carlos Lértora [Santiago: Mosquito Editores, 1990], and *A horcajadas/Astride,* translated and edited by Analisa Taylor, with translations by Amanda Powell and others [Santiago: Editorial Asterión, 1992]), together with Analisa Taylor (for excerpts from the translation *A horcajadas/ Astride*); David Benavente (for material from ICTUS, David Benavente, and TIT, *Pedro, Juan y Diego/Tres Marías y una Rosa,* "Ave Félix" [Santiago: CESOC Ediciones Chile América, 1989]); Ariel Dorfman (for quotes from the poem "Esperanza," *Desaparecer/Aus der Augen verlieren* [Bornheim-Merten: Lamuv Verlag, 1979], the novel *Viudas* [1981], 2d ed. [Buenos Aires: Siglo XXI, 1985], and its translation, *Widows,* translated by Stephen Kessler [New York: Vintage, 1984], together with Stephen J. Kessler for excerpts from the translation *Widows;* Diamela Eltit (for material from *Lumpérica* [Santiago: Ediciones del Ornitorrinco, 1983], *E. Luminata,* translation and afterword by Ronald Christ [Sante Fe, N.M.: Lumen, 1997], *Por la patria* [Santiago: Ediciones del Ornitorrinco, 1986], *El cuarto mundo* [Santiago: Editorial Planeta Biblioteca del Sur, 1988], and *The Fourth World,* translation and foreword by Dick Gerdes [Lincoln: University of Nebraska Press, 1995]), together with Ronald Christ for quotes from *E. Luminata* and Elaine Maruhn of the University of Nebraska Press for material from *The Fourth World.* I am grateful to the artist Guillermo Núñez for permission to reprint his painting *¿Qué hay en el fondo de tus ojos?* [What's there, deep in your eyes?] on the book's cover.

I thank all those who read the manuscript in its entirety and offered challenging suggestions at various stages in its preparation. In particular, my work has benefited from many years of unwavering engagement and generous support by Ariel Dorfman and Kathleen Ross, my original dissertation advisors, and insightful comments by Alice Y. Kaplan, Gustavo Pérez-Firmat, and Daniel James, my committee members. Over the years, they have continued to be both inspiring mentors and supportive friends. I am grateful as well for the discerning feedback offered by other colleagues and friends, including Verónica Feliú, Peta Henderson, Patrick Hub, Manuel Jofré, Greg Mullins, Jean O'Barr, Alejandro Rupert, Therese Saliba, Naomi Schor, Silvia Tandeciarz, Tom Womeldorff, the anonymous reviewers of the manuscript, and Aníbal González Pérez, the wonderful series editor for Bucknell University Press. Several of my team-teaching partners at The Evergreen State College shaped this book in ways they may not even be aware; I especially thank Nancy Allen, Caryn Cline, José Gómez, Peta Henderson, Hiro Kawasaki, Josie Reed, Therese Saliba, and Tom Womeldorff for their varied and stimulating perspectives on the social meaning of cultural forms. I also thank my students at Evergreen, especially in the programs "Self-Determination" and "Political Bodies," for their engagement with many of the ideas contained here. While the book is stronger for the impact of all these people on it, I am of course ultimately responsible for its perspectives and limitations.

It is always most difficult to find words adequate to thank those nearest by, without whom not only academic work, but most essentially, daily living, would be far less rich and rewarding. For those who offered friendship and hospitality to me in Chile—Queno, Alejandra, Carlos, Erwin, Pepe, Soledad, Dánica and Emilio, Elizabeth and Tomás, Ariel and Angélica—I am very grateful. I also thank those who gave substantial encouragement during the various stages of this project, especially Gayle and Silvia in Durham; Nancy, Tom, Therese, Peta, Josie, Greg, Jean, R&E, and Marv in Olympia; and Alex, from many locations. I thank my parents and family for their constant support, and occasional irreverence, offered at just the right moments. And finally, to my beloved Patrick, an unfailingly generous and creative partner, and the anchor of our home, my greatest thanks.

Note on Translations

Although my analysis relies on the original Spanish language source[s, I] have quoted in English translation throughout the text. In the case of [pri]mary literary sources, I include both the original Spanish citation an[d the] English translation, in order to provide nuance for readers of Spanish. [On a] few occasions, I have included key words from the original Spanish [in] secondary sources as well. Given the range of discourses I discuss—f[rom] the slang of shantytown women to the complex work of the *avanzad[a]* neo-avant-garde—such references have proven essential for conveying [ap]propriate linguistic specificity in each case. When possible, I have re[lied] on published English-language translations and have referred to those w[orks] in the body of my text by their English language titles; I cite both the [En]glish and the Spanish versions in the notes. In a few instances, I pro[vide] my own translation as an alternative to the published version, and likew[ise] have indicated this in the notes. Where no published translations exi[st, I] have provided my own, but have referred to the work using its orig[inal] Spanish title, after offering a parenthetical, unitalicized title translatio[n at] its first mention. Finally, I provide the original Spanish terminology [for] various Chilean institutions and organizations, but refer to them therea[fter] in English.

Political Bodies

1
Introduction

On 4 September 1990, Salvador Allende received the funeral he had been denied on the day of the 1973 coup. After his shooting death in La Moneda, caused by military betrayal though he may have pulled the trigger himself, Allende's corpse was unceremoniously deposited in an unmarked grave in Viña del Mar.[1] The junta had hoped to erase Allende's memory by leaving no name, no headstone that could become a monument to Unidad Popular [the Popular Unity coalition]. Seventeen years later, less one week, Allende's remains were exhumed from their anonymous tomb and transported to Santiago for an official burial. The city was cordoned off to contain the crowds, the streets lined with metal barriers and uniformed officers. As I walked early that morning along the funeral route, I gradually became part of a sea of red and white carnations, banners of all sizes, memories voiced quietly or loudly. The flow of the crowd led past Morandé 80, the door through which Allende's body had been removed, the door no longer in existence because Pinochet had walled it in, erased it from the official story, substituting for it "The Bunker" (a subterranean entrance named after Hitler's). I was told that the funeral procession would go by that door, extant only in memory, "para cerrar el ciclo," to complete this historical cycle. Eventually, I joined a group gathered at La pérgola San Pablo, a flower store on the corner of Avenida La Paz, the street leading to Santiago's General Cemetery. There stood an arch of flowers placed to receive the procession, with the message, "Hasta siempre, compañero presidente" [Farewell, *compañero* president]. A modest-looking older woman whispered to me, "Me compro unas florcitas, y de aquí no me muevo" [I'll buy myself a few flowers, then I'm not moving from this spot]. I nodded, clasping a single white carnation to the cold metal railing that separated the mourners from the guards.

As I stood there that day, caught up in the emotion of the event, I began to realize that Salvador Allende's funeral was emblematic of the larger moment in Chilean history. It played out a widespread necessity to make collective, public meaning for overcoming the many official silences of the previous seventeen years. At the same time, Allende's funeral reenacted a drama that had become commonplace since 1973: the contest over a body, over human bodies, as sites of domination and resistance, an all-too-familiar terrain of struggle—simultaneously symbolic and materially real—between the civilian opposition and the authoritarian regime. The ability to reclaim Allende's body, denied for so many years, signaled a triumph in the first months of civilian rule, and implicitly opened the possibility that other bodies, other anonymously buried *compañeros*, might also be recuperated. And insofar as these individual bodies progressively emerged from the shadows of official silence, the collective body, the body politic of civil society, would itself regain integrity, in the literal and figurative senses of the word. On that September morning, I realized that the processes of excavation, recognition, naming, and in some cases, burial, of all that died or disappeared during the Pinochet years had only just begun.

During that particular research stay in Santiago in 1990–91, I did witness many more excavations: of human bodies (discovered based on information by witnesses of human rights abuses), of stories of disappearance and death (by the government-appointed Committee for Truth and Reconciliation in its Rettig Report), of denunciatory art (at Museo Abierto/Open Museum and the Encuentro Nacional de Arte/National Encounter for the Arts), of previously forbidden texts (from *testimonios* to Cuban films) and formerly suppressed acts (from Communist Party rallies to an Amnesty International concert in the infamous National Stadium). I also saw some burials with names and dates—acts of remembrance—and some pleas for reconciliation and pardon before responsibility for violence had been assigned—potential acts of forgetting, of "moving on." I came to understand that the overall impulse to unearth publicly what had happened during the Pinochet years, or alternatively, to keep it underground as part of the unwritten past, was simultaneously a debate about how the future might be constructed, about who might narrate that future, about the values upon which Chilean society would be rebuilt.

This ongoing contest to name and narrate both individual bodies and the social body of Chile from 1973 until the present is what I call, in the upcoming pages, the struggle for narrative power during the postcoup years. That is, I have drawn upon a notion of history as a material and symbolic struggle for the ability to tell one's story and the story of one's community, and to enter into social dialogue. In a context in which a single official story had been imposed to replace a multiplicity of voices—"order" was to replace "chaos"—vast sectors of Chilean society had been excluded from collective discourse, officially denied their participation in history by the military regime. Telling alternative stories (and by "stories," I mean communicative forms like performances or demonstrations, as well as texts with words) was therefore one of the most basic functions of resistance culture during the dictatorship.[2]

Moreover, the national narrative continued to be powerfully contested after the beginning of the democratic transition in 1990. Allende's mourners' insistent remembrance of the walled-in door on Morandé provides one small but potent example of this contest over history at the beginning of the transition process. At that time, the very notion of democracy was pregnant (I choose the metaphor intentionally) with a range of possible meanings, including all that the dictatorship was not: multivocality, pluralism, economic alternatives, and reconceived power relations among the multiple axes of society (class, gender, ethnicity, sexuality, and so forth). Though the transition could not conceivably encompass the entire range of these sometimes conflicting possibilities, it was nevertheless not suspected in 1990 that today's institutional democracy would exist within such dramatically narrowed political and economic parameters. By exploring this ongoing struggle for narrative power, I hope to reveal points of continuity and rupture in these ostensibly very different periods of recent Chilean history. For these reasons, I use the term "postcoup years" to include the period from the military coup and dictatorship through Chilean democracy today. In the sections that follow, I will provide the contexts for the two organizing ideas of this book: that the recent struggle for narrative power in Chile has been a contest about gender ideologies, and that this contest has been enacted literally and figuratively on the stage of human bodies as sites of domination and resistance.

Historical Contexts: Gender, Class, and Nation

As a literary scholar who has learned enormously from teaching at a liberal arts college organized around team-taught interdisciplinary programs, my approach to these issues may be best described by the broad term "cultural studies." In their influential volume on this emergent cluster of methods, Nelson, Treichler, and Grossberg note that "cultural studies draws from whatever fields are necessary to produce the knowledge required for a particular project" and that "the choice of research practices depends on the questions that are asked, and the questions depend on the [historical] context."[3] They also rightly note that, despite the range of scholarship the term may embrace, cultural studies "shares a commitment to examining cultural practices from the point of view of their intrication with, and within, relations of power."[4] These observations capture in very large brushstrokes the major characteristics of my research practices and priorities over the last decade.

In thinking about the particular issues surrounding the struggle for narrative power in Chile since 1973, I have drawn freely from insights generated within feminism,[5] the new cultural anthropology, historical materialism, and poststructuralism, always privileging the historical context of postcoup Chile over any single theoretical apparatus. Since it seemed very clear to me that daily life was where political culture received its expression in postcoup Chilean society, I found that the most effective strategy for me was to focus on **specificity**, to go as deeply into day-to-day postcoup life as I could, given my own limitations as an outsider. I have done so not to claim some ephemeral sense of cultural authenticity, but simply because this approach is the most congruent with my goal of exploring how Chileans understood and represented themselves within this particular historical moment.

Another consideration for me was that, even as the postmodernism debate raged on in the U.S. academy while I conducted my research in Chile, I felt that defining the postmodern could be useful only if the concept meaningfully took into account Latin America's historical and cultural particularities. While theorists such as Fredric Jameson have offered useful ways for understanding a global context of late capital within which various manifestations of postmodern "symptoms" have appeared, most theories of postmodernism (including Jameson's) seemed to me insufficient in accounting for the precise circumstances of postcoup Chilean (or any particular Latin American) culture.[6] Latin America's uneven modernity—in which noncapitalist, capitalist/modern, and late capitalist/postmodern cultures intertwine and coexist in both peaceful and violent ways—clearly requires such nuance. While the community-based narratives by men and women in postcoup Chile in some respects did embody the postmodern—in that a unitary subject no longer made sense, or that literature could not tell the utopian stories it did only a few decades ago—most U.S. theories ignored that these texts were produced in a context in which the unitary and utopian had become distinctly associated with authoritarian violence. So even as postcoup Chilean culture provided a Southern "body" upon which Northern theory could write, the theories themselves risked erasing the specificity of Chile's locally produced forms of authoritarianism and resistance.[7] In response to these concerns, I have sought to provide a strong sense of context throughout the chapters that follow.

Any historically grounded discussion of Chilean culture over the last thirty years must begin with consideration of the 1973 coup. It is difficult to overstate the traumatic impact of the coup for Chileans on the left, for whom it meant a brutal interruption of the collective historical process, a devastating *crisis de proyecto*, in the broadest sense of the phrase. During the 1960s, of course, revolution had been the watchword that represented a range of visions for national and regional liberation throughout Latin America and the world. In Chile, such dreams for social change found their expression through the 1970 election of Salvador Allende, presidential candidate for the left-wing Popular Unity coalition. As is well known, Popular Unity's unique political experiment (*la vía chilena al socialismo,* the Chilean path to socialism) attempted to combine traditional democratic institutionality—highly valued in Chile throughout its history—with widespread socialist reforms, including nationalization of the copper mining and banking industries, land reform, and equal distribution of food, health care, and education. The Popular Unity government held that social transformation could be achieved by constitutional means since, as Allende stated in 1971, "A nation which is self-aware, organized and as politically mature as ours can achieve the goals it sets itself."[8]

Under Popular Unity, many Chileans for the first time had an enormous stake in political expression, and in shaping the direction that this socialist experiment would take. The Allende years produced an explosion of public participation, and a multiplicity of sometimes deeply conflicting interpretations of the present, past, and future of Chilean society. Few suspected then that this exceptionally productive time—as expressed in the proliferation of public voices and social actors—could provoke ideological rifts so deep as to explode in the extreme violence of a military coup. But on 11 September 1973, Chile's socialist experiment came to its calamitous end. The "tower of Babel," as David Benavente describes public expression during Popular Unity, crumbled alongside democratic institutionality, giving way to an abject "tower of silence," the void that signified a crisis of all previous models for imagining history.[9]

Although an in-depth assessment of Popular Unity and of the causes of the 1973 coup surpasses the scope of this study, I feel compelled to address the overwhelming pressures that Allende's coalition faced, even before its victory in 1970.[10] As a U.S. citizen, I am especially appalled at the role played by the Nixon administration and the CIA, along with multinational business interests such as ITT (International Telephone and Telegraph, Inc.), to foster social conflict and violence in Chile and to support the eventual military regime. The 1975 U.S. Senate Report of the Select Committee to Study Governmental Intelligence Activities, *Covert Action in Chile, 1963–1973*, amply documents expenditures of over $14 million dollars spent on financing actions "from simple propaganda manipulation of the press to large-scale support for Chilean political parties, from public opinion polls to direct attempts to foment a military coup."[11] With full support from the White House, the CIA manipulated the news published by the opposition daily *El Mercurio* (including and suppressing articles as it saw fit), funneled millions of dollars to the Christian Democratic Party (playing a decisive role in Eduardo Frei's 1964 presidential victory over Allende), passed money to private organizations that most likely funded the truck owners and other anti-Allende strikers in 1970–73, and eventually supported neo-Nazi right-wing terrorist organizations, such as Patria y Libertad [Fatherland and Liberty], that emerged in violent opposition to Popular Unity. The hypocrisy of U.S. advocacy of self-determination and human rights in the world, even as it conspired to sabotage a democratically elected government and fostered years of brutal repression in Chile, is wholly unconscionable.

At the same time that the U.S. generously funded Allende's opponents, it also sought to "make the [Chilean] economy scream,"[12] by cutting off the country's access to international loans and commercial credits, as well as by eliminating the supply of replacement parts and machinery for crucial sectors of the economy, including the copper and petroleum industries and transportation.[13] These measures, combined with financial support for anti–Popular Unity strikers, crippled the economy and heightened the public perception of chaos within the country. Such perceptions, fostered by newspaper propaganda as well, helped garner public support for the eventual military coup.

Meanwhile, U.S. intelligence officers and anti-Allende military plotters maintained very close contact throughout the Popular Unity years and beyond. During this period and later under Pinochet, members of the Chilean armed forces were trained in "antisubversive" techniques, including torture methods, at U.S. military bases in Panama and elsewhere.[14] The supplying of machine guns by U.S. officials for the first coup attempt in 1970 (a conspiracy ending in the assassination of the General René Schneider)[15] was but one early revelation of the widespread, systematic backing of antidemocratic, violent tendencies in the Chilean military offered by the U.S. for over two decades. In the wake of Pinochet's current legal battles, more information has come to light, if selectively, about the extensive U.S. knowledge and promotion of the regime's highly abusive tactics.[16]

Yet the strength of the Chilean political process was such that these external pressures, by themselves, would not have produced the 1973 coup. We must recognize this if we hope to avoid the kind of paternalism sometimes directed by U.S. leftists toward their Latin American counterparts. The Chilean political scientist Manuel Antonio Garretón has been an articulate proponent of the importance of examining factors internal to the country and to Popular Unity, not only as a means for more deeply understanding the past, but as crucial for creating alternative political projects in the future. According to Garretón, some of the major shortcomings of Popular Unity included its failure to adequately incorporate the middle classes culturally and ideologically in the process of social change, its unresolved relationship with the armed forces, its incomplete ability to channel the multiple and diverse impulses of the popular movement into a coherent project, and an insufficient ideological depth and cohesion on the Chilean left overall.[17] In particular, Garretón contends that Popular Unity's "contradictory ideological formation . . . sacrificed originality and specificity for the sake of abstract theoretical political schemes."[18]

What remains apparent today is that for Chileans across the political spectrum, Chile's long-standing democratic institutionality collapsed under the weight of overwhelming external pressures, and of the country's own internal contradictions. This failure brought a deep questioning of the very notion of Chilean "exceptionalism," the concept that Chile was immune to the authoritarian tendencies that marked the histories of many of its Latin American counterparts. In recent years, this has caused historians to rethink the country's modern trajectory; for example, Alfredo Jocelyn-Holt Letelier contends that the myth of Chile's strong democratic tradition actually veiled a steady undercurrent of authoritarian tendencies of the state, expressed variously from Portales to Pinochet.[19]

In the largest sense, then, the 1973 coup meant not only a violation of democratic social structures, but also signaled the end of an entire way of life, a way of understanding self, community, and nation. The coup meant a crisis of language and of history, for the previous ways of conceiving of historical continuity and change had failed to eclipse the possibility of the violent authoritarianism that became embodied by the Pinochet regime. After the coup, many Chileans were left without a means of participation in history, and attempted to find a language with which to represent self and community in the radically altered circumstances of postcoup society. In short, the 1973 coup dramatically reconfigured the terms with which the collective struggle for narrative power could be waged.

Furthermore, I contend that gender centrally frames this trajectory of recent Chilean history. Specifically, the process of struggle to reshape the national narrative, I argue, should be understood as a **gendered process**, in which ideologies of gender and sexuality, cultural structures of family and sex roles, and informal values and expectations all come into play, and are continually contested, reproduced, or rewritten. As an example, we might recall those well-to-do conservative women who had so ardently opposed Popular Unity, which they viewed as a threat to traditional family values (and of course, though they didn't say so, to their own class privilege). They demonstrated in the streets, banging pots and pans *(cacerolas)*, symbols of their own domesticity, to denounce the material scarcity and moral corruption in society, and to incite the Army to be "manly" enough to establish order in that "chaotic" time.[20] Using such sexualized slogans as "¡La Tencha [Allende's wife] nos decía que Allende no servía!" [Tencha told us Allende couldn't do it], and calling military men *maricones* (faggots) for not "straightening up" society,[21] these conservative women questioned the virility/masculinity of Allende and the military alike, and explicitly called for the reaffirmation of traditional gender (and implicitly, class) roles and hierarchies. According to these right-wing women, since the "effeminate" men of Popular Unity had failed to protect them as housewives from public contradictions, only a decisive authoritarian intervention could reestablish a clarity of roles within the divided family-nation.[22] These conservative women, known collectively as Poder Femenino [Female Power] eventually became the backbone of the Centros de Madre [Mothers' Centers] and the Secretaría Nacional de la Mujer [National Secretariat for Women] under Pinochet.[23]

The gender script laid out in the *cacerola* protests violently culminated in the military assertion of strength against Allende, who was forced to don an ill-fitting helmet and gun and to "act like a man" in the attack on La Moneda on 11 September 1973.[24] The contrast between the sensitive Allende's awkward appearance in military garb and the portrait of the four members of the junta that evening—an impenetrable wall of uniforms, squared shoulders, and dark glasses—reveals the very different gender ideologies they embodied. The military junta immediately set out to assert its authority by violently eliminating the "masses," feminized like Salvador Allende, from the center stage of the country's history. During the days and weeks following the coup, agents of the military state slaughtered hundreds of Chilean leftists—including the folk singer-guitarist Victor Jara, whom the military "emasculated" by breaking his hands before murdering him in the National Stadium.[25] The exaggerated character of the regime's violence against a largely unarmed civilian population was geared toward creating a tabula rasa upon which to inscribe the "new" foundational narrative of militarized and masculinist Chile.

In official discourse under Pinochet, the traditional nuclear family became a metaphor for the state, and its symbolic organizing principal. *La gran familia chilena* (the great Chilean family) was comprised of certain stereotyped members: the father-governor-patriarch, whose duty it was to protect and defend his home and family; the abnegated mother, relegated to the private sphere, and dedicated exclusively to socializing the children; and the unruly children-civilian population, in need of tutelage and protection.[26] As María Elena Valenzuela aptly notes, the military continued to view as feminine any values outside of its own:

> [T]he Chilean Armed Forces have "feminized" society, converting it into an object to be protected against any potential "violation"—particularly by those ideologies and values that might emancipate it from military tutelage.[27]

Clearly, this model held long-term consequences, in that the working class, and leftists more generally, were viewed as symbolic women and children within the military's paternalistic worldview. The family metaphor thereby couched authoritarianism, including its anti-Communist and classist dimensions, within the familiar terms of patriarchy, in order to justify military dominance as the "natural" order of things. Discrimination toward women specifically—and violence towards a feminized civil society generally—could at once be institutionalized and rationalized through this military worldview, making the patriarchal family a powerful ideological instrument of the regime.[28] It is therefore hardly surprising that Pinochet's Constitution of 1980 explicitly prohibits any ideological stance that would undermine the traditional family.[29]

As will become evident in the upcoming chapters, however, the discrepancy between this conservative rhetoric and the violent realities of postcoup society proved to be one central contradiction that eventually led to the regime's demise. At the same time that official discourse had strictly reinforced the separate and gender-associated public and private spheres, the violence employed by agents of the state overtly and systematically violated the boundaries between them. Thus, while the notion of public and private continued to exist as a social construct, the military's agents routinely penetrated homes, bodies, and psyches, politicizing private life. The personal crises resulting from this overt and covert violence in turn provided a catalyst for political action (especially since the junta had closed down all previous, traditional channels for political participation). The regime's efforts to depoliticize the country therefore ultimately backfired, creating the impetus for a wide variety of new social actors to organize collectively and publicly, in order to question and denounce the ways in which the dominant exercise of power intersected with their daily lives.[30] Under Pinochet, hundreds of working- and middle-class women organized themselves to expose human rights abuses, to ensure the economic survival of family and community, and to critique authoritarian social structures "en el país y en la casa," in the country and in the home.[31] Paradoxically, in the midst of the fiercest authoritarian regime in the country's history, the Chilean women's movement had been dramatically reborn.

In the pages that follow, I attempt to show that this vocal presence of women of diverse social backgrounds in the postcoup context challenged Chilean history and culture in fundamental ways. If the regime's official story—its gender script—was continually contested by mothers of the disappeared dancing alone, publicly negating the silences surrounding those bodies excised from the national narrative after 1973, it was also interrogated by those authors who, in response to the new social movements, began to narrate the collective, social body of Chile from the position of characters feminized in their relationships to a centralized power. Such alternative stories located the problem of authoritarianism within traditional structures of gender, family, sexuality, and within language itself, as a structure codified by the same institutionalized hierarchies operating within society at large.

In considering authoritarianism and this range of responses to it, I have found useful the research done by Chilean social scientists such as Manuel Antonio Garretón and Julieta Kirkwood, whose work has raised difficult questions about the eventual possibilities for social transformation in their country.[32] In particular, Kirkwood articulated a body of written knowledge about the history of feminism in Chile, the tensions between party politics and feminist politics, and the connection between traditional patriarchy and authoritarianism. While reading Kirkwood, I began to see that the emergent social movements protagonized by women after the coup were related to postcoup literary texts in that both were fundamentally about envisioning democracy locally and personally, about its past limitations and future possibilities.[33] For Kirkwood, the violence of the Pinochet years marked a difference of degree, but not kind, vis-à-vis the sorts of phallocentric oppression operative at every level of Chilean society. Unlike those thinkers who posited the coup as a definitive rupture with the past, Kirkwood emphasized the continuities in Chilean politics and culture, particularly the hegemonies of liberalism, capitalism, and patriarchy, which she saw as producing and reproducing insidious forms of authoritarianism throughout the country's history. Since democratization is clearly still one of the most difficult and urgent issues of today—in Chile, throughout Latin America, and in many parts of the world—the dilemmas represented by Kirkwood and the authors I study here seem particularly pertinent for unearthing those hidden structures of power that most insidiously limit the parameters of social change imaginable at this time.[34]

From the panorama of postcoup literary writing, I have chosen five authors—two men and one woman from the generation of 1970 (Ariel Dorfman, David Benavente and the Taller de Investigación Teatral/TIT [Investigative Theater Workshop], and Isabel Allende), and two women from the generation of 1980 (Pía Barros and Diamela Eltit)—to explore suggestive commonalities and differences within postcoup cultural production. As I stated in the prologue, I have attempted to balance gender and generational considerations in choosing this group, while also including work written inside (Benavente/TIT, Barros, Eltit) and outside (Dorfman, Allende) the country. While these writers display considerable stylistic differences, they share a feminist orientation toward social structures of power (including gender, class, sexuality, and language). All five began to publish between the mid-1960s and the mid-1980s, and came up against the obstacle of censorship, an immediate constraint until 1983. All were subject, directly or indirectly, to the pressures of militarized postcoup society. Finally, most of these authors produced a deeply troubled literature, a literature struggling to find its way through the crises of authority and truth that the coup left in its wake, a literature whose integrity lay in exposing its own contingent nature and its own contradictions.

With the possible exception of Isabel Allende, whose cross-generational perspectives I examine in chapter 6, the scope of these contemporary writers differs substantially from that of their forebears in the generation of 1950 (José Donoso, Enrique Lafourcade, Jorge Edwards, Isidora Aguirre, Mercedes Valdivieso, and others). That generation had begun writing from another historical moment and worldview, post–World War II, and in general had developed a strong critique of the decay affecting the Chilean oligarchy.[35] That generation portrayed a human incapacity to take action, individually or collectively, and viewed social change as yet another fleeting human gesture ultimately doomed to meaninglessness. For this reason, writers such as Donoso, geographically and intellectually peripheral to the experience of Popular Unity, were severely criticized by their younger colleagues for the seemingly apolitical perspective of their work.

Yet even Donoso was disconcerted by the 1973 coup, moved to question deeply authority and authoritarianism, gender and class, in his *Casa de campo* [*A House in the Country*] (1978). Who could forget, among a number of memorable characters, his cross-dressing, gender-indeterminate Wenceslao in the ciphered role of Salvador Allende? Donoso also acknowledged the importance of feminist voices in the postcoup context in *El jardín de al lado* [*The Garden Next Door*] (1981), in which the female narrator of the entire text is revealed only in the final chapter.[36] The issues of gender and authority are also prominent in *Maldita yo entre las mujeres* [I, Cursed Among Women] by Mercedes Valdivieso, who after a long silence published this historical novel on "La Quintrala" in 1991.[37] And finally, the crisis of male-centered authority was still thematically evident at the end of the Pinochet years, with Roberto Parra's extremely popular *La negra Ester* (1989),[38] a play that transgressed the regime's limits on both public expression and gender, by occupying large outdoor spaces like the Cerro Santa Lucía (in downtown Santiago) for its performances, and by focusing on its male protagonist's failure to triumph in life and love. These texts provide suggestive links between responses to the post-1973 context by writers of this older generation and the dilemmas presented by those younger writers whose work I discuss here.

While Donoso's generation was most basically marked by the post–World War pessimism or *desesperanza*,[39] the rapid changes of the 1960s and early 1970s by contrast shaped the following generation, known as *los novísimos* (Dorfman, Antonio Skármeta, Poli Délano, Fernando Jeréz, Cecilia Vicuña, and others).[40] This generation of 1970, strongly influenced in the early 1960s by the liberating promise of the Cuban Revolution, and by the Popular Unity experience itself, worked within the realm of the imaginary and the emancipatory potential of language. Intimately connected with Latin American writers of the 1960s, particularly Julio Cortázar, this generation of *intelectuales comprometidos* (politically committed intellectuals) strongly believed in the possibility of creating utopias in literature and society, and in a collective hope for the emancipation of Latin America.[41]

It is perhaps this generation that most directly felt the defeat of Popular Unity in 1973 as a profound crisis of every personal and political project they previously had known. For example, Antonio Skármeta's *Soñé que la nieve ardía* [*I Dreamt the Snow Was Burning*] (1975),[42] a very early post-coup novel, reads as a failed individual and collective *Bildungsroman*. Since several of these writers had been energetic participants in the transformation of their society, many experienced the coup as the failure of their most basic worldview, not to mention the fact that several were exiled or imprisoned by the Pinochet regime as a result of their political and cultural activism during the Popular Unity years. These writers struggled to reforge their ideals within the most horrific and stifling of circumstances after the military coup.

The texts I examine by authors of this generation, specifically Dorfman and Benavente/TIT, also provide important challenges to some aspects of theoretical works that have informed my analysis. Whereas Ernesto Laclau and Klaus Theweleit both offer keys for my understanding of fascist violence as continuous with certain masculinist expressions of desire[43] (a theme I treat principally in chapter 2), I think that the emphasis in Theweleit on a sort of psychosexual "everyman" is potentially reductive in a context such as Chile's. As is evident in the works by these Chilean authors, many civilian men were themselves both feminized and feminist, in that they reacted very much in opposition to the dominant (military) paradigm of masculinity.[44] However, for these authors, such a stance implied coming to terms self-reflexively with the tensions and complexities of their own gender privilege. This nonliteral, antiessentialist perspective—and its potential contradictions—merits exploration as an important aspect of Chilean resistance culture of the Pinochet years.

For their part, the generation of 1980, or those young writers who first began producing after the 1973 coup (Eltit, Barros, Ramón Díaz Eterovic, Diego Muñoz, Ana María del Río, and others), initiated their careers within the context of social repression enforced by the military regime. This generation discovered the utopian impulse when, in a sense, it was too late: Popular Unity, and the large ideals it represented, had already been defeated.

Yet they found their voices in much the same ways as did the new social movements that emerged under Pinochet, by attempting to tell another, radically contingent, story, conceived in response to the multiple internal and external pressures of postcoup society. And because potential mentors had been exiled or were otherwise inaccessible to them in this fragmented social context, this generation fostered a strong sense of collective purpose within literary workshops *(talleres literarios)*, including the Unión de Escritores Jóvenes [Union of Young Writers] (1976–79); the Agrupación Cultural Universitaria [University Cultural Association] (1977–81); the Colectivo de Escritores Jóvenes [Young Writers' Collective] (1982–85), and others.[45] Their aesthetic of *desencanto* or disenchantment (the term is Pía Barros's),[46] created in a context in which writing itself posed a tremendous risk, demonstrated a critical irony toward the political dimension of any literary project, as I will explore at length in the upcoming pages.

On the whole, the chapters that follow represent an effort to place the literary critic in dialogue with those concerned with large questions about Latin America's future. I believe that ahistorical analysis is clearly inadequate for understanding the urgent sociocultural problems consciously addressed in contemporary Chilean literature. The central dilemmas explored in these literary texts—issues of language and power, gender and class, and as I will discuss further in the next section, the struggle to narrate the national body politic—are clearly bound up within the mass cultural movement of postcoup society. Because these texts are tied so centrally to the movement of society at large, they demand a response in a literary criticism which accounts for the complex historical and cultural conditions of their production. This move away from ahistorical literary analysis toward interdisciplinary study of Latin American literature recognizes the vital interrelationship of cultural discourses, the resonance of questions raised by writers to those raised by their societies, and the role of literary narrative in historical movements, and places the task of both writers and literary critics within the broad social realm.

No other study of postcoup literature that I am aware of—written in the U.S. or in Chile—focuses so centrally on women and resistance as the key to unlocking a deeper understanding of the broader cultural context. Moreover, studies of postmodernism in Latin America have fallen short of understanding feminism as a central component of the 1990s resistance cultures widely associated with it, as Beverley and Oviedo acknowledge.[47] Scholars have written valuable sociological studies of the emergence of feminism in Chile's authoritarian context, works on Chilean women writers, and books focusing on single genres of postcoup literature.[48] But by teasing out the connections between the various displacements resulting within an authoritarian context such as Chile's, and the emergence of feminist organizations across social classes at that time, I hope to address feminism as a central component—not merely as a parallel development—comprising Chile's "postmodernist turn" in the postcoup years.

As Chile sustains the long process of democratic transition, the issues of social narrative and social voice, power and empowerment, and the cultural redefinition of public and private arenas, continue to be hotly debated in many sectors of the country—and throughout the Americas. By engaging literature in dialogue with the sociocultural context in which feminism was reborn in postcoup Chile, it is my hope that *Political Bodies* might contribute to these debates, filling a gap both in the discussions of the many Chileans actively engaged with these issues, and in the studies of Latin America pursued in the United States.

POLITICAL BODIES: LITERAL AND METAPHORICAL MARKINGS OF POWER

> The example of the human body is comparable to that of the social body.... When one member threatens to infect [*gangrenar*] the whole social body, that member can be eliminated, or its action impeded, with even more justification than in the case of the human body. This is because members of the social body [unlike the human body] act voluntarily.
> —G. Ibáñez, *El Estado de Derecho* [The State of Law] (1978)[49]

Under Pinochet, the human body became both a metaphor for the body politic of Chilean society, and a stage upon which the violent contest for narrative power was literally played out. The act of torture, for example, clearly represents a direct, political appropriation of the body, a literal inscription and violation of bodily boundaries by the dominant power. However, any other claims to that body potentially contest the hegemony of such an act, making the body the most local and intensely personal site for historical struggle. As illustrated by Salvador Allende's funeral, the attempt by excluded communities to reclaim the body, fighting for its literal and symbolic incorporation into the collective body, thereby became fundamental to resisting both the regime's official rhetoric and its violent practices. Moreover, alternative narratives of individual and social bodies served not only as oppositional responses to the regime's discourse, but also as acts that could reaffirm excluded communities' own capacity for self-representation. Because the body became such an important terrain for contesting and rewriting the national narrative after 1973, I have structured this book around various kinds of bodies—disappeared, hungry, erotic, or marginal—to explore multiple dimensions of dislocation and struggle in Chilean resistance culture during the postcoup years.

For approaching issues related to the body, a few key theoretical concepts have informed my work. It is thanks in large part to insights developed within feminism, cultural anthropology, and poststructuralism—constituting "a major paradigm shift . . . over the last hundred years,"[50] in the words of Susan Bordo—that the human body may be understood as an historically, socially, and culturally mediated space. Anthropologists like Mary Douglas have held that the "central rules, hierarchies, and metaphysical commitments"[51] of a given culture are constantly played out on the body's surface, making the body the most intimate site where cultural norms are produced and reproduced. In addition to cultural anthropology, we should credit poststructuralism (particularly Derridian thought) for this notion that bodies are cultural, and for the understanding that any interpretation of the body is always mediated by language, by the stories that organize our experiences. At the same time that the body's surface provides a cultural text, however, it also constitutes "a **practical**, direct locus of social control,"[52] as Michel Foucault and others have persuasively argued. That is, if bodies are cultural, they are also political, and the dominant power relationships in society are materially contested in the ways that bodies are codified and controlled, resist and rebel, within their specific contexts over the passage of time. This is not to say that bodies are not biological, for they are, but that their functions are always touched by, and interpreted through, culture. In short, the physical shape of the body, the material practices associated with it, and the stories always mediating our relationships to the body, **all** take place within an historical and social web of dynamic power relationships.

Two works by Foucault, *Discipline and Punish* and *The History of Sexuality*, have been especially crucial for my understanding of this cultural reproduction of power relationships on and through the human body (after the coup, he began to be cited in Chilean academic work as well). In *Discipline and Punish*, Foucault analyzes an historical shift in the West from the pre-eighteenth century ancien régime to the subsequent modern paradigm of "power without the king."[53] Within the former system, power was exercised directly by the sovereign who physically restrained and literally punished the real bodies of his unruly subjects. Within the latter, self-surveillance and bodily compliance to internalized social norms become the modes by which the predominant hierarchies are reproduced. In Foucault's work, Jeremy Bentham's Panopticon (with its omnipresent "gaze") provides both a model of the modern prison, and a potent metaphor for the ways in which surveillance broadly engenders self-regulation—whether in factory assembly lines, schools, church confessionals, or the home.[54] Because individuals internalize ostensibly external norms and expectations, and act accordingly, they become agents in the social reproduction of power relationships. Foucault explains:

> There is no need for arms, physical violence, material constraints. Just a gaze. An inspecting gaze, a gaze to which each individual under its weight will end by interiorising to the point that he is his own overseer, each individual thus exercising this surveillance over, and against, himself.[55]

Of course, Pinochet's regime relied on a **combination** of the literal, exterior, direct exercise of violence associated with the sovereign (in its most brutal extremes), with the more subtle and efficient mechanisms of modern surveillance (and, as we shall see, of economic regulation). While Chilean feminists like Kirkwood argued that Pinochet represented an exteriorizing of those hidden forms of authoritarianism operating culturally, it is nevertheless crucial for the context of my work to remember that the violent markings of power on human bodies under Pinochet were both literal and metaphorical.

Closely related to *Discipline and Punish*, Foucault's *History of Sexuality* develops and extends his meditation on power. Here, Foucault writes of the notion of power "from below": as fluid, interactive and dynamic, and as exercised together with resistance in all relationships.[56] For the context of postcoup Chile, this leads away from the notion that one group simply and straightforwardly wields power over another, toward the more complex understanding of power as "capillary" and contested, a process (or set of processes) occurring at every level of human relationships. Thus, Foucault insists that: "Where there is power, there is resistance, and yet, or rather consequently, this resistance is never in a position of exteriority in relation to power."[57] If individuals are agents in the reproduction of power relationships, then they are also potential agents of resistance, able to act within multiple (and sometimes contradictory) local struggles to contest the hegemonic hierarchies and rules of a given society. With this understanding, the micropolitical activism so crucial to the new social movements in Chile may be seen as just as important, and just as relevant a form of resistance as (some would say more important than) the disputes over macropolitical power relations that characterize modern politics.

All of this said, Foucault's work does have some important limitations. Like Foucault's *History of Sexuality*, the Chilean literature I study here in each case emphasizes the manner in which domination may engender resistance. But in contrast with Foucault's own discourse, each Chilean author examines power in its most locally specific expressions, to such a degree that the literary language they use to do so sometimes seems to burst at the seams, reflecting the violence that their words at once describe and contain. In this regard, the fractured and fragmentary aesthetics of many of the literary works I study here offer a differently compelling meditation on power relationships as they are constructed in language, surpassing in this way the focus of Foucault's (and other) more theoretically oriented texts.

Second, despite Foucault's insights on the social constructedness of sexuality, he never adequately explores its links with discourses of gender, an aspect stressed in the Chilean works. I have found Susan Bordo's feminist rereading of Foucault, in the context of her work on the body in Western thought, to be absolutely essential for correcting this limitation. While Bordo's work is centered in the West (with resultant silences on international power relationships and on some issues of cultural difference), she has successfully mined the richness of U.S. feminisms, particularly the Anglo-American and African-American radical and socialist strains, for their important historical—but often unacknowledged—contributions to any current understanding of the body as a politicized space. Bordo argues that

> neither Foucault nor any other poststructuralist thinker discovered or invented the idea . . . that the 'definition and shaping' of the body is 'the focal point for struggles over the shape of power.' **That** was discovered by feminism, and long before it entered into its marriage with poststructuralist thought.[58]

Bordo credits especially those Anglo- and African-American thinkers and activists in the U.S. second wave who "imagined the body as a socially shaped and historically colonized territory."[59] Rereading Foucault through this lens, Bordo contends that "[O]ur bodies are trained, shaped, and impressed with the stamp of prevailing historical forms of selfhood, desire, masculinity, femininity," and insists that "normalization of the female body" historically has proven to be "an amazingly durable and flexible strategy of social control."[60]

Of course, the notions of the body as a colonized space and as a locus of social control clearly have been familiar realities for, and theorized by, women living in colonized societies around the globe—and are not merely the purview of U.S. or Western feminisms. We need only think of work as varied as Leila Ahmed's on the complexities of women's embodiments of Islamic cultures in resistance to Western hegemonies, Molara Ogundipe-Leslie's call to multiple alliances for a feminist "Stiwanism" (Social Transformation Including Women in Africa), or the Christian Chinese feminist Kwok Pui-Lan's meditations on female sexuality and feminist theology, to remind us of a vastly diverse range of international feminist contributions on the politics of the body.[61] In my own discussions, for the historical reasons discussed, I have placed Chilean conceptions of these issues at center stage. However, because Chilean feminisms themselves dialogue with Western and U.S. feminisms, and because my own work will be read in the U.S. context and elsewhere, looking closely at Bordo's contributions to debates on Foucault and the body seems useful as a point of departure for engaging an ongoing set of feminist dialogues and practices whose relevance is not limited to the West.

Bordo situates her analysis of U.S. feminist interpretations of power and the body within a long trajectory in Western philosophy (including "Plato, Aristotle, Cicero, Seneca, Machiavelli, Hobbes, and many others"[62]), in which the body served as a metaphor for the body politic of society. This was certainly a trope of the Chilean junta's official discourse, as the epigraph to this section illustrates. Bordo writes:

> In the old metaphor of the Body Politic, the state or society was imagined as a human body, with different organs and parts symbolizing different functions, needs, and social constituents.... Now, feminism imagined the human body as **itself** a politically inscribed entity, its physiology and morphology shaped by histories and practices of containment and control—from footbinding and corseting to rape and battering to compulsory heterosexuality, forced sterilization, unwanted pregnancy, and (in the case of African American slave women) forced commodification.[63]

In this way, Bordo places the concept of a "politics of the body" back in the context of historical struggles for social change organized originally around dimensions of identity such as gender, race, and sexual orientation. This seems politically important as a gesture that refuses to privilege feminist theory out of the context of a range of feminist praxes as they have unfolded historically—an emphasis shared by most Latin American feminists as well.

Importantly, Bordo also acknowledges the interrelationship between the issues of gender and race and the historical materialist discussion of class in works by Marx. As Bordo so aptly notes, both Marx and feminists have insisted that "it makes a difference . . . **whose** body you are talking about"[64] for understanding its specific relationship to multiple systems of power. While Marx emphasized that the body is an historical arena "shaped by the social and economic organization of human life, and often, brutalized by it . . ."—but **differentially**, if one is a day laborer, a factory worker, or a manager[65]—feminism has held that the "direct grip" of power on human bodies is variable in degree and kind, and depends centrally on the gender and race (as well as class) associated with a particular body, within a given cultural context. Like Bordo and Foucault, then, I understand these dimensions of identity not as unchanging essences, but as historically specific markers (or rather, sets of markers, along various dimensions) which culturally situate individual bodies among a web of interwoven social systems of power.

By emphasizing the importance of both the materiality and the textuality of the body (in contrast to some poststructuralists' dismissal of the material, and of some Marxists' de-emphasis on the discursive), Bordo has provided a model of poststructuralist-inspired cultural criticism that is not afraid of the material world. Bordo takes to task those forms of postmodern culture, poststructuralist thought, and feminists like Judith Butler, who "embod[y] . . . fantasies of transcendence of the materiality and the historicity of the body, its situatedness in space and time, and its gender."[66] In so doing, Bordo has managed to appreciate the role of language in contesting power relationships, while criticizing those who celebrate the "free play" of cultural forms as the predilect arena of resistance. Bordo holds that

> No matter how exciting the destabilizing potential of texts, bodily or otherwise, whether those texts are subversive or recuperative or both or neither cannot be determined in abstraction from social practice.[67]

I value Susan Bordo's work for its insistence on the contextual and historical, without eschewing language and cultural forms as important sites of political struggle. Within my own focus on the words and bodies of Chilean men and women, I attempt to relocate and expand upon Bordo's work on the body, in order to explore the complex relationships between social rupture and cultural resistance, between authoritarianism and the emergence of feminist-oriented social and literary protagonists, and between narrative strategy and the struggle to participate in history, within the local specificities of Chile since 1973.

My work also dialogues with that of Hernán Vidal, a Chilean Marxist literary critic living in the United States, who has contributed several fundamental pieces to the analysis of the body within postcoup Chilean culture. In his insightful essay on the Junta's Declaration of Principles, Vidal shows how military discourse under Pinochet systematically suppressed the materiality of the human body, in favor of a mythologizing discourse geared toward reifying the regime's own authority. This discourse harnessed the old Western binary between the spiritual and the material (and, we may add, between mind and body, good and evil, and as I discussed in the previous section, masculine and feminine) to build its own ostensibly moral character. Vidal explains:

> [In] the vision . . . proposed by the Declaration of Principles . . . all of humanity is reduced to a spirituality animated and dignified by the divine. As a spiritual being, man tends to fulfill something called the "ultimate

good," which is inspired by, and originates through, God, while what is material becomes condemned as a satanic and corrupting force that leads man to stray from his true mission. The human body, as a material nexus of necessities and work, does not appear within this ideological frame.[68]

Within the terms of this discourse, the "sacred" military-technocratic "mission" was to purge Chilean society of the base temptations of the Allende period, in order to restore Chile to its pristine spiritual grandeur supposedly existent before "the fall."[69] According to this ideology, Vidal argues, history ("the narrative of human acts"),[70] like the human bodies targeted by the regime, simply does not appear: it has been banished, like the serpent from the garden. Although Vidal does not address the gender content of this discourse, it seems quite clear, too, that what is good, spiritual, and orderly becomes aligned with the military patriarchs, while what is material, corporal, and evil is aligned with the feminine and effeminate, the unstable and disorderly, the weak Eve-like Allende followers to be straightened out—or eliminated—by the "real" (military) men.

Official discourse recast this moralizing story using a medical metaphor as well. As is clear in the epigraph at the start of this section, this version conceived of the country/body as ill due to an "infection" or "Marxist cancer," such that any "diseased members" threatening the values of the fatherland must be extirpated from the social body. The military patriarch was thereby likened to a physician who cures society of its ills, in order to restore the transcendental values (or the bodily "wholesomeness") essential to *la chilenidad* (Chileanness). His intervention, as sanitized and distant from violence as a surgeon's, becomes an absolutely justifiable crusade for saving the life of the patient.

The political consequences of these metaphors are twofold.[71] First, violence is both invited and justified, its materiality hidden behind an official discursive guise. Second, the defense of the social body becomes implicitly aligned with a specific economic model—neoliberal capitalism—as a cure for the chaos and "disease" of Marxism. Hence, the mythologizing or epic language of the regime's discourse systematically evaded the materiality of the human body, even as it invoked the body as a metaphor for society. In this way, official discourse symbolically "disappeared" individual bodies from its concept of the social body. Since the regime was simultaneously disappearing (and torturing, disciplining) **real** bodies after the coup, this discursive cover paralleled the material cover-up of its own violent atrocities, a not-so-gratuitous second throwing of "diseased members" into clandestine graves.

In response to these official ideologies and practices, Vidal points out that the key task for resistance cultures was to focus on the materiality and historicity of the human body, to restore its dignity and "reweave the most basic fabric of social life."[72] In *Dar la vida por la vida* [Giving Life for Life], his book-length analysis of the protests and discourse of the Association of Family Members of the Detained-Disappeared (referred to here as the "Agrupación"), Vidal writes:

> The argument in favor of human rights stems from the materiality of the human body as a focus for respect, from which flow all other values that make society a space for life. This discourse is the inverse of that contained in the Doctrine for National Security. That Doctrine makes the material body an object, a presumed or real target for military attacks. . . . While militarism makes the human body a site for closing down an order based on life, the Agrupación makes caring for the material bodies of family members, whether dead or alive, the opening point for a new order.[73]

Vidal points out, then, that the human body as a metaphor for Chilean society provided a common language for both the junta and human rights organizations like the Agrupación. But while the military regime considered itself the patriarchal guardian of the family/social body/Fatherland, the Agrupación exposed the military's violent severing of the very bodily and social integrity it claimed to protect. From that position, the Agrupación could offer a different narrative, and an alternative order, based on corporal and communal dignity.

Without a doubt, my work builds on the conceptual foundations laid by Vidal in these readings of the body in postcoup culture. However, I have significant differences with him that merit discussion here. First, as my comments above have shown, Vidal does not address the substantial gender content operative in both the official discourse and the resistance strategies of groups like the Agrupación (predominately women, many of them mothers). Gender is not a mere undercurrent in these discourses: it is a central ideological frame of the postcoup cultural context overall.

Second, Vidal conserves an old left (and modernist) predilection for the *grands récits* or "great narratives" approach to history and resistance. He conveys a strong skepticism about both the micropolitical strategies developed by the new social movements and those practiced by the *avanzada* or neo-avant-garde under Pinochet. Vidal writes:

> [The] strategy of micropolitics . . . requires that the defeated dilute their presence in the everyday world and disguise themselves with the discourse of the conquerors in order to mock them at a distance so that no punishment can reach them.[74]

He criticizes the new social movements as middle class radicalism, unstable, and organized around "very limited objectives related to the defense of human rights, the quality of life and the environment, and to the redefinition of sexual and gender identities."[75] In trivializing the importance of local activism and of these specific issues, Vidal makes clear his perspective that what counts as social change involves a privileging of class struggle, of political parties and labor unions as the chief mechanisms for creating change, and that a movement's impact on the macropolitical sphere of the nation-state provides the ultimate measure of its success. From my perspective, while those arenas are clearly significant, Vidal systematically underestimates the concrete political importance of the new social movements, protagonized by both working- and middle-class members, many of them women, in achieving the defeat of the dictatorship in the 1988 plebiscite.

And while Bordo maintains a simultaneous emphasis on the material and the textual politics of the body, Vidal invariably emphasizes the material over the textual, in the Marxist tradition. In my view, it is by **retrieving the human body through the telling of stories** that the atomized body of civil society could be pieced together during the Pinochet years. By contrast, Vidal is mainly interested in stories that minimize their own presence, providing a kind of transparent window on the social world they portray. Referring to key post-1973 novels like Donoso's *A House in the Country*, Vidal criticizes their authors' "inability to elaborate an organic discourse based on historic facts," indicated by the texts' "non-functional ruptures of episodic sequences," "strong allegorical abstraction," and their "thematic reiteration apparently out of synch with their [historical] moment."[76] He explains:

> [My] hypothesis . . . is based upon a conception of literature as a discourse that typifies and totalizes social experience, integrating the immediacy and limits of daily life into a global vision of the national culture. The proliferation of fragmentary texts, allegorical abstraction, and thematic reiteration [in postcoup texts] may be interpreted as a momentary incapacity to formulate symbolically, metaphorically, and thematically the flow of a vast and contradictory history.[77]

Vidal's assumption that fragmentary texts are dysfunctional, and conversely, that the best-elaborated discourse is the most totalizing and seamless one, I argue, runs exactly counter to the literary tendencies that emerged from progressive intellectuals in the country in the wake of the crisis of paradigms produced by the 1973 coup. For many leftist intellectuals, generating such a "totalizing" or "globalizing" discourse became not only difficult, given a reality that was anything but "whole" (as Vidal rightly acknowledges), but also highly **problematic**, because of the connections between any totalizing narrative and the authoritarian political project. In my view, Vidal's desired novel (one "that totalizes and typifies social experience") may be precisely the literary form that was most delegitimated by the complexities and contradictions of history revealed after 1973.

Given these positions, Vidal's attitude toward Chilean postmodernists (among whom he includes literary writers like Diamela Eltit, artists of the *avanzada* art scene, and intellectuals involved with the *Revista de crítica cultural*) is hardly surprising. Citing Hopenhayn, Vidal describes these artists' work as "fragments of a cryptic aesthetic, which almost tribally decides its own codes for interpreting itself, making itself indigestible to those who are not part of the tribe."[78] Ironically, Vidal implicitly maintains the old dichotomy between art and politics, between the concern for aesthetics and the concern for social change, which he sees as mutually exclusive—as if a focus on one by definition precluded the other. In his view, this group of Chilean artists and critics evades moral and political responsibility through their deliberately aesthetic focus.[79]

By contrast, thinkers like Nelly Richard (editor of the *Revista de crítica cultural*) have insisted that such aesthetic work **is** political, but within the carefully circumscribed, insistently local realm of cultural practices. Writing from inside Chile, Richard explains:

> Modestly, the *Revista* directs itself primarily and specifically to the **cultural sphere**, with its highly particular networks of discourses, practices, and institutions. Its collaborators can express solidarity with human rights issues and work on their behalf without necessarily obliging the journal to become the bearer of "great narratives of human redemption"—especially when these discourses (of totality, or of the Revolutionary Proletariat) are themselves implicated in the repression of the critical potential of **localized interventions**. . . .[80]

In short, Richard insists that the *Revista* and its authors "take seriously a function that Vidal seems to consider excessively modest on our part: that of being an agent of the dynamic reactivation of cultural discussion and critique."[81] Although I find myself more sympathetic to Richard's view in this debate, Vidal's concern about the hermeticism of works produced by the postmodern avant-garde merits further discussion, which I undertake principally in chapter 5.

In addition, returning to Bordo's insistence that the subversive potential of cultural texts "cannot be determined in abstraction from social practice,"[82] I must ask in the context of each work I explore how, concretely, it relates to social practices of resistance in Chile under Pinochet. In this regard, it is important to recognize that within Chile, along with human rights activists like the members of the Agrupación, who actively contested narratives about the body from the earliest moments after the coup, cultural activists involved in the *avanzada* also worked with the body in ways uniquely relevant to this period. In *Campos minados*, Eugenia Brito writes:

> During the first years of the dictatorship there emerged a battle zone that was previously unthinkable in Chile: the body . . . as a signifier of transgression against the system. It is a body that would reveal, as an icon of itself, a system of writing, whose marks [*grafos*]—wounds, exhibitionism, histrionic drama—become a metaphor, a distilled response to the battered national body.[83]

Brito examines work by Diamela Eltit, Raúl Zurita, Carmen Berenguer, Carlos Leppe, Juan Luis Martínez, Eugenio Dittborn, Lotty Rosenfeld, and others, to make a strong case for the body as a stage for writing, for cultural ciphering and performance of meaning, during the Chilean dictatorship. She asserts that this work sought to posit a challenging, suggestive, and refractory message, one that would not reproduce the regime's ideology, but would rather "confront the oppressive structures of power by generating a language impossible to repeat, to be acquired or bought by the Chilean bourgeoisie."[84] Unlike Vidal, Brito suggestively points out the politics behind narrative complication as a mode of resisting the totalizing stories consumed by bourgeois capitalists and offered by the regime. Whether such a stance consists of a link to social practice, or an abstraction from it, is a question I return to, especially in chapters 5 and 6.

Finally, there is an important subtext to the Vidal-Richard debate, which has to do with who might best claim authority or the power to interpret postcoup culture—those who, like Vidal, observe from a critical distance, or those who, like Richard, write from within the context itself. The answer is not as straightforward as it may seem. Both positions, I contend, have advantages and drawbacks, issues I explore in my discussions of the complexities of authorial (dis)placement throughout this book. Bearing in mind the Vidal-Richard debate overall, then, I shall attempt to tease out the range of tensions between those working inside and outside the country, between "old" and "new" progressive politics, between modernism and postmodernism, as played out in each of the postcoup Chilean texts I examine here.

Each of my chapters explores a differing kind of claim on the body in the struggle for narrative power in the postcoup context. I place each literary work alongside the forms of activism developed by women and men of diverse social backgrounds in response to the specific circumstances of the period, thereby reflecting on the blurred text/context distinction in postcoup cultural production. Building on my discussion of Vidal's work above, I begin in chapter 2 by examining how the Association of Family Members of the Detained-Disappeared and Ariel Dorfman's *Viudas* [*Widows*] (1981) narrate the disappeared body, in order to bear witness to—and symbolically retrieve—huge sectors of a country metaphorically "disappeared" by the military regime. As hopeful as that process sounds, the novel reveals it to be both difficult and contradictory.

In chapter 3, I turn to hungry and working bodies in postcoup culture. As Vidal noted, citing Pinochet's famous statement that neoliberal Chile would become a country "de propietarios y no de proletarios" [of property owners and not of proletarians], workers had become symbolically disassociated from the physicality of work during the postcoup years, even as their bodies were assumed to be agents of consumer culture.[85] One of Dorfman's essays aptly captures this paradox:

> Neo-colonial fascism takes the bourgeois dream to its totalitarian culmination: eliminating the materiality of the body while at the same time benefiting from its production and consumption.[86]

Predictably, just as overt violence was discursively swept under the rug by the regime, so was the economic violence resulting from the regime's neoliberal policies. It is hardly surprising that Pinochet declared the spirit to be free from all bodily processes, at the same time that dire economic necessity became the daily reality of more Chileans than ever before in the country's history. In chapter 3, I discuss the issues stemming from postcoup society's hungry body, as expressed in artisan's workshops and other working-class women's organizations, and in the alternative theater movement. The material presence of work in plays like David Benavente and the TIT's *Tres Marías y una Rosa* [Three Marías and a Rosa] (1979) countered the regime's denial of hungry bodies and their physical needs. Moreover, through their collective work, the women in *Tres Marías y una Rosa* develop a language of self-representation, by claiming their own bodies as a necessary first step for their political intervention. Yet the constraints on their actions, including their own gender expectations and the influence of the economic system itself, undermine the possibilities for lasting transformation.

This focus on the body receives a different twist in works produced by the generation of 1980, especially by those women writers who burst onto the literary scene after the 1983–84 National Protests. In chapter 4, I explore these protests, along with middle- and cross-class feminism, and literary workshops, with relation to expressions of erotic desire in Pía Barros's *A horcajadas* [*Astride*] (1990). Since the military ideology had depended so centrally on a traditional conception of gender, one of the greatest threats to the regime's hegemony was losing control of female sexuality. The magazines and pamphlets produced by official government organizations for women, the Mothers' Centers and the National Secretariat for Women, both directed by Lucía Hiriart de Pinochet, describe sexuality outside of marriage as "monstrous and even puerile, characteristic of immature peoples," and therefore to be forbidden. Hiriart concludes:

> Therefore it is urgent to return sexual relations to their true magnitude and to all their spiritual and physical grandeur, as a mystery emanated from God, and as a foundation for the projection of humanity [into the future].[87]

In questioning this ideological script, Pía Barros views the body as the cultural space where the public and the private merge, and where desire gains its potentially transgressive expression, particularly for women. The frontiers between eroticism and violence, the political and the intimate, and the objective and the subjective, constantly permeate each other in Barros's texts, through her own use of irony and through the fantasies of her female characters. Barros's focus on female sexuality challenges every norm proposed in the official story, calling into question the foundation of the military's patriarchal ordering of society. At the same time, Barros shows how her characters' (as well as language's) internalized forms of authoritarianism reproduce the very power structures that they had hoped to contest.

In chapter 5, I explore Diamela Eltit's work in CADA, a neo-avant-garde performance art movement, and her novels *Lumpérica* [*E. Luminata*] (1983), *Por la patria* [For the Fatherland] (1986), and *El cuarto mundo* [*The Fourth World*] (1989), which provide radical innovations on this same theme. For Eltit, the female body is marginal from before birth, and is violently inscribed by the power exercised within the social realm. Through the metaphor of families besieged by illness, insanity, and incestuous desire, Eltit's work portrays a crisis of both individual identity and of traditional institutions. Eltit represents bodies deeply fragmented by the social structures that exclude them, yet she also reveals their precarious grounds for resistance. Crucially, for all of the authors studied, and especially so for Eltit, telling another story of the social body—establishing a sense of historical and narrative grounding in postcoup society—is an extremely precarious process, involving both conflict and contradiction. Yet it is only through that process that another, always unidealized and locally contingent, version of history might be "reborn."

Returning to the regime's **idealized** gender script (and in contrast to its violent practices), "woman" became the epitome of a bodiless spirit, belonging to a world of values, not material necessities. In another editorial, Lucía Hiriart de Pinochet stated that: "The value locked inside the small, delicate body of the Chilean woman is as great as that contained within the heart of a soldier, who is of her flesh and blood."[88] Here, woman's only embodiment is through the body of her offspring, just as her only social value resides in her ability to produce sons of the Fatherland. Although women of course figured among the many members of the social body who had suffered violations of their **material** human rights after the coup, all women were instead interpellated (in the Althusserian sense) as agents of **spiritual** human rights, their presumed superior calling. In chapter 6, I explore Isabel Allende's phenomenal popularity, and the tensions between material bodies and bodiless spirits in her work, as complex indicators of Chile's contemporary cultural crossroads. It seems worth considering, to recast a phrase from Lovell's *Consuming Fiction*, that while Allende's work is not "unambiguously subversive," it may not be "unambiguously conciliatory," either.[89] A closer look at Allende's novels seems especially necessary for glimpsing the popular *imaginario* in (and about) Chile after Pinochet.

Finally, in the epilogue, I will examine briefly what has happened in the first decade of democracy in Chile, as it has impacted cultural production. Returning to Kirkwood's warning that the return of democracy would not necessarily mean the end of authoritarianism, I ask: Have the fundamental societal changes enacted in postcoup resistance literature "become real," incorporating the feminist-oriented protagonists that emerged during the crisis? Or has the return of the basic structures of liberal democracy also meant a return to (a more friendly version of) the standard patriarchal ordering of society? In short, what gender (political, and class) scripts predominate in Chile today? In looking at these issues, I will explore the powerful influence of liberal ideology, the patriarchal exclusions of traditional politics, and the country's continuing course of neoliberal capitalism, which together have enabled a **dismembering** of collective bodies during the democratic transition—a crisis of the new social movements that had emerged under Pinochet. Yet this is a drama whose ending has not yet fully been determined: Regardless of his supposed "unfitness" to stand trial in Chile, what have Pinochet's failed extradition to Spain and his loss of legal immunity meant for the **remembering** of Chilean society and its future?

Overall, *Political Bodies* is a story of social rupture, resistance, and the decidedly human—and therefore fallible—efforts to reconstruct cultural meaning in the wake of a profound collective sense of personal and political defeat. It is an exploration of the achievements and limits of the cross-class feminism that re-emerged within recent Chile's hierarchical, militarized social context. It is a portrait of men and women who pieced together fragments of an atomized social body through telling stories, and through reconceiving interpersonal relationships within families, groups, and the nation, in order to reaffirm those "imagined communities"[90] that authoritarian discourse had aspired to eliminate or diffuse. And it is a tale with aspects familiar to many Latin Americans, who at the beginning of the twenty-first century face the hegemony of economic neoliberalism in the global context, and a concurrent crisis of representation within their local democracies. By reading recent Chilean literature within the broad discursive and material contexts of postcoup social movements, I hope to unearth, recognize, and narrate some of those "bodies" whose meaning for the future remains as unresolved as the deposed dictator's eventual fate.

2

The Disappeared Body and the Exiled Voice: Displacement and the Struggle for Narrative Power

> We have the responsibility to remind everyone that thanks to the women who took to the streets, we have this little bit of democracy that there is. ... Thanks to all the mothers.[1]
> —Adriana, member of the Agrupación de Familiares de Detenidos-Desaparecidos [Association of Family Members of the Detained-Disappeared] (1990)

> Dicen que lo reconocieron
> por la voz, por los gritos,
> dicen.
>
> [They say they recognized
> his voice his screams
> they say.]
> —Ariel Dorfman, "Esperanza" [Hope] (1978)

IN ORDER TO DEVELOP THE CONNECTIONS BETWEEN GENDERED BODIES, POWER, and postcoup resistance culture, we must begin one place where those relationships were most directly played out: with the disappeared. If physical bodies provided the most local sites for struggle during the Pinochet years, how might we understand the terrifying drama of disappearance, in which the regime attempted to rewrite the material body as an absent signifier of military power? How might that body's story instead be contested, be made present as a sign of resistance, by opposition communities themselves feminized by the regime? These questions are at the heart of the struggle for narrative power—over the ability to name the body, and as I will argue, to engender the nation's future—that unfolded during the Pinochet years.

Although the general phenomenon of disappearance is all too well-known—with distinct versions taking place not only in Chile, but also in

Argentina, Guatemala, El Salvador, and South Africa, to name a few—it is worth retelling the story here to reflect both the specificity of the Chilean case and to develop terms for thinking about the issues of representation played out on and over the bodies of the missing. Direct military abuses in Chile (e.g., disappearance, torture, murder) reached their most acute levels between 1973 and 1976.[2] It is important to remember that, from the moment of their disappearance, missing people were relegated to a perverse limbo in which the State not only denied their **deaths**, but also attempted to negate their **lives**, by claiming that the disappeared never had existed.[3] Even without a body to serve as physical proof of their existence, however, missing people did continue to exist through the ways in which other people reconstructed them discursively, by telling stories that bore witness to those individuals' lives within a community. As the community continued to tell stories (i.e., to represent itself), those narratives explicitly reaffirmed the existence of the absent person and resisted the social fragmentation that the regime sought to impose. In order to disappear a person completely, then, the State's task involved an extended battle to silence such community-based narratives. As a response to the official version of the nation's history, in which extensive sectors of the population were silenced or declared nonexistent, family and friends of the disappeared contested the discourse of the regime by speaking for themselves. In this way, each attempt to recuperate the life of a disappeared person also functioned as a metaphor for what was happening throughout postcoup Chile, as the struggle to represent the body became a struggle for the power to participate in, or narrate, history itself.

In contrast to Argentina, where the State's elimination of "subversives" regularly crossed class and gender lines, the disappeared in Chile were in the vast majority (about 95 percent)[4] male and most frequently (though by no means exclusively) from working/peasant class backgrounds.[5] This is especially revealing of the military State's patriarchal and classist view of just who might be considered a threat: not women, but men, especially those publicly active in political organizing; not the middle and upper classes, so much as *el pueblo*, the Marxist-inspired masses who had overtaken Chile, in the minds of the elite, during the Allende years. The fact that the State targeted these groups, while being blind to activism by others, left a space for political work rapidly occupied by "invisible" members of the opposition, particularly women. In effect, as Hannah Arendt wrote in her *Origins of Totalitarianism*, "[t]otalitarian domination," in this case, did "[bear] the seeds of its own destruction."[6] Similar to the "Europeanized" Muslim women who effortlessly crossed military checkpoints in Pontecorvo's classic film *The Battle of Algiers* (later to bomb their French occupiers where they least expected), Chilean women of various classes played upon cultural expectations of their roles to contest the regime's hegemony after 1973.

And yet it was not, for the most part, women previously active in political groups or parties who organized the first public resistance to the regime's terror, but the many women, of diverse social backgrounds, who had lost their husbands and children in the aftermath of the coup. Once they discovered the collective nature of their situation—having crossed paths while searching for missing family members—such women joined together to collectively demand the regime's accountability and the return of the disappeared.[7] Even as the regime fiercely repressed any groups expressing social discontent, these women relied on their moral authority **as mothers** to publicly condemn the regime's abuses. Thus commenced one of the first major social mobilizations during the Pinochet years, protagonized by women who stretched traditional roles to achieve specific political (if not, in their view, explicitly feminist) ends.[8] One of the earliest and most visible of such organizations, the Agrupación de Familiares de Detenidos-Desaparecidos [Association of Family Members of the Detained-Disappeared], which I will refer to simply as the "Agrupación," was formed at the end of 1974 by those women who sought to make a collective, public response to the acts of terror perpetrated by the State.[9]

In his anthropological study on the symbolic importance of the Agrupación, Hernán Vidal maintains that its work reaffirms the materiality of the human body as the base from which the value of human life takes on meaning in the social context.[10] Though Vidal stops short of exploring the discursiveness of the body that I wish to develop here—the process of **metaphorization** by which the body becomes a locus for historical struggle—he does contribute to an understanding of the relationship between the disappeared and the community, as represented through the form of the Agrupación protests. As Vidal notes, the Agrupación began to organize a series of public acts to demonstrate the **continuity** of their own bodies with those of the disappeared, that is, to show the interconnectedness of a unified **social body**. Thus, their forms of protest, which included wearing photographs of missing persons, hunger strikes, and *encadenamientos* (literally "chainings," such as the 18 April 1979 protest of fifty-nine people who shackled themselves to the gates of the National Congress), represented the corporal continuity of the community with the disappeared.[11] Likewise, women of the Agrupación recast the Chilean folk dance *la cueca*, by performing it as a public act of women dancing "together" with their absent family members. This dance with the disappeared simultaneously dramatized each woman's personal loss as well as the regeneration of a community which incorporated both its present and its absent members.

Through these and other methods of representing the continuing horror of the State's violation of personal and communal integrity, the Agrupación rejected the illusion of social normalcy propagated by the regime. That is, Agrupación members refused to conform to the military's demand that they, or their loved ones, become Foucauldian "docile bodies."[12] Moreover, because they publicly renounced the silence that surrounded the bodies of the disappeared, while showing their own bodies as unified in a collective struggle, Agrupación members reclaimed the capacity for organized public expression that the State had sought to eliminate. Rather than function merely as negative, oppositional responses to official discourse, then, these acts served as a positive reaffirmation of the community's own capacity and need for self-representation.

Just as the women of the Agrupación participated in political activity based initially on their familial roles, many female journalists were granted interviews with military officials precisely **because** they were women. It is hardly surprising that among the most revealing *testimonios* and works of investigative journalism produced during the Pinochet period, a majority were written by women: the works of Mónica González, Patricia Politzer, Raquel Correa, Patricia Collyer, and Patricia Verdugo, among others, come to mind here.[13] I spoke with Mónica González about how the regime's biases paradoxically worked in the opposition's favor during the postcoup years. González emphasized that even though anyone who questioned the regime's methods was automatically suspect, female journalists were viewed by the military as less aggressive, and less politically dangerous, than their male colleagues. If a female journalist also had the physical appearance of an upper-class woman—light skin and hair color, taller stature and tailored clothing, connoting that she was a "lady" *(mujer bien, mujer decente)*—then it was nearly unthinkable that she might be a political "subversive." (However, the prevailing stereotype for secret police agents in the DINA and the CNI was nearly the opposite—that a "woman dedicated to her cause" was more dangerous than a man—which accounts for their development of perverse torture practices, based on sexual humiliation and psychological manipulation, to be employed specifically with women.)[14] But because the stereotypical and idealized notion of "ladies" was especially prevalent among military officers, and a linchpin of official discourse on women, female journalists used these codes to their advantage.[15] As a result, many female journalists were selectively granted access to military personnel and secret documentation, enabling them to claim narrative power, to initiate the process of reconstructing the prohibited history of the Pinochet years.

For González, a handsome blonde woman, the official gender/class ideology constantly intersected with her professional and personal experiences. This became particularly useful to her when she was in prison.[16] She recounts that the women with whom she was incarcerated urgently desired to speak of the horror they had survived, and they discovered how to take advantage of the guards' attitudes toward them to do so. The women secretly taped testimony on a cassette, which was then hidden inside González's sanitary napkin and snuck out of the prison when she was released. Since González claimed that she was menstruating, no guard searched her. When González carried the women's **narrative** as a part of her own ostensibly unclean **body**, she risked her body, and those of the other women with whom she was connected, in order to make **public** those women's words. Similar to the Agrupación protests, this strategy not only took advantage of the regime's sexism and classism for the opposition's ends, but also reasserted the vital link between bodies and stories necessary for the rearticulation of a communal narrative.

In the broadest sense, the regime's denial of the existence of the disappeared extended to its negation of the existence, voice, or visible presence of **any** person in the opposition, whether inside or outside of the country. Yet the gaps and contradictions in the regime's all-encompassing discourse were made clear by the actions of the Agrupación and the journalists: in both instances, women took advantage of the regime's ideological blind spots to piece together and embody local forms of community representation that contested the official story. It is crucial to remember that, during the Pinochet period, all efforts at social representation inserted themselves into this specific material and discursive context. That is, the ability to speak took place within a contextual frame marked by official gender and class assumptions, by fierce repression, **and** by the specific forms of organized resistance that had emerged during the postcoup years.

Given this context, the immediate challenge to literary writers on the intellectual left was to make visible the deepest contours of a country threatened on a very broad scale with discursive nonexistence. Such writers searched for a symbolic means to narrate the country out of disappearance, and to imagine a future without the self-declared unifying figure of Chile: Pinochet. In contrast to the ways in which bodies were literally and figuratively disappeared through the regime's univocal discourse, Chilean writers began to explore the process of the **metaphorization** of the absent body: that is, the ways in which communities struggled to narrate and recuperate the missing through representation of linked individual and collective social bodies. Contesting disappearance was always simultaneously a struggle on at least two interrelated fronts: for the physical recovery of the missing person, and for the symbolic restitution of a ruptured body politic. Because of the political reciprocity of individual and social bodies, the move toward recuperation of one was necessarily a move toward recuperation of the other. At the same time, this contest over the nation's social body was a struggle over gender and class boundaries, over which version of Chile would prevail in the future: a country like Pinochet's disciplined, masculinist, and exclusionary Fatherland, or one more akin to the feminized Mother Country of the unruly masses? In short, for writers on the left, narrating the country out of disappearance, and engendering a nonmilitary future, necessarily began with recovering the specifically feminized social body of the community's absent men, as I will show in this chapter.

This struggle for narrative power was hardly straightforward. Most immediately, the artistic community was itself a disarticulated one, for the coup had sent many writers to prison, into exile,[17] or to their deaths. Those who remained in the country worked in isolation, living out the daily pressures of "incile," a symbolic exile within the borders of their own country.[18] The immediate political contingencies conditioning the lives and work of leftist Chilean writers posed the dilemma of how they could coherently and fairly represent their communities when, in many cases, they were themselves radically displaced from their former positions within those (now fragmented) communities. Many writers therefore struggled to develop a language capable of bearing witness to Chile's deep social rupture and of representing the ways in which emergent collectives actually were able to express themselves. One such literary effort is Ariel Dorfman's novel *Viudas* [*Widows*], written during his exile, and published in Mexico in 1981.[19]

Widows presents the drama of disappearance as a struggle for narrative control between military personnel and the women who resist the official silence shrouding the disappeared men of the village. But even as *Widows* explores **how** the story of the disappeared might be told, it also asks **who**, morally and politically, should tell that story. Given the shared struggle of Chileans to represent themselves in the postcoup context, Dorfman necessarily questions the bases of his own authority to speak for the women and men represented in the text. While questioning this authorial position, *Widows* also probes the hidden ways in which political violence may be perpetuated through traditional structures of social relations. The novel prompts readers to ask: What is the social value of keeping the disappeared alive through telling their stories? How does one make the disappeared body coherent within a context of social fragmentation, particularly when one's own body has been absented from the country in exile, or when, like the women in the text, one has been excluded from history? What is the interrelationship between authoritarian repression and the ways that men and women traditionally relate to one another? Written from Dorfman's position in exile, *Widows* is itself a product of the implicit and explicit violence it portrays. This stylistically fragmented text is a testimony to the complex struggles to narrate or "authorize" a version of history, and to imagine an alternative future for the country, in a context in which the bases of authority (and paternity, a parallel concept for Dorfman) are fraught with contradictions.

Displaced Bodies, Displaced Narratives

The prologues to *Widows* immediately introduce displacement as the fundamental link between Dorfman's personal situation in exile and the treatment of the disappeared in the remainder of the novel. Rather than merely describing this situation, the opening pages of *Widows* inscribe displacement as a narrative issue involved in establishing a position from which to represent self and others in the context of postcoup Chile. Hence, the novel begins with an apparently disjointed series of narrative mediations: a title page ("ariel dorfman * *viudas* [novela]" [WIDOWS, Ariel Dorfman]), Dorfman's "A modo de dedicatoria" [By way of dedication], a second title page ("*Viudas*, novela de Eric Lohmann" [WIDOWS, a novel by Eric Lohmann]), and finally the "Palabras preliminares del hijo del autor" [Foreword by the author's son], Sirgud Lohmann. Who, then, is the author of *Widows*? Dorfman? Lohmann? Or might there be another "author" behind this novel—the military regime that disappeared so many people? What of the authority of the women who reclaim their faceless relatives on the banks of the river? And of the reader who "witnesses" these events?

As the novel proceeds, the "author" of *Widows* seems to be an amalgamation of all of those who struggle to interpret, or to narrate, the significance of the bodies that resurface throughout the text. The displaced structure of authorship that begins the novel foregrounds the general difficulty of claiming representational power in the context of a military regime that seeks to negate any author-ity but its own. The concept of authorship is questioned to the degree that the many "authorized" and "unauthorized" versions of this story, variously believed to be true, are ultimately incompatible with one another. Moreover, the novel's narrative displacement reflects Dorfman's particular struggle to write when he had officially been made a nonauthor, and to narrate a path to his country when that path was laden with obstacles. In order to approach the widows' struggle to recuperate disappeared relatives by narrating their absent bodies, the author had to confront the ways in which his own position conditioned the language he could use to do so.

The first section of *Widows* is Dorfman's dedicatory note dated "Amsterdam, 1980,"[20] which traces *Widows*' disjointed path to its appearance as a novel. Because of the political difficulty of publishing a novel in Chile with such an explicit focus on the disappeared, Dorfman recounts that he devised a strategy:

> Mi plan consistía en hacer traducir primero al danés mi novela, y luego sacar "traducciones" a otros idiomas, entre los cuales estaba, claro que sí, el castellano en que de veras se encontraba escrito originalmente. (7)

> [My plan was that we would first bring the book out in Danish, and then publish "translations" in other languages, among which would figure the Spanish in which it had actually been written.] (translation mine)

This plan, and the elaborate steps he took to make it possible, demonstrate Dorfman's continuing desire for his former public and published place in Chilean society. Such a desire for a broad, public intervention, shared also by David Benavente and the theater collectives with which he worked (treated in chapter 3), poses a direct contrast to the notion of a more intimate intervention, as in the cases of Pía Barros and Diamela Eltit (discussed in chapters 4 and 5). This disjuncture between these two male authors (who were literarily active before the coup) and two younger female authors (who began writing after the coup) demonstrates two very different visions of the intersection of literature with history, visions that certainly reflect both gender and generational differences. However, because Dorfman had been exiled from the public place he desired (even his words were prohibited), *Widows* was necessarily and deliberately produced with a form distinct from his previous work.

In fact, the circumstances of Dorfman's exile demanded that the novel be formally displaced, that it follow an indirect and winding path:

> Para que **mi novela** no sufriera, entonces, el destino de **mi cuerpo**, y fuera prohibida también, la situé en Grecia en algún período del siglo XX, y se la atribuí a Eric Lohmann, un danés que, supuestamente, la habría escrito hace cuarenta años atrás. (emphasis mine, 7)

> [So that **my novel** wouldn't suffer the same fate as **my body**, and be banned from Chile too, I decided to place the story in Greece, at an undefined moment of the twentieth century, and publish it under the name of a Dane, Eric Lohmann, who had supposedly written it forty years earlier.] (translation and emphasis mine)

Political exigency required a Cervantine series of masks: pseudonyms and a "discovered" author, "translators" and "translations," a different narrative style, a setting in another place and time. Dorfman explains:

Al verme forzado a escoger cada palabra con precaución, al forzarme a presenciar una experiencia tan traumática e **inmediata** desde una **distancia casi alegórica**, al forzarme a explorar un lenguaje que no podían lectores o críticos identificar como el que yo solía utilizar, me parecía que me estaba también aproximando a la situación de los desaparecidos **de una manera menos local y más universal**. Esa tragedia podía ocurrir **en todas partes y en cualquier momento y a cualquier persona.** (emphasis mine, 8–9)

[By forcing myself to choose my words with caution, by forcing myself to witness such a traumatic and **immediate** experience from a **distance** {almost allegorical}, by forcing myself to explore a language which could not be traced to the style that Latin American critics and readers might have recognized as my own, it seemed to me I had managed to make the plight of the missing people into something **{less local and} more universal, which could happen anywhere, at any time, to anyone.**] (emphasis mine, vi)

This tension between the "immediate" and the "distant," or the "local" and the "universal," is symptomatic of the particular circumstances of the novel's production. Though Dorfman aspired to a public, written, "universal" (masculine-centered) history, in the postcoup context, those spaces no longer existed in the same way for him. As the subject matter of *Widows* suggests, Dorfman was feminized by his displacement, and his marginality sensitized him to the local trauma from which he nonetheless was physically removed. Dorfman's attempts to draw closer to his own distanced society necessitated his creation of narrative bridges that could reinscribe a larger community of **all** those who could recognize themselves in this plight. Those bridges, however, could only be partial and fragmentary.

In exile, Dorfman's plan could protect neither author nor novel, as the novel's final destiny illustrates. *Widows* was subsequently refused by a prominent Southern Cone publishing house, whose authorities had previously accepted it, though they had suggested a careful treatment of military characters (8). Banished to publication elsewhere, Dorfman's novel **did** suffer the same fate as his body, and the context of Chilean political repression dictated that this could not have been otherwise. That is, from the perspective of both the author and the Chilean authorities, the author's novel was nothing if **not** a representation of his body. Displaced temporally, spatially, and linguistically, it was an attempt to narrate multiple forms of self-representation that he could not control. Yet at the same time that the novel attempted to narrate other displaced bodies, it also functioned reciprocally, as a way to make Dorfman himself textually "reappear." Hence, Dorfman at once dissimulated his authorship and claimed this text as his own, "esta novela que recojo con humildad bajo mi propio nombre" (9) [this novel for which I take responsibility] (vii). Both despite and because of Dorfman's displacement, the author of *Widows* was necessarily inside **and** outside of the text. Ultimately, what had begun as a formal pretext became, by necessity, a narrative strategy: both novel and body shared the same historical and contextual limitations on how they might be told.

But how such narrative "embodiments" continue to be represented remains in the hands of others, as part of a collective history. In their prologues, both Dorfman and Sirgud Lohmann emphasize this history as a patrilineal one, which may be shaped by women, although it is protagonized, and written, by men. Dorfman concludes:

> De esa manera, quienes lean el libro podrán juzgar si también pudo haber sido escrito—y así fue, no se necesita a nadie que lo certifique—por ese danés resistente, ese **hermano** mío cuarenta años mayor, ese **padre** que no alcanzó a conocer a su **hijo**, y a cuya memoria dedico las páginas que él logró terminar unos días antes de morir. . . . (emphasis mine, 9)

> [This way, whoever reads the book can judge whether it also could have been written—and it was, nobody has to certify it so—by that Danish resistance fighter, that **brother** forty years my senior, that **father** who never got to meet his **son**, to whose memory I dedicate these pages he managed to finish a few days before his death. . . .] (emphasis mine, vii)

As Dorfman remarks early in his dedicatory note, the Dane Eric Lohmann was supposedly disappeared by the Nazis in 1942, before the birth of his son. In his foreword, Sirgud Lohmann states, "Yo nunca conocí a mi padre. Vinieron a buscarlo los hombres de la Gestapo un mes antes de mi nacimiento, en abril de 1942" (13) [I never met my father. Men from the Gestapo came for him in April 1942, one month before my birth] (3). It is hardly a coincidence that 1942 is the year that Dorfman was born, like Sirgud Lohmann (who perhaps also is Jewish), in the month of May. Dorfman situates himself within a patrilineal history, already in progress before his birth, in order to emphasize the importance of his own place within an historical continuity. (That this historical continuity is also literary becomes reinforced by the echoes of Cervantes running throughout the prologues.)[21] However, the future form of that history (which here remains male-defined) depends **not** on official "certification," but on the collective judgment of a social lineage: the known and unknown readers of his **corpus**; "brothers," "fathers," and "sons" perhaps as yet unborn.

The continuity of this narrative therefore depends upon knowing what came before. If Sirgud Lohmann never met his father, the recuperation of three interrelated "texts" facilitates Eric Lohmann's fragmented remembrance. Appropriately, each of these is a distinct form of self-representation: a photograph, Sirgud's dialogue with his unnamed mother, and finally, the novel:

> Sólo años después, cuando comencé a hacerle a mamá preguntas más específicas acerca del hombre cuyo retrato retenía yo al lado de mi cama, averigüé lo de la novela. (13)
>
> [Only years later, when I began asking my mother more specific questions about the man whose picture I always had beside my bed, did I find out about the novel.] (3)

The novel, Sirgud tells us, was placed in his Aunt Gertrudis's trunk for safekeeping a few days before his father's disappearance (Gertrudis and Eric were twins, the first of three sets in the novel). Gertrudis became ill after her brother's disappearance, and the novel, whose existence was known to Sirgud's mother, remained untouched in the trunk since that time.

Hence, the male Lohmanns view their family lineage and the novel as two intertwined threads that comprise the family's historical continuity. The surfacing of Eric's lost text and its eventual publication not only imply "un acto de respeto a su memoria" (14) [an act of respect for his memory] (4), as Sirgud Lohmann maintains, but bear witness to—and textually embody—the Eric Lohmann that his "son(s)" come to know (the service that Dorfman's novel does him, as well). Sirgud revives his father through recuperation of the novel, the narrative of his father's memory. Through incorporating that memory, Sirgud continues his father's struggle against the historical amnesia produced through collective silence. If the novel was saved because someone (Sirgud's mother) remembered it, Eric Lohmann and other members of his community would not completely **disappear**. Moreover, if past and present terrors are incorporated as part of historical remembering, then a different future may be imaginable, and perhaps possible, according to Dorfman's "aesthetic of hope."[22] In the prologues to *Widows*, the struggle to reclaim historical continuity is emphasized as a strategy necessary to resist the officially severed link between the social subject and history, a key concept to be developed in the remainder of the novel.

But who might participate or claim a voice in that history? Although both Sirgud's mother and his Aunt Gertrudis served as guardians of the novel, and of oral family history, they appear to be mere conduits for Sirgud's principal search for his father, and for the written text. As in Dorfman's prologue, Sirgud emphasizes the quest for a narrated history of "fathers," "sons," and "brothers," **not** of the women who were incidentally involved in the production of that narrative. In both of the prologues, the authors place women in a parenthesis of implied orality, marginal to a masculine lineage of written history. As in the social setting of *Widows*, the valorized sphere of history into which this novel is inserted is public (published) and male-centered. By framing the main body of the text in these terms, the male authors beg the question of what the justification is for their authority to represent the women, texts, and bodies portrayed in the novel. The narrative cracks in these prologues reveal the reflexive conditions under which Dorfman and the Lohmanns must operate, despite their own feminization: they are men claiming to represent women who are, both in the novel and in Chile, threatened with exclusion from the men's version of this story.

Yet the novel would have been literally and figuratively lost without these women. Because the main body of *Widows* represents a crisis in which women emerge to tell their own stories, the novel itself demonstrates the instability of the masculine-centered framework (the prologues) through which the novel emerges. Moreover, as the widows gain narrative power in the text, the very definition of history set out in these prologues (a written, male-authored lineage) is necessarily unsettled as well. In this way, *Widows* reveals itself as a product deeply challenged by the circumstances it narrates, demonstrating the historical breakdown of totalizing (or modernist) narratives in Chile after 1973. The emergent instability of Dorfman's narrative ground inscribes the failings of utopian political projects and of univocal language to account for the devastating forms of domination and the vital sources of resistance embodied by Chileans during the Pinochet years.

Authoritarian Discourse, Gender, and the Body

Given the narrative position that *Widows* takes in favor of historicity, and against collective amnesia, how can the novel suggest that there is potential for this tragedy to happen "en todas partes y en cualquier momento y a cualquier persona" (9) [anywhere, at any time, to anyone] (vi)? In my view, Dorfman's answer is that certain fundamental social structures have been culturally constructed, and reconstructed, via the same deep exclusions and violence over time, such that similar crises have been triggered at various points throughout modern history. In *Widows*, Dorfman meditates not simply on the authoritarianism embodied by military men, but instead probes the connections between military violence and the more general ways in which gender and class operate culturally. Like Klaus Theweleit's work on ascending Nazism, Dorfman reveals that fascism hinges on a misogynist (and I would add, homophobic) dread of femininity, as represented by the desire to conform the self—and the nation—to an exclusively masculinist image of the disciplined military man. (According to

Theweleit, the "other" for the German Freicorpsmen was categorically "woman," and the feminized "masses," as opposed to Hitler's disciplined *Volk*.)[23] In the Chilean case (the implicit focus of Dorfman's novel), the military men fear the dissolution of both the masculinist self and the Chilean Fatherland—a disintegration or chaos culturally linked with unbound femininity and with the uncontained working/peasant class activism of the Allende years. In response to this fear, the military man violently excludes the feminine "other" (women, the feminized masses) in order to reaffirm his own authority, and to remasculinize the Nation. Counterpoised to this concept of the disciplined Fatherland, however, is the social body of the Chilean Motherland, the composite body of the disappeared men in the arms of community women who collectively refuse the misogynistic exclusions of the fascist state. When Dorfman explores these connections between gender, class, and violence, however, he simultaneously and self-consciously questions **language**'s role as a social structure also imbued with the potential to replicate—or to question dialectically—the dominant constructs of the social context he represents. It is in these respects that Dorfman surpasses Theweleit's work and inscribes his text within the specific coordinates of cultural resistance in Chile after 1973.

Widows consists of thirteen narrative segments comprising eight chapters. The first three segments of the novel (chapter 1) present a study of authoritarian psychology, as they develop the narrative conflict between Sofía, the Angelous family matriarch, and the unnamed officers of the town. These segments focus upon masculinist military culture, as narrated in the third person by an omniscient narrator. In similar fashion to the prologues, both the exchanges between the officers and the narrative mode in chapter 1 of *Widows* work to exclude women from the story, for the linear structure coheres through a singular focus on the military perspective. However, as Sofía's claims unsettle the officially hermetic, masculine world of the military headquarters, the instability of the captain's rule is revealed, and the novel's linear structure starts to break down.

When Sofía Angelous appears at the captain's office, she wants him to give her the body she identified as that of her father when it was pulled from the river. For her, the issue is not merely that her father be buried (the soldiers had already done that), but rather that it is her right to bury him in the family **plot**, to narrate his death, and to consolidate her family's history (23). Identification of the body through naming it would retrieve it from the status of "bloody mass" (the term is Theweleit's), a voiceless void shrouded by the anonymity of official silence. Sofía's positive identification of her father thus challenges the body's ostensible nonexistence as represented in military discourse. Yet the struggle for control over the power to name and narrate the body becomes a vital issue concerning not only the military's stability, but also the stability of military **identity** as well. Because he is unsure of himself, the captain thinks that he must be decisive: "No era el momento para solicitar mayores antecedentes. Recién arribado, había que demostrar control, absoluto control" (23) [It wasn't the time to find out the history of the case. He had to show he was in control, absolute control, now] (12).

The captain's sensation that in fact he may be unable to control this moment, that perhaps someone else's actions are indirectly narrating **him**, manifests itself in his struggle to control **time**. This is demonstrated in the third segment, which traces his visit to the village church. Because the captain is unable to suppress Sofía's authority to narrate her father's body, he seeks an alliance with the priest in order to pacify the widows. Representative of the captain's uncertain authority, this segment breaks with linear structure, as it begins and ends at the moment the priest opens the church door. Segment iii zigzags between two narrative threads: one portrays a future moment of the captain's arrival at the church and his conversation with the priest; the other, the past moments of conversation with Gheorghakis and his personnel about the problem of gaining the priest's cooperation for the transition period. Through this zigzag structure, the captain appears to be caught between two points in time, two spaces (the church and the military headquarters), and two sets of interests, each governed by narratives that negate his own.

The sense that the captain **is** controlled by "alguien aquí o en otra parte" (24) [someone here or elsewhere] (12) emerges through the use of the future tense to describe his actions, thoughts, and even his body. The omniscient narrator appears to be distanced from the captain, who seems to be a mere puppet manipulated by the official narratives he embodies. For example, it is deterministically stated that he "will feel" an unidentifiable weight overcoming him: "Aún así, el capitán sentirá que los pies le pesan, que una fatiga de muchos años le ha ganado los muslos . . ." (40) [Even so, the captain will feel the heaviness of his feet, the years of fatigue collected in his thighs . . .] (27). The interplay of this distant voice with the captain's memories suggests that what is happening to the captain is at once real and unreal (an "immediate" and "distant" reality, to return to Dorfman's prologue). The narrator at once identifies and dis-identifies himself from the captain's position, as if the narrator's **own** identity depends upon grasping the character of the captain—and distancing himself from it—in this segment. The narrator redoubles control through the back-and-forth narrative structure: if the captain's role cannot be controlled, the narrator's bases of authority—and the text—also threaten to fall apart.

This threat to the captain's authority is linked to the escalation of Sofía's activities, as her version of history gains momentum in the text. Although the captain must enlist the priest's help for negotiating with the widows, his colleagues all discourage the captain's interaction with the priest. The military men hold that a visit to the priest would be "una señal de debilidad" (41) [a sign of weakness] (27), because "los hombres de acción tienen poco que ver con esta fauna rara" (40) [Men of action have little to do with his sort] (27), the priestly protector of "los elementos anti-sociales" (40) [antisocial elements] (27) and "defensor de las mujeres" (48) [the women's defender] (33).

Wary of the priest's nonmasculine status, the military men seek to distinguish themselves from him. In doing so, they intimate that the captain risks becoming less masculine through association with the priest, so they disassociate themselves from the captain as well. As a result, the captain fears the disintegration of his identity, and in turn attempts to differentiate himself from the priest. He homophobically accentuates and despises the other's physical characteristics, which he perceives as indicating weakness and softness, in a description markedly similar to his earlier vision of the widows themselves:

> Le repugnará el olor a ropa vieja, a encierro, a cocina pobre, a polvo libresco, la cara mansa, demasiado dulce, del hombre que lo invita a sentarse, las mejillas excesivamente rosadas y blandas, los labios débiles y carnosos, las manos que delatan susceptibilidad y sufrimiento. (42)

> [He'll be disgusted by the smell of old clothes, closed rooms, cheap food cooking, dusty books. That mild face too, {so sweet,} of the man inviting him to have a seat, those cheeks excessively soft and pink, those {weak} fleshy lips, those hands so patient and vulnerable.] (28)

As he contemplates "las mejillas femeninas, rosadas, casi risueñas del sacerdote, y esa mano benigna" (49) [the feminine, rosy, almost pleasant cheeks of the priest, and that benign hand] (34), the captain fears that his own orders to proceed evenhandedly ("con mano blanda") will lead him to identify with the priest's "mano benigna."

In order to keep the upper hand, so to speak, in his bargain with the priest (that the priest will pacify the widows in exchange for the return of the boy Alexis, who "will" have been disappeared), the captain struggles to maintain the boundaries between himself and the priest. The captain therefore seeks to separate the masculine from the feminine—and to differentiate politics from matters of the soul—distinctions that the priest rejects:

> —La guerra— [dirá el cura] y el capitán odiará nuevamente los ojos profundos y vacunos del sacerdote, la ternura acumulada en esa boca endeble y sensual, los movimientos de una mano acostumbrada a las páginas de los libros y las noches solitarias, las pestañas casi femeninas, casi exquisitas—
> . . . .

—Entonces, entreguen los muertos a sus familias.... Lo más cristiano y lo más político también.
—Déjenos mejor la política a nosotros los militares— el capitán le recomendará— y usted ocúpese de asuntos del alma.
—De eso me estoy ocupando, capitán, de eso precisamente. (53)

["War, Captain . . ."
And again the captain will feel a surge of hatred for the priest's deep, cowlike eyes, the tenderness gathered in that sensual mouth, the motions of a hand accustomed to turning pages and to solitary nights, the almost feminine, almost exquisite eyelashes.
". . . Then return the dead to their families. . . . More Christian and more political as well."
"Better leave politics to us military men, and you tend to matters of the soul."
"That's what I'm tending to, Captain, precisely that."] (37)

When the priest, like Sofía, rejects the captain's masculine-centered view of history and politics, he suggests why the captain is on such tenuous grounds for controlling an official version of this moment. If the captain were to suppress the women's actions right away, he would be standing on firm authoritarian ground, but he would betray his orders to act "blandly."[24] Conversely, if he does not suppress the widows or seems unsure of himself, he risks loss of control, which casts doubt upon his ability to maintain order, the cornerstone of his masculinity within the terms of military culture. The struggle for narrative control is therefore a struggle which questions the validity of gender boundaries, and when the captain disassociates himself from the priest's apparent femininity, it is not clear if he can maintain his sense of masculine self—or his control of history—without exercising violence.

Segment iii closes as it had begun, at the church door. Instead of marking the future moment of the priest's opening the door (the beginning of this segment), the segment closes at the moment that the door open**ed** and the captain enter**ed** (57). This segment's circular structure thereby leaves the future undetermined: is what "will happen" actually what happened in the unwritten moments after the men entered? The omniscient narrator's seeming inability to exert absolute control over the exchange between the captain and the priest parallels the captain's own questionable authority in this segment. Because the women's claims have begun to undercut traditional bases of authority, both the narrator and the captain must seek alternative strategies for intervening in this story.

Ultimately, the entire first chapter works as a unit describing a moment of sociopolitical transition in which the captain and the villagers, like the author(s) of the novel, are necessarily unsettled due to their radically altered positions vis-à-vis their own authority. Segments i to iii focus upon the narrator's and the military's struggle to contain the representations of this moment—of the women, of the bodies, and of themselves—by establishing coherent narratives. The captain redoubles his misogynist/ homophobic quest for self-integrity, a strategy that resurfaces in the later segments on his sexual advances toward the female journalist (with obvious resonances with the experiences of the actual Chilean journalists I discussed earlier). In effect, the captain makes clear that justification for military control lies in an **extended**, and simplistic, metaphor of the traditional gender-role-based family, with virile military fathers in charge, sacred mothers in the home, and a general population of children in need of the father's tutelage.[25] From this perspective, **all** others are placed in a feminized or infantilized position with respect to the soldiers, who attempt to enforce a monopoly of masculinity by distinguishing themselves from the "barbarian," uncontrolled, or womanly "masses" (75–76). However, since they all live in a moment marked by a crisis of roles, their former identities, as they are narratively constructed, are also inevitably destabilized.

Through his narrator, Dorfman self-reflexively questions his own claim to narrative power in this context. At those moments in which the narrative perspective coincides with the captain's subjectivity, the narrator is implicitly aligned with the military struggle for coherence. In the first chapter, the narrative mode remains linear as long as the captain himself is sure of his personal boundaries, as long as he (and the narrator) can maintain some self-coherence by containing the unsettling narratives of the Angelous women. Although the captain's insecurity leads him to desire control, both the captain and the narrative itself become increasingly destabilized from segment iii on. This ostensible divergence of the narrator and the captain suggests the captain's real instability and functions to distance the narrator from the captain's militaristic struggle for self-identity. The narrator therefore attempts to maintain control of the text while tactically avoiding a connection to military means of authorially controlling the social narrative.

In contrast to the first chapter, chapter 2 of *Widows* breaks into a more chaotic narrative style, for in segment iv the women's voices emerge more explicitly to vie for control with the omniscient narrator. Segment iv traces the women's trajectory from the private strategy of individual or **silent** family claims for the body, to a public, collectively **voiced** representation of it. Through a process of collective discussion, the women become their own narrators, taking control of the (con)text they are creating within the community. The process of their becoming aware of the social consequences of their personal concerns develops as the chapter unfolds. As a result, the plural narrative voices in this segment disrupt the male-centered, omniscient perspectives through which the women were represented in the preceding segments.

This segment's narrative mode interweaves the omniscient perspective, the individual voice, and the emergent, collective female "we" ("nosot**ras**"). The chapter begins with these words:

> Algo tenía que pasar. Eso lo sabían todas las mujeres, desde el día del funeral lo habíamos sabido, desde que Fidelia le había visto la cara a su hermano entre los dos soldados y mamá le había apretado más fuerte todavía la mano. Mamá me apretó la mano con furia cuando trajeron a Alexis, pero ella no le preguntó nada, no le quiso preguntar. (61)

> [Something was going to happen. All the women knew that much, since the day of the funeral we had known it, since the day Fidelia had seen her brother's face between the two soldiers and Mama had squeezed her hand. Mama squeezed my hand even harder when they brought Alexis back, but she didn't ask my brother a thing, didn't want to ask him.] (43)

This passage moves from the abstracted "Algo tenía que pasar" [Something was going to happen] to an objectified awareness ("lo sabían todas" [all the women knew]), and, through the concrete experience of the funeral, a personal "we" evolves ("lo habíamos sabido" [we had known]). As when she spoke by the riverbank, Fidelia advances and recedes as a narrator in this segment (as both "yo"/I and "ella"/she, within the more encompassing female we, "nosotras"). This **organic** "we," which evolves out of the concrete elements of the women's struggle to claim their history and to speak via the community, is counterpoised against the **hegemonic** "we" of the single, universalizing, military voice that claims to speak for (in place of) all others. As illustrated by the breakdown of the narrator's omniscience, the claims of the women themselves could not be excluded, for they emerge as the main force defining the shifting social context of the story.

In this respect, Dorfman shows that he is narrated by the context he seeks to narrate. The author, himself displaced by sociopolitical crisis, cannot afford to maintain omniscient coherence, because his own position, identity, and the bases of his author-ity are also decentered. For these reasons, Dorfman philosophically aligns himself with the organic "we" of segment iv.[26] However, as Dorfman reminds the readers of his prologue, he ultimately does retain authorship of this text, "esta novela que recojo con humildad bajo mi propio nombre" (9) [this novel for which I take responsibility] (vii). His desire to raise the women's struggle to public awareness by equitably representing **them** depends upon his ability to publish him**self**. His relationship to the texts/bodies he interpolates is therefore inevitably a double one (again, it is "immediate" and "distant"). Dorfman's displacement aligns him with those on the margins (including the women, the disappeared), but his desire for, and eventual access to, public representational power (the published written word) already implies his separation from those he represents.

In contrast to the utopian quality of the women's resistance portrayed in chapter 1 (and of the men's view of them as an undifferentiated mass), the women's dilemma is placed within the specific terms and conditions of their particular situation in segment iv. As the women converse, a conflict develops that undercuts any homogenizing or essentialist vision of them. Here we learn that all of the men of the family are disappeared, with the exception of Alexis, and that fear has taken hold of the young women of the family. It is Alejandra (Alexandra in the English translation, mother of the twins, and Sofía's daughter-in-law), who breaks a tacit silence among the young women by telling Sofía: "—Estamos matando a nuestros propios hombres abuela —dijo Alejandra—. Usted los está matando" (63) ["We're killing our own men, Grandma," Alexandra said. "You're killing them"] (45). The collective narrative voice gives support to this public emergence of the private, echoing Alejandra's words:

> Matándolos, abuela, y se estaba cometiendo un error, un error que terminaría costando caro a toda la comunidad, y a la familia también, y lo que es más, no lo pensaba solamente ella. (64)

> [Our own men, Grandma, a mistake was being made, a mistake that the whole community would end up paying for, and the family too, and what's more, she wasn't the only one who thought so.] (45)

The young women are afraid that the older woman's claims to individualized corpses, and her always speaking of death, may produce the literal and discursive death of the family men that may still be alive. If Sofía insists on retrieving the corpses, Alejandra fears that the military will continue to produce just that: **dead** bodies.[27] Though Sofía senses the necessity of community support for her actions, she retains a localized interest in only the bodies of family men, for herself alone to identify.

The need to reconcile these partial visions of the political consequences of the widows' actions becomes urgent when other women begin to claim the bodies washed up on the riverbanks. Both Angelous women understand this development as a personal threat: for Alejandra, it brings the death of Dimitriou closer, and for Sofía, it lessens her singular hold on the corpses of family men. However, all of the women realize that they must struggle collectively against the universalized official story that the military sought to impose. The inclusive projection of the women's claims, in contrast to the military discourse, can only take shape through a voiced reconciliation of Sofía's and Alejandra's positions within their social community. They must recognize the link between the individual bodies they claim and the feminized social body of which they are all a part.

Thus, in the midst of the cries of a screaming child (a hint of the childbirth metaphor discussed in my next section), Alexis, who had formed a silent part of the choral "nosot**ras**" until that point, speaks to the importance of a humanized, cohesive community. He steps forward, as his twin Fidelia had done in the preceding segment, to position the women's claims within the context of the entire community's struggle for historical continuity:

> —O lo tenemos todos —dijo Alexis— o no lo tiene nadie. Que todas las mujeres vayan a reclamarlo para el entierro, todas las familias.
> —¿Y después?
> ¿Quién preguntó eso? ¿Yo, nosotras, la abuela, Alejandra, quién lo preguntó?
> —Y después —respondió Alexis con cuidado, y era la voz de Dimitriou ahora, **era la voz matriz y tierna y áspera de papá**— y después veremos. (emphasis mine, 74)

> ["Either he belongs to us all or he belongs to nobody. All the women have to claim him for burial, all the families."
> "And then?"
> Who asked that? Me, us, Grandma, Alexandra, who asked?
> "And then," Alexis answered carefully, with Dimitriou's voice now, it was **Papa's own tough and tender and pregnant voice**, "and then we'll see."] (emphasis mine, 53)

Alexis's response to the conflict expressed by Alejandra and Sofía shows that the family has discovered that theirs is not a private struggle over an individual corpse. Instead, it is a collective struggle to reconnect themselves to the *voz matriz* (fecund or "pregnant" voice) of their absent forebears, of the feminized social body/Motherland excluded from the military narrative. Instead of conserving the gendered boundaries that structure the militarized masculine Self, they deconstruct the correspondence of biology to stereotype. Alexis/Fidelia/*nosotras* speak through an integrated voice, at once *matriz* and *de papá*, feminine and masculine, present and past. Here the text suggests that Alexis is not merely acting as a man on behalf of the women's struggle: instead he is a part of an articulated social body. The community struggle depends upon this sense of integration in order to resist the military's totalizing and misogynist literality of the present, and to project a potentially hopeful alternative future.

Despite this narrative emphasis on nonmisogynist community integration, the fact that the only Angelous man is the person stepping forward to have the last word in this segment does pose several complications. Alexis is, after all, especially valued in the family and social contexts precisely because he is the last remaining (not disappeared) man. Why is it only the last Angelous **male** who can speak through "la voz matriz y tierna y áspera de papá" [Papa's own tough and tender and pregnant voice]? Does Alexis in effect subsume the women's voices through this gesture? Or are the women's voices made more effective through the intervention of Alexis/Dimitriou?

In this passage, Alexis moves within the collective of Angelous women as a counterpart to Dorfman's function as author of *Widows*, enacting Dorfman's own **desire** to join with and represent the women in the text. The boy Alexis is feminized within this body of women, and he takes part in the community-based narrative they represent, at the same time as his social value derives from his status as male within the family. As such, he is in a double position similar to Dorfman's: both are socialized and privileged as men, even as they are feminized by displacement in their respective social contexts. Alexis's capacity for speech (particularly his having the last word in this segment), like Dorfman's authorship, socially indicates his privilege. It is the displaced privilege of his masculinity that enables him to claim his own femininity as well.[28] The same is **not** true for the widows, because their displacement can never imply any "given" social status of masculine privilege.[29]

To establish a position from which to represent these men and women without reinscribing the author-itarian gesture, Dorfman justifies himself through showing the possibility of gender and community integration within the social body of a feminized Motherland. This possibility emerges through the very instability of personal identity as socially constructed (in these particular historical circumstances), a situation common to both the author and the characters. The community of women would have been more clearly established had Fidelia, not Alexis, stepped forward at the end of this segment. But because it is Alexis, Dorfman not only contests the literality of the military worldview, but also self-consciously inscribes the contradictory privilege of "la voz matriz y tierna y áspera de papá" [Papa's own tough and tender and pregnant voice]. In doing so, the author suggests that the complexities of social privilege do not simply disappear, even while self-identity may be radically redefined by an unstable sociopolitical context. Hence, Dorfman's own authorial position is at once self-affirming and self-contradictory. It is his position of social privilege that allows him to author, even as the text signals that the transformative potential of collective redefinition is a process beyond his individual control.

As Dorfman moves increasingly from an exploration of the male-centered sphere of military culture to a more complex analysis of interpersonal relationships (e.g., between the captain and the priest), he shows, like Theweleit, that domination does not derive solely from extreme versions of masculine military ideals. Instead, domination is produced through the sometimes hidden ways that gender boundaries are established culturally. Authoritarian terror is therefore **not** an aberration of history (in accordance with Laclau),[30] but a direct consequence of any particular historical moment, and of the predominant ways people interact with one another and construct their experience in language. *Widows* reveals that the ways that authority is maintained through socially established boundaries of gender and class operate via a violent logic of exclusion that extends from language to the realm of politics and back again. When these boundaries are violated, however, the very bases of authority necessarily fall into crisis.

In the above segments, normalcy—as understood by the military, the women, and the narrator—has already been violated by the violence manifested in such deep ruptures of traditional social relations. Moreover, this deep social instability has also necessarily produced textual instability, as indicated by the complex narrative postures developed up to this point in *Widows*. While Dorfman, through Alexis, aligns himself within the feminized social body/Motherland, it is unclear how this drama will be resolved within Chile itself. Because of these complications, any possibility of narrative resolution is left with the readers, and with those who would participate in history beyond the novel's frame. Only then will the outcome of the novel's dilemmas potentially be known: an eventual reconciliation of tradition and crisis, or of tradition and its transformation.

THE CHILDBIRTH METAPHOR:
WOMEN AS REPOSITORIES OF THE FUTURE?

As seen in the previous section, the first half of *Widows* examines the discursive struggle of two concepts of history. On one hand, the military (and initially, the omniscient narrator) work to impose an exclusively masculine, univocal, and universalized History: the narrative of the disciplined social body of the militarized state. On the other hand, the widows (and their emergence in the novel itself) develop an inclusive, multivocal story, and claim an historical continuity for their social body, through narrative incorporation of the absent members of their communities, of the feminized country. How each of these narratives might **give birth** to a different future (to return to a prominent theme in the Dorfman and Lohmann prologues) becomes a primary issue of the text in the segments dealing with Emmanuel and Cecilia (chapter 6, or segments ix and x), and later, Alexis and Sofía (chapter 7, or segment xi).

As we have seen, Dorfman makes explicit his troubled authorial position, vacillating between two narrative options in *Widows*. The first involves the necessity of textually **controlling** the possibilities raised by his characters and their representative contexts (an ethos dangerously similar to that which guides the military). The second requires that he relinquish control, thereby reflecting the extent to which the **community** narrates and delimits the author's personal possibilities for direct social participation through (and beyond) the text itself. By focusing increasingly on the options developed by the two "sons" in the novel, Emmanuel and Alexis, Dorfman simultaneously explores his own possibilities for participation, as a displaced "father" of this story, to effect social change. Ultimately, Dorfman suggests that the main force defining the social context of the novel is not the widows' claims as such, but the ways in which masculine culture might be challenged by and come to incorporate the community-based values that the widows represent. Through Alexis and Emmanuel, Dorfman most directly addresses the connection between the struggle to narrate the social body and the future of the country itself: will the Chile of the future more closely resemble the Fatherland of the captain and Emmanuel, or will it draw closer to the Motherland of the widows and Alexis? And how can the novel, by definition a univocal form, embrace multivocality as a narrative possibility?

Segment ix involves the temporal interplay of two alternating narratives of the orderly's visit to Felipe Kastoria's estate. The first thread of this segment takes place after the visit, in a debriefing session in which Emmanuel (as "el ordenanza" [the orderly]) responds to the captain's questioning about his exchange with Kastoria. The second thread narrates the dialogue between Emmanuel and his fiancé, Cecilia, who accompanies him on the afternoon of his drive to the Kastoria home. Through the narrative interweaving of these two threads, the **continuity** of masculine domination in Emmanuel's private and public lives emerges. Moreover, by revealing this continuity, the narrative crossover simultaneously exposes the distinction between gendered public and private spheres as a masculinist cultural construction implicitly contested by the narrative movement.[31]

While Emmanuel is placed in a submissive, feminized position with respect to the captain and Kastoria, he seeks to consolidate his own fiction of personal power by differentiating himself from Cecilia in the second narrative thread. When Emmanuel describes his youth to Cecilia, he claims that the most important thing he learned from his childhood was to seek an alliance with a father figure that was a "winner." Emmanuel's opportunistic view of male alliances at the center of his story leads him to accept his biological father's harsh punishment for Emmanuel's "betrayal" (his leaving home, 130) as a wartime defense of father-son hierarchies. He justifies the violence inscribed on his body as a discipline necessary for being a man. Although Emmanuel left his impoverished family to serve more powerful men, he did so because he felt that he had no other choice, if he did not want to "disappear" from history as his father had. From his childhood, Emmanuel therefore submits himself to this extreme version of reproduction of self: a militaristic masculinity, based primarily upon denial of desire and of human subjectivity.

So when Emmanuel recounts various personal details to the captain, the interplay of public fathers and wartime loyalties stimulates the captain to intervene, symbolically cutting off the orderly's ties with his childhood. The captain's interruption illustrates the truncation of personal continuity necessitated by military culture, whereby denial of subjectivity becomes the only thing which is reproduced:

> Ellos habían sido como padres para él cuando.
> —Cierto que te pedí detalles— se lamentó el capitán— pero todo lo que sea historia personal la puedes suprimir. . . . (133)

> [They had been like parents to him when he—
> "It's true I asked for details," complained the captain, "but you can skip the personal history.". . .] (101)

As the narrative itself illustrates, the captain suppresses any idea of the importance of Emmanuel's childhood by interrupting precisely when he might have completed the phrase, "cuando [era niño]" [when he {was a child}], which would have articulated a connection with the past that the captain could not accept. Despite the orderly's efforts to ensure his presence in the winner's history, then, the threat of his own disappearance becomes a real possibility, as seen by the fact that the captain repeatedly narrates **him**. Disappearance itself therefore can be understood as a metaphor for how the dictatorial masculine ideology strives to construct **all** identity, so that there ceases to be a self for any-body which is not comprehensively defined by military (and ruling class) interests.

However, just after this same moment, the captain refers to the orderly by name for the first time:

> Después dijo: —Emmanuel— y era la primera vez que pronunciaba su nombre, que no lo trataba con formalidad—, dime algo. ¿De veras han sido como padres para ti? (last words before narrative break, 133)

> [Then he said, "Emmanuel"—it was the first time he had pronounced his name, that he hadn't addressed him formally—"tell me something. Were they really like parents to you?"] (narrative break, 101)

Here the captain implicitly recognizes that Emmanuel's personal history is circumscribed by his official role: ideologically, the orderly's private and public selves amount to the same thing, as this segment's overall narrative movement suggests. The ultimate inability of these two men to suppress the personal connections that military culture denies, as seen in each of their struggles for authority, suggests the complexity of their social positions and narrative roles. Neither of them can simply be dismissed as inherently evil. Moreover, in belying the distinction between the public and the private, Emmanuel's assertion that the Kastorias "habían sido como padres para él" [had been like parents to him] emphasizes how deeply militaristic ideology is embedded in paternalistic notions of the family (and vice versa, as in the captain's exaggerated discourse to the nation, 98). Yet Emmanuel's fragmented history ultimately reveals that such a narrowly inscribed family/nation has little hope of survival.

When Emmanuel places a premium in his story on his search for a winning father, he seeks to control absence by determining how it will be filled. He also does this in his relationship with Cecilia. Emmanuel's desires for a woman become fulfilled through his own ability to fill in Cecilia's story (which he thinks of as "una ausencia física," 138 [an empty space, 105]) with his own narrative presence. While Emmanuel had been narrated by the dominant men, he creates a version of himself which excludes any version of Cecilia's identity but his own. Emmanuel's need for a woman is therefore a negative expression of his search for a father, and for his own masculinity. Both are means for self-affirmation in a context that threatens to "disappear" him, to subordinate his desires according to the ideology that disciplines his body. Since Emmanuel has resigned himself to this ethos, he, in turn, attempts to negate Cecilia's claims to self-determination beyond his control of her. Yet Emmanuel does not see that the dominance implicit in this vision of his relationship with Cecilia, and his denial of her, parallel the futility of throwing stones into the river (137).

In the passage that follows, the omniscient narrator makes explicit Emmanuel's negation of femininity. Here, the text reveals how Cecilia's perceptions of the river raise doubts for Emmanuel's version of masculinity, doubts which are necessarily dismissed by him, for they threaten his coherent self:

> Y como ella sólo murmuraba, es él, es él, es él, en voz muy baja y disonante, . . . Emmanuel decidió [investigar] . . . el río. Se veía mal. **Lo que parecía ser un hombre muerto (¿o era una mujer, podría ser una mujer con algo que se arrimaba a una cabellera escalofriante, eso que fluía negro?), el hombre estaba sumergido bajo el agua,** y las ramas . . . impedían **identificar con exactitud la forma** que las olas agitaban, subían, hacían descender, volvían a estrellar y ocultar detrás del follaje y las piedras. (emphasis mine, 142)

[Since she just kept muttering, it's him, it's him, it's him, in a very low toneless voice, . . . Emmanuel decided {to investigate} . . . the river. It looked bad. **What seemed to be a dead man (or was it a woman, could it be a woman with some sort of shivering long hair, that flowing blackness?), the man was submerged in the water**, and the tangled branches . . . obstructed the **clear identification of the form** the waves were agitating, lifting, sinking, dashing against the rocks, hiding behind the foliage.] (emphasis mine, 108–9)

Cecilia, like the Angelous women, sees the corpse/corpus of her history (presumably in the shape of her disappeared father, though this remains ambiguous) in the waters of the river, and she enters into the collective history that the river represents, the forces that Emmanuel does not and cannot know: the continuity of the feminized social body from which he has severed his ties. When Cecilia runs forward to reclaim the body, however, Emmanuel seeks to prove that her visions are false. Drawing from the logic of Theweleit, this passage highlights Emmanuel's need to distinguish forms from masses, the floating bodies from the chaotic limitlessness of the river (associated with the widows). The self-conscious narrative exposes this need by acknowledging, and later excluding, the possibility that the form/body in the river be "una mujer" [a woman], as the parenthetical revelation of Emmanuel's doubt is resolved with the affirmation that it was "el hombre" [the man]. This closure excludes the possibility of "woman" as "form"—a question raised and then closed down—narratively revealing the misogyny implicit in Emmanuel's necessary nonidentification of self with the river.

The sterility represented by Emmanuel's inability to situate himself within a continuous story—or as he had emphasized, his lack of "water" inside (130)—as well as the violence implied in his means of self-construction, all call into question his ability to project himself into the future. Moreover, he is incapable of dealing directly with Cecilia's identification with what the river represents. Emmanuel cannot interpret her cognitive distance from him or the plurality of her body, except literally, in its potential biological function in motherhood. Illustrative of this point, Emmanuel picks up a small pebble, which he calls the stone of truth, and asks Cecilia: "¿Estás esperando un niño?" (narrative break, 152) [Are you pregnant?] (narrative break, 116). When the text returns to this thread, Cecilia angrily answers that she is fine, but without picking up the pebble (154, end of segment ix). The narrator implies that Cecilia deceives Emmanuel due to her connection with the river of her personal history, which is intimately connected with the history of her community. Because she is aware of these connections with others, Cecilia does represent the symbolic possibility of carrying life within her, including (but certainly not limited to) potential motherhood. But due to Emmanuel's denial of his community, it seems doubtful that Emmanuel and Cecilia will together "give birth" to a common future.

Through the interweaving of the two threads of this segment, Dorfman attempts to portray the ways in which Emmanuel combats his own marginality by excluding femininity from his life story and values. Because he shows Emmanuel's solution to be a barren one, by demonstrating how and why Emmanuel excludes women, the author self-reflexively attempts to question the traditional father-son paradigm established in the prologues of the novel. In this segment, Dorfman shows how masculine exclusion operates and creates its own sterility (in terms of projecting a collective future): the narrative juxtaposition of multiple perspectives becomes truncated at the moment that feminine values must be repressed to assure the authority of masculine culture. Because Dorfman's fragmented style invites readers to participate in constructing this story, the interwoven narrative contests this repression of community-based values. Hence, Dorfman's self-reflexive meditation on masculine culture at the interpersonal level also reflects his concern with how he and his text might, from his own simultaneously marginal **and** empowered position, participate in the process of giving birth to a society with a fecund future. Because neither text nor author can engender this society themselves, Dorfman struggles to recuperate the community-based connections necessary to its becoming possible.

In contrast to Emmanuel's personally stifling solution portrayed in chapter 6, the next chapter focuses on alternative strategies for dealing with the dilemma of male marginality. Chapter 7 struggles with how masculine culture might come to include, and not repress, feminine values, how these sons (like the widows) might express desire for (and through) community, and how this community might, in turn, collectively "give birth" to a different future. Alexis, the other feminized son in the novel, offers an alternative to Emmanuel's repression of desire and community.

As discussed earlier, Alexis's function within the collective of Angelous women—as "la voz matriz y tierna y áspera de papá" (74) [Papa's own tough and tender and pregnant voice] (53)—enacts and thereby justifies Dorfman's own desire to represent the women in the text. For Dorfman, representation of the community women is basic to participation in a collective future, but what the author desires is for the community to authorize his representation of its members. This response is textually invited by the narrative gaps in the text (including the missing segment x, itself also evocative of the disappeared). When Alexis faces his grandmother in the prison cell in segment xi, he (like Dorfman) attempts to take on and represent her values, and further, to justify his survival (and his voice) as an authorized representative of this collective.

Like segment ix, segment xi intertwines two versions of a present moment. The first thread narrates between quotation marks the voiced (officially authorized) negotiation between the captain and Sofía regarding Alexis's incarceration, while the second thread narrates the interior (unauthorized) dialogue of Sofía and her grandson in the presence of the captain. While the first thread underscores the captain's inability to understand the Angelous's sense of community (because of his nonproductive self-affirmation), the second explores how life might be passed on from one generation to the next (symbolic childbirth). As this juxtaposition implies, the present is not unitary (as the military would hold), but multiple, and contains within it the many other moments (pasts and futures *in potentia*) that each person brings to it. The narrative voice is aligned with this multiple perspective of time from the opening words of the segment: "Antes de que le sacaran el capuchón, bastante antes de eso, Alexis ya sabe dónde se encuentra, recordó este lugar. Conoces esas escaleras . . ." (159) [Before they take the hood off, well before that, Alexis already knows where he is, he remembered this place. You know those stairs . . .] (123).

This "you," object of the implied narrative voice, is Alexis, who seems to be narrated by the silent caresses of his grandmother. Sofía's tracings of Alexis's **body** represent the connections with community which the captain cannot understand. While the captain awaits Sofía's response to his offer to free Alexis if she were to give up her cause—"—Aconséjeles a las mujeres que se vuelvan a su hogar" (162) ["Advise the women to go back home"] (125)—Alexis and Sofía debate about how to best ensure the present and future survival of their community. If Sofía refuses to cease her activities, remaining loyal to the principles of the women's struggle, Alexis (and perhaps she, too) will be sent to a violent end in the city. Even the other women may be subject to violent retaliation. If she gives in to the captain's requests, she and Alexis will presumably be freed, but they will have sold out their integrity, and their struggle, to the structures of the military regime.[32] How then can they guarantee their own survival? The text continues with Sofía's words:

> que los seres humanos no están nunca solos. que en las peores encrucijadas, era cosa de doblarse hacia adentro y ahí él, tú, cualquiera, encontraría algo que, bueno, uno llevaba a la gente que ama adentro. . . . [a] estos militares, . . . había que tenerles lástima, finalmente, porque eran tan ciegos que habían olvidado sus adentros. . . . cuando creían estarnos mirando sólo se veían a sí mismos, creían mirarse adentro y sólo lograban reflejarse su propia imagen como en un charco. (*sic*, 171–72)

> [that human beings are never alone. that at the worst moments it was a matter of turning inward and there he, you, whoever, would find some-

thing which, well, you carry the people you love inside. . . . one should feel sorry for these military men, finally, because they were so blind that they had forgotten their own insides. . . . when they thought they were looking at us, they only saw themselves, when they thought they were looking inside themselves, they only saw a reflection of their own images on the surface of a puddle.] (translation mine, *sic* from original)

While the military are capable of seeing only themselves in themselves, due to their totalizing vision of their own presence, Sofía notes that the real value of the Angelous family's claims to the body consists of each member of the community carrying the lives of others within. The matriarch does so herself: "ella estaba llena, repleta, hinchada, requete, de personas. y si no, cómo, cómo podría haber atravesado estos años" (*sic*, 173) [she was full, stuffed, totally swollen with people. and if not, how, how could she have gotten through these years] (*sic*, 134). Sofía therefore maintains that history lies in this potential of the symbolic **pregnancy** of carrying people **buried** deep inside themselves: "puedes estar seguro, alexis [*sic*], de que si tienes por lo menos una persona **enterrada** adentro, bien firme, creciente, que vas a volver" (emphasis mine, 173) [you can be sure, alexis {*sic*}, that if you have at least one person {**buried**} inside you, solid, growing, you'll make it back] (134). Sofía communicates to Alexis what she would not in the second chapter of the text, that Dimitriou is symbolically buried deep inside Alejandra. Are women, then, the repository of the future, the conceivers of a fecund Motherland? The text seems to answer "yes," insofar as they represent community-based values, and "no," insofar as this ability is not limited to biological females.

Thus, Sofía not only passes on to Alexis those bodies she carries inside, but also the community-based values (or femininity, in the terms of the novel) represented by the river and the widows. This fusion of death (burial) and life (birth), of past and future, hinges upon the integrity of a community that nourishes its historical continuity—that is, that tells its own story, narrates its own composite body. Sofía therefore is confident that Alexis will return. In contrast to Emmanuel, Alexis's relationship with the community means that his story will be retold, and, since he is connected with other human beings, he has a conceivable future. Childbirth, or the birth of the future, therefore becomes something general that men and women may share, an awareness by which each member may be a representative of the whole community. Ultimately, then, Dorfman's "utopia" is solidarity: an ideal materially embodied by those resistant communities who live out the values embraced in *Widows*.

Like Alexis's alternative to Emmanuel's "son-hood," Dorfman's version of fatherhood (authorship) is valorized as positive because it is pro-motherhood. But Dorfman's authorial position is a tricky one, for it is through the privilege of his masculinity that he claims his femininity, giving written form to the materiality of the women's struggle "aquí o en otra parte" [here or elsewhere]. It is his own replication of the quest for a father (a model for his authority), likewise, that leads him to produce a "son," "esta novela" [this novel], as stated in the prologue. However, because of the real challenges to traditional modes of representational power being waged in the communities from which he was displaced, Dorfman's search for a father leads him to discover, and to depend upon, a mother figure (the widows) that textually embodies the possibility—and, importantly, the limits—of his own resistance.

Widows' focus on complex male characters, its fragmented style, and its displaced language therefore show how the widows' claim to narrative power deeply challenges any construction of masculine identity. Their claims challenge not only military culture (which violently excludes femininity), but also any nonmilitarized version of masculinity that seeks to fairly represent femininity as well. It is Dorfman's desire-based need—however contradictory—to take into account the challenges posed by real women to masculine-centered cultural constructs that most fundamentally characterizes *Widows*—and, in my view, the postcoup work of several male Chilean writers of his literary generation (e.g., Benavente, to be discussed in chapter 3) and the next (e.g., the younger poets Raúl Zurita and Diego Maqueira, among others).

In fact, it is this response by Chilean men on the left that most distinguishes the country's literary relationship to resistance movements from those of other Latin American contexts also experiencing the rebirth of women's movements, whether under dictatorship or in the context of revolutionary change, in the late 1970s and early 1980s. Unlike the Argentine playwright Eduardo Pavlovsky's *Paso de dos*, which as Diana Taylor eloquently writes, "reaffirmed the continuity of a misogynist version of Argentine nationhood as well as the gendered structure of representation itself,"[33] the Chilean writers studied in these pages set out to break the links between misogyny and nation, and between authoritarianism and language. And unlike the Nicaraguan Omar Cabezas's wonderfully engaging focus on the revolutionary "New Man" in *La montaña es algo más que una inmensa estepa verde* [*Fire from the Mountain*], this new Chilean literature says that perhaps one flaw of Latin American revolutions has been the "new" society's blindness to the entrenched forms of domination that they, too, reproduced.[34] If not seeing those errors in part led to the failure of Allende's Popular Unity project, these Chilean writers suggest, we must now learn the lesson if we are ever to rid ourselves of "the Pinochet within"—each person's piece of the authoritarianism generated from among ourselves. This literature also says that change cannot happen within a closed feminist enclave, but must instead cut across the strata of society where forms of domination are most entrenched. Ultimately, Dorfman argues, it is not enough for Chilean men to thank the mothers, as Adriana says in my epigraph, but to **be** mothers (in the figurative sense), with an eye toward society's revolutionizing motherhood altogether.

Of course, framing change within a structure such as motherhood, rendered problematic because of its status within masculinist discourse, is not without irony. But counter to Diana Taylor's thoughtful remarks about the Argentine Madres de la Plaza de Mayo [Mothers of the Plaza de Mayo], in which she suggests that feminist transformation will never come out of the "bad script" of motherhood, it seems to me that it is important to recognize the transformational potential of acts "disguised" within the terms of the dominant ideology (which James C. Scott terms the "use-value of hegemony"). In his *Domination and the Arts of Resistance*, Scott writes:

> [Cultural forms of the powerless] insinuate a critique of power while hiding behind anonymity or behind innocuous understandings of their conduct. These patterns of disguising ideological insubordination are somewhat analogous to the patterns by which, in my experience, peasants and slaves have disguised their efforts to thwart material appropriation of their labor: for example, poaching, foot-dragging, pilfering, dissimulation, flight. Together, these forms of insubordination might suitably be called the infrapolitics of the powerless.[35]

About the Mothers of the Plaza de Mayo he further states: "By clothing their defiance in hegemonic dress, these women were able to challenge the regime in other respects."[36] Taylor may be right to signal that the Madres' "scripting" of motherhood does not **necessarily** lead to social transformation, but my point is that it **may**. Whether the forms of resistance embodied by the Agrupación members and represented literarily in texts like *Widows* end as "bad scripts," or rewrite the terms of the story, obviously depends on Chileans themselves. Certainly nothing will be gained, however, if feminists and leftists cede the entire discursive and political terrain of motherhood and the family to the patriarchal right.

At the close of *Widows*, dawn arrives, and the soldiers take Alexis away. Nonetheless, Sofía is confident that Alexis (as "mother") will return. The last words of the chapter complete this characterization, as they point to Alexis's own birth as a narrator of himself and of his future. For the first time in this segment, he ceases to be the "you" [tú], narrated by and through his grandmother, to join with others as an empowered "I" within the community: "El, Alexis, iba a sobrevivir. Me iba a la capital a encontrar a mi papá" (177) [He, Alexis, was going to survive. I was going to the capital to find my father] (137). Like Dorfman, Alexis claims that he is prepared to give birth to and narrate his displaced history, to shape his destiny. Through Alexis, Dorfman intimates that if he struggles to break the literality of misogyny and the violence of gendered constructs, even if he alone cannot completely succeed, the sterility of the patrilineal paradigm may also be broken.

The contradictions of Dorfman's authorial position highlight the difficulty of this prospect, as well as the impossibility of a total escape from the dominant cultural codes within which resistance necessarily functions. By incorporating these contradictions, and showing himself as struggling to narrate (while himself being narrated by the contexts he attempts to represent), Dorfman implies that there are (complex) alternatives to the expansive sterility of military worldviews. Though he inevitably does so from the risky position of a male who authorially narrates his version of these contexts, he enacts his own desire for community-based narratives that would negate the necessity for him to tell this story ever again.

In the closing segments of *Widows* (chapter 8, segments xii and xiii), the captain faces his last chance to consolidate his personal and political position through direct, material violence. When he meets his armed troops at the scene of the women's final gathering at the banks of the river, he once again feels weak, out of control, dazed by the spiraling process of throwing more stones into the river, as had Emmanuel, without changing its course. The battle over gender boundaries at the center of the military worldview lies bare, as the squadron prepares to fire upon the unarmed women.

As if to mock the captain, a third body washes ashore, and the narrative *nosotras* again emerges as the widows claim it. The collective social body of the women stands not only between the soldiers and the river, but represents the very basis of historical continuity that the soldiers must eradicate. Precisely because this collective represents more than its own group of bodies, the text emphasizes that Alexis, the community, and other collective bodies will keep on returning, keep on "giving birth." The novel ends with these words:

> Esperaron la orden del teniente.
> Mientras **el muerto** se mecía entre nuestros brazos como **un recién nacido**. (emphasis mine, 187)

> [They waited for the lieutenant's order.
> While the body {**the dead man**} was rocked in our arms like a **newborn child**.] (emphasis mine, 146)

While the novel resists closure—we do not know whether the soldiers fire or not—there remains the idea that formal finality does not matter: it would only replicate the absolute determinism latent in the cultural boundaries enforced by the military. The parallel of the dead man ("el muerto") with a newborn ("un recién nacido") consolidates the connection of past, present, and future through community-based narratives of the feminized social body. Because such narratives exist, resistance is possible, and *el muerto* comes to represent life, the reclamation of collective history which parallels giving birth to the communal future of a Chilean Motherland that has struggled deeply with eradicating "the Pinochet within." The bodies of the disappeared exist through the ways in which people tell their stories, in the way they have been, are, and will be narrated. The social text, produced from the social body, is therefore projected toward all men and women who open themselves to their communities, and who attempt to exorcise authoritarianism in their lives, despite inevitable contradictions. As future communities empower themselves through collective self-representation, any univocal representation might then, according to Dorfman's ideal, become unnecessary.

3
The Hungry Body and Patchwork Histories

> It will be women who turn the tables [que darán vuelta a la tortilla]. They are the most affected by the situation. The humble, calm housewife is not what she used to be. She is no longer bound to the home. And this is a process where there's no going back.
> —Isolda, shantytown dweller (1987)[1]

> *Maruja.* ¿Y qué fue lo que hizo sin el Mario, señora María Luisa, por Dios?
> *María Luisa.* Apechugar, ¿qué es lo que iba a hacer?
>
> [*Maruja.* My God, señora María Luisa, what did you do without Mario around?
> *María Luisa.* Keep a stiff upper lip. Carry the weight. What else was I going to do?]
> —David Benavente/TIT, *Tres Marías y una Rosa* (1979)

THE COMING OF AGE OF ALTERNATIVE CHILEAN THEATER[2] AFTER THE 1973 COUP depended upon each theater collective's ability to bear witness to the resistance of the social body to being officially disappeared from postcoup history, a project shared by Ariel Dorfman and other leftist intellectuals as well. But while Dorfman approached the realities of his country from the "immediate and distant" experience of exile, independent theater groups in Santiago had to face the pressures of the context from within it—including real and threatened violations of human rights, the effects of economic neoliberalism and increasing poverty, and an overall social climate of distrust. However, direct experience of this context included not only those negative dimensions, but also a heightened potential for awareness of, and connection to, the nascent forms of dissent slowly surfacing from various officially excluded sectors of postcoup society. Independent theater's **coming to terms** with these conditions, then, literally meant finding the words and the movements, and developing overall artistic strategies adequate for representing emergent alternatives to the master narrative of Chile under Pinochet. This process occurred while theater itself struggled materially in a context officially hostile to cultural productions dealing even obliquely with recent historical contingencies. Yet independent theater groups in Santiago simultaneously responded to the immediacy of the institutional crisis and participated in the slow, ongoing process of social rearticulation being pieced together within Chilean society during the late 1970s.

Like the captain's situation in Dorfman's *Widows*, the Pinochet regime faced an early need to consolidate its own authority after the initial wave of violence following the military coup. In contrast to the captain, however, the Pinochet regime sought to articulate an economic model that would lend apparent coherence to its specific political project.[3] Such a model was proposed in 1975 by Pinochet's economic team, known as the "Chicago Boys" for their personal and intellectual ties to the University of Chicago economist Milton Friedman. The Chicago Boys advocated an anti-Keynesian, neoliberal restructuring of the Chilean economy, in which national and international "free" market forces alone would regulate all economic activities—a radical experiment that led Chile to be proclaimed an economic showcase for the world to watch.[4]

Using words appropriately similar to the regime's own discourse, Friedman likened this early restructuring of Chile's economy to the application of a "shock treatment" necessary for "curing" its main "ill," the big government spending associated with the Allende years. Advocating strict discipline for a social body/country in need of intervention, Friedman stated:

> I don't think that gradually implemented economic policies make sense for Chile. **I'm afraid that the patient could die before the treatment takes effect.** . . . I believe Chile stands to gain if it considers **shock treatment** [as a cure] for the problems of inflation and disorganization.[5]

The disturbing correspondence between the literal shock treatments taking place in Chilean torture chambers and Friedman's description of the economic "shocks" employed to restructure a "chaotic" socialized economy could not be more revealing. In both cases, Chile became a laboratory for nongradualist treatment of a social body that was assumed to be diseased. The violence of intervention was thereby justified as a means for achieving economic and political "health," regardless of the pain or social costs incurred along the way.

In *La herencia de los Chicago Boys* [The Legacy of the Chicago Boys], Manuel Délano and Hugo Traslaviña hold that only within such a violent authoritarian context could the radical economic experiments conducted in Chile beginning in the mid-1970s have taken place. Not only did the pervasive security apparatus ensure social order, but also the sanitized, technocratic appearance of the economic plan itself seemingly depoliticized subsequent policy decisions. The effects of the regime's economic shock treatment, in symbiosis with the repressive political system, were indeed startling. Both economic and political power became concentrated within the hands of a very few Chileans (a fact ignored by official proclamations of an economic "miracle"), while extreme poverty further marginalized the same working-class people who were seen as the internal enemy of the military regime.[6] Whereas the military had relied on direct repression (and had even relocated many *pobladores* to the outskirts of the city, thereby fragmenting shantytown organizations and "cleansing" the city center of the poor), its economic policies provided a more indirect mechanism for social control.[7] Widespread unemployment became a continuous, systematic form of excising the social body's "diseased members," since those who lost their jobs also lost access to formal workplaces, a traditional channel for public participation and organization.[8] Economic neoliberalism therefore served several of the regime's key political interests: the dominant classes were appeased and rewarded for supporting the military government, while economic inequity and hunger became the regime's indirect (and ostensibly legitimate) tools for excluding lower-income people from the formal exercise of political power.

As unemployment became a particularly severe problem among working-class men, a number of those who remained working in informal economic sectors or in the home (mostly working-class women) were compelled to find new ways to meet the most pressing material needs of their families. Many subsistence organizations, including cooperative shopping *(comprando juntos)*, collective neighborhood soup kitchens *(ollas comunes)*, and artisans' workshops *(talleres artesanales)*, were formed under the auspices of the Vicariate of Solidarity, and a majority of them were sustained by shantytown women *(pobladoras)*.[9] Since increasing numbers of these women, motivated by their traditional roles as food providers for husbands and children, became organized to treat domestic economic problems collectively, the public–private distinction—a construct serving the regime's interest in social fragmentation—increasingly broke down. Many *pobladoras* came together to (re)discover that hunger and other issues affected them similarly as working-class women, and were therefore not merely private, individual problems. Instead, these issues provided a material base for active social intervention.[10]

The first specifically **artisan**-oriented workshops grew out of distinct needs that arose immediately after the coup. One of the earliest petitions placed by political prisoners in 1974 to the Comité Pro Paz [Committee for Peace in Chile, later the Vicariate of Solidarity] was for an outlet for selling handicrafts made in the prisons and concentration camps from available scraps (including soup bones, matches, and the like). Simultaneously, groups such as the Association of Family Members of the Detained-Disappeared began to produce *arpilleras*, colorful appliquéd and embroidered burlap-backed wall hangings, as a means for representing their personal and collective pain. When people working in the Vicariate programs for the unemployed *(bolsas de cesantes)* also began to make handicrafts, the Vicariate strengthened its network to sell these products locally and internationally as symbols of Chilean resistance.[11] By the late 1970s, small workshops had formed in a majority of Santiago shantytowns, each with a regular meeting place at the local church, at the neighborhood center, or at a member's home.

While most workshop members began to produce handicrafts to sell as a means of economic subsistence, the development of any community-based form of representation necessarily began with facing the mistrust and fear that had so radically altered the ways in which interpersonal relations could take place. As the playwright David Benavente observed in his ironically titled essay "Ave Félix" [Bird of Happiness, also a wordplay on "Phoenix"], postcoup society was like a "tower of silence,"[12] in which even the most intimate aspects of human relations were marked by suspicion and self-censorship:

> In that context, the suppression of language became the language of repression, which wasn't limited to public spaces, but which penetrated the intimate realm, blocking and interfering with interpersonal relationships and private conversations.[13]

The act of joining together to meet shared material needs provided the basis for dealing with this deep social fragmentation. Over time, artisans' workshops became a space to address the fear of communicating about repression, to regain personal dignity through work, and to piece together the organizational skills necessary for collective problem-solving. The workshop network likewise provided a realm for reestablishing some democratic modes of social participation, despite official prohibition of any collective form of organization.[14]

In several workshops, this process of shared communication among women outside of their homes also stimulated reflection on the combined gender and class dimensions of their situation as *pobladoras* (shantytown women), including not only issues of marginalization and hunger, but also of domestic violence, birth control, sexuality, and child care. For many of the women with whom I spoke, this process of shared reflection began with discovering the ability to speak publicly about interrelated personal and community needs, despite feeling culturally silenced as working-class women. For Yolanda, who described herself as a stutterer, and several others who mentioned prior physical or psychological inhibitions from speaking in public, participation in workshops had meant overcoming several very real obstacles. Elizabeth, a shantytown dweller and *arpillerista* (*arpillera* maker) from Puente Alto, maintained that a major consequence of this collective participation was the workshop members' greater sense of independence as women:

> Making an evaluation of all the work done with women during all these years, I think there has been a lot of progress, in personal growth, in learning how to face life and society as a woman, and not as dependent upon men.[15]

Arpilleristas like Elizabeth and Yolanda developed a particular, materially grounded language for representing daily life in the shantytowns, by literally and figuratively piecing together local history. In the *arpilleras*, artisans would join together bits of discarded clothing and other used materials, including newspaper scraps, grains of rice, or even locks of hair, which would be sewn onto a backing made of burlap (a fabric typically used for feed sacks and from which the craft drew its name). As is well known, the colorful wall hangings often depicted working-class neighborhood scenes that had become commonplace after the coup—people gathered around the community soup pot, nocturnal police arrests, power outages, closed factories and schools, and even women stitching *arpilleras*—but nearly all were portrayed on a background including the Andes and a bright sun. Somber realities were represented with vibrantly colored images, and in this way, the *arpilleras* reflected both the repression and loss, and the bottom-up struggles for change emerging from local communities. Because the *arpilleras* portrayed daily life as a collective, community-based activity, they reconstructed the connections between the personal and communal situations of the shantytown dwellers, and became a means for telling the stories that were systematically censored from political history under Pinochet.

In her book on the *arpilleristas*, aptly titled *Scraps of Life*, the Chilean poet and literary critic Marjorie Agosín observes that the early *arpilleras* of 1973–74 ("when the lives of so many had been shattered")[16] were composed of many disparate visual images. Only when the women's collective organization had strengthened did the *arpilleras* become more holistic compositions, because, as Agosín states, "the world was being put back together again."[17] Of course, the women's increasing skill and experience over time, and the successful sales of *arpilleras* in the international market context, also very likely influenced this trajectory. But Agosín is right to suggest that the development of a visual language for representing local, collective experiences depended upon the rejoining of communities through the development of functional organizations. For this reason, it is significant that the representations of daily community scenes in the *arpilleras* sometimes included part of a *pobladora*'s physical body (e.g., her hair). Like the actions of the Agrupación discussed in the previous chapter, the *arpilleras* reflected the vital continuity of individual and social bodies, of personal and collective stories. The *arpilleras* not only pieced together the shared local history of daily life in the shantytowns, but also served to reaffirm the community's ability to speak for itself.

Within the postcoup context, then, what began as a material struggle to subsist—literally, to provide food for hungry bodies—became a collective locus for claiming narrative power, for participation in local history. The act of feeding the individual, physical body depended upon a **rearticulation** of the social body, in both senses of the word: as a simultaneous rejoining and revoicing of community during a time of fierce social fragmentation. By combating both hunger and silence, the collective survival strategies pieced together by the *arpilleristas* in subsistence workshops gave testimony to the resistance of the social body's "diseased" members to being officially eliminated—politically and economically—from the social narrative of Chile after 1973. For the *arpilleristas*, developing a language of community-based representation was an integral part of their struggle to survive.[18]

The need to tell this story of community survival likewise stimulated leftist professionals to respond to the changing roles of women as social protagonists, particularly in the shantytowns, after 1973.[19] Independent professional theater in Santiago was one major area of cultural production that rediscovered its own ability to speak by taking into account the postcoup experiences of organization that had fostered working-class community claims to representational power. This trajectory is particularly clear in two plays marking alternative Chilean theater's late 1970s renaissance,[20] *Pedro, Juan y Diego* [Pedro, Juan, and Diego] (1976) and *Tres Marías y una Rosa* [Three Marías and a Rosa] (1979).

The theater collective ICTUS and David Benavente's *Pedro, Juan y Diego*, produced in 1976, portrays Chile's sociopolitical context through a focus on the struggles, humor, and frustrations of three unemployed working-class men, who find work in the state-subsidized Programa de Empleo Mínimo [Program for Minimum Employment].[21] The protagonists receive scant pay for building a wall with no apparent function, and their attempts to maintain a sense of purpose through their work are systematically thwarted by their government supervisors. The three men also compete to gain the favor of the only female character in the play, "La Muda," a woman who became mute, "hace como dos años, por un susto muy re'grande que tuvo" (33) [about two years ago, because of a really big scare she had], or as the audience would infer, as a consequence of the 1973 coup. Because of the terror linked with her muteness, La Muda incarnates the paralysis of fear, isolation, and an absolute incapacity to speak in the repressive context in which all of the characters lived. In this 1976 play, the most seemingly marginal character of all—a working-class woman, characterized by an extreme version of the stereotypically feminine traits of silence and passivity—represents the state of terror that had taken over in a populace emasculated by the widespread violence exercised by the military regime.

In this early postcoup play, however, the community remains defined through a traditional male-centered lens. Throughout the play, La Muda's capacity to speak depends upon the ability of Pedro, Juan, and Diego to join together in a collective project, and to maintain their dignity despite the governmental mechanisms that deny it. By the end of the play, the male protagonists decide to decorate and inaugurate their useless wall, a ceremony in which La Muda participates. As a government bulldozer drives forward to demolish the wall, the men sing in celebration of their work, and La Muda spontaneously joins in, signaling with her voice the triumph of their collective dignity over the silence, fear, and humiliation propagated by the regime. In doing so, however, La Muda implicitly reaffirms the male protagonists' sense of worth as men fulfilling their traditional roles as public workers and satisfiers of (what they perceive to be) women's needs.

Three years after *Pedro, Juan y Diego*, in which the survival of the community—the ability of the silenced to speak—hinged upon the incorporation of La Muda into the activity of the male protagonists, *Tres Marías y una Rosa* (1979),[22] cowritten by David Benavente and the Taller de Investigación Teatral [the Investigative Theater Workshop, for which I will use its Spanish acronym TIT], dramatized community-based survival as dependent on the organization of working-class women themselves. This play took as its focus the female-centered world of the *arpillera* workshops. While *Pedro, Juan y Diego* must be credited with opening the path for independent theater to reemerge in the late 1970s—because its indirect, but clear, reference to the crisis demonstrated that critical expression was again possible within alternative plays—it was *Tres Marías y una Rosa* that touched a cultural nerve, attracting record audiences during its extended run in Santiago.[23] By the end of 1979, nineteen *obras alternativas-críticas* (alternative-critical plays) had been produced in Santiago playhouses, a figure that nearly doubled by 1981.[24] As I will discuss in the following sections, the representation of shantytown women as social protagonists in *Tres Marías y una Rosa*, as well as the circumstances surrounding the play's production, provide an illuminating view of how the changing social participation of working-class women and men reshaped both the dominant social narrative and the production of alternative professional culture in Chile after 1973.

REARTICULATING THE SOCIAL BODY: "DOMESTICATED" THEATER AND THE TALLER DE INVESTIGACIÓN TEATRAL (TIT)

Before approaching the play specifically, it is important to note the ways in which independent professional theater groups had withstood similar pressures to those levied against other publicly oriented and collective organizations immediately after the military coup. The Pinochet regime initially relied on direct repression tactics (such as mandatory closings of plays, arrests, or violent "accidents" that befell theater spaces and artists) to curb the production of alternative theater during the early postcoup years.[25] After a 1977 incident—the late-night burning of the tent housing a production of Jaime Vadell and José M. Salcedo's *Hojas de Parra* [Pages by Parra]—drew international repudiation, the regime set aside direct violence in favor of more indirect economic pressures as the preferred means for disciplining alternative theater collectives.[26] Any theater event not accepted by the Ministry of Education as "cultural" would carry a 22 percent tax (IVA) added to the ticket price. Clearly, this designation of plays as cultural or not was a political decision, as the regime supported foreign classics, particularly Spanish Golden Age and French theater, while taxing plays it considered referential to contemporary Chile. Such economic pressures effectively reduced the public who could afford to attend alternative plays, while also undercutting the economic stability of the independent theater groups themselves. After the regime's neoliberal economic policies also took effect, the reduced buying power of the middle and working classes further limited the theatergoing public.

These pressures, coupled with the generalized strain of censorship and self-censorship, subjected alternative theater to an overall process of "domestication."[27] Theater spaces were reduced in number and size, and dramatic subject matter focused upon the personal manifestations of sociopolitical crisis, rather than referring directly to the military regime. As it turned out, representing day-to-day conflicts framed by a backdrop of social uncertainty provided a rich metaphorical structure for exploring many forms of authoritarianism and resistance enacted within specifically local contexts. Such indirect representations also fostered a sense of complicity between the characters and the audience, which served for overcoming, however fleetingly, the inability to criticize the regime publicly. As Manuel Antonio Garretón succinctly noted in 1980, the collective action of coming together in the space of a theater led to a ritual of rearticulation, for audience members would leave with the sense that "there aren't so few of us, because so many people applauded."[28] At the same time that alternative theater relied upon an intimacy established through its indirect language, then, it used that language to reforge social connections, joining other precarious local struggles for representational power taking place in pockets scattered throughout postcoup society.

So while alternative theater groups, like the *arpilleristas*, necessarily came "home" to the domestic conflicts resulting from the sociopolitical crisis, both did so in order to contribute publicly to the formation of alternative discourses and practices elsewhere in the country. But while the *arpilleristas* took daily life in the shantytowns as their referential base, independent theater took the metarepresentational stance of reflecting in its own discourse other new forms of resistance culture, like the *arpilleras*, that both composed and reshaped the postcoup cultural context itself. This proved to be both a productive and a contradictory relationship, as the process of producing *Tres Marías y una Rosa* illustrates.

Based on direct observation of women artisans in the Santiago shantytown Lo Hermida, a group-oriented methodology was used to create the play. This collective endeavor aimed to generate a dramatic language which could represent the lived experiences of women in the officially excluded periphery of the city. In contrast to the efforts of an individual exiled author like Dorfman, as mentioned previously, the members of the TIT sought to participate in a project that would contest the univocality of militarized society from within very local circumstances inside the country. Like Dorfman, though, the TIT's public authorship in the postcoup context implied coming to terms with the contradictions of social privilege implied by any such claim to authority.

Thanks to efforts by the Centro de Indagación y Expresión Cultural y Artística [Center for Research on Cultural and Artistic Expression] or CENECA, there is a surprising amount of documentation about the early postcoup activities of theater collectives such as the TIT, ICTUS, Imagen, and La Feria. As Hurtado and Ochensius note in the Introduction to their *testimonio* series "Maneras de hacer y pensar el teatro en el Chile actual" [Ways of creating and thinking about theater in Chile today], this research had three main objectives: to see how theater reemerged as a movement grounded in national realities, to study the social effects of artistic praxis, and to systematize the experience.[29] That is, CENECA worked to create bridges between the various threads of theater activity, so that distinct experiences could expand rather than be lost. It is important to note that CENECA was a collective formed by intellectuals and artists displaced from Chilean universities after the coup. Its substantial thinking about postcoup alternative theater practices and theory marked what Hernán Vidal has called the inauguration of a new discipline, the sociology of theater, during the military dictatorship.[30]

According to volume 3 of CENECA's *testimonio* series, the TIT came together in 1974 as a self-supported, independent theater group consisting of ten members, the majority of whom were students of Raúl Osorio, the director of the group, at the Catholic University in Santiago. Osorio noted that the TIT initially formed to combat the institutional fragmentation of the theater movement after 1973. It sought "to propose alternative lines of [creative] action and to say what people were thinking about theater as a vehicle of communication and as art."[31] From its beginnings, the TIT's bottom-up methods of collective creation, inspired by Augusto Boal's "theater of the oppressed,"[32] contested the hierarchical nature of traditional theater groups—and implicitly, of the authoritarian regime. Osorio describes that paradigm as "a very precise model: there is a vertical mode of government, with a group of people who don't participate, who instead only follow orders."[33] Though the TIT began its work with the impetus to produce *teatro de servicio*[34]—that is, theater about conflicts of the working class, performed for working-class audiences, and stimulating audience reflection—the TIT's precarious economic position required that it change production strategies over time. The subsequent changes not only reflected the difficult position of independent professional theater after the coup, but also required that the TIT justify its claim to represent working-class collectives in the postcoup context.

In order to approach the untold realities of daily life in militarized Chile, the TIT based its work on direct participatory observation of those social sectors made invisible by official discourse and the mass media, and by the bulk of theater classics being produced at the time. The TIT began with investigation of the *bolsas de cesantes* and the artisans' workshops (especially of *arpilleristas*) formed through the Vicariate of Solidarity. They chose to work with these groups because they represented "a new type of organization" under the military regime, in which the unemployed developed the manual skills necessary for their economic subsistence.[35] After each session of participatory observation with workshop members, the TIT actors would write *memorias* (memories, or notes). These *memorias* were first or third person narrations about the actual or potential actions of their "characters" (workshop members), which emphasized sensory, physical, or emotive aspects over the stated goal of the action. That is, the actors privileged what people **did**—and how they did it—over what they **said** about their situations. Using the perspectives gleaned through writing these *memorias*, the actors would improvise onstage interactions between their working-class characters. These improvisations in turn provided material to be used in the play, which would link together the conflicts, reactions, and gestures of working-class characters to dramatize their daily lives.[36]

The TIT's reliance on physical action over dialogue was essential to their goal: "doing plays . . . not writing plays."[37] Given the danger of overtly politicized speech in the early postcoup context, the TIT chose to ground theatrical language in the materiality of community-based acts of survival. Rather than focus on the ontological meaning of repression, the TIT's method recuperated the small gestures of opposition and resistance that were absent from official discourse. According to the TIT's methodology, such resistance emerged from the materiality of personal necessities, work, and daily living, grounded in the most local site for narrating those experiences: the body.

Hence, the TIT relied upon the antirhetorical, subjective, and bodily emphases of the various actors' *memorias* as a base from which to articulate and embody the hidden aspects of the collective memory. In the words of TIT actor Luz Jiménez (Maruja in *Tres Marías y una Rosa*):

> I think that if anything characterizes our way of working with our characters, it is the emotion [la afectividad] that ties us to them. For example, when I observe a woman, I think that the difference between what I do and what a professional imitator does is that I have a commitment to this woman, an emotional, ethical, and artistic commitment [un compromiso afectivo, ético y artístico]. . . . Without such a commitment, I'd be left only with a sketch. . . .[38]

Actor Loreto Valenzuela (María Ester) adds:

> The emotional commitment [el compromiso afectivo] that is produced with this method is something that we've been learning to channel in practical terms. It can happen that you produce things in the character you're developing that aren't really about her, that are only about your own needs. It's very difficult: you are a human being and your character, in our case, is also a human being.[39]

Despite the rigorous nature of their documentation, the members of the group did not claim objectivity, but instead focused upon the reestablishment of emotional links ("el compromiso afectivo") with the people and communities that they would represent on stage. Such a commitment was posited as the base for bridging the blocks in interpersonal relationships Benavente described as the postcoup "tower of silence." By filling in each "sketch" with the flesh of a human being, the TIT embodied a theatrical language that represented affective connections in interpersonal relations, thereby playing a part in the reconstruction of an emotionally repressed social body. In this regard, the TIT's work shares a common stance to that of Pía Barros, whose short stories on desire-based interpersonal connections provide the focus for the next chapter.

After the TIT's first collective production, *Los payasos de la esperanza* [Harlequins of Hope] (1977), a play based on the grinding sensation of waiting experienced in a Vicariate workshop for unemployed clowns, the history of the group took some turns that in part paralleled the women artisans' dilemmas represented two years later in *Tres Marías y una Rosa*. Because the male actors in *Los payasos de la esperanza* became inactive after that production, the group split, leaving only its female members and the director Osorio, who assessed the situation as follows:

> It was not a political or artistic schism. . . . There was a series of circumstances like the fact that the play being prepared, TMYR [*Tres Marías y una Rosa*], had only female characters, and they were already working when *Los payasos de la esperanza* debuted. But once the work on TMYR was advanced, the men in the group weren't working on anything. If we had had a parallel project to TMYR for the men, it is most likely that the Workshop [TIT] would have retained its original composition.[40]

While Osorio believed that the group's split was neither political nor artistic, it was actually both, insofar as the group had been challenged by the same "absent" antagonist as the characters of the plays: the pervasive context of social rupture of late 1970s Chile. The resulting difficulties caused by the marginalization of the men from the TIT echoed in part the gender-based division of activities documented in *Tres Marías y una Rosa*, in which no men appeared on stage. Despite class differences, for both the working-class *arpilleristas* portrayed in the play and for the TIT itself, the displacement of men from the center of (public) activity was the catalyst for a crisis of authority in their collective organizations.

But the group's difficulties were not limited to the political dimension, or to the aesthetic challenges resulting from the new context. In addition, economic pressures to produce the play quickly pushed the TIT to change its production strategy. *Tres Marías y una Rosa* would be produced in a central Santiago playhouse in order to attract a larger audience, and to guarantee infrastructural stability for the production, since it would not have to move from location to location.[41] While *Los payasos de la esperanza* had been performed in various Santiago shantytowns, according to the group's desire to perform *teatro de servicio* for the working class, the group now moved to the more lucrative center of the city, though a central Santiago playhouse would be less economically accessible to working-class people. This move, in effect, paralleled the movement toward integration into the market economy that was happening on a much larger scale throughout neoliberal Chile. Due to the inescapable pressures of the market, the TIT had to face new philosophical contradictions.

In the TIT's conversations with CENECA, members of the theater group maintained that this decision to move the play to the center did not reflect a change in its initial goal of service. Instead, they argued that distribution through a playhouse was a less paternalistic way to reach the working classes,[42] and that the potential diversification of their audience (including upper and middle classes) would allow for broader reflection on the situations represented on stage. However, the TIT's arguments highlight their philosophical struggle to justify this move away from the marginal neighborhoods. The most striking explanation for this change is given by actor Soledad Alonso (Rosa):

> The fact of being in a theater, trying to sustain and defend an identity that corresponds to the group's chosen path of evolution, is what producing culture is all about. Otherwise, you just **disappear** [porque si no, se **desaparece**].[43]

Alonso holds that theater itself was threatened with the marginality basic to the postcoup experience of the working-class sectors it had sought to serve. According to Alonso, if alternative theater did not make itself available to the dominant economic center, by drawing middle- and upper-class (as well as some working-class) spectators, it would have been subject to the same invisibility (or symbolic disappearance) as the shantytown dwellers themselves. However, in the shantytowns, disappearance was not a metaphor alone, but was a literal, everyday reality. The TIT's ability to choose the physical site for its productions is evidence of the social (middle class) privilege that did distinguish it from the *pobladores*—and that distinguished its activity from *teatro poblacional* (plays produced in shantytowns by working-class people themselves). Though the TIT actors attempted to "become" their working-class characters, it was, in part, their social **difference** from those characters that allowed the TIT to represent them on stage in a central Santiago theater. Alonso begs the question of how the play (and audience reflection) would be compromised by this change, since the "other" realities of the shantytowns would necessarily be "translated" to the more privileged audiences.

The TIT's second decision was to streamline the slow process of piecing together the play itself. Because of the overwhelming amount of documentation gathered in nearly three years of field work, the members of the TIT called playwright David Benavente to assist in the synthesis of their materials. However, the TIT's incorporation of Benavente, as an independent, male authorial figure, inevitably compromised the collective dynamic of the group. All members would have to assume their traditional functions in the distinct roles of (male) playwright and director, and (female) actors, "with the formula of 'collective creation' followed in the previous play simply vanishing."[44] Benavente's presence stemmed from, and exacerbated, the identity crisis of the TIT, which, in the collective sense of the word, was a workshop no longer.[45]

In order for the group to survive economically, it had to produce, which paradoxically led to its reliance upon playwright Benavente. Because of this compromise, the TIT's testimony in the CENECA documents reflects the TIT members' painful process of self-justification. While Benavente can be credited with the development of the festive aspects of the play, using the actors' improvisational skills instead of purely didactic material, his intervention nonetheless left the group uneasy. Actor Loreto Valenzuela (María Ester) notes that Benavente "asked us to please respect his role, and that we not get into big debates, because the key thing in that moment was to complete the play."[46] On one hand, Osorio maintains that Benavente's authority yielded "a more rigorous piece of work,"[47] and actor Soledad Alonso (Rosa) acknowledges that the use of a traditional role-based theater structure provided "a very effective formula"[48] for achieving satisfying aesthetic results. On the other hand, the members of the group seem to resist valorizing that method as anything but an emergency measure. These difficult explanations indirectly acknowledge that any justification of the group's return to a "vertical" hierarchy was philosophically continuous with the rhetoric validating the military intervention of 1973. The actors therefore refused to institutionalize any future intervention of a playwright, unless incorporated into the collective from the beginning of a project.[49]

Taken together, the TIT's conversations with CENECA highlight the contradictions involved in claiming representational power in neoliberal Chile. Despite the group's heightened awareness of the need for collective work and attention to the economic margins, their own production had to conform, at least in part, to the dominant, market-driven, postcoup society, or else be excluded from it altogether.

The work of alternative independent theater groups such as the Taller de Investigación Teatral illustrates the complex search for a theater practice or "language" with which to join the process of social rearticulation of atomized local communities. For the TIT, development of this language depended upon recuperation of the organizational process of working-class women artisans' workshops in Santiago shantytowns after the military coup. However, the TIT's history shows that their professional claim to representational power was not free of the gender and class contradictions, or the economic parameters, of the context in which their work was inserted. Their play was further limited, as art, to opening the possibilities, envisioning or pointing towards the sorts of material social change potentially developed by its absent protagonists (real shantytown women). Hence, *Tres Marías y una Rosa* was necessarily a self-reflexive play,[50] for telling the complex story of community-based resistance implied that the TIT simultaneously struggle for its own survival and that of its absent protagonists, however mutually conflictual those processes proved to be.

The Hungry Body and Patchwork Histories

Three years after the production of *Pedro, Juan y Diego*, in which collective survival hinged upon La Muda's finding a voice alongside the three male protagonists, Benavente and the TIT's *Tres Marías y una Rosa* dramatized community-based survival as dependent on working-class women themselves. The play's four protagonists—Maruja, the workshop leader; María Ester; María Luisa; and a newcomer, Rosita—are all spouses of unemployed men who form a *taller artesanal*, an artisans' workshop, in order to earn enough money to feed their families in the absence of other income. As the play unfolds, the parallel functions of **work** in the *taller*—earning in order to eat ("parar la olla"), being strong in the face of hardship ("apechugar"), and telling stories through artistic creation ("hacer arpilleras," making *arpilleras*)—become linked as processes of self-expression mutually necessary for collective survival. As the women's organization grows stronger, the stories stitched together in their *arpilleras* come to represent their collective struggle to articulate the suppressed histories of their daily lives. Through their activities, the women contest the official policies and dominant narratives that attempted to make invisible the public presence of the shantytown dwellers—their literal and symbolic bodies—through hunger, unemployment, and the physical displacement of community members.

Throughout the play, the physical process of work is therefore always at center stage. There, the material act of sewing serves not merely as a trope, but as the basic condition for the characters' social interaction. The women constantly stitch together a sense of community from which all other relationships, actions, and dialogues become meaningful.[51] The sense of the play comes precisely from the materiality of these staged elements. Consistent with the philosophy of the TIT, what the characters **do** is a precondition for what they **say**, as it represents the active process of constituting a position from which to speak collectively.

Although both *Pedro, Juan y Diego* and *Tres Marías y una Rosa* examine the importance of work in postcoup society, Pedro, Juan, and Diego's jobs depend upon government support of their official (though marginal) job space. The men still function within a precarious public sphere from which they derive a sense of self-worth. In order to maintain their sense of themselves, they form a common front against the external bureaucratic apparatuses that condition their labor. By contrast, the work space in *Tres Marías y una Rosa* is simultaneously domestic (the workshop is located at Maruja's home) and public in a redefined, unofficial way. It is one of many workshops that produce handicrafts through an alternative network, that of "la Central" [the Central Office], a coded reference to the Vicariate of Solidarity. However, despite this extragovernmental system of work, the women are not free from the demands of the dominant culture, and they still respond both to their husbands and to the Central officials and priests who market their handicrafts. By focusing on the difficult position of these women, whose efforts involve a questioning of gender- and class-based claims to authority, *Tres Marías y una Rosa* examines the transformative potential—and the limits—of these women's actions, in a society which would negate their public capacity to speak for themselves.

While the women work, they simultaneously make the *arpilleras* that visually represent their daily lives **and** they verbally "sew" tales that also articulate their experiences. Through both "texts," the audience becomes aware of the milieu in which the play takes place, and of each woman's relationships beyond the stage. These stories convey to the audience that displacement (of men) and structural rupture (of family roles, and of traditional social organizations such as unions) characterize the social crisis that shapes the personal circumstances of the women's lives. While all the women must deal with the unemployment of their husbands, it also becomes clear that Maruja's oldest son is exiled in the United States (208), presumably for political reasons, while Rosita, the newcomer to the *taller*, had to move in with her in-laws, due to her family's financial troubles (163). The rupture of the economic, emotional, and role-based stability of these families has undercut the bases from which they traditionally had conceived of themselves. As the play's focus makes very explicit, the economic and political crisis has therefore affected the relationships and identities of both the community men and the women who adapt to the changing pressures on their daily lives.

In order to emphasize this shift, no men appear on stage at any point during the play. That is, social rupture is represented by the women's central **presence** as workers in the men's **absence**. From the opening scene, a bicycle and an offstage voice (both metonyms of Negro, Maruja's husband and an ex-union leader, 185) offer the only explicit evidence that there are any men nearby. As if to highlight the sense of male displacement, the onstage bicycle is taken apart, "toda desarmada" (151). However, despite their displacement (and because of it), the men exert a great deal of influence over the women, as illustrated by the fact that several scenes open or close with a verbal intervention by Negro.[52] Act 1, scene 1 of the play begins with his words:

> *Negro.* (En off. Desde el interior de la casa) ¡Apaga esa huevá, Maruca!
> (Maruja baja de la escalera, apaga el receptor y regresa a su trabajo, martillando más fuerte).
> *María Ester.* (Entrando, con anteojos ahumados) ¿No ha llegado nadie?
> *Maruja.* ¿¡Qué le pasó, Estercita, Por Dios!?
> *María Ester.* ¡El Román me pegó!
> *Maruja.* ¿¡Otra vez!?
>
> (149–50)

> [*Negro.* (Offstage. From inside the house.) Turn that junk off, Maruca!
> (Maruja descends the stairs, turns off the radio, and returns to her work, hammering even louder).
> *María Ester.* (Entering, with dark eyeglasses) Nobody's here yet?
> *Maruja.* My God, Estercita, what happened to you!?
> *María Ester.* Roman beat me!
> *Maruja.* Not again!]

Negro's aggressive shouting from inside the house serves to mark his authority in that interior space, in the absence of his authority in any other space. Similar to Emmanuel in Dorfman's *Widows*, Negro attempts to reestablish traditional gender boundaries by exercising control over Maruja while she is at work. If he is able to condition Maruja's expectations and determine such details as the volume of music played in the workshop, he would recuperate a sense of masculine self, despite the fact that Maruja has necessarily assumed some of "his" work in the present circumstances.

The men's attempt to establish boundaries receives a more explicitly violent expression through María Ester, who enters the workshop visibly beaten by her husband. The bruises on María Ester's battered body add a visible sign of the men's reaction to their own feminization: Román's unemployment translated into the signs of domestic violence inscribed on the woman's skin. In this scene, however, the figure of paralyzing silence is no longer "La Muda" (the mute woman, as in *Pedro, Juan y Diego*), but rather "[el] mudo" (151), the mute man, according to the adjective María Ester uses to describe Román's responses to her accusations. It is Román's perceived inability to control any circumstances—or metaphorically, to narrate himself or others—that leads him to exercise a violent marking of her body, as a sign for himself of his own authority. Domestic violence thus falls principally upon the bodies of working-class women, a gender-specific consequence of the generalized feminization of the working class.

This is one important insight that distinguishes *Tres Marías y una Rosa* from *Pedro, Juan y Diego*.

Yet María Ester's response to domestic violence hints at the contradictions that surface in this context of ruptured gender identities. While the violent marks on her body indicate Román's attempts to regain his sense of self by exercising control over her, María Ester nonetheless attempts a similar control, albeit figurative, over Román's body. María Ester becomes an agent of violence in her interactions with her husband, as she literally throws her work in Román's face, a gesture both reflecting and reinforcing her estrangement from him. María Ester's fight with Román indicates her desire that he act like a man, in the traditional sense of being productive in the public sphere, getting a job, and leaving behind the frivolity of primping (with his John Travolta hairdo) in front of a mirror. But because his traditional manhood, as well as his public place, no longer exist as such, both characters flounder in their attempts to reimpose such "normal" structures, which seem to be elusively beyond their reach. Neither has as yet discovered a position from which to critique their roles in this violence.

The issues of violence (e.g., between María Ester and Román) and a marked individualism (evident in the lack of coordination in the work of María Ester and Maruja in this opening scene) both demonstrate that the women are not exempt from the dominant characteristics of their society, as they unwittingly reproduce those paradigms without as yet being able to establish a point of resistance to them. As I have discussed in relation to the TIT itself, the ability of any group to produce in this context also required a compromise with the dominant economic system; its influence was inescapable. The interior or personal elements of conflict and the exterior, political, and economic pressures thus are portrayed in the play as fundamentally intertwined. Moreover, the characters' relationships demonstrate that the social context serves to antagonize to the degree that they have internalized it, and reproduce it through the ways they relate to one another. As the play gradually reveals, the women's ability to organize depends as much on their dealing with interiorized conflicts—within their own reproduction of authoritarian behaviors, within their home situations, within their attitudes towards family and work—as on the seemingly exterior pressures of the postcoup context itself.

Act 1 portrays these internalized ideologies within the distinct languages each María uses in her individual *arpillera* craft. In this sequence, the three Marías instruct the novice Rosa on the art of sewing *arpilleras*. Throughout this scene, however, Rosita's naïveté as a newcomer to workshop procedures not only challenges the others to clarify their positions, but also provides a motivation for humor. This humor, enjoyed principally by the audience and increasingly by the characters themselves, provides an index of the women's growing cohesion throughout the remainder of the play. Laughter develops complicity and a sense of community both within the *taller* and potentially beyond it. That is, in *Tres Marías y una Rosa*, humor provides a mechanism for creating the kinds of emotional or affective ties among the characters, and between the characters and the audience, that the TIT actors emphasized as central to their collective project. On every level, this play embraces daily life—the cultural locus of humor—in a way that *Widows*, written at a strategic but unavoidable narrative distance, could not. Throughout the play, humor is validated publicly as a source for personal and collective resilience and for mitigating the potentially overwhelming pressures and fragmentation of postcoup society.

Maruja begins to teach Rosa by noting that incidents from one's life provide the basis for themes to depict in the wall hangings:

> *Maruja.* De las cosas que le han pasado en la vida suya tiene que ser el tema. Porque la gente se interesa en las cosas de una, Rosita. Una cree que no se interesan, pero la gente se interesa . . .
> *Rosita.* Se me hace que no voy a poder, yo . . .
> *Maruja.* Tiene que mirar pa'atrás, y acordarse de algo que le haya pasado en la historia suya, ¿me entiende?
> *Rosita.* No . . .
>
> (170–71)

> [*Maruja.* The theme of an *arpillera* should be things that happened in your life. Because people really are interested in those things, Rosita. You might not think they're interested, but they really are . . .
> *Rosita.* I don't think I can do it, I can't . . .
> *Maruja.* You have to look way back, and remember something that's happened in your own life, you see?
> *Rosita.* No . . .]

In Maruja's view, expression of one's own history allows a connection with others to be made. Individual experience and memory should therefore be the basis for the visual narrative of the *arpilleras*. Behind Maruja's notion of the public's interest in personal histories, however, lies the marketability factor: if the *arpillera* sells, one's own history is validated by the public—that is, by the international market. The international market indirectly becomes the target audience and the broker of personal histories. In order to conserve one self-expressive *arpillera* as her own, as a symbolic point of resistance to the ostensibly all-determining market forces, Maruja refuses to sell her first and most personal wall hanging. It depicts her husband's loss of his factory job in the aftermath of the coup, and she keeps it carefully tucked away in her sewing box, a poignant reminder of the deeper motivations behind her *arpillera* craft. The large issue of how the workshop might develop a sense of self-expression and survive market pressures comes into more explicit relief as Rosa's lesson continues.

When Rosa is baffled by Maruja's approach, Maruja cleverly leaves María Ester, the person who had opposed Rosa's membership, in charge of teaching her the process of making *arpilleras*. In so doing, she leaves Rosa's integration in the hands of the person who most resisted it, a move geared toward strengthening the commitment of **both** María Ester and Rosa to the workshop. In contrast to Maruja, María Ester teaches Rosa through the mechanics of the process. In the following dialogue, María Ester's short-tempered attitude is countered by Rosita's well-intentioned clumsiness and good humor, qualities which make it very difficult for María Ester to remain angry at her:

> *María Ester.* Aquí, cada una tiene su modo de hacer las cosas. Si quiere que yo le enseñe, tiene que hacerlas a mi manera. ¿Entendido? Punto uno. Agarra un trapo de cuarenta por sesenta. Ni más grande ni más chico, porque tiene que ser de cuarenta por sesenta. ¿Oyó?
> *Rosita.* Cuarenta por sesenta. . . .
> *María Ester.* Punto dos. ¿Tiene listo el trapo de cuarenta por sesenta? Lo primero que hace es pegarle la cordillera.
> *Rosita.* ¿La cordillera de los Andes?
> *María Ester.* La cordillera de los Andes, no la cordillera de la costa. Porque, como estamos en Chile. . . . Pa'que se sepa en el extranjero. . . . **Para ahorrar tiempo, puede hacerse una cachá de cordilleras, y después, llegar y pegar.** El Román, mi marido, es como tonto pa'hacer cordilleras.
> *Rosita.* ¿Qué él le ayuda a usted?
> *María Ester.* Hay que incorporarlos también. O sea, participación. Porque si no, los huevones se acomplejan donde no tienen pega. . . . Punto tres. Abre la ventana, mira pa'afuera. ¿Y qué es lo que ve? Conteste.
> *Rosita.* ¡Es que no sé, puh!
> *María Ester.* ¡La población! Eso es lo que se ve por la ventana. La realidad de la vida. O sea, **tema de población**: casas, chiquillos, pilón de agua, perros y moscas . . .
>
> (emphasis mine, 175–77)

[*María Ester.* Here, each of us has her own way of doing things. If you want me to teach you, you have to do things my way. Got it? Point number one. Grab a piece of cloth, 40 by 60 centimeters. No bigger, no smaller, it has to be 40 by 60. OK?

> *Rosita.* 40 by 60. . . .
> *María Ester.* Point number two. You have your 40 by 60 cloth ready? The first thing you do is sew on the Andes mountains.
> *Rosita.* The Andes?
> *María Ester.* Of course the Andes, not the coastal mountains. Look—because we're in Chile, right? It's so foreigners can tell. . . . **To save time, you can make a whole bunch of mountain ranges, and then just stick them on, one after another**. Román, my husband, is just crazy about making those mountains.
> *Rosita.* You mean he helps you?
> *María Ester.* You have to get them involved, you know, get them to share in whatever you're doing. Because if you don't, the bums get uptight because they don't have jobs. . . . Point number three. Open the window, look outside. And what do you see? Tell me.
> *Rosita.* Uh, I really don't know!
> *María Ester.* The shantytown! That's what you see out there. That's reality. I mean think about it: houses, little kids, the communal sink, dogs and flies . . . **The shantytown: that's the theme** for your *arpillera* . . .]

For María Ester, her work is solely a means of earning money, and therefore must be approached pragmatically, taking into account the mechanisms and tastes of the market. She has learned to work like a machine, to (re)produce her depictions of the "tema de población" [theme of the shantytown] or the "tema de extrema pobreza" (176) [theme of extreme poverty] as mechanically as Román with his "cachá de cordilleras" [bunch of mountain ranges]. At the same time, María Ester also points out the advantages of incorporating her husband into the production process. Including her husband is a means by which to rebuild a relationship with him and, she hopes, to diminish the problem of domestic violence.

Though María Ester is the character who most obviously reproduces dominant worldviews (in her individualism and heeding of market mechanisms, as well as in her autocratic teaching style), she seeks to take advantage of consumer society only in order to subsist. According to María Ester's logic, the more she produces, the more she can sell, and the better off she will be economically. The difficulty with María Ester's pragmatism is that she acquiesces to dominant sociopolitical messages (in which she herself represents "extreme poverty," for example) at the same time that she attempts to establish a point of difference from them (e.g., by making visible the dominant culture's exclusions of the *pobladores*). Although the neoliberal culture excludes her, effectively erasing her material presence, as well as her desires and needs, she caters to the dominant market in search of her own economic inclusion and fulfillment of those needs.

By showing this paradox, María Ester as a character represents the contradictions expressed by the actor Soledad Alonso in her description of the TIT's changed production strategies. According to Alonso, the TIT needed to produce within the (economically dominant) center in order to survive as a theater group. Though the dominant economic system did require production within its own (neoliberal capitalist) terms, the TIT occupied a different position within that system than did the shantytown dwellers. Because of their social difference, the TIT actors' relationship to the characters they represent is inevitably a double one, like Dorfman's with the widows. Working-class women are made present on stage, and are placed in this history, by the TIT actors. But the actors' presence also indicates the *pobladoras'* real absence, as women and as members of the working-class, from the stage and from the dominant worldview. Since that worldview negated the existence of working-class women (beyond their role in production and consumption), the actors' embodiments **of** them is at once a recuperative and an exclusionary gesture.

In contrast to the other two women, María Luisa views free use of the imagination as the key to the process of representation. María Luisa begins her explanation:

> *María Luisa.* Lo primero que tenís que hacer es ponerte un paño en la vista, bien apretado. Porque cuando se hace arpillera, hay que mirar pa'dentro y pa'ni una otra parte. Entonces, con la vista cubierta, una se va metiendo, metiendo, metiendo . . . Hasta que, de repente, ¡zas! comienza a salir el chorro. Con ese chorro usted dibuja la arpillera ¿Me comprende?
> *Rosita.* Con tanta profesora, cómo no voy a comprender, puh . . .
> (185–86)

> [*María Luisa.* The first thing you gotta do is put on a blindfold, tied really tight. Because when you make an *arpillera,* you need to look deep inside and nowhere else. Then, with your eyes shut, you go deeper, deeper, deeper . . . Until suddenly, whoosh!, everything starts to flow like water. And you use that stream to set up the *arpillera,* understand?
> *Rosita.* Gosh, with so many teachers, how could I not understand!]

Despite her light-hearted irony, Rosa dutifully follows María Luisa's creative exercises, seeing stars when she covers her eyes too tightly, and through free association comes up with a surreal scene: UFOs and Mickey Mouse in the Andes (187). This comical image combines the artistic perspectives that Rosita had learned, for the Mickey Mouse toys she has sold are symbolic of her personal history (Maruja's strategy), the Andes are part of the *arpillera* formula (María Ester's method), and UFOs form a favored part of María Luisa's imaginative repertoire.

In contrast to Maruja's and María Ester's methods, however, María Luisa's imaginative artistry proved to be counterproductive on the market. Throughout the play, the Central Office consistently rejects her work, much to her frustration, because its abstract representational style showed versions of local history that were not recognizable (or saleable) to a wide public. In a sense, María Luisa is an avant-garde *arpillerista*, whose highly imaginative but hermetic work remains marginal because the Central Office cannot make it accessible to the public. But María Luisa (like the TIT) must sell in order to survive; she must therefore translate her work into more acceptable terms for the Central Office. María Luisa's case shows how the dominant economic system (and the nongovernmental Central Office) did require the women's conformity with (at least some of) its terms, and more importantly, how the market excluded **or rendered incomprehensible** those imaginative projects that did not reflect back its own terms in a "legible" way. María Luisa's case thus provides a sort of metacommentary on Chilean culture generally, and on literature and theater specifically, after the inauguration of neoliberalism in the authoritarian context. In chapters 5 and 6, I will discuss this with respect to experimental works by Diamela Eltit, on one hand, and to Isabel Allende's best-sellers, on the other.

Though none of the Marías' strategies provides Rosa with a way to narrate her theme, or to negotiate her relationship with the market, she does gain exposure to three distinct bases for making *arpilleras*, and for telling stories: personal history, formulaic production, and individual imagination. All of these approaches presuppose that the *arpilleras* provide a means of subsistence that depends on communicating some aspect of one woman's life to others: all view this craft as necessity. What remains at the end of act 1, however, is for Rosa to find her own language for stitching together her version of history. Likewise, all of the women have to deal with the contradictions created by the influence exerted upon them by both the marketplace and their husbands, inside and outside of the workshop.

Act 1 culminates with a crisis: the Central Office not only has rejected the majority of their pieces, but also has suspended the *arpillera* program until further notice. These circumstances push the women to polarize as well, in terms of their individual interests versus their solidarity with the group. While Rosa remains with Maruja in the workshop, in order to seek a collective solution ("entre todas," 203), María Ester and María Luisa decide to sell their work in the uptown boutiques, and, like Carmen (the boutique owner is a former *arpillerista*), ostensibly sell out their collective enterprise to dominant interests. While this response is rather predictable in María Ester's case, due to her consistent adherence to market principles, it is somewhat surprising that María Luisa joins her, that it is the avant-garde *arpillerista* who responds to the market's rejection of her work by overtly capitulating to its terms. Of course, there is no doubt that her extreme economic desperation fueled this move; how much María Luisa will be required to compromise her aesthetic and political values only later becomes clear to her. Likewise, the TIT's 1977 decision to produce the play "uptown," also based on severe economic pressures, required redefinition of a collective production that would be viable in this context. In act 2 of *Tres Marías y una Rosa*, the two pairs of women play out the tensions between individual and collective goals, and struggle to reestablish their sense of personal and artistic integrity without undermining their capacity for economic survival.

Sewing a Sense of Community: Women's Voices and Collective Bodies

During act 2, all four women eventually acknowledge the ways in which they reproduce aspects of the dominant narrative in their lives: Rosita and Maruja, through a self-abnegating attitude toward husband and family;[53] María Ester, through her conflicting responses to the cycle of domestic violence, and along with María Luisa, through complicity with the market-driven worldview of the Providencia boutique owners. They begin to realize that their internalization of these ways of interacting has exacerbated the fragmentation of their communities, as well as worsening their material necessity within this context. The women's complicity with the systems that exclude them has produced not social inclusion, but the women's further marginalization, along with their sense of betrayal of self and principles, as expressed in María Luisa's conflict with Carmen and the class interests she represents. However, the severity of the women's needs, and the limitations of their individual efforts both outside and within the *taller*, eventually force them to find a means for working collaboratively toward common goals.

Act 2 opens with Rosita and Maruja sorting through large bags of materials, which were given to them by the *gringo* priest for creating a giant *arpillera* altarpiece for the new local church (218). The *taller* thus has work to support itself, and importantly, the project is one which requires a joint physical and conceptual effort. In this act, María Ester and María Luisa return to the workshop to make amends, after having faced political conflicts with the paternalistic boutique owners whose favor they had previously cultivated. Rosita and Maruja eventually accept María Ester and María Luisa's return, though not without requiring their greater commitment to collective work. Having failed with independent entrepreneurism, the two women are better positioned to understand the necessity of reestablishing a basis for unity among all members of the workshop.

In order to take the next step toward collective creation, the women celebrate their reincorporation as a group. They create a space in which to imagine collectively and to affirm themselves, beyond their material roles in production and consumption. In this safe space among women—as Maruja states, "[A]quí estamos entre puras mujeres" (225) [Here we're among women only], and "No se preocupe, Rosita, que aquí mandamos nosotras" (230) [Don't worry, Rosita, we women are in charge here]—they begin to rediscover the issues uniting them as *pobladoras*. Moreover, they start to **dramatize** their imaginative responses to some of those issues: a clear evocation of theater's own function in the process of social rearticulation. For example, when Rosa recounts the circumstances of losing her virginity, the other women clothe her pregnant body in ironic representation of the Virgin of Lourdes:

> *Rosita*. El Rafa siempre me decía: "vamos, vamos . . .". Total, que un día yo le dije: "Bueno, ya, vamos." Enamorá. A Las Vizcachas fuimos, en el cerro, detrás de la Virgen. No había nada de gente ahí. De vuelta, en la micro, yo iba todo mojá, donde uno sangra la primera vez. . . . Entonces, el Rafa me dijo que se quería casar conmigo. "¿Qué?," le dije yo, si tenía quince pa'dieciséis no más, puh.
> *María Luisa*. (Terminando de arreglar a Rosita) Listo. ¿Cómo quedó?
> *Maruja*. ¡Pero si quedó igualita a la Virgen de Lourdes! Le falta el puro lazo celeste, no más. (Le pone un lazo celeste en la cintura) . . .
> *María Ester*. ¡La Virgen de Lourdes esperando guagua!
> *María Luisa*. ¡No iba a salir del aire Nuestro Señor Jesucristo!
>
> (226)

> [*Rosita*. Rafa would always say: "Come on, let's go . . ." So one day I said to him: "OK, let's." True love. We went to Las Vizcachas, on the hill, behind the Virgin. Nobody else was there. On the way home, on the bus, I was all wet, the way you bleed the first time. . . . Then, Rafa told me he wanted to marry me. I couldn't believe it, since I was only 15 going on 16 back then.
> *María Luisa*. (Putting the final touches on Rosita's outfit). All set. What do you think?
> *Maruja*. She looks just like the Virgin of Lourdes! All that's missing is the light blue ribbon around her waist. (She puts on the ribbon) . . .
> *María Ester*. The Virgin of Lourdes expecting a baby!

María Luisa. Well, Our Lord Jesus Christ wasn't just going to fall from the sky!]

Here, the women actively rewrite—re-present—religion from their experience, and this experience is grounded precisely in their narration of Rosita's body, in its specificity as a working-class woman. The Virgin is thereby reappropriated as a functional, and sexual, being. She is not the disembodied suffering servant of traditional Catholicism (the vision echoed both in official discourse and in Rosita's earlier self-effacement). Instead, she is a practical figure, embodied through the material terms of this working-class religiosity. By reclaiming the Virgin's materiality (and her desires), they take a creative step toward imagining and claiming for themselves a position of resistance to the dominant culture.

Because Rosa never had an official marriage ceremony, the three Marías decide to act out her wedding, distributing materials for performing and exaggerating gender roles: Maruja, as the groom, wears a spool of thread as a mock penis; Rosita dons a veil to play the bride; María Ester gains her authority as priest by riding Negro's metonymic bicycle; and María Luisa plays her part as matron of honor *(madrina)* by telling Rosita, tongue in cheek, that she must be an obedient wife (229–31). However, from the moment that the women are able to acknowledge, and parody, the functional consequences of these gender stereotypes, they begin to identify more closely with each other—a moment of mutual recognition symbolized by their gathering around a mirror before the ceremony begins. Due to its central function in the play, the mock wedding dialogue is reproduced here at length:

María Ester. (Engrosando la voz) "¿Habéis venido a unirnos en matrimonio?"
Maruja. (Da un codazo a Rosita) "Sí."
Rosita. Sí.
María Ester. "Sra. Rosa Martínez...."
Rosita. Sí.
Maruja. No se contesta sí.
María Ester. "Señora Rosa Martínez, ¿acepta seguir a este hombre en el dolor, la adversidad, la desgracia, la miseria, el hambre y los terremotos?"
Rosita. No.
María Ester. "¿Acepta que la cachetée, que le ponga el gorro, que la llene de chiquillos, que no traiga plata pa'la casa, que llegue curao?"
Rosita. No.

María Luisa. ¡Así me gusta!

María Ester. "¿Y usted, don Rafael, promete solemnemente ante este altar sagrado no cachetearla, no ponerle el gorro, no llenarla de chiquillos, no llegar curao, y traer plata pa'la casa?"

Maruja. ¡Bravo, señor cura! ¡Otra vez, señor cura! ¡Otra vez!

María Ester. "¿Promete que no le va a dar todas las noches con la custión, porque aburre también?"

María Luisa. ¡Que prometa! ¡Que prometa!

María Ester "¿Promete pedirle el favor solamente cuando ella tenga deseos?"

Todas. ¡Prometido!

María Ester. "¿Promete que después de ocurrido el hecho, hacerle por lo menos un cariñito?"

Todas. ¡Sí! ¡Sí! ¡Sí!

María Ester. "Entonces, en ese caso . . ."

Todas. ¡De nuevo! ¡De nuevo!

María Luisa. Pídale que le ayude a educar a los cabros, señor cura.

Maruja. Y que le ayude a arreglar la casa, también.

María Luisa. Y a no enojarse porque hace arpillera.

Rosita. Quedarse cuidando a los chiquillos.

María Luisa. Comprarle lavadora, pa'que no eche los pulmones lavando.

Maruja. ¡Claro! Si no hay que dejarse atropellar.

Rosita. Porque se aprovechan de una.

María Ester. Pa'eso están los derechos de la mujer.

Rosita. ¡Una también es persona!

Maruja. No hay que aguantarles ni la puntita de ahora pa'delante.

(232–34)

[*María Ester.* (Deepening her voice) "Have you come together to unite yourselves in holy matrimony?"

Maruja. (Elbows Rosita) "Yes."

Rosita. Yes.

María Ester. "Señora Rosa Martínez. . . ."

Rosita. Yes.

Maruja. Don't answer yes.

María Ester. "Señora Rosa Martínez, do you agree to follow this man in pain, adversity, disgrace, misery, hunger and earthquakes?"

Rosita. No.

María Ester. "Do you accept that he'll rough you up, bug you to death, fill you up with kids, bring no money home, and show up drunk?"

Rosita. No.

María Luisa. That's more like it!

María Ester. "And you, don Rafael, do you solemnly swear before this sacred altar not to beat her, not to bug her to death, not to fill her up with kids, not to show up drunk, and to bring money home for the family?"

Maruja. Way to go, señor priest! Encore, señor priest! Encore!

María Ester. "Do you promise not to ask for some every night, because that gets boring, too?"

María Luisa. Go on, promise!

María Ester. "Do you promise to ask her that favor only when she's in the mood?"

All. Consider that promised!

María Ester. "Do you promise that when you're through, to at least caress her a little bit afterwards?"

All. Yes! Yes! Yes!

María Ester. "Well, in that case . . ."

All. One more time! Say it again!

María Luisa. Ask him to help her educate the kids, señor priest.

Maruja. And to help her with the housework, too.

María Luisa. And not to get mad because she makes *arpilleras*.

Rosita. To stay home taking care of the little ones.

María Luisa. To buy her a washer, so she doesn't wear out her lungs doing the laundry.

Maruja. Of course! You don't need to let men walk all over you.

Rosita. Because they take advantage of you.

María Ester. That's why there are women's rights.

Rosita. We're people, too!

Maruja. We don't need to put up with any more crap from here on out.]

In this wedding scene, the women create together for the first time a space in which they simultaneously represent their common dilemmas and celebrate their collective capacity to imagine alternatives. The women's specific critiques of dominant gender paradigms, as reinforced by institutions such as traditional weddings, emerge as they make the connection between general material needs and their specific socialization as women. The protagonists begin to overcome the interpersonal conflicts that had divided them in act 1, precisely through reidentification of the difficulties they share: hunger and material adversity, domestic violence, appropriation of their sexuality, their husbands' lack of contribution either in completing domestic tasks or in earning money outside the home. All of these problems are related to the double pressures of their gender and class status, and the protagonists become "wedded" to each other through their shared commitment to represent their collective selfhood as working-class women.

Furthermore, the wedding scene traces the process behind the emergence of this feminist consciousness, as the scene moves from an oppositional logic of negation, in which Rosita answers "no" to the priest's (María Ester's) description of her future role as abnegated wife ("acepta seguir a este hombre en el dolor . . .") [do you agree to follow this man in pain . . .], to an affirmation of a negative logic in which the relationship of the spouses could be different ("promete . . . no cachetearla, no ponerle el gorro, no llenarla de chiquillos, . . .") [do you solemnly swear . . . not to beat her, not to bug her to death, not to fill her up with kids, . . .]. The list of demands then moves to agreement: an acceptation by the husband to participate in domestic tasks, and likewise to accept his wife's participation in public work. When Rosita exclaims "¡Una también es persona!" [We're people, too!], she not only critiques the exclusion of (working-class) women from the "universal" (male-defined) category of public personhood, but she also affirms the women's right to participate in history as "people" who do not need to "aguantarles ni la puntita de ahora pa'delante" [put up with any more crap from here on out]. In short, this scene in the play clearly prefigures the reemergence of explicitly feminist thought in Chile in subsequent years (to be discussed in chapter 4), particularly two of the concepts explored by Julieta Kirkwood's work in the 1980s: the notion of "personhood," and that of feminism as a negation of authoritarianism.[54]

Most crucially, in *Tres Marías y una Rosa*, the women's empowerment lies not only in their claiming the **bodies of their men** through telling those men's stories, as in *Widows*, but also depends on their establishing a position from which to speak for and represent themselves, grounded in the claim to **their own bodies**. While *Widows* sought to rewrite the national narrative of Chile to incorporate present and absent community members and to embrace the communal values the widows represent (an ideal, as we have seen, not free of contradictions), *Tres Marías y una Rosa* suggests that the solution to working class exclusions from the collective body of the nation (due to unemployment, hunger, repression) must begin with working-class **women's** claims to their own visibility within the national script. That is, the TIT/Benavente play clearly posits the terrain of collective struggle in the *pobladoras'* hands, within the realm of their collective bodies (the *talleres*), and aligned with their capacity to piece together alternative narratives like the mock wedding and the giant *arpillera*. The women's demands do not take the form of a dour manifesto, but rather draw on imagination and humor in shaping these alternative stories.

As is evident from this self-reflexive scene of the play, however, the characters (like Benavente and the TIT) cannot, in this context, completely reconfigure the institutions they critique. An implicit question is raised, for example, when the protagonists claim their ability to retell the wedding from their perspective, calling it a "un matrimonio moderno" (30) [a modern wedding]. The women's evocation of modernity is not simply a positive nod toward capitalist models of development, but rather connects to the fact that their nascent feminist consciousness may rest on classical liberal assumptions that they do not question. Furthermore, the women's party comes to an abrupt halt when the voice of Negro interrupts the scene:

Negro. (En off. Gritando desde la calle) ¡Maruca!
Maruja. ¡El Negro!
   (Silencio. Recogen rápidamente el plástico con todas las cosas y se arrinconan en la puerta de la casa sacándose el disfraz)
Negro. (En off) ¡Maruca! Ayúdame a bajar estos paquetes.
Maruja. (Duda un instante) ¡Voy! ¡Voy! (Sacándose el disfraz, se dirige hacia la puerta).
Rosita. Estuvo linda la fiesta ¿ah?
(close of scene 4, 234–35)

[*Negro.* (Offstage. Yelling from the street) Maruca!
Maruja. It's Negro!
   (Silence. They quickly gather up the plastic with their things and huddle in the doorway taking off their costumes).
Negro. (Offstage.) Maruca! Help me unload these packages.
Maruja. (Hesitates a moment). I'm coming! Coming! (Taking off her costume, she heads for the door).
Rosita. Nice party, huh?]

The women's imaginary script emerges within the present (contextual) constraints on the women's work space. After a momentary vacillation, Maruja removes the costume of her potentially liberated self, to heed Negro's call for help. Negro's words again represent the male-centered demands shaping the women's creative possibilities. Those demands limit these characters' reconfiguration of their social roles, even as postcoup history opens up the possibility of the women's collective work. Thus, Benavente and the TIT leave several large issues unresolved: that the operative categories of the women's discourse appear to be mostly liberal, not socialist or radical, and are based on a selfhood continually in tension with collective goals; that the men remain marginal, not visible or reintegrated into the social body, and never rewrite their own scripts of masculinity; and that the play (and the play within the play) themselves remain necessary, but insufficient, ingredients for creating social change.

By showing how the imaginative act is framed by the context in which it emerges, this play echoes the ways in which the TIT felt it had to adapt strategically to the dominant sociopolitical context, including its move to the center of Santiago and the incorporation of Benavente as the principal authorial figure. Since the male playwright Benavente, like the invisible Negro (and the Central Office), has the power to delimit the workshop members' imaginative project, one tension in the play lies with how the protagonists might become truly empowered to tell their own stories. Like the dilemma faced by Dorfman in *Widows*, Benavente's authorial position is at once self-affirming and self-contradictory. Benavente is like Negro (and Dorfman) insofar as he is in some sense marginal (in opposition to the dominant regime) at the same time that his social privilege as male allows him to circumscribe the women characters' actions. Benavente's situation (like Dorfman's) is distinct from Negro's, however, because his privilege also entails representing working-class women as a middle-class man with access to a public space (and a middle-class theater group). Benavente aspires to make public the shantytown women's struggle, but in so doing, he suggests that validation of their activity comes from outside of that activity itself.

However, where Dorfman must look to the universal ("menos local y más universal") due to his displacement from the local context, Benavente delves as deeply into local circumstances as he possibly can, given the limits of his own gender and class status, and of the context of resistance in Chile itself. Because Benavente (unlike Dorfman) works with a collective (the TIT) inside the country, his own work is directly and constantly affected by the contextual pressures of the postcoup context. Those pressures not only included day-to-day interpersonal repression and economic hardship, but also the positive and urgent need to nurture collective work, in whatever ways possible, in order to contest the fragmentation of communities—and suppression of interpersonal desire and expression—propagated by the regime.

The final scene of act 2 opens with the "Juicio Final" [Final Judgment] hanging unfinished on the clothesline,[55] while the women (minus María Ester) work furiously to finish it. It is only when Rosita points out that "Pa'mí que está quedando demasiado triste el Juicio. . . . Como bailando cueca tiene que quedar" (254) [I think this Judgment is turning out way too sad. . . . It needs to be more like dancing the *cueca*], that the women begin to reassess the giant *arpillera*'s content in terms of their own specificity. That is, they begin to see the possibility that they produce not a grim indictment of the dominant authoritarian discourse, but a piece that incorporates themselves into the narrative (work and story) through showing the vitality of shantytown culture (much as *Tres Marías y una Rosa* itself does). The *gringo* priest also had commented that the "Final Judgment" seemed "triste y poco chileno" (257) [sad and not very Chilean], underscoring that a foreign-authorized version of what was Chilean also shaped their work. But in a whirlwind of revisions, the women turn the tables on the official discourses of neoliberal Chile, taking on the roles of judge and seekers of justice. They place the uptown boutiques in Hell, while members of the working class dance the Chilean *cueca* in Heaven, eating *empanadas* with all the trappings ("Everything Free" reads the sign on the Independence Day food booths).[56] The *arpilleristas* thus portray a utopia in which working-class women **and** men are fed: their collective body is full; it is central and not marginal in this social portrait.

In the folklore song[57] that they improvise together for performance at the church dedication, it is the women, not God or the courts, who judge in the end:

> Juicio Final, ¡ay, sí!
> de las mujeres . . .
> Será con empanás
> pal'que las quiere.
> ¡Huifa Ayayay!
> Con empanadas sí,
> Pa'regodearse.
> Porque el Juicio Chileno
> tiene que darse.
>
> (268–69)

> [Final Judgment, that's right!
> by the women . . .
> And we'll have *empanadas*
> For all who want some—
> With *empanadas*, oh yes,
> to stuff yourself.
> Because the Chilean Judgment
> is going to come.]

The women entitle their giant wall hanging "La Cueca del Juicio Final" [The Final Judgment Cueca], happy that its content was renovated to reflect their own values. The four women effectively represent themselves in a triumphant position in the this "Juicio Chileno" [Chilean Judgment], which suggests the potential retribution of those particularly repressed by the regime. Like the women's wedding, this performance not only allows them to reclaim the materiality of their bodies (here, through showing the social nature of food distribution), but also constitutes a community-based act of self-representation. This reference to a Chilean Judgment Day would certainly have invited the audience to cheer the women on—thus reaffirming and celebrating the silenced alternative dreams of the theater public in 1979.

At the same time that theater voiced these repressed possibilities, the play's content suggests that social transformation would ultimately hinge upon resistance activities becoming pieced together from within disparate corners of Chilean society at large.

The trajectory of *Tres Marías y una Rosa* explores the conflicting positions of its protagonists: doubly marginalized, as shantytown dwellers and as women, but also empowered through crisis to organize and represent themselves. The play at once posits this aperture, raising hopeful possibilities for both the working-class female protagonists and for rewriting authoritarian Chile, even as it anticipates the kinds of fundamental limits that both the women's movement and the political left would face during the transition to democracy after Pinochet. The fact that the *pobladoras'* capacity to narrate in their own right never escapes deep structural constraints—ideological liberalism, market demands, pressures from their husbands, and even the foreign pressures placed by the parish priest on their work—bears out this point. It is nevertheless significant in the context of postcoup Chilean culture that **female** characters speak for and embody the larger resistance agenda, through their dramatized discovery of how to feed themselves cooperatively, in both the literal and symbolic senses of the phrase.

Like many real Chilean women who were increasingly active during the institutional crisis, the fictional *pobladoras* in *Tres Marías y una Rosa* by necessity discover a strategy for telling their own stories. Only when the women become capable of imagining collectively are they able to sew the representational text of a giant *arpillera* that will allow the marginal community to survive, both materially and discursively. In the play's closing moments, Maruja is the last workshop member to leave for the church dedication,[58] and she hesitates at the door, as if wondering if Negro will be back. In contrast to the end of the wedding scene (as well as all previous scenes), she simply turns and departs from her home/workshop, leaving behind her acquiescence to Negro's anticipated demands, in order to celebrate with the group their collective work. For the first time, through the collective process of storytelling, Maruja has chosen to feed herself first, by joining the collective body "sewn" with the other women of the workshop. At the very least, by grounding themselves firmly in local postcoup history, and affirming their capacity to imagine alternatives, neither the *arpilleristas* nor independent postcoup theater remained locked in the silence of "La Muda."

The overall movement from crisis, to an individual search for language, to a stitched together sense of community in *Tres Marías y una Rosa* parallels the first steps in the process of "coming of age" of independent Chilean theater (and the Chilean opposition generally) after the 1973 coup. By stitching together community-based histories, nonfictional women, their fictional versions, and eventually independent theater itself, **came to terms** with the profound effects of recent Chilean history. Whether the four characters' imaginative potential remains merely a "linda fiesta" [a nice party], or whether this is indeed "a process where there's no going back," as the *pobladora* in my epigraph maintains, clearly depends on what might happen beyond the play itself. *Tres Marías y una Rosa* suggests that social transformation depends upon the ways in which these characters—and the members of the theater public—continue to develop of representing themselves. Certainly the Chilean opposition, including male authors such as Benavente and Dorfman, continued to be moved by the experiences of those women who sustained their communities after the 1973 coup. Yet as I will discuss in the next chapter, the 1980s augured an increasingly public protagonism of women in resistance movements and a new explosion of women writers themselves energized to narrate these experiences otherwise.

4
Erotic Desire and Bodily Violence

> Women . . . confronted with [military] authoritarianism, are in a certain sense facing a known phenomenon: authoritarianism as a culture frames their everyday experiences [el autoritarismo como cultura es su experiencia cotidiana].
> —Julieta Kirkwood (1982)[1]

> I believe that there is no greater or more profound gap between masculine and feminine than through sex . . . that deep and absolutely unspoken solitude of the body of a woman facing the body of a man.
> —Pía Barros (1990)[2]

IN THE PRECEDING CHAPTERS, I HAVE DISCUSSED HOW TWO MALE AUTHORS FROM THE generation of 1970 both arrive at the same issue—the intimate reproduction of authoritarianism—through their narrative processes of exploring domination and resistance in the context of postcoup Chile. Writing in exile, Ariel Dorfman first examines the main public actors—the military and the widows, who struggle to narrate the bodies of disappeared community men—and then discovers the resonances of their conflict in the private lives of Emmanuel and Cecilia. He particularly questions the ways in which masculine identity may be constructed without replicating authoritarianism, through the recuperation of what he sees as the feminine values necessary for (the country's) survival. Such values stem from establishing desire-based links with present and past communities, through the public telling of collective stories. Furthermore, Dorfman opens up narrative structures and invites readers to reevaluate their own positions in this story, and to examine how each person perpetuates domination and resistance through interpersonal interactions.

David Benavente, working with a predominantly female theater collective inside of Chile, also presents an awareness of how militarized society has affected working-class men and women, for *Tres Marías y una Rosa* takes as its point of departure the men's complete exclusion from public activity. The women, as social protagonists, develop a means to provide materially for the hungry bodies of their families and communities, discovering that they must first develop a way to work together as a collective if they are to survive. As represented in the wedding scene, the women's ability to imagine alternatives to their gender and class exclusion implies that they must first claim and narrate themselves (express their own desires and needs) as *personas*. Yet their self-expression is always linked to their production of goods to sell, an activity conditioned both by the men's opinions and by the exigencies of the neoliberal marketplace. The women's *arpilleras* thus simultaneously represent the opportunities and obstacles shaping their public emergence as collective actors in the postcoup context.

Taken together, both *Widows* and *Tres Marías y una Rosa* are texts written by men who examine how women's roles as social protagonists challenge the ways in which gender norms may continue to operate culturally. Both texts move from public to private situations, revealing the link between the two, and returning finally to questions of public social transformation. The parallel journey here is the evolving emphasis from collective bodies to individual bodies and back again. Both authors ultimately valorize intervention in a public sphere as the means by which history takes place, a priority also evident in the production and distribution of their work (e.g., Dorfman's elaborate plan to get *Widows* published in Chile, Benavente's increased role as playwright when the TIT moved to Santiago's center).[3] For both Benavente and Dorfman, gaining access to public bodies (and public circulation) is a fundamental precondition for any personal, aesthetic, or political act to potentially impact history.

As I turn to literature by those writers who began to publish during the second decade of the Pinochet dictatorship, I move forward chronologically, generationally, and perhaps most significantly, I turn from the work of men to the work of women. For her part, the young short story writer Pía Barros (b. 1956), a woman committed to telling stories about women, shares with Dorfman and Benavente the presupposition that the public and the private, and that collective and individual bodies, are inextricably intertwined. In contrast to the works by Dorfman and Benavente, however, Barros's *A horcajadas* [*Astride*] (1990) begins and ends with the most private of acts, suggesting that the claim to narrate, to participate in history (particularly as a woman) must begin with the bodily expression of erotic desire. In other words, for Barros, the sexual act becomes a metaphor for creating a collective future. If women are to participate in that future, they must first claim the ability to name and narrate within the sexual realm. At the same time, Barros ultimately reveals that her characters' expressions of desire do not escape the same culturally determined structures of power operative in society at large. Hence, while Dorfman and Benavente discover private bodies through their emphasis on public history, Barros reveals problems in the social body through her insistent look at the potentials and prohibitions shaping sexual intimacy, especially specific women's expressions of erotic desires and needs.

Clearly, each of these three authors' narrative positions is influenced by generational and gender differences, and by their differing experiences of (dis)placement, inside or outside of the country. In the context of the increasingly public emergence of feminism in Chile, it is no wonder that among the younger writers who began to publish during the 1980s figure a remarkable number of women. For this new generation of writers, the intense sociopolitical circumstances of the 1970s and 1980s had a particular impact on their sense of themselves and of their literature. Most of the prose writers of this generation—which includes Pía Barros, Diamela Eltit, Sonia Montecino, Ramón Díaz Eterovic, Ana María del Río, Carlos Franz, and others[4]—were under eighteen years old at the time of the 1973 coup, and lived inside the country during the entire dictatorship. Most began their writing careers in relatively small, and initially clandestine, *talleres literarios* (literary workshops).[5] The terms used by critics to describe various groupings of these writers, "La vigilada generación del 80" [the generation of 1980, a generation under surveillance], "La generación dispersa" [the disperse generation], "Los escritores de la orfandad" [the orphaned writers], "La generación N.N." [the unidentified {"Ninún Nombre" or "no name"} generation], "La avanzada" [the front line {or avant-garde}][6]—referring to military vigilance, internal and external exile, disappearance, and vanguard resistance, respectively—indicate this basic link between the act of writing and the repressive facts of life under the military regime. These young writers not only initiated their literary development after the coup, but also gained their entire sense of individual and collective identity while living within the context of militarized society.

By contrast, writers of the previous generation, such as Benavente and Dorfman, had lived and written throughout the 1960s and 1970s—with the liberating promise of the Cuban Revolution and of Salvador Allende's Popular Unity, paralleled by "large" modernist literary projects such as those of Cortázar and García Márquez, as I discussed in chapter 1. They had also lived through a failure of those discourses in 1973.[7] Many became immediate targets of postcoup repression. Literature written after the coup by authors such as Dorfman and Benavente therefore demonstrated the ways in which this turn in history had deeply and violently challenged their claims to any authority in language. Both *Widows* (1981) and *Tres Marías y una*

Rosa (1979) reflect the authors' literal and symbolic displacement in relation to community-based struggles for representational power after the coup. As I have discussed, Dorfman's vacillation between the "universal" and the "local" is symptomatic of both his social displacement and his contradictory desire to grow closer to that which was far away: a country, a time, a public space or large narrative that was no longer imaginable for him as before 1973.

For the young writers of the generation of 1980, however, the history that they were living was not the story of a search for utopias lost or for universal truths. Instead, it was a history of suppressions in interpersonal relationships, small gestures of resistance, and the daily struggle for survival. Pía Barros describes the *desencanto* (disenchantment) of her generation: "My generation has tremendous dreams of utopias, but at the same time we know that we can't believe in them. It's like feeling brutally ripped off by your history [Es como sentir{t}e brutalmente estafado por tu historia]."[8] This generation distrusted discourses of Truth and of History, due to their similarities with the totalizing bases of the regime's univocal interpretation of reality. From the time they began writing, the new generation of authors by necessity searched for a language capable of telling stories that examined the contaminated relationships and local struggles of daily life, to reveal what Foucault has described as the dynamic of power and resistance at work in every social exchange.[9]

By the 1980s, this same distrust of utopian discourses was true of the older generation as well (as seen in my readings of Dorfman and Benavente), and their generation became more *desencantada*, more disenchanted, the longer Pinochet remained in power. However, the difference between these groups hinged upon the older generation's having directly lived another national reality, versus the younger generation's having known only militarized society. The sense of *desencanto* was therefore qualitatively different for each generation: if the older generation had "loved and lost," in its experience with Popular Unity, the younger generation never had "loved" at all. As Popular Unity had by the 1980s become part of a mythical past (gone the way of other large or totalizing narratives), the older generation felt the bitter loss of having once believed in collective myths, while the younger generation simply yearned to believe—despite cynicism—in the possibility of telling stories at all. Both generations had to deal with their respective senses of *desencanto* during the 1980s, in order to imagine alternative aesthetic and political orders in their writing and in their future society. For the generation of 1980, however, this first meant searching for different ways to tell the story of what they were presently experiencing at the most intimate levels of their daily lives.

The struggle of the generation of 1980 to claim narrative power in postcoup Chile is evident in the literary production of Pía Barros. Her first collection of short stories, *Miedos transitorios (De a uno, de a dos, de a todos)* [Transitory Fears (By ones, twos, and everyone)][10] is clearly a product of the years immediately following the coup. It illustrates an immediate need to call things by their names, in order to overcome fear, both of words and of their referents.[11] The collection's subtitle indicates its movement from stories about individuals, to those about couples, and finally to those about "everyone," each expanding Barros's examination of how repression, fear, and resistance are operative and mutually reinforcing on all these social levels.

The collection's frugal economy of language (manifested in the short sentences, halting rhythm, and brevity of the texts, some of which are only four or five lines long) reinscribes the urgency of the mid-1970s, a moment which required the rapid and sometimes clandestine dissemination of literature. Their brevity also made these stories **memorable**, which enabled the regeneration of collective memories that the regime had sought to censor. In these respects, the form of these stories invokes the link between literature and other forms of protest, including street theater, *acciones de arte* (art actions), and the *manifestaciones-relámpago* ("lightning fast" protests) of the late 1970s and early 1980s.[12] And as was the case with alternative theater, this collection's indirect references to the sociopolitical context (e.g., in the very short *microcuento* "Golpe")[13] required the complicity of readers willing and able to decipher the stories' literary and political codes. By fostering such complicity, these texts sought to articulate a sense of community despite the official prohibition of that possibility within the military order. Thus, *Miedos transitorios* attempts to piece together a fragmented historical corpus, written from (and directed toward) the officially excluded margins of militarized society.

By the mid-1980s, concurrent with broader and more public social protest, including the visible emergence of a feminist movement to which Barros was committed, the author's initial urgency to contest the regime's discourse gave way to a specific need to elaborate political and aesthetic alternatives to the dominant order. In *A horcajadas* [*Astride*], a collection of short stories written between 1986 and 1989, and published in 1990,[14] Barros is less interested in explicitly showing how agents of the State exercise violence, than in exploring how systems of power are perpetuated at the most intimate levels of cultural practice. By revealing how gender-based violence is culturally reproduced, Barros demonstrates, like Dorfman, that authoritarianism is not a political aberration (nor a "transitory fear"). In contrast to Dorfman, however, Barros is most concerned with the effects of authoritarianism on those who stayed home, with the phenomenon of incile in its most interiorized expression.

Barros's originality lies especially in her language, in an aesthetic that goes against the grain of transparency of official discourse, consumerist propaganda, or simplistic political slogans. There is an ambiguity, a kind of double movement, in Barros's *Astride*. At the same time that Barros's thematic foci emphasize the interpersonal violence and absolute alienation characterizing postcoup society, her language seeks to fuse disparate elements using what I will call an aesthetic of synesthesia. Employing techniques of inversion, tension, neologisms, indeterminate narrators, and ambiguous situations, Barros aesthetically joins what society (and sometimes her own characters) render apart, thereby enacting the kinds of desire-based links between people necessary to defeat the fear and solitude they otherwise experience. But Barros never does so glibly. Like her characters, Barros struggles through her work to claim the right to self-representation through narrative, through the politically and aesthetically challenging act of telling stories, always cognizant that the context of alienation, and her social status as a woman, condition the very possibility for her to do so.

Barros's textual focus on the interior, personal means of social intervention is paralleled by her view of the production and distribution of her literature. In contrast to Dorfman's and Benavente's desire for broad, public literary intervention, Barros produces in slim volumes published by alternative presses, in literary magazines, and within the space of the literary workshops she directs (composed mostly of middle-class women). Similar to others of her generation, Barros faced not only the obstacle of censorship, but also the prohibitive expense of publication and distribution (with the IVA tax), which had led many writers to publish themselves in *autoediciones* (self-financed editions) or in small alternative editorial houses. Unlike Benavente's and Dorfman's preference for larger narrative forms, Barros utilizes her genre of choice, short stories, to focus on slices of interpersonal interactions, which (taken together) develop a dialogue, or a partial and incomplete whole. As I will explore further in chapter 5, Diamela Eltit's work is the most radically fragmentary and indirect of the authors I discuss, and yet, her trajectory in the 1980s leads her back to a kind of novelistic whole in *El cuarto mundo* [*The Fourth World*]. By comparison, Barros's short stories only obliquely aspire to such a sense of wholeness, through the unstated thematic and political continuity that indirectly connects the disparate, but internally coherent, "slices" (short stories) of *Astride*.

On both the textual and contextual levels, then, Barros's vision of the intersection of literature and history is much more local, private, and intimate than that of Dorfman and Benavente, which raises several questions. Does Barros merely claim sexual self-determination while ceding the public sphere as a terrain of struggle? In addition, Barros's engagement with the ostensibly middle-class dilemmas of authoritarianism "en la casa" [in the home] reflects a shift away from Dorfman's and Benavente's attention to the working-class women protagonists of the early postcoup years. So while Barros's work on the whole may gain (middle-class) feminist ground, does it risk making working-class women invisible? Finally, can her (or any) aesthetic stance actually contest social alienation? In my analysis of *Astride*, I will explore the contradictory potential for Barros's focus on intimate expressions of authoritarianism and resistance to intersect with broad public efforts, shaped by women and men, aimed toward achieving social transformation.

"DEMOCRACIA EN EL PAÍS Y EN LA CASA"
[DEMOCRACY IN THE COUNTRY AND IN THE HOME]

In order to consider how Barros's feminist critique in *Astride* squares with a need for collective social change shaped by both women and men, it is important to recognize how the Chilean social context itself had shifted by the early 1980s. Two main events—the progressive reemergence of (middle- and cross-class) feminism and the National Protests of 1983–84— had an indelible impact on Chilean society at large, and on literary production in the country. Both of these events demonstrated the dramatic momentum gained by resistance movements during the late 1970s and early 1980s. Local groups had moved from private expressions of opposition to public criticism of the regime, from subsistence measures and clandestine politics to public protest, and from the early postcoup demands for social justice, voiced first by working-class women (as represented in *Widows* and *Tres Marías y una Rosa*), to a general demand for democracy voiced by working- and middle-class women and men (such as Barros's protagonists). By the early 1980s, many more Chileans had discovered truth in the message of those first few protesting mothers of the disappeared: that the most effective way to imagine a future without Pinochet was for each person to tell—and to embody publicly—her/his local story of survival. By bringing such stories into the open, civil society showed that community-based history had gone on, despite military efforts to silence it.

In a general sense, the rejuvenation of feminism in Chile was not unique internationally during this time period, but its relevance for the country did evolve from experiences specific to the Chilean context. International feminist projects flourished after the U.N. declared 1975 to 1985 the Decade for Women.[15] Riding their own Second Wave of feminism, industrialized nations in Western Europe and North America offered funding for nongovernmental organizations (and other independent feminist projects) within "developing" countries in Africa, Asia, and Latin America. Chilean feminists, like those in other countries that were experiencing authoritarian (or otherwise exclusionary) governments, benefited from the increased global awareness of authoritarianism as a feminist issue and took advantage of available funding. In addition, because many (mostly middle-class) Chilean students, scholars, and politicians had been exiled in Europe, North America, and elsewhere in Latin America, they were increasingly aware of (and participants in) both this rising international feminist consciousness and the increasing financial and political support for feminist projects within Chile itself.[16]

However, channeling these international feminist experiences and funds to Chile could have been highly problematic, had not the country's own process of resistance to authoritarianism been well underway. The movement within Chile needed to be sufficiently self-determining to avoid capitulation to any "strings" implicitly attached to the international funds—that is, to shape its own agenda, rather than simply adopting a feminism created in and for the industrial North. In Santiago, the progressive feminist awakening of the 1970s and 1980s culminated in an eventual union of the grassroots social organizations developed by working-class women in the years immediately following the coup with a rapidly expanding network of middle-class, professional women.[17] The cross-class feminisms that emerged out of this recent Chilean history shared basic assumptions about the interrelatedness of gender, economic, and sociopolitical transformation as necessary for liberation: this was predominantly a socialist feminist agenda for social justice (as opposed to a liberal or radical one, though these lines of praxis also existed). Within the postcoup context specifically, members of the diverse feminist groups therefore shared two fundamental commitments: they sought the demise of the Pinochet regime, and they sought to question the multiple ways in which authoritarianism was perpetuated through gender and class-based exclusions. During the 1980s, international funding was used largely to support, not determine, these locally generated goals.

In building a broadly-based coalition, contemporary Chilean feminists deliberately invoked the repressed historical lineage of Chilean struggles for women's rights early in the twentieth century. On 20 June 1983, twenty-four women's groups created an umbrella organization to coordinate their activities, MEMCh'83. This group revived the acronym of the Chilean suffragist organization, Movimiento Pro Emancipación de las Mujeres de Chile [Movement for the Emancipation of Chilean Women], thereby situating themselves in an historical trajectory of political struggle that predated the Pinochet regime.[18] By representing themselves as part of an historical, social *corpus*, these feminists reestablished links among present and past members of a community of women actively pursuing social transformation. At the same time, by creating symbolic links to the suffragists, they based themselves within a broadly accepted liberalism associated with the Chilean mainstream and Western democracies alike, despite the socialist leanings of most of their member groups. In the context of creating a united front for defeating the common enemy embodied by Pinochet, potential contradictions between these feminist political positions were repressed during the 1980s—and have only emerged, painfully, during the first decade of the transition to democracy.

The slogan coined by the Movimiento Feminista [Feminist Movement] in 1983, "Democracia en el país y en la casa," "Democracy in the country and in the home,"[19] sums up both the theoretical content and the political strategy of the feminist and women's organizations that had emerged in the early 1980s. As I mentioned in the Introduction, Patricia Chuchryk points out in her analysis of Julieta Kirkwood's work that Chilean feminists made the important claim that authoritarianism in Chile did not begin with the coup of 1973. Chuchryk states:

> [Kirkwood] argues that military rule has only made visible an authoritarianism which is embedded in the Chilean social structure. It has enabled us to see that the family is authoritarian, that education, factories and even political parties are based on authoritarian relationships and structures.[20]

Since the extreme violence of the Pinochet regime built upon the traditional authoritarian structures that governed family life, Chilean feminists argued that the critique of women's personal experiences of gender- and class-based discrimination necessarily implied challenging the underlying core of authoritarianism in Chilean society overall. Political change, they maintained, must be actively sought on all levels, public and private, "en el país y en la casa," in order for a more inclusive democracy to be possible.

Hence, the most convincing reason for the feminist renaissance in postcoup Chile was, ironically, that the authoritarian context itself made the feminist critique particularly relevant. As I have discussed in chapters 1 through 3, the coup began a period of crisis, in which politics became a very personal matter and personal issues were likewise politicized. In the postcoup context, civil society **was** feminized, to the extent that it was made vulnerable and was systematically excluded by the misogynist military State. As leftists assessed the past, searching for answers as to how such terror could have emerged from within a long-standing democratic society (a question that Dorfman's *Widows* poses), one answer lay in the notion that traditional society was not so deeply democratic after all. That is, some of the most basic structures governing traditional democracies (i.e., the ways relationships of power are structured culturally) were imbued with the extreme mechanisms of exclusion made manifest in authoritarian violence. The context of struggle against the regime and for democracy had led civil society, and most particularly women, to question what sort of "democracy" that "they [we]re struggling **for**."[21] The feminist critique opened a window of understanding on both the authoritarian regime and on the cultural exercise of power in Chilean society at large.

The National Protests of 1983–84 brought together those who had remained precariously and clandestinely organized in participatory structures that predated the coup (such as political parties, labor unions, and student organizations), those who had emerged as strong social actors after the coup (including various women's organizations and working-class subsistence collectives), and those who had not organized at all after the coup, despite their dissatisfaction with the Pinochet regime (mostly disparate sectors of the middle class).[22] In an atmosphere of systematic exclusion, the economic crisis of 1981–82, coupled with the fraudulent plebiscite staged to approve Pinochet's 1980 Constitution, had provided powerful catalysts for a nationwide explosion of discontent.[23]

Since the dictatorship had affected even the most private aspects of everyday life—a point that the mothers of the disappeared had made many years before—it was appropriate that the protests began with a call for dissatisfied citizens to modify their daily activities in some denunciatory way. Participants in the first of the protests (11 May and 14 June 1983) did just that. The diverse responses ranged from work slowdowns, banging on pots and pans, and school absenteeism, to bonfires and sit-in barricades in the shantytowns.[24] Though it was working-class women who had first dared to protest years before, this was the first time after ten years of military rule that various social sectors acted simultaneously in protest against the military regime.

However, the renewed predominance of party politics and unions—which had taken the public lead in calling for the days of protest[25]—was questioned by women's groups who felt they had done the hard work of leading the way in contesting the regime throughout the 1970s. Furthermore, to them, party politics (on both the right and the left) had historically meant subsuming gender issues to supposedly "larger" struggles dominated by men.[26] Many women therefore pursued a *doble militancia*—a double activism, in parties and in feminist organizations—to combat this tendency. During the protests, MEMCh'83 staged a series of acts to supplement those organized by political parties and unions, including demonstrations by women at the National Library and the Plaza de Armas in downtown Santiago, between the third and fourth protests. MEMCh'83 also issued a public statement that denounced the regime's violent treatment of women specifically (in contrast to its hypocritical exaltation of them). This statement powerfully articulated the link between the women's struggle against various authoritarianisms and the opposition's fight to end the Pinochet dictatorship.[27]

De la Maza and Garcés find the degree of women's unity during the National Protests remarkable, as they state:

> We should point out the arrival of a new sociopolitical agent, one that has achieved very significant results: women. Gradually, there developed an overarching coordination of all the functioning women's organizations, from the various instances of women organized at the working-class level (especially in the shantytowns) . . . to the political coalition of women called Mujeres por la vida [Women for Life]. . . . and various other groups. Together, these women produced an event that was previously unthinkable: a protest by women only, in the Caupolicán Theater in Santiago, **where a unifying atmosphere predominated, which the rest of the acts and protests did not achieve.**[28]

According to de la Maza and Garcés, **only** the women's organizations—which insisted on autonomy from political parties—were able to maintain their common, unifying referent ("Democracia en el país y en la casa") throughout the National Protests. The drawing power of this December 1983 event (organized by the new umbrella group, "Mujeres por la vida") surprised both the regime, which began stricter repression of women, and the political parties, led by men who did not realize the degree to which these women had organized a stable base of working- and middle-class support.

It is also important to note that this feminist gathering followed what had been, one month earlier (18 November 1983), the largest antigovernment protest ever. The failure of civilian dialogue with the regime about ending military rule had led to the protest.[29] It brought together between 400,000 and one million people,[30] including the two major factions of the party-based opposition (center and left, which differed strongly on their views of the utility of negotiating at all with Pinochet), and some 150 other groups, in Santiago's Parque O'Higgins. Despite this show of unity, the civilian opposition remained deeply divided in subsequent months, and the division between center and left political party blocks grew worse throughout 1984. After the long-planned days of National Protest and Strikes on 29–30 October 1984, Pinochet finally declared an end to any dialogue, reimposing a state of siege on 6 November 1984.[31]

Overall, the 1983–84 National Protests did achieve a measure of success. They had articulated the population's generalized dissatisfaction with the regime (thus redefining the regime-opposition relationship) and had energized diverse oppositional sectors to sustain their support and to develop political alternatives to the military government. Student organizations and professional groups gained the right to elect their leaders (instead of Pinochet's appointing them), and book censorship was lifted.

Yet the protests also made the weaknesses of the opposition evident. Labor unions, political parties, and (to some degree) poor working-class *pobladores* had all clearly been debilitated by the regime's sustained attacks upon them. In particular, the lack of a viable alternative to the pre-1973 political party system—which reappeared with the same leaders as before the coup, but devoid of its political base and spaces for interparty negotiation—highlighted the opposition's initial inability to develop a coherent political project. The traditional party system had been criticized as exclusive (nonrepresentational) by members of the new social organizations that proliferated during the late 1970s, but none of those organizations offered an overarching alternative. The tensions between a traditional notion of politics and the new reality of heterogenous popular demands—expressed in the struggle to move from *protesta* to *propuesta,* from protest to concrete proposals—was to last until the 1988 plebiscite, and in many ways, still continues today.[32]

This evolving political scene of the early 1980s had an indelible impact on the literature produced in the country. Just as many forms of local resistance became vehicles for more overt public protest in 1983–84, the literature produced and distributed among small groups of people in the late 1970s and early 1980s—principally through the phenomenon of literary workshops—could finally be published without prior censorship after 1983.[33] Moreover, the increasing social participation by women of diverse class backgrounds after the coup was mirrored by the increasing numbers of women writers (of prose, poetry, and literary criticism) to be published and to gain public attention in subsequent years.[34] This emergence of Chilean women authors in the 1980s, and the increased critical attention in Latin America to the cultural production of women writers more generally, culminated in what was perhaps the most significant literary event of the dictatorship: the Primer Congreso de Literatura Femenina Latinoamericana [First Congress on Latin American Literature by Women], an international gathering that took place in Santiago in August 1987.[35] This conference demonstrated that the relevance of women as social actors after the coup—and feminist critiques of various cultural forms of authoritarianism—had set the groundwork for public reception of the women writers who had begun to publish after 1983. The writers themselves also rediscovered a sense of community and of common concerns (about aesthetics, politics, and practical exclusions vis-à-vis the institutions of literature) that each had confronted since she began writing. Most importantly, this Congress made obvious a dominant characteristic of Chilean culture after 1973: in literature, as in society, many women had become narrators of postcoup history.

Unwittingly, the regime's interference with even the most intimate aspects of daily life after the coup had created a context in which feminism flourished. Yet the capacity for women to find their voices in the literary world, in feminist organizations, or as cohesive political actors in the National Protests, to a great extent depended upon their creating a space **apart** from those outlets, where their stories may have been diluted by the dominant (and culturally validated) voices of men. For the women involved, this apartness seemed to be both the consequence of the militarized context (e.g., the marginalization of men in civil society) as well as a necessary aspect of their developing autonomous critiques of political and cultural authoritarianism. It carried the risk, however, of leaving the traditional hegemonies largely uncontested on their own terrain.

These observations bear a crucial relationship to the work of Pía Barros, who was both a participant in, and a product of, the resurgence of Chilean feminism. In *Astride*, Barros emphasizes how the possibility for women to tell their stories is culturally conditioned by those various, and sometimes invisible, forms of authoritarianism. As a prerequisite for this exploration, however, Barros creates spaces apart to validate women's struggle to find their voices: from the imagined spaces of her protagonists' fantasies, to the slim volumes of stories she publishes, to the real space of her literary workshops. This question of the relationship between the local, ostensibly private, story, and the potential for overtly public social transformation— whether a local apartness limits public action, or whether it is a precondition for women's participation in social change—brings me to analysis of the stories comprising *Astride*.

TEXTUAL BODIES: DESIRE AND VIOLENCE IN PÍA BARROS'S *A HORCAJADAS* [*ASTRIDE*]

The short stories in *Astride* explore the most local site where power relations between people and cultural institutions are played out: the human body,[36] and more specifically, woman's body. Since the authoritarian regime viewed the "feminine" as a form of excess (or unruliness) to be codified or contained (like the "masses"), the **specificity** of woman's body (defined both symbolically **and** literally as feminine by masculine-centered culture) made it a negatively "privileged" space within the postcoup social order. The specifically female body represented the nexus between the local and the social in a society broadly feminized by the exercise of military violence. For Barros, the struggle by women to reclaim their own bodies, particularly through expression of erotic desire, necessarily contested the militarized masculine culture that would negate both the female social subject's expression of desire and her capacity for self-representation. Woman's body thus becomes in *Astride* both the site of, and a metaphor for, the historical struggle for social participation, for contesting the national narrative, within feminized Chilean society as a whole.

In *Astride*, Barros asks: How might one tell the story of woman's body, particularly in a context in which it must be negated in the service of military authoritarianism? How might she claim narrative power in a society characterized by **various** forms of authoritarianism, many of them invisibly reproduced within the structures of gender and family, erotic desire and sexuality, and even language itself? Given that cultural structures such as language are founded upon the violent exclusion of her experiences, can she use them for her purposes without destroying herself? In *Astride*, Barros's female characters' struggles for narrative power show how the potential for violence is present within any attempt at self-expression, whether real or imaginary. Hence, the possibility for a female social subject to claim self-authority through embodied erotic desire—and her capacity to imagine alternatives to the dominant order—are acts which necessarily imply contradictions.

"Prefiguración de una huella" [Foreshadowing of a Trace], the story that opens *Astride*, serves as a frame and prologue to the entire collection. It invokes a woman who actively claims the power to narrate herself, an act metaphorically expressed through an erotic encounter taking place between herself and her lover. The story is composed of a single extended sentence, which establishes eroticism as a changing position—or a horizon of possibility—from which the protagonist may claim narrative authority as a woman who is at once the subject and the object of her own representational power. In this way, "Foreshadowing of a Trace" demonstrates that points of resistance are indeed inscribed *in potentia* within the dominant discourses of society. The female narrator elaborates this potential through the construction of her own self-authority, but she must also confront the limits of the past—of history—on that authority. Hence, what the text proposes involves a simultaneity of potential opposites, a suggestive aesthetic based on the tense fusion of disparate elements. As its final phrase indicates, the woman's story is **at once** "indeleble e imposible" [indelible and unattainable {impossible}], it is articulated but not unchanging, it is the ironic "huella" or "trace" that insists it is nothing more, and nothing less, than a "prefiguración" [a foreshadowing].

From the beginning, the narrator's desire propels forth the narrative. She describes herself and her body, only implying the presence of her lover through her commands, as is evident from the story's first words: "Lame mis rodillas, devocióname, los muslos, lengua a lengua, lame mi pubis aguardante, sométete, succióname, lame **mi deseo y el dolor** . . ." (emphasis mine, 11) [Lick my knees, zeal me and entreaty me and devotion me, these thighs, tongue to tongue, lick the eager arch of my pelvis, {submit}, suck me, lick all **my desire and {pain}** . . .] (emphasis mine, 15). The narrative hinges upon this tension—which Juan Carlos Lértora appropriately calls an erotic "friction"[37]—between "mi deseo y el dolor" [my desire and pain]. While pleasure and pain are connected (she **aches** with desire), the narrator attempts to distinguish between their positive and negative aspects by claiming "**mi** deseo" [**my** desire] and subtly distancing herself from "**el** dolor" [the pain {or generically, "pain"}]. In doing so, the narrator associates the positive aspects of both pleasure and pain (i.e., subjective desire) with her own self-authority, while linking the negative aspects (i.e., objective violence) with her lover.

In this first moment of the story, however, it is the narrator who exercises violence, as she attempts to empower herself through subjecting the one who "licks," the one who traces her body with his tongue (the adjectives referring to the lover are masculine). Because the narrator assumes the ability to speak—and to narrate her own body, an "unpublishable" act according to the dominant order—she transgresses the cultural codes that would repress that possibility. The relationship established through the story is therefore a simultaneously erotic and violent one between the woman who writes her story and the language that she uses to do so. The protagonist establishes herself as a narrator only after dominating her lover, both as physical being and as language. Through this process, she establishes her "self," and seizes the opportunity to narrate this self as well as the body of her lover, that is, to invent new words and rewrite the codes of a masculine-centered order that excludes her experiences.

However, this transgressive act is an unstable process, for it necessarily functions within the violent cultural dynamics (represented in language) that it also seeks to transform. Transformation therefore remains as a possibility *in potentia* in the present textual moment, as indicated by the change to the future tense after the narrative "yo" [I] is founded: "yo seré poderosa e invincible ante ti y no podrás tomarme, ahora que eres tan vulnerado" (11) [I'll be mighty, womanly, invincible before you and you will not be able to take me, now that you are so wounded] (15). Only after she establishes her own control through violence does she feel safety to join her lover, as a third moment of the story states: "entonces, sólo entonces, abrazaré tu cabeza a mi pubis, descenderé hasta ti" (12) [then, and only then, will I embrace your head at my pelvis, then I'll descend to where you are] (15), and it continues, "**ahora** que habrás comprendido, **ahora** que el rostro del tiempo se te ha mostrado, **ahora** que mi huella es indeleble e imposible" (emphasis mine, 12) [since by **now** it must be clear to you, **now** that the face of time has revealed itself to you, **now** that any trace of me is both indelible and unattainable] (emphasis mine, 16). Upon constructing herself as the subject of this story, the protagonist enables herself to articulate her own pleasure during the struggle to make her mark ("mi huella") on her lover and on language. However, the violence culturally inscribed within the relationship of language, power, and eroticism does not disappear, but rather is dramatized through the narrator's search for self-authority in this context. Given that her resistance always functions in relation to power,[38] her resistance cannot exist outside of that relationship: history is always there.

Hence, the "ahora" [now] at the end of the story has not yet fully occurred. It remains in a future accessible through narrative imagination, and through the desire expressed in the story itself. Within the context of "Foreshadowing of a Trace," this "now" is decidedly not a fixed foundational moment. Instead it is an evocation of transformative potentials within the dominant discourses of society, which carry (and reproduce) their own limits. That is, there is no space **entirely** outside of the codes of the dominant culture itself. This is why the female narrator's "trace" is "indeleble e imposible" [indelible and unattainable]; it represents the contradictory place of her voice in history. For these reasons, it is unthinkable to celebrate the narrator's self-authority in any pure utopian sense. To read this text, for example, through the lens of Hélène Cixous's view of woman's body as endlessly multiple—and as escaping the limits of the dominant language, and by extension, of history[39]—would be to miss Barros's most essential point.

The stories that follow "Foreshadowing of a Trace" in the collection reinforce this sense that utopian purity is not a material possibility in *Astride*. "Iniciaciones" [Initiations] is the story of the loss of innocence of two adolescent friends, while "Conmiseración" [Commiseration] depicts a woman who expresses love and sadness, after finding and then cradling an unknown dead man in her arms for hours. In "Diccionarios" [Dictionaries], Barros explores how language replicates deep cultural exclusions, which in turn impede desire-based solidarity between men and women. In these stories, it is no coincidence that the woman in each pair takes charge of the man, narrating his body with her own (as in "Foreshadowing of a Trace"). The themes of a lack of innocence and death as commonplace run throughout the collection, though one source of hope for the characters lies in fleeting moments of physical solidarity with others (like the dead man). However, the characters in these stories are ultimately alienated from one another by death, by their status as anonymous strangers, or by their incapacity in a fragmented society to achieve any real sense of communication with another human being. This alienation or irreconcilable solitude—often rooted as much in gender-based differences as in the sterile (implicitly postcoup) landscapes of the stories themselves—is a common experience for both Barros's male and female characters in *Astride*. Thus the collection implies that the lack of real desire-based connections between people is the deepest consequence of the reproduction of authoritarianism in people's intimate lives. In all three of these stories, however, the ambiguous (and inclusive, interpellative) first and second person narrative voices create an intriguing tension with—and potentially contest—the overwhelming alienation they describe.

Barros's fourth story, "Olor a madera y a silencio" [Scents of Wood and Silence] is one of the starkest portraits of miscommunication between a woman and her lover(s) in *Astride*. In this work, as in "Foreshadowing of a Trace," Barros dramatizes the female protagonist's efforts to make a mark ("dejar huella"), to tell her own story. "Scents of Wood and Silence" interweaves two narrative spaces, which represent two simultaneous worlds for the female protagonist. In one space, "de este lado del umbral" [on this side of the threshold], the protagonist faces the banality of fulfilling her roles as "dueña de casa" [housewife] and "esposa fiel" [faithful spouse]; this world is narrated with an ironic simplicity that reveals the subtle cruelty of those roles. Since the protagonist cannot express herself in that realm (because it represents her codification via gender role-based norms), she seeks refuge in her dreams, in the space "del otro lado del umbral" [on the other side of the threshold].[40]

Following the legacy of the Chilean writer María Luisa Bombal (e.g., "El árbol" [The Tree] from *La última niebla* [*The House of Mist*], 1941),[41] Barros's protagonist explores fantasy as a space of potential freedom. By building on Bombal's "The Tree," Barros inscribes her work within, and recuperates, the history of a larger body of narrative written by Chilean women many decades before her. In Barros's story, the protagonist's fantasies are narrated with long lyrical phrases; through this flowing, sensuous language, the protagonist imagines her lovers and voices her repressed erotic desires. Just as the protagonist crosses over the "threshold" between the two "sides," likewise the private and the public, the indoors and the outdoors, the intimate and the political, converge throughout the story. Barros subtly intertwines the real and the imaginary so completely that we, as readers, must recognize the reality of the protagonist's experiences on **both** "sides." And although the protagonist attempts to escape the banality of daily life through her erotic fantasies, worldly violence eventually overtakes this refuge, leaving no escape for her (except death). In contrast to "Foreshadowing of a Trace," where the narrator employs force for her own ends, the narrator in "Scents of Wood and Silence" becomes a victim of the latent violence conditioning even the imaginary world of her erotic dreams.

At the beginning of the story, the protagonist's husband (appropriately named Ismael)[42] notices that something is unusual about her behavior:

> —Amaneces distinta.
> —Es que soñé con gaviotas, dijo ella saltando de la cama a las tostadas y huevos, al café humeante y el cotidiano ritual de desayunos compartidos. No lo escuchó cuando dijo:
> —Es extraño, traes pasto verde entre los dedos. (19)

> ["You seem different this morning."
> "It's just that I dreamt about sea gulls," she said, jumping out of bed to toast and eggs, steaming coffee and the daily ritual of shared breakfasts. She didn't hear him when he said:
> "That's strange, you've got green grass between your fingers."] (23)

As this passage suggests, the protagonist's dream seems out of place within the codes of "el cotidiano ritual de desayunos compartidos" [the daily ritual of shared breakfasts]. The juxtaposition of "gaviotas" [sea gulls] and "pasto verde" [green grass], signs of life brought in from outside, alongside "tostadas y huevos" [toast and eggs], emphasizes the protagonist's and Ismael's distance from one another, and their unconnected communication, inside their home. As the story continues, Ismael attempts to comprehend his wife's behavior according to his own codes, while she, in turn, becomes increasingly involved in the more fulfilling reality of her dreams.

The second paragraph of the text stylistically invites the reader's identification with the protagonist's perspective, as it traces how erotic fantasy evolved out of her daily circumstances. Barros fuses first- and third-person narration to show the interrelationship between the objective and the subjective, the interior and exterior spaces of the protagonist's parallel worlds. Out of an omniscient third-person voice emerges a more personal third-person perspective, closely identified with the protagonist's subjectivity (following her unstated "I" as she invents hands that touch her). Drawn into the view of this "I," readers are invited to share the protagonist's fantasy as it happens:

> Había sido un juego para que el lavado no fuese tan anodino. Empezó soñando con unas manos que salían de las sábanas en busca de sus pechos, deberían ser grandes, toscas, huesudas y descuidadas, de dedos largos, que la palparan sin dolor, vigorosas, subiendo y bajando por sus pezones, dibujando la erizada piel, recorriéndola. (19)

> [It had been a game so doing the laundry wouldn't be so dull. She began dreaming about hands that reached out of the sheets searching for

her breasts, they should be large, coarse hands, bony and neglected, with long fingers, that would touch her painlessly, vigorous hands, rising and falling over her nipples, tracing her bristling skin, roaming all over her.] (23)

The protagonist experiences the cultural expectations regimenting a housewife's "normal" behavior as the emptiness of domestic tasks, and her stifling environment motivates her to search for an alternative. Doing the laundry is described as "anodino": not only is it a boring task, but it is also "dull" like a muted pain, symptomatic of the implicit violence that confines her within banal, day-to-day routines. By contrast, the invented hands stimulate her, touching her with strength but without pain, qualities she desires in her invented lover, whose hands provide a vehicle for her self-discovery. His hands are transgressive, too, because they are working-class hands—rough and unkempt—freely touching this middle-class woman within her self-generated fantasy world.

As in "Foreshadowing of a Trace," the narrator attempts to distinguish between the positive and negative aspects of pleasure and pain by claiming "mi deseo" ("my desire," as self-authority) and distancing herself from "el dolor" ("pain," associated with the objectifying codes of day-to-day routine). This fictitious disassociation is necessary to the construction of her dream world, to the creation of an ostensibly separate alternative to domestic discipline. The hands that she engenders become the "author" that tells her story, the means for her self-recognition; the hands explore her body, "dibujando la erizada piel" [tracing her bristling skin], and with them, the protagonist draws out her desire, narrating her own body in the process.

By contrast, Ismael finds his wife's desire for sleep to be incomprehensible, because for him, the juxtaposed, ironic narrative voice indicates, "La vida era segura y se sentía pleno" (20) [Life was secure and he felt fulfilled] (24). However, Ismael's sense of security seems to depend upon his ability to create an escapist world of fiction that is as much a denial of their material surroundings as is his wife's dreaming. When Ismael contemplates her at the beginning of the story, he does not see her as a friend or as a lover, but rather in terms that objectify her; he sees her as a transparent, nearly sacred woman who is "embellecida y diáfana" (20) [beautiful and transparent] (24). When he first noticed her dreaming, Ismael

[d]ejó el portafolios sobre la mesa y deseó hacerle el amor allí mismo, pero se contuvo, porque esa imagen le parecía virginal y ella era tan delicada, que no quiso agredirla y se sentó largo rato sonriendo, viéndola dormir tan abandonada, dulce, con el rostro aniñado por los sueños.
Pero ella estaba lamiendo caderas, besando nalgas, rasguñando. (20)

[put down his briefcase on the table and wanted to make love to her right there, but he controlled himself, because the image seemed virginal to him, and she was so delicate that he didn't want to attack her, and he sat down for a long while smiling, watching her sleep, so abandoned, sweet, with a face made childlike by her dreams.
But she was licking hips, kissing buttocks, clawing.] (24)

Ismael comes to represent a benevolent father-patriarch, whose gaze denies not only his wife's sensuality but also her independent subjectivity. For him, making love is tantamount to brutality, and since he cannot admit to himself that he could "attack" her ("agredirla"), he creates an image of his wife as virginal and childlike. However, as the narrative irony reveals, she is neither; unknown to Ismael, she was "lamiendo caderas, besando nalgas, rasguñando" [licking hips, kissing buttocks, clawing]. Ismael's assumptions about gender and sexuality, as represented by his unstated expectations about his wife's conformity with both the domestic space and her role in it,[43] **create** the fiction of her innocence, of her childlike appearance. Hence, Ismael becomes especially concerned about his wife's obsession with sleep only when it interferes with her assigned duties: "cuando la casa empezó a ostentar el descuido le pidió que viera a un médico" (21) [when the house began to show neglect, he asked her to see a doctor] (24).

Since neither his wife, nor the house, fits his images of them, Ismael begins to reassert himself, gradually becoming a voyeur: "trataba de ver por el espacio entreverado de sus pupilas somnolientas en dónde hacían el amor, hacia donde miraba" [He . . . tried to see through the intermingled space of her drowsy eyes to where they were making love, toward where she was looking], but "los sueños lo dejaban a él vulnerado, inerme . . . humillado por la niebla que no sabía combatir" (23) [the dreams . . . left him injured, defenseless . . . humiliated by the mist that he didn't know how to fight] (27). Since Ismael is shut out of this imaginative space of desiring, he is rendered impotent, both sexually and in terms of his control of the situation. But his solitude and bewilderment, traits shared with other male characters in the collection, reveal him to be a sympathetic character. Because he seems unaware of the masculine-centered codes culturally invested in him ("no sabía combatir" [he didn't know how to fight]), he naïvely seeks to enter her world: "miraba hacia dónde miraba" (23) [he looked toward where she was looking] (27). In this way, Ismael hopes to become an accomplice to his wife's fantasy, by abandoning his familiar postures in the domestic space. Though he relinquishes himself to her, she is now so far away that she is no longer aware of Ismael's presence. The protagonist's now deepened involvement in her dream world, with her imaginary lover, is signaled by the change of which "side" is **"this** side" ("**este** lado"), the space with which she identifies and within which she places herself:

> Ella sabía que **de este lado todo era propio**, que él la amaría dolido y desgarrado, llena de caballos el alma. Del otro lado quedaban las urgencias, las culpas, los horarios. (emphasis mine, 22)

> [She knew that **on this side everything was her own**, that he would love her, aching and torn, his soul full of horses. On the other side remained pressing tasks, guilt, schedules.] (emphasis mine, 26)

Though the protagonist desires communication with another body, and a means for discovering herself, the contradictions latent within her desires eventually begin to emerge. First, the body that reciprocally authors the protagonist's own body remains under her control only as long as she dreams small fragments of it. As long as the "other" is fragmented, it is assimilable by her "self," but such total self-centeredness means that intimate communication with another is thereby made impossible. Second, if the protagonist creates her desired author-lover as a whole, she must relinquish control, making herself vulnerable to the power he may assert in the relationship. Once she enters into such a relationship with her lover, she begins to feel guilty for dreaming, for having challenged her expected obedience as Ismael's wife:

> Fue entonces que le hizo rastro y pensó estremecida que a partir de ese momento, estaba siendo infiel. Sacudió la idea porque él no existía, era sólo múltiples trozos de muchos alguien, fragmentos de atracción que no la hacían culpable de nada que no fueran sus sueños. Sonrió liberada y ansiosa y lo quiso con mirada verde y horizontal . . . y se sintió a salvo, porque supo que quedaba lejos, del otro lado del umbral, donde era posible inventarle una piel salada para lamer poco a poco, sin apremios, hasta tomarla, hacerla suya, desandarla. (21–22)

> [It was then that she gave him a face, and she thought with a shudder that from that moment on, she was being unfaithful. She brushed aside that idea, because he didn't exist, he was only multiple pieces of many somebodies, fragments of attraction that made her guilty of nothing but her dreams. She smiled, relieved and anxious, and she desired him with a green horizontal gaze . . . and she felt safe, because she understood that he was far away, on the other side of the threshold, where it was possible to invent his salty skin to lick bit by bit, unhurriedly, until taking it, making it hers, reshaping it.] (25–26)

At this point in the text, the protagonist begins to invoke her desired lovers in order to exorcise them through the authority she still wields over them. In this way, the protagonist may assure her own safety and her own subjectivity, but she inevitably reenacts domination (violence) within the erotic relationship. It is she who invents the skin-object of a desiring tongue, and it is she who empowers herself by narrating that invented skin, "hasta tomarla, hacerla suya, desandarla" [until taking it, making it hers, reshaping it], but it is also she who objectifies and molds her lovers using the kind of force she had originally sought to escape. However, the eroticism of Barros's own daring language—the "lover" which Barros reshapes and makes **her** own (in such innovative expressions as "la mirada verde y horizontal" [the green horizontal gaze])—implicitly fuses words and fragments that the context would otherwise render apart. Once again, the double movement between separation and unity, solitude and synthesis, plays itself out aesthetically in Barros's synesthetic use of language.

In the above passage, the protagonist's desired author-lover takes on a life of his own, once she dreams him as an integral human being with his own voice (21–22). The protagonist turns herself over to her romance with him, an experience that she hopes will free her through the "horizontal" (egalitarian) lovemaking they share (22–23). This freedom proves to be temporary, however, for the "hombre horizontal" [horizontal man], who coauthored her erotic fantasy, becomes the violent "hombre vertical" [vertical man], surrounded in her dreams by disturbing images of domination, suggesting a subtext of torture:

> Ella quiso volver a soñar las gaviotas, pero cada mordida la arrojaba a imágenes extrañas, una boca gritando en la oscuridad, una semisonrisa entreabierta por un cigarrillo, los zapatos de un hombre sobre el pasto. . . . (24)

> [She wanted to dream about sea gulls again, but each bite hurled her towards strange images, a mouth crying out in the darkness, a half-smile slightly parted by a cigarette, a man's shoes on the grass. . . .] (28)

The imaginary lover eventually makes her submit, and he appropriates her dreams and desires, fragmenting her body. Likewise, Barros's narrative violently fragments, as her protagonist's vision clouds over, leaving narrative gaps indicated by ellipses. While erotic fantasy had permitted the protagonist to free herself briefly from her role-based limits as *esposa fiel*, the (re)emergence of violence demonstrates her internalization of the pervasive social inequalities that she had sought to escape.

In these passages, the cruelties of the unequal relationship between the narrator, her voyeur, and the imaginary man who violates her dreams—a relationship that both Ismael and the dreamer carry inside—shape the expression of her desires. It is not that she desires violence, but rather that violence conditions and limits any of her **possible** desires. Hence, the following passage marks a reassertion of the cultural scheme that marks the narrator's body in submission to "el hombre vertical" [the vertical man]:

y el mar estaba allí, rugidor, lamiendo las pantorrillas que ella subió para quedar a horcajadas sobre el hombre vertical al que el mar parecía tratar de derribar con el oleaje y la espuma rugiendo sobre las nalgas y las piernas entrecruzadas en la espalda a la que ella clavaba las uñas tratando de marcar, de dejar huella, y el hombre la embestía hasta nublarle los ojos y dejar un hilillo en las comisuras de los labios. . . . (24)

[and the sea was there, bellowing, licking the calves that she raised to keep astride the vertical man whom the sea seemed to be trying to topple with its waves, and the foam roaring over her buttocks and her legs crossed over the back into which she dug her nails trying to mark, to leave a trace, and the man attacked her until her eyes clouded, leaving a small thread in the juncture of her lips. . . .] (28)

Threatened with exclusion from the story by the authoritarian vertical man who dominates her, the protagonist searches for a way to exorcise him through expressing herself, through making her own meaning. (Crucially, the narrative perspective in the above passage likewise is aligned with the clouded subjectivity of the protagonist, not with the vertical man's now-green gaze).

Since the protagonist may not remain **astride** the man, she violently struggles to leave a trace ("marcar, dejar huella") on his body. His body offers the place and the means for the narrator's self-expression, but his body also represents the historical and textual institutions that hierarchically (vertically) repress her self-expression. Because the narrator reconstructs her own struggle (and deals with her "guilt") in her dreams, she wills a symbolic triumph over her objectification by attempting to narrate the man who would censure her body. But she must exercise a form of domination in order to do so; violence is thereby presented as a perpetual mechanism defining—directly or indirectly—every relationship among human beings in authoritarian society.

At the end of the story, absolute freedom is denied by both the text and the protagonist, who becomes a person who depends on Ismael for her most basic needs:

En el delirio, ella pedía que le ayudara a recordar, a rememorar el lago y sus ojos, y cómo le hice el pecho, Ismael . . .
Pero Ismael sólo acercaba agua a sus labios y sonreía. (25)

[In her delirium, she was asking him to help her remember, to reconstruct the lake and his eyes, and how I made his chest, Ismael . . .
But Ismael only put water to her lips and smiled.] (29–30)

She has exhausted herself (as her illness and delirium reflect) trying to recreate a love scene with her desired "horizontal" lover, instead of with the cruel "vertical man," but she is incapable of reaching any-body else at this point. The memory of the protagonist, just like her own (textual) body, fragments violently. The voice that she had engendered "ya no era una voz, era el recuerdo de haber oído alguna voz y el horror y el vacío y las caderas y los hombros y la mirada verde aguándose hasta desaparecer" (26) [was no longer a voice, it was the memory of having heard some voice and the horror and emptiness and hips and shoulders and the green gaze diluting until it disappeared] (30). Ismael then opens the window, letting out her memory (26). In the end, the banality of the dominant order reasserts itself:

> La ventana era sólo un ancho marco mostrando edificios y calles y cemento; . . . y las sábanas volvieron a ser anodinas manchas, a las cuales le sería imposible restituirles el olor a madera y a silencio. (26)

> [The window was only a wide frame, displaying buildings and streets and pavement. . . . {T}he sheets became dull stains once again. It would be impossible for her to restore in them the scents of wood and silence.] (31)

Barros's protagonist shows that the capacity for a female social subject to imagine alternatives to the dominant order, even as she explores repressed erotic possibilities, is ultimately circumscribed by the limitations of the culture within which she imagines.

While the first stories in *Astride* build upon an implicit referentiality to militarized society, "Mordaza" [Muzzle], the fifth story in the collection, provides its most explicit, unflinching focus on the material execution of violence. The story takes place as a woman is being tortured. The woman's perspective is narrated as a stream of associations that objectify the violence she experiences. As in "Scents of Wood and Silence," the third person is used to narrate an "ella" [she] identified with a first-person subjectivity. This process of objectification allows her to resist by re-creating a version of herself even as she is being violated. Like the other stories in *Astride*, "Muzzle" retraces the connections between various forms of authoritarian domination which predated (but reached a most obvious expression in) postcoup Chilean society. Unlike the rest of the collection, however, the critique of gender hierarchies in "Muzzle" becomes a vehicle for exposing a wide range of social mechanisms of power, including ethnic, class, colonial and neocolonial domination, and sources of resistance.

In "Muzzle," Barros employs the concept of gender-based violence simultaneously to expose its most literal consequences and to explore its broadest resonances as a metaphor for any politics of exclusion. For Barros's protagonist, torture is an explicit expression of the bodily appropriation (or "domestication") of "woman" in the construction of Latin America's history since the Spanish conquest. In the narrow sense, this act of appropriation is perpetuated by society's grooming of woman's conformity with extant power structures that exclude her, by socializing her to behave like a *señorita* and to internalize her own discipline (in the Foucauldian sense of self-regulation of the body for maximum political obedience within the dominant regime).[44] In the more metaphorical sense, however, the tortured female in "Muzzle" comes to represent the emblematic colonized subject, the feminized social body of "the masses" throughout Latin America's history. The story portrays this social body—as *señorita*, "Malinche," mestizo culture, or Latin America itself—in perpetual struggle to rewrite the official story of its own violation. (According to traditional, and sexist, versions of the myth elaborated by Octavio Paz and others, Cortés's indigenous mistress and translator, Malinche, embodies the betrayal of the Mexican/colonized people, who as a result take on an identity of inferiority as "los hijos de la chingada" [children of the fucked woman].)[45] In Barros's story, the female narrator resists by bending, attempting to break, and then reshaping language to expose the colonized experience, to rewrite the script relegating her to powerlessness.

The story begins with these words:

> Cuando el hombre introduce los electrodos en su vagina, ella propone pasto-pastizal-pastedumbre y los ojos le huelen obstinados a verde. El campo entero le galopa en las pupilas. Ante la primera descarga el dolor la desmembra, le seca la boca, parto-partir-parir, el gorgorito de su hija sin rabia de nacer desde el sometimiento colonizado. . . . (27)

> [When the man shoves the electrodes into her vagina, she thinks "grass-grassland-grassiness" and her eyes smell stubbornly of green. The whole countryside gallops in front of her. At the first surge the pain dismembers her, dries her mouth, apart-split-splinter, the sounds of her daughter in no hurry to be born from her submissive, colonized belly. . . .] (33)

The disembodied man (conquistador, torturer, patriarch) violently inscribes her body with electrodes, positioning her as both the material and the matrix upon which the conquest is written. He seeks to erase the possibility of her self-definition by denying her the authority to narrate. He does this by "dis-membering" her, by attempting to fragment her body, her memory, and her history. Only by erasing her past can he achieve, through her vagina, the tabula rasa—the "virginal" blank slate—upon which to (re)inscribe the authority of the dominant culture. (This inaugural scene might also be read as a gender-specific version of the Chilean military's exaggerated razing of the Moneda Palace, and the symbolic emasculation of Salvador Allende, on the day of the 1973 coup—as well as the violent feminization of the opposition in its aftermath). And yet "el hombre" [the man] only exists through her pain in this story; he has an integral self only insofar as she is "dismembered."

In the face of this absolute brutality, "ella" [she] resists through proposing an alternative, through her obstinate nonconformity with the man's narrative hegemony. Though the man tries to reduce her—or rather, to reduce her body—to pain, the woman attempts to explode that sign into various permutations that invoke life, countryside, and sensuality: "pasto-pastizal-pastedumbre" [grass-grassland-grassiness]. Despite the fact that she must use his terms to tell her story, she pushes his language to the breaking point, just as she is pushed to her physical and psychological limits through his torture of her. The cracks created by this broken language, which is then patched together in remarkably fresh synesthesias, effectively unite her stake in life and her pain in the immediacy of the narrative moment. While life/pleasure and death/pain are central issues in the other stories ("Scents of Wood and Silence," "Foreshadowing of a Trace"), it is in the language of "Muzzle" where the two forces most explicitly, immediately, and defiantly clash and join together in several recombinations before the reader's eyes. By stubbornly holding onto life during torture, the woman narratively reclaims meaning for herself as representative of a spectrum of pain-pleasure, destruction-creation, death-life ("parto-partir-parir": a play on the Spanish "I split apart/give birth"). It is through this dynamic language that Barros, like her narrator, performs (or **prefigures**) a response to the extreme situation she narrates.

As the torture continues, the protagonist contemplates the connection between this physical violence and her socialization as a little girl. As she remembers her father's insistence that she behave like a *señorita*, she thinks:

> que es ser señorita, a lo mejor es el miedo, ese terror que le enrosca la lengua y le impide hablar, insultar o dar nombres, ser señorita es ser muda cuando hablan los otros y cuando no también . . . ser mujer, no ser, ser a partir de lo que no se es. (28)

> [what is it to be a lady, it's probably fear, that terror that curls her tongue and keeps her from speaking, or insulting or naming names, being a lady is keeping quiet when others speak and when they don't . . . to be a woman, not to be, to be on the basis of what she is not. . . .] (34)

She therefore attempts to renounce this dominant version of femininity in order to reaffirm herself, in order to redefine "woman" against the cultural norm. Her resistance takes shape through the creation of a counter-memory, a reinterpretation of the myth of Malinche, who is seen **not** as the figure of betrayal, **nor** as the indigenous woman who sold her tongue and her body to Cortés and the Spanish conquerors. Instead, she is a figure **herself** betrayed by the history that "ellos" [they], the male conquistadors (or military torturers), inscribed upon and through her body:

> sólo queda la franja anaranjada del dolor, dolo, falso, falsos mitos de Malinches, no venderá el secreto de la voz, Malinche no era tan malinche, es que son ellos, . . . son ellos los que nos retacean la historia. (27)
>
> [all that's left . . . is the pain's orange fringe, fraud, false, lying myths of Malinches, she won't give away the secret with her voice, Malinche wasn't so malinche, it's them, . . . they're the ones who sell us remnants of our history.] (33)

While the torturer attempts to force her to give her history to him (on the literal level, to give names of comrades in the opposition), she refuses to give away "el secreto de la voz" [the secret with her voice]. At the same time, she resists by identifying with Malinche's tongue(s). That is, she becomes daringly **unlike** the *señorita* precisely because she **does** "dar nombres" [name names]: not to betray her comrades, but to convey her world. She unflinchingly names her experience, thereby revealing the contradictory social status of any woman—or colonized subject—who refuses to be muzzled.

Barros's own language—and her ability to speak the unspeakable—likewise attempts to challenge the codes of silence and to express multivocality as a generative possibility of language, and of a textual corpus that resists reduction to the mute signs of pain. The narrative voice demonstrates the central tension of the protagonist's situation: to be subject or object of this history, to narrate or be narrated, or to embody the simultaneity of the two. The narrative itself proposes this last option in its vacillations between first- and third-person perspectives. This simultaneity enables the narrator to tell her own story, even if it is the story of her betrayal by history. Torture objectifies her—"El grito la aulla hasta desfallecer" (28) [The scream howls her to fainting] (33)—but she reincorporates her narrative by retrieving this memory (refusing to be "desmembrada" [dismembered]), and by revealing and working against language's historical limits.

In this way, the protagonist reinterprets the cultural myth of Malinche to recuperate the unidealized possibility of hope (her self-representation within an historical lineage) in the midst of horrific circumstances. At the close of the text, she is raped, signs a statement, and is taken away:

> trasladada a la iglesia mientras vocifera, cree ella, mientras en realidad musita, Llévense sus dioses y sus cruces . . . no los necesitamos, ni a ustedes ni a los otros normadores, Malinche y yo los venceremos alguna vez, cuando remen mar adentro con sus dogmas y nuestra tristeza . . . (30)

[she is transferred to the church while she shouts, she thinks, while she really mumbles, Take away your gods and your crosses . . . we don't need you, not you or the rule makers, Malinche and I will win one day, when you go paddling back out to sea taking with you your dogmas and our sorrow . . .] (36)

While dominant history imposes the silence of the muzzle, the protagonist recuperates Malinche to maintain her own voice. Yet her hope and her triumph (as in "Scents of Wood and Silence") are largely symbolic, for they involve the physical destruction of the woman who resists—even though her text remains. The dominant culture's betrayal of her involves her own demise.

It is important to recall that, while Barros posits the need to reestablish counter-memories based on intimate connections among people or through **erotic** expression, the Dorfman and Benavente/TIT texts had emphasized a sort of **maternal** solidarity at the base of their ethical visions. That is, an underlying supposition of both *Widows* and *Tres Marías y una Rosa* is the positively valued alliance between feminine values and motherhood (associated with the life of the community), in opposition to masculinist authoritarianism, linked to sterility and death. Both texts return us to Sonia Montecino's concept of "maternal politics,"[46] mobilizations of women making a claim, as mothers, for the survival of their communities. This maternal-communal association is particularly strong in Dorfman (e.g., the Emmanuel-Cecilia, Alexis-Sofía exchanges, the final segment of the novel). *Widows* suggests that, in an early postcoup context in which most men are disappeared and the others embody authoritarianism, erotic love is made virtually impossible. Hence, in *Widows*, hope necessarily resides more with maternal love (the symbolic, feminine value of childbirth) than with erotic love.

By contrast, "Artemisa" [Artemisia], the ninth story in *Astride*, posits a very different attitude toward maternal love. In it, Pía Barros examines her protagonist's claim to a voice based on the claim to her own body, this time radically questioning the necessary correspondence of such a claim to the culturally accepted position for staking it: the moral high ground of motherhood, seen in both the Dorfman and the Benavente texts. "Artemisia" dares to express the feeling of repugnance that the protagonist feels towards her own body as maternal. This story reveals the violence latent in the act of breast-feeding, in order to question the naturalness with which women are culturally expected to fulfill (literal and symbolic) reproductive functions. Here, Barros turns from Bombal toward Marta Brunet, that "indecorous" mid-twentieth-century Chilean writer who unflinchingly explored the darker impulses of her female protagonists.[47] Barros's reference to the Greek goddess Artemis, whose father Zeus granted her wish that she never have to marry, and who combines beauty with an active desire to kill, is an appropriately ironic choice for this story's title.

In "Artemisia," the first-person narrator suffers from the fact that her corporeal changes, after being pregnant and giving birth, signal a cultural recodification of her body. As both she and her husband view her, she is no longer a sensual lover, for she is now a superior being ("madre") beholden to her offspring. Her son, rather than being an innocent creature, is a small man who redefines her body based on his biological needs. Her own needs for erotic self-expression are therefore undercut by her son's demands, and she views her husband as her son's accomplice in the physical domination of her—"la tortura, la pestilencia de la leche" (47) [And the torture, the stench of the milk] (53). The protagonist's rejection of the ostensible pleasure of nursing her offspring translates into subjective anguish, a search for the memory of her former body, and the rejection of that small being who enslaves her to her breasts. She plays out a double bind: her quest to reject one male-defined narrative (maternity) risks embracing another (the thin female body of advertising, also to be consumed by men). In the end, her breasts, the sign of the maternity she rejects, consume her: she effectively becomes only "breast," sprouting nipples from every corner of her body (55).

Insofar as her maternity negates the protagonist's capacity for self-expression, her motherhood does not allow her to share more fully with other human beings. Instead, it represents her enslavement to cultural codes that require her self-abnegation and exclusion from history, a reduction of her womanhood to her function in the cultural reproduction of gender-based domination. When Barros questions those reductive definitions, she actively combats the military definition of "woman," even as she shocks her readers' valuing of tradition through revealing her protagonist's horror. In doing so, Barros radically unsettles the patriarchal system from which the regime drew its support.

In contrast to Dorfman, then, Barros finds hope in the search for shared expression of erotic love, rather than maternal love, though she does not posit erotic love as an uncomplicated (or ideal, utopian) enterprise. Alienation, social fragmentation, and the constant threat of violence mark all of her "inciled" characters' experiences. Unlike Dorfman's work, Barros's nonutopian writing clearly aligns her with the younger generation, and its particular sense of *desencanto*, shaped fundamentally by the process of growing up during the postcoup years. In *Astride*, there is no moment of innocence nor any space free from the interchange of domination and resistance. While violence gives evidence to this shared lack of innocence (as the adolescents discover in "Initiations"), the desire for solidarity through erotic expression, however foundationally impossible, creates a point of resistance and of survival within the dynamic interplay of power relations.

Maternal love, for Barros, can be related either to **giving** as erotic expression (such as the maternal cradling and licking as an act of solidarity in "Commiseration") or as the violent and absolute **repression** of her female protagonist's self-expression (as in "Artemisia"). In either case, Barros does not present maternal love as a uniformly positive or uniformly negative value, but rather she subjects motherhood to the same critiques as other social structures that in cultural practice limit her female protagonists' communication of desire. Herein lies Barros's radicalism: social structures, including language, must be examined critically and never trusted, for they have historically served to limit woman's ability to tell her own story, to recognize and name her own body, and to enter into nonviolent erotic relationships with other human beings. Woman's body becomes a sign for the range of feminized social subjects that experience the symbolic and literal forms of violence inscribed by the dominant culture.

That said, Barros does better in her critique of some social structures than she does with others. Of all of the stories in *Astride*, "Muzzle" makes the most explicit statement about the interconnectedness of systems of power. However, we must acknowledge that even in this story the issue of class is only weakly represented. In fact, given the assumptions about *señoritas* in the story, we could conclude that the story shares the same middle-class bias as many of the others (e.g., the narrator's obsession in "Artemisia" quickly becomes absurd if we imagine her stripped of middle-class privilege). Barros's work undoubtedly gains middle-class feminist ground on important issues of gender and sexual oppression, but it only vaguely makes working-class women and men visible. It does so, for example, in those story lines crossing class bounds, as with the experience of terror in "Duerme" [Go to Sleep], which could take place in any but the most privileged of Chilean homes, or the poignant portrait of death in "Commiseration." She also understands the historical marginality of Latin America in the colonial and neocolonial contexts. However, in no story does Barros carry off explicit integration of class and gender critiques. In this sense, then, she does risk the sort of working-class invisibility that Dorfman and Benavente seek to contest. At the same time, all three of these writers' contradictions in representing "the other" anticipate the kinds of very real exclusions (of marginal voices) that have taken place during the process of Chile's return to democracy.

Overall, *Astride* returns time and again to the questions of what impedes relationships between men and women, and what obstacles prohibit the creation of desire-based forms of self-expression that would intimately bind communities together. In several stories of the collection, Barros shows the solitude of one body before another body, metonyms of people who hope to narrate themselves collectively. However, the insurmountable lack of communication between those desiring bodies, Barros suggests, is perhaps the biggest mark of authoritarian domination on the expression of erotic desire. In "Go to Sleep," the fearful protagonists believe that State terror lurks just outside, threatening to violate their home and their sense of themselves at any time: "Sé que van a entrar" (41) [I know they'll come in] (47). "Go to Sleep" demonstrates that this daily pressure of fear in a militarized society both represses interpersonal contact and makes it absolutely necessary: "Tal vez fue una mala broma, un invento y es sólo el miedo a que existan. . . . Como el amor o lo contrario, una necesidad de que exista . . ." (41) [Maybe it was just a bad joke, a lie and they wouldn't exist if not for our fear. . . . Like love or {its} opposite, like creating a need for it to exist . . .] (47). In "Lo había odiado con pulcritud" [He Had Hated it with Pulchritude {though following the story's deliberate ambiguity, it could just as well be "She Had Hated Him Bitterly"}], a younger couple eerily and indeterminately becomes the older, emotionally dysfunctional, and entirely alienated couple haunting the female narrator's imagination and her home. Likewise, "Desfiladero de iguanas" [Procession of Iguanas] portrays solitude as the seemingly immutable mark of the erotic relationship, while such solitude—"el desamparo de mi deseo" (66) [the abandon of my desire] (72)—is associated with the sterility, incommunication and neurosis of modern urban life in "Deshabitados ante la ventana" [Desolate Before the Window].

In "Desolate Before the Window," the final story in the first edition of *Astride*, the parallel desires of a man and a woman, who each masturbate in front of windows in opposite buildings, only precariously and impersonally join together through the narratives they recount to the same psychiatrist—who himself represses the connection between the stories he has heard. The entire collection thus ends with the theme of incommunication, with Benavente's "tower of silence," the repression of desire marking and fragmenting interpersonal communication in postcoup Chilean society. In this sense, the collection also closes in the ostensibly private sphere, wherein each individual desperately desires a public sense of community that is ultimately denied, due to the sterility of authoritarian society.

In *Astride*, militaristic violence and the female/feminized social subject's desire are intimately mediated by distinct claims to self-authority, as much in spaces such as the torture chamber as in fantasy—that is, in any narratives produced by the woman whose body becomes the site of discursive struggle. If she can narrate herself, Barros holds that she implicitly contests the reproduction of social mechanisms that require her conformity to culturally determined gender and sexual norms. Yet the protagonist's potential for social intervention through self-narration is necessarily contradictory for at least two reasons. First, the protagonist can never take a position exterior to culture, outside of the conflictive mechanisms of power and resistance at work in every social relationship, real or imaginary. Second, the protagonist's capacity for communal expression is circumscribed by her ability to imagine with others, to achieve a shared, collective expression of desire. This last bridge between people itself remains a desire latent in the collection, a petition for other readers to imagine the potential and limitations of their own narrative power. In this sense, the nonutopianism (or nonfoundationalism) of *Astride* is **itself** the foundation from which social transformation is projected. Barros thus acknowledges the limits of literature in and of itself to effect social change, even as her aesthetic of synesthesia narratively enacts the desire for solidarity.

Does Barros then risk marginalization from a public, collective history shaped by both women and men? In a sense she does. Like the protagonists in *Astride*, Barros views all social structures as historically exclusionary of her; paradoxically, she must test boundaries of those structures, even risking further marginalization, if she is ever to be heard. Like the feminist critique that emerged in postcoup Chile in the late 1970s and early 1980s, Barros enacts in her literature the position that woman must find her own voice, tell her own story, before any really collective history, shaped by both women and men, may emerge. Moreover, Barros also holds that telling the story of mostly private interactions is an effective point of departure toward social transformation. To return to the terms used by MEMCh'83, Barros's narrative demonstrates how and why there will be no democracy "in the country" unless it begins "in the home." However, the eventual marginalization of the women's movement from the centers of public power established during the democratic transition unfortunately reveals that the separate activism of women, coupled with the reappearance of political structures dominated by men, has left uncontested many structures of gender-based exclusion in Chilean society today. Clearly, much work remains to be done.

Published in 1990, *Astride* is a metaphor of the sociopolitical circumstances within which it was produced: a metaphor of the possibilities and the limits of a woman who writes in a society that censures her, as "feminine" in relation to man, military masculinity, and the neocolonial order. Barros herself consistently struggles with such prohibitions using her own unrepressed, violent, and erotic narrative language. In contrast to the univocality of the hegemonic official discourse characteristic of the military regime, which suppresses its own contradictions, Barros takes on the complex relationship—at once erotic and violent—between language and the woman who claims self-authority. The narrative of Pía Barros is, therefore, an attempt to embody the textual corpus of a woman who desires to be the subject of her own story, and who seeks to leave a trace, at once "indelible and unattainable," in the multiple and contradictory spaces in which her story is written.

5
The Social Body and the Rebirth of History

> During the first years of the dictatorship there emerged a battle zone [una zona de barricada] that was previously unthinkable in Chile: the body, which became a stage for protest and dramatic action, . . . the body became a signifier of transgression of the system.
> —Eugenia Brito (1990)[1]

> —Métete, me dice, empecemos esto de nuevo.
> Y yo hundiendo la cabeza presionando, haciendo fuerzas para abrir el túnel y sumergirme en la oscuridad cálida de adentro.
> Hablé:
> —Páreme. Páreme otra vez, guárdame un tiempito.
> Fue un acto desesperado.
>
> ["Come inside," she says to me, "let's start over."
> And I push, burying my head, trying hard to open the tunnel and submerge myself in the warm darkness of her insides.
> I spoke:
> "Give birth to me. Give birth to me again, hold onto me for a little while."
> It was a desperate act.]
> —Diamela Eltit (1986)[2]

AMONG THE LITERATURE PRODUCED AFTER THE 1973 COUP, AND PERHAPS AMONG all Chilean literature ever written, Diamela Eltit's work stands out as one of the most radically challenging critiques of **all** basic structures of narrative, language, and society. In her rigorous examination of the relationship between society and literature—bodies and texts—each of Eltit's highly experimental novels is a product of a distinct moment of postcoup history. Her literary journey, from the deeply ruptured language of *Lumpérica* [*E. Luminata*] (1983) and *Por la patria* [For the Fatherland] (1986), to the more cohesive narrative of *El cuarto mundo* [*The Fourth World*] (1989), parallels the trajectory of a Chile first traumatized, and then empowered, through local responses to authoritarianism within the postcoup context. As civil society struggled during the 1980s to come together again, so, too, did each of Eltit's first three novels explore the slowly growing potential and the incredibly powerful limits conditioning the stories that could be born from within militarized society.

Written during the late 1970s, Eltit's first novel, *E. Luminata* (1983), portrays a context in which history itself has become nothing more than successive fragmentary scenes, in which a female protagonist struggles, time and again, to gain narrative power vis-à-vis the authoritarian and urban marginal characters who directly shape her world. Eltit's deeply ruptured language reenacts the social fragmentation of the early postcoup years, and challenges the reader to make meaning in a world in which excluded communities have nearly ceased to do so. The novel demonstrates how Eltit-as-author, and her readers, must develop alternative codes for interpreting this seemingly incoherent world, and by extension, for telling the story of the fragmented and traumatized social body.

By contrast, Eltit's *Por la patria* (1986), her second novel, was written in the years following the National Protests of 1983–84. While it is, like *E. Luminata*, a deeply fragmented text, *Por la patria* portrays marginal characters who eventually begin to interpret and represent themselves, and who generate alternatives to the official discourse of the authoritarian regime. By the time Eltit finished writing her third novel, *The Fourth World*, in 1988, Chile was headed toward the plebiscite and toward the opportunity to take civilian control of the future once again. In *The Fourth World*, for the first time, Eltit used a language and narrative structure that were as outwardly "healed"—if very partially and imperfectly—as the collective body of civil society in the late 1980s. By 1988, both the social body and the literary text showed that, despite substantial lingering tensions, community-based history had begun once again.

In considering Eltit's trajectory, however, it is important to bear in mind that her prose, even in *The Fourth World*, never portrays an ideal world in which history is slowly recomposed. For Eltit, both society and language still bore the deep scars of military rule, and would continue to do so for an uncertain time to come. Both, as cultural structures, also carried within them the very authoritarianism they were contesting. In fact, the three novels taken together explore increasingly internalized and less visible forms of domination. While authoritarianism is located primarily in exterior spaces and specific characters in *E. Luminata* and *Por la patria*, it appears more diffusely and corrosively in the claustrophobic family home and womb, and in subjective desires and fears, in *The Fourth World*. Thus, even as Eltit shows the birth of a "new" social text in her third novel, she clearly anticipates "pinochetismo sin [without] Pinochet," the insidious internalized reproduction of domination that has characterized the Chilean democratic transition.³

All three novels emphasize that it is precisely within the margins of society that the effects of official discourse become most excruciatingly clear, and where ruptures in that discourse—sometimes entailing the madness or violation of the protagonists—can open other (always unidealized) possibilities. In the testimonial work *El padre mío* [Father of Mine], Eltit explains her view of the dialectical relationship between the city's center and its periphery or "marginal zones":

> I sought, especially, to capture and convey an aesthetic which would generate cultural meanings. I saw the vital movement of those marginal zones as a sort of negative—**like a photographic negative—, necessary for configuring the positive—the rest of the city—**, through powerful territorial exclusions, thus revealing the strong, sustained hierarchies that structure our social system.⁴

When Eltit's protagonists move in function of the public sphere, then, they either occupy a place in it (for example, E. Luminata's presence in the public plaza), or as is more often the case, define its exclusions and hierarchies through their own marginality to it. In this sense, Eltit portrays an **inverse** public sphere, focusing on the social margins to reveal (like a photographic negative) the effects of the center's power. For Eltit, the margins represent not only what the dominant society does not **want** to see, but also what it cannot **afford** to see, if its basic structures are to remain intact. Hence, for Eltit, community-based history could only be "reborn" in the postcoup context from the excluded margins, from people acting locally and sometimes perversely within the contaminated and incestuous confines of the social periphery.⁵

Because Diamela Eltit, like Pía Barros, began her writing career during the dictatorship, she shares some common experiences—and a basic sense of *desencanto*—with Barros and other members of the generation of 1980. As in Barros's *Astride*, Eltit's work portrays interpersonal relationships as marked by suppressed desires, indirect communication, and by a fundamental lack of innocence, due to the mistrust and pressures characterizing daily life under Pinochet. Like all of the authors studied, Eltit holds that contesting the ability to name and narrate the body was the most local struggle to be waged by all officially excluded members of postcoup society—if "Chile," as (re)defined by the community, were not to disappear. Among the four authors, however, it is no coincidence that both women writers focus upon the **specificity** of female (and sometimes gender indeterminate) bodies as exemplary spaces for the enactment of domination and resistance, in a society feminized by the use of military violence.

In spite of these similarities between Barros and Eltit, the two authors differ dramatically in terms of **how** they explore these issues. While Barros uses middle-class characters to examine questions of eroticism and violence, focusing on language, sexuality, and woman's struggle to narrate her body, Eltit pushes that focus to its most extreme limits. Eltit's characters are social outcasts, characters struggling with their precarious psychosexual and gender identities in a public world that cruelly ostracizes them. Whereas Barros emphasizes the private, intimate operation of power to reveal the political implications of gender and (hetero)sexuality, Eltit shows just how **public** every body is, inevitably scarred and degraded by the official privatization of privilege and power in authoritarian society. For Eltit, no body was clean—politically, sexually, economically, or linguistically— in the postcoup world.

Likewise, while Barros forcefully but sensually bends and rejoins language to make it her own (what I have called her aesthetic of synesthesia), Eltit's novels radically dismantle the most basic structures of language itself. Eltit fractures the centers of institutionalized language by irreverently "rubbing" them against various forms of marginal expression (the aesthetic of the *frote* or "rub" in *E. Luminata*,[6] and of social and linguistic "incest" in *Por la patria*), thereby generating a vast range of hybrid linguistic permutations. Of all of their works taken together, Eltit's **least** fragmented novel, *The Fourth World*, has the most in common stylistically with Barros's **most** fractured texts in *Astride* (such as "Muzzle"). By the late 1980s, however, paralleling civil society, these two authors had come more closely together in terms of narrative strategy: while Barros had opened her language to increased instability and complication, Eltit explored the benefits and liabilities of establishing a more overtly cohesive (if still suggestively unstable) narrative ground.

At the same time, Eltit's emphasis on the public sphere as a powerful and defining center of society more closely parallels Dorfman's and Benavente's work than Barros's. In this regard, it is crucial to recognize that Eltit (b. 1949) exactly splits the age difference between Dorfman (b. 1942) and Barros (b. 1956). Eltit was twenty-four years old at the time of the coup, so she did have experiences and memories of the years of Popular Unity (like Benavente and Dorfman), though her literary career did not begin until several years afterwards. Like Dorfman, Eltit published her work in increasingly prestigious editorial houses over time—though her first work was published by small alternative presses, like those tapped by Barros—signaling her gradual consecration by the literary establishment and the expanding possibilities for distribution of her work. After Eltit won the Guggenheim in 1985, and helped organize the 1987 International Congress on Latin American Literature by Women (discussed in chapter 4), she became the most publicly-acknowledged—though perhaps also the most widely misunderstood—of the postcoup women writers. Critics simultaneously praised her innovation and criticized her writing as overly hermetic, piquing readers' interest in Eltit as female *literata*, while scaring them away from her literature.[7] As a sanctioned but "strange" writer, Eltit found herself neither wholly inside, nor entirely outside, the literary establishment of her country.[8]

Due to these differing experiences, there is an intergenerational quality to Eltit's writing. For example, Eltit's focus on the psychosexual conflicts of her protagonists always explicitly refers to broad, historical issues: the marginality characterizing Eltit's postcolonial, violent, and solitary characters is the same issue that connects them with other marginal peoples in Latin America and in the world. All three "large" titles of her novels—*Lumpérica* (the original Spanish plays on "lumpen[proletariat]," "mujer" [woman], and "América"),[9] *Por la patria* [For the Fatherland], and *The Fourth World*—evoke national and international contexts; in this sense, Eltit's work, like Dorfman's, tests the connections between "local" and "universal" versions of history. Nonetheless, the epic resonances of Eltit's titles may be best understood as ironic in the context of the novels themselves, in which Eltit develops her decidedly anti-epic, anti-utopian, and anti-universalist view of history. In contrast to Barros's inability to escape or idealize history (her **non**utopianism)—that is, her inability to believe in (or write) large stories like her predecessors could—Eltit "negatively" acknowledges foundationalist narratives (epics, large stories, the center) through her explicit, **anti**foundationalist, countering of them. Barros simply omits the large stories; Eltit actively deconstructs them. This is the most intergenerational aspect of Eltit's work, putting her in dialogue (like Dorfman and Benavente) with both the "large" modernist (political and literary) projects of the 1960s and with the "small," local, postmodern narratives of the 1980s.[10] In terms of her language, Eltit has at least as much in common, perhaps more, with experimental postcoup poets such as Diego Maqueira, Soledad Fariña, Juan Luis Martínez, and Raúl Zurita (each of whom, like Eltit, confronts the epic from the position of a feminized or androgynous subject), as with the prose writers of the generation of 1980.[11]

The differing trajectories of Barros's and Eltit's narrative strategies may also be traced to the very different aesthetic and political paths the two took at the beginning of their literary careers. As I mentioned in chapter 4, both authors began to write in *talleres literarios* (literary workshops).[12] However, the group that supported Eltit's first work differed significantly from Barros's first *taller*, as well as from the small middle-class feminist literary workshops that Barros later organized. Barros had joined Enrique Lafourcade's officially sanctioned and more traditional workshop, while Eltit participated from 1979 to 1985 in a neo-avant-garde collective concerned principally with visual and dramatic representation as its means for contesting official discourse. This interdisciplinary group, the Colectivo de Acciones de Arte [Collective for Art Actions], or CADA, consisted of Eltit, visual artists Lotty Rosenfeld and Juan Castillo, the poet Raúl Zurita, and a sociologist, Fernando Balcells. Hence, during the time in which Barros pursued a contestatory stance through her late 1970s *microcuentos*, focusing ever more sharply on very short narratives, Eltit experimented with visual art, performance, and poetry—practically any medium besides prose—as her initial genres of expression. One consequence of these differences is that, while Barros developed her social critique through a focus on personal politics, Eltit explored **the politics of literature and artistic institutions themselves** as symbolic of the public exclusionary power most explicitly embodied by the regime.

Aesthetically, CADA viewed the space of the **city**—the militarily occupied public sphere—and the more intimate space of the **body** as parallel stages where the terrible drama of the dictatorship played itself out.[13] On those stages were rewritten all previous means of reading the culture of day-to-day life after the coup. Influenced by older visual artists such as Carlos Leppe and Eugenio Dittborn (considered proponents of this *avanzada* [neo-avant-garde] or *nueva escena de arte* [new art scene]),[14] CADA began to produce brief public performances, or "art actions," to show just how insidiously regulated daily routines had become under the military regime. Through their performances, CADA members sought to contest the regime's censorship (like other emergent forms of street protest before them) **and** to show how the human body itself both demonstrated and resisted the hegemony of the dominant discourses (military, sexual, and religious).[15] Like other grassroots movements discussed in previous chapters, CADA's art actions were created on the premise that individual and social bodies were reflexively bound to one another, but they sought to demonstrate this connection publicly through visually oriented art.

While critics have described CADA's experimental work as "avant-garde," "postboom," "postmodern," or even like the "Cuban neobaroque of Sarduy"[16]—comparisons that have some merit—it can be more meaningfully understood **only** by taking into account the specific circumstances of postcoup Chile. Within a context in which members of the Association of Family Members of the Detained-Disappeared were telling the community-based stories of the missing, CADA's particular orientation toward the body resulted from, and produced, very specific sociopolitical resonances. As members of CADA explained in 1982:

> [C]ertain art practices that were in vogue in the urban centers ten years ago, such as body and land art, as well as performance . . . constitute in our cultural landscape utterly immediate realities, regardless of their status as forms of art. . . . For example, the meaning of **the body as a stage, for us, stems from concrete facts that are all too familiar** [given the context of repression], and we must not forget that this familiarity has been won at the cost of many types of hardship. What defines this new scene, then, is not its relationship to art history per se, but rather, its **direct engagement with the precarious and painful elements of our social context, and with the vulnerability of concrete lives**.[17]

In essence, it is because of the complex ways that power operated through and upon the body in postcoup Chile that CADA's aesthetic practices held **particular** political relevance as a response to the military regime.

The connection between telling the story of the individual body and representing the history of the collective body is especially evident in CADA's 1979 art action "Para no morir de hambre en el arte" [So as not to die of hunger in art]. For this early action, CADA went to Santiago shantytowns to distribute one hundred half-liter bags of milk. This symbolic act denounced the literal and metaphorical hunger of the community under Pinochet, at the same time as it evoked Allende's "half liter of milk per child per day" campaign under Popular Unity. The milk itself also connoted growth, plenitude, and motherhood, similar to the life-affirming moral symbolism drawn on by the Agrupación, the *ollas comunes* (communal soup kitchens), and later, the umbrella organization Women for Life. The day after distributing the milk, CADA collected the empty bags, and gave them to one hundred artists and intellectuals, who in turn fashioned artworks out of them, knowing that the milk had been consumed by people who had no steady food supply.[18]

The artists' works were then exhibited in an art gallery (Centro Imagen), along with an acrylic box containing milk left to decompose. A sign on top of the box read: "Para permanecer hasta que nuestro pueblo acceda a sus consumos básicos de alimentos. Para permanecer **como el negativo** de un cuerpo carente, invertido y plural" [To remain here until our people gain access to basic food for consumption. To remain **as the negative** of a suffering, inverted, and plural body].[19] Meanwhile, ten milk trucks, proceeding as if military tanks, headed to the Museo de Bellas Artes [Museum of Fine Arts], which was draped with a cloth suggesting its closure as an institution. This ironic procession through downtown Santiago to the museum was simultaneously a public statement about generalized hunger in postcoup society, and a denouncement of the elitism of the officially sanctioned (and antihistorical) museum in this context. Ultimately, CADA's procession emphasized the need for artists to redefine art, in response to the starving social body under Pinochet. In this regard, CADA's work insistently did "defy any facile opposition between political commitment and aesthetics," as Mary Beth Tierney-Tello has aptly noted.[20]

The following year, Eltit's contributions to CADA's work came into particular relief in the art action "Maipu" (1980), filmed on video by Lotty Rosenfeld in the marginal Santiago neighborhood of the work's title. Eltit was the sole protagonist of this action, in which she ritually wounded herself, by making several lacerations and burns along both arms. Afterwards, she penitently washed the stone sidewalk in front of a brothel in Maipu, then went inside to read early material from *E. Luminata* to the prostitutes present there. During and after her reading, CADA projected slides of Eltit's face on two exterior walls opposite the brothel.

Through this act, Eltit invoked a sort of religious self-sacrifice or martyrdom, by marking her own body as wounded, using pain as a means for making materially evident the link between individual and shared experience in the fragmented postcoup context. For Eltit, suffering connected her own body to the social body.[21] According to Eltit's act, self-destruction (or painfully transgressing the boundaries of self), was absolutely necessary for this collective connection to be made[22]—perhaps especially for a middle-class woman, whose body did not so overtly manifest suffering as did those of urban marginals.

By performing this act in front of a brothel, Eltit's art action further suggested a criticism of the dominant codification of women's sexuality in authoritarian culture. According to the terms of this action, the repressed connections between women/prostitutes and the social body, and among women themselves, could be best expressed through alternative discursive means. In other words, Eltit could "decir lo indecible," speak the unspeakable, by revealing shared pain, through making visible and horribly explicit the invisible marks and violations of the feminized social body inflicted by the dominant regime.

At the same time, the aesthetic developed by CADA in both of these examples ("Para no morir del hambre en el arte" and "Maipu") raises questions about the privilege of the artist-intellectual to represent (or speak for) marginal communities—an issue that neither Nelly Richard nor Eugenia Brito, the main critics of this work, ever adequately addresses. By relying upon images constructed from her own body to represent collective pain in "Maipu," Eltit risks appropriating or subsuming the collective "we" (the social body) within an authorial—and authoritative—"I," readily identifiable with Diamela Eltit. The larger-than-life slide of Eltit's face projected onto the brothel's exterior walls could be (mis)read this way.

However, the key here is that Eltit's evocation of an authorial "I"—in her work with CADA and within her literature—occurs with maximum self-consciousness, which at once affirms **and** undercuts her ability to speak as an individual woman-author in the militarized context. The physical sacrifice of body experienced by herself and her female characters dramatically renegotiates privilege, enacting what "woman" and "marginal" have in common, as social subjects violently marked as "eccentric" to institutional forms of power. In this sense, the artist, as individual or ego, becomes effaced, or rendered only quite complexly. Perhaps the better question, then, is if such self-destruction is worth it, or if it simply replicates society's violence in another form. I will return to this issue in my analysis of *E. Luminata* below.

CADA's art actions also beg the question of what sort of audience there could be for their representations of social trauma. Since one critical linchpin of CADA's work was to stress the relationship between "art" and "life,"[23] we must ask what communities CADA could reach with its fleeting art actions, whether in the shantytowns, on Santiago's main avenues, or in the museum. Eltit admits that not many people were reached by CADA's performances; in fact, she attributes the lack of direct repression of CADA members to this minimal public attention:

> We didn't have problems with persecution . . . because actually, our work didn't matter to the authorities, because people were mostly staying at home . . . , art just didn't matter. Why should they censor us, if there was no audience for our work?[24]

Hence, it appears that the contestatory power of CADA's *acciones de arte* in the early 1980s was already circumscribed by the regime's silencing of public activity, especially in the center of the city. Since the people that would receive and interpret the action either already lived marginally ("Maipu") or were the artists themselves ("Para no morir del hambre en el arte"), there is a marked self-referentiality inherent in CADA's work. The challenging insights presented within these art actions, for better or worse, largely remained isolated interventions on the margins of postcoup society.[25]

This impression of CADA's self-containment was also produced by the nature of the criticism of its work, written by critics very near to its inner circle, particularly Brito and Richard. Richard, for example, has shown how CADA and the *avanzada* forged a unique path, through taking on the totalizing tendencies in both the traditional left (as well as the modernist avant-garde)[26] and the authoritarian right—which constituted the *avanzada*'s specific representational power.[27] At the same time, taken as a body of work unfolding over time, Richard's essays have served to make marginal cultural experiences visible beyond the moment of their production, thereby conveying and expanding their political relevance within the particular emergent—if narrow or "modest"[28]—context of an antiauthoritarian, locally contingent aesthetic. By teasing out these relationships and tensions, Richard's critical texts have both reciphered **and** reinscribed CADA's (and the *avanzada*'s) marginal positionality. Thus, as was the case when I considered the "apartness" of Barros's work, the tension around the *avanzada* in general and Eltit's work in particular is whether its political-aesthetic content might be recuperated socially beyond its own borders, and within and beyond the Pinochet years—despite the fact that, and at the same time as, the artists themselves disavow any interest in their work's "transcendence."

In many respects, Eltit's highly innovative texts clearly occupy a special position vis-à-vis both the sociopolitical context and the institution of literature after the coup, crossing traditional gender, genre, and generational boundaries. Linguistically, Eltit's novels make it very clear that history—even the most marginal community-based claims to representational power—could not be told in the same way after the 1973 coup as before. In fact, Eltit's early postcoup works (CADA, *E. Luminata*, and to a degree, *Por la patria*) show how both literature and history had become so fragmented, and social meaning so elusive, that telling any story at all had become at best a precarious enterprise. In order to approach these works, I must ask: In her ability to reflect the difficulty of producing social meaning, and the exclusions of the dominant discourse, does Eltit ultimately reinscribe only language's limitations? Or does she succeed in challenging her readers to seek new meaning, to contest dominant cultural codes at the various levels at which they operate?

Fragmented Bodies, Fragmented Narratives (Eltit's *Lumpérica* [*E. Luminata*])

> Chile is a fractured country, with a ruptured and fragmented history. The language that I use is fragmented, broken, insufficient, deceptive [fragmentado, roto, fallado, enmascarador], and for these reasons, emanates from a very precise situation: our own [i.e., that of Chile today].
> —Diamela Eltit (1985)[29]

In an interview published after the appearance of her first novel, *Lumpérica* [*E. Luminata*] (1983),[30] Eltit described the continuity between her work with CADA and her writing: "I don't distinguish so clearly between my visual and literary activities, in fact, I would say they both form part of one and the same creative practice."[31] Certainly this cross-fertilization of Eltit's visual and literary art—the singleness of her aesthetic stance—had a particular impact on *E. Luminata*'s form and content. On the most basic level, just as Eltit's literature had played a role in CADA's 1980 "Maipu" (the author's readings came from *E. Luminata*), so too did "Maipu" provide photographic material that became part of the published novel: the cover photograph (of Eltit's face projected on Maipu walls) and a video still shot of Eltit's wounded arms (preceding chapter 8). More importantly, this relationship between visual and literary practices deeply informs the structure of the novel itself. In it, Eltit repeatedly uses the "languages" of video and spacial techniques of visual representation to structure the text.[32] Lacking a plot in the traditional sense, the novel is more like a performance piece than a conventional narrative.[33]

E. Luminata is composed of ten chapters, each of which consists of at minimum one—and up to thirty-one—subsegments. In these segments, Eltit explores a single central image: the female protagonist (L. Iluminada in the original Spanish, E. Luminata in the English translation) violates curfew by remaining in a public plaza in Santiago after nightfall. Her only interactions take place with marginal characters (the lumpen or urban poor, known as "los pálidos" [pale people]), while the authorial/authoritarian figure of "el luminoso" [the lighted sign] shines down upon them all. The relationship between these beings, and their negotiation of the power to name and narrate their own bodies (versus being narrated by "el luminoso"), is played and replayed in a number of successive photographic-like "takes" in each of the chapters of the book. *E. Luminata*'s series of "freeze frames" suggests that collective history, in effect, had come to a near standstill within this starkly fragmented context, in which both body (feminized society and marginal individuals) and text (language, what Eltit calls "literature," and history itself) were almost totally dominated by authoritarian discourse.

At the same time, the fact that any body at all remains in this public plaza, and in particular, that a woman and the lumpen occupy this sphere (from which they were ostensibly banished), provides a fragile hope that community-based history might survive. Likewise, the multiplicity of languages in the text also points to the persistence of various versions of this story; each chapter is written in a distinct register or voice, juxtaposing ("frotando," rubbing together) different literary and syntactic strategies, irreverently mixing slang, Renaissance Spanish, police interrogation, and other discourses, over the course of the novel. Eltit's narrative is therefore not "one," not monolithic or linear, but rather generates the enigmas and questions resulting from competing and contradictory versions of the story or "scene." Readers are clearly challenged to abandon traditional ways of reading, and to develop alternative and intuitive ways for interpreting this (novelistic) world.

As in Eltit's work with CADA, *E. Luminata* emphasizes the parallels between literary politics and the public exclusionary power most explicitly embodied by the regime. The novel suggests at the outset that within the deeply fragmented postcoup context, individual bodies had been completely severed from one another, except insofar as they shared the dominant story (which, in parallel criticism of an exclusive literary history, Eltit calls "ficción" [fiction] or "literatura" [literature]). This official story is inscribed upon E. Luminata's body from above:

> [L]a luz eléctrica la maquila fraccionando sus ángulos, esos bordes, en que se topa hasta los cables que le llevan la luz, languideciéndola hasta la acabada de todo el cuerpo: pero el rostro a pedazos. Cualquiera puede constatar sus labios entreabiertos y sus piernas extendidas sobre el pasto—cruzándose o abriéndose—rítmicas en el contraluz. (7)

> [{T}he electric light makes her up by splitting her angles, those outer edges at which she jostles toward the cables that carry the light to her, languishing her right up to the finishing touches to her whole body: but her face in bits and pieces. Anyone can testify to her half-open lips and her legs stretched out on the grass—crossing or opening—rhythmic against the backlight.] (14)

The totalizing and godlike electric light falls upon the bodies in the plaza, at once marginalizing them **and** sanctioning them by naming them as citizens—"les dará la vida: su identificación ciudadana" (7) [the process that will definitively give them life: their civic identity] (14).[34] The light therefore simultaneously excludes any other marking of the body and makes it (marginally) exist, within the "contraluz" [backlight] where the beam intermittently reaches.[35] The light also casts E. Luminata's fragmented female body as sexually inviting, as a potential object of desire, in contrast to the other (unsexed) bodies surrounding the edges of the plaza.

This act of bodily inscription by the dominant discourse—a literary act that "garantiza una ficción en la plaza" (7) [guarantees a fiction in the city] (14)—establishes the market **value** of each of those bodies (and stories, literatures) in society. This is the "Santiago de Chile" (8) of neoliberal economic policy, where everything has a price, where bodies can be bought and sold. The text states:

> Aunque no es nada novedoso, el luminoso anuncia que se venden cuerpos.
> Sí, cuerpos se venden en la plaza.
> A un precio no determinado. . . . Sus palabras caen en el vacío ampliando sus moléculas para petrificar lo eterno de la producción. (10)

> [Though that's nothing new: the sign announces bodies for sale.
> That's right, bodies are sold in the square.
> Not at a fixed price. . . . Their words fall into the emptiness, amplifying

their molecules in order to petrify the production's everlastingness.] (18–19)

The light of "el luminoso" [the lighted sign] assigns this value, making possible the exploitation of them as material beings, by naming them within the dominant order. Eltit later makes explicit the parallel with commercialized literary discourse: "Y lo que se vende por la irradación del luminoso . . . es la equivalencia a la plusvalía que alguien pudiera sacarle a unas palabras desplegadas sobre un libro" (33) [And what's sold by irradiation from the sign installed atop the nearby building is equal to the surplus value someone could take from a few words spread out across a book] (47).

Like Eltit-as-author, E. Luminata struggles to find points of corporeal and textual resistance to the official discourse, by seeking to tell her own story. In this painfully fragmented context, E. Luminata discovers one strategy for doing so: by violently rupturing the dominant codes and boundaries of both body and text. In this way, she might address the marginal place she occupies in her immediate context, a metonymy of her continent's place in the world. That is, if she could speak, or in the novel's terms, if she could cry out ("producir un grito"), E. Luminata's story would at least partially and momentarily pave the way—or as chapter 8 suggests, provide an "Ensayo General" or "Dress Rehearsal"—for representing as social subjects the marginal "lumpen," "mujer" [woman], and "América" fused in the book's original Spanish title, *Lumpérica*.[36]

In *E. Luminata*, the possibilities for producing textual and corporeal counternarratives emerge through self-destruction, or more often, pain, the scarring of one's own body in the desperate need to sacrifice self for the community. E. Luminata uses self-directed violence to affirm her difference from "el luminoso" [the lighted sign] and to contest his/its narration of her:

> Estrella su cabeza contra el árbol una y otra vez hasta que la sangre rebasa su piel, le baña la sangre su cara, se limpia con las manos, mira sus manos, las lame. Va hacia el centro de la plaza con la frente dañada—sus pensamientos—se muestra en el goce de su propia herida, la indaga con sus uñas y si el dolor existe es obvio que su estado conduce al éxtasis.
> Se exhibe esperando la caída del luminoso sobre la herida:
> Si yo misma tuve una herida, pero hoy tengo y arrastro mi propia cicatriz. Ya no me acuerdo cuánto ni cómo me dolía, pero por la cicatriz sé que me dolía. (15)

[She smashes her head against the tree again and again until the blood overflows the skin, it bathes her face that blood, she cleans her face with

5 / THE SOCIAL BODY AND THE REBIRTH OF HISTORY

her hands, looks at her hands, licks them. She moves toward the center of the square with her forehead wounded—her thoughts—she parades her pleasure in her own wound, she probes it with her fingernails and if there is pain it is obvious that her state leads to ecstasy.

She exhibits herself waiting for the fall of the sign upon her wound.

Yes, I had a wound myself, but today I have and drag my own scar. I no longer remember how much or what way I suffered, but from the scar I know I did suffer.] (24)

In this horrifying world, the violence done to one's own body provides the only possibility to claim narrative power, to make one's mark, to gain a scar that would validate one's own memory of the incomprehensible pain of recent history. The resulting scar then continues to be a reminder of this pain, a lasting textual mark. In this very material way, E. Luminata transcends her individual body, as suggested in the above passage (and in CADA's "Maipu"). Her "éxtasis" [ecstasy] is the union of her story with a collective body, however damaged it may be.

In an eroticized echo of this violent contest between "el luminoso" and E. Luminata to narrate her body, Eltit turns next to the issue of power in literary discourse. Chapter 4, "Para la formulación de una imagen en la literatura" [Toward the formulation of an image in literature] begins as follows:

> Entonces/
> Los chilenos esperamos los mensajes
> L. Iluminada, toda ella
> Piensa en Lezama y se las frota
> Con James Joyce se las frota
> Con Neruda Pablo se las frota
> Con Juan Rulfo se las frota
> Con E. Pound se las frota
> Con Robbe Grillet se las frota
> Con cualquier fulano se frota las antenas.
>
> (69)

> [So then/
> We Chileans, we look for messages
> E. Luminata, undividedly she
> Thinks about Lezama and rubs them together
> With James Joyce rubs them together
> With Neruda Pablo rubs them together
> With Juan Rulfo rubs them together
> With E. Pound rubs them together

With Robbe Grillet rubs them together
With any Tom, Dick or Harry rubs {her} antennae.]

(77)

Since the author suspects the exclusionary social power and privilege represented by traditional (male-dominated) literary paradigms, she irreverently and suggestively "rubs" her "antennas" together with them to produce frictions and resistances—or multivocality (the aesthetic of the *frote* made explicit here). Eltit's other chapters practice this aesthetic, but this chapter is the first to reveal the irreverent, almost tongue-in-cheek eroticism of the female who dares to narrate alongside the male literary "prophets."[37] Such a woman is seen as promiscuous, since her genre-bending literature entails her committing the sexualized act of the *frote* with a range of representational languages.

Because of her transgression—this promiscuity—she becomes a "public" (and published) woman. Her body/text is read differently, since her action would go against the grain of the patriarchal canons:

> Para ese nuevo amanecer de una imagen en la literatura en que se expresa cabeza abajo colgando de su cuerpo luminoso. Una cabeza de perfectas dimensiones rapada a todo lo largo.
> Planteando lo que se creía inadmisible; que bajo su pelada estuviese oculta su verdadera belleza
>   su promiscuidad
> todo su talento/ ya uno se pierde con tantas vueltas que impiden distinguir lo impostado de lo real. (72)

> [For the new dawning of an image in literature in which she expresses herself head hanging down from her luminous body. A head of perfect dimensions razed from front to back.
> Stating what was thought inadmissible: that beneath her razed skull lay hidden her true beauty
>   her promiscuity
> all her talent/ now one gets lost with all the switches that prevent distinguishing what's faked from what's real.] (80)

The textual body of the woman who transgresses generic (gender and genre) boundaries is marked, "la cabeza rapada" [her razed skull]. Through this writing, she becomes double: she is body, but she is also text; she is herself and her story; she is at once real and an imposter. In short, she performs—or embodies—her fiction.

At the end of segment 4.4, the ambiguous identification between narrator, protagonist, and author—suggested from the cover of the text onward—becomes explicit:

Su cintura ¡ay su cintura! es gemela a la mía en la transparencia al alma.
Su alma es material.
Su alma es establecerse en un banco de la plaza y elegir como único paisaje verdadero el falsificado de esa misma plaza.
Su alma es cerrar los ojos cuando vienen los pensamientos y reabrirlos hacia el césped.
Su alma es este mundo y nada más en la plaza encendida.
Su alma es ser L. Iluminada y ofrecerse como otra.
Su alma es no llamarse diamela eltit [sic]/ sábanas blancas / cadáver.
Su alma es a la mía gemela. (80–81)

[Her waist—oh, her waist!—is the twin to mine in its transparency to the soul.
Her soul is material.
Her soul is being established on a bench in the square and choosing as the only true landscape the falsification of this same square.
Her soul is shutting the eyes when thoughts come and reopening them on the grass.
Her soul is this world and nothing else in the lighted square.
Her soul is being E. Luminata and offering herself as another.
Her soul is not being called diamela eltit {sic}/ white sheets / cadaver.
Her soul is to mine the twin.] (90)

Her doubleness—and her duplicity—emerge as the material world ("alma"/ soul, "banco"/bench, "césped"/grass, "este mundo"/this world) is narrated or fictionalized ("falsificado"). Only then can "she" **be** E. Luminata and **pose** as another, perhaps as "diamela eltit," even without calling herself by name. For her part, "diamela eltit" (as twin) is at once conceded E.'s status and denied it; she is like E., but she is not E. What the two have in common for certain is the material body, marked female and feminized, upon which they attempt to make "literatura." The marginal text is made "literatura" through the author's own *frote* with literary tradition and the official story. In a sense, then, "E. Luminata" **is** the photographic negative of "diamela eltit."

However, Eltit's increasing use of self-referential elements to explore how her story (and E. Luminata's) intersect with the pain and fragmentation suffered by the marginal communal body entails considerable political risk. Eltit had to present both the common marginality of woman ("E. Luminata") and the urban underclass ("los pálidos"), while also providing a sense of the fundamental differences between them. Eltit narratively confronts these issues by describing the challenge that "los pálidos" or "pale people" place to any text that would represent them. In segment 5.3, E. Luminata dares to mark the plaza, confronting both "el luminoso" and "los pálidos" with her chalked words: "dónde vas." This implied question— where do you go, where are you going, and even, where do you fit—is also a statement. It is about the problem of a woman who writes, who takes up language, who faces both the dominant discourses (of "el luminoso," as well as of the literary "fulanos") **and** the silences of the margins ("los pálidos"). It is about imagining or figuring one's place in this story, when one is decentered. It is about the marginality of a city, country, and continent narrated by authoritarian discourses and the difficulty of telling another story under those circumstances. It is a question/statement that, depending on the inflection with which it is voiced, may promise another place or future, or may require stopping dead in the tracks of an eternally present place (the limits of "where are **you** going?"). In *E. Luminata*, which is based on the search for words, for a genre and a place, despite "occupied" language's potential for disintegration and betrayal, those two words "dónde vas" seem to encapsulate the novel's form and content, its openings and its foreclosures of meaning in the postcoup world of the "freeze frame."

Segment 5.1 sets the stage for the uttering of that "dónde vas."[38] This segment establishes the tension involved in E. Luminata's hope to narrate the scene of the plaza from herself (from the threads of her gray dress) and from the materials within the plaza (the branches), while being monitored by the disturbing, definitive presence of "los pálidos":

> Podría así tejer inumerables historias tan sólo decantando la trama de su vestido de lana gris. Desenmarañar esa hebra para extenderla como escritura en la plaza.... Subir hasta los árboles y rompiendo las ramas, completar con ellas la novela.... hasta llamar por espectáculo a **los pálidos que ordenarán una lectura posible, corrigiendo algunos textos, sacando otros,** manteniendo en apogeo las baterías, toda esa luz eléctrica que contraría la lluvia. (emphasis mine, 93–94)

> [She would be able to weave that way innumerable yarns just by untangling the web of her gray wool dress. Unraveling this strand in order to extend it as writing in the plaza.... To rise up into the trees and breaking the branches, complete the novel with them.... until summoning by spectacle **the pale people who will order a possible reading, revising some texts, deleting others**, keeping the batteries at their peak: all this electric light opposes the rain.] (emphasis mine, 101)

What she writes is conditioned irrevocably by the readings enabled or prohibited by the mere presence of "los pálidos." This story cannot be told, represented, or interpreted—history cannot be revised—without this conditioning limit:

> —Para ser leídos desde atrás de los plásticos que los salvan de la lluvia y por eso, descifrados, mirada y texto, cuerpo y mente se refrotan. Se abre

5 / THE SOCIAL BODY AND THE REBIRTH OF HISTORY

así la novela, surgen los personajes, se los lee bajo la iluminación de la plaza. El plástico evita el deterioro, como cubierta, como forro. Se ambienta la pupila y los chorros de agua gustan la caída sobre la piel—
Pero no: marcan el cemento, nutren los árboles, desafían la electricidad. (97)

[—So as to be read from behind the plastic sheets protecting them from the rain and that's why deciphered like that, gaze and text, body and mind are rubbed together. That's how the novel opens, the characters appear, they are read under the square's light. The plastic prevents deterioration, like a sleeve, like a book jacket. The pupil adjusts itself and the streams of rain enjoy falling on the skin—
But no: they mark the concrete, feed the trees, defy the electricity.] (105–6)

In this culminating moment of segment 5.1, "los pálidos" make this story possible ("se abre así la novela" [that's how the novel opens]). Through making their mark ("marcan el cemento" [they mark the concrete]), they challenge the dominant narrative of them, that of "el luminoso" ("desafían la electricidad" [they . . . defy the electricity]).

But because of this large role "los pálidos" play in the plaza, they also must challenge the authority of E. Luminata's narrative power. In segment 5.3, E. Luminata again attempts to write:

Se agacha con la cabeza entre las piernas y con las manos eriza sus cabellos. Asoma su sonrisa natural. Con su lengua limpia los dientes: el cemento recogerá la imagen. Teñidas las mejillas se para bajo el farol y sobre el metal su dedo caligráficamente escribe en forma imaginaria—como los niños—"**dónde vas**" con letras mayúsculas y con la mano completa borra lo escrito. (emphasis mine, 103)

[She bends over with her head between her knees and with her hands bristles up her hair. Brings out her natural smile. Cleans her teeth with her tongue: the concrete will pick up the image. Cheeks tinted she stops under the lamp and on the metal her finger writes in imaginary calligraphy—like kids—WHERE YOU GOING and with her whole hand completely rubs out the writing.] (113)

The tentativeness, and self-consciousness, that she feels when faced with her readers, "los pálidos," leads her to erase her mark time and again. When she finally leaves her message written, "los pálidos" examine it from every angle. Then follows the inevitable moment of confrontation:

Ellos, a su vez, comienzan a detener sus movimientos. Sus labios murmuran la frase acercándose cada vez más a las palabras, incluso algunos de ellos las pisan. Por fin las cubren totalmente con los pies. Permanecen rígidos

encima. Así nada está escrito sobre el suelo, siguen como protagonistas ocupando el cemento. **Es evidente que se sienten expulsados hasta los bordes de la plaza como notas al margen. Por eso tapan el rayado. Han comprendido la agresión.**
No la miran y lentamente sus pies **refrotan** contra el suelo. Como en un baile improvisado, rítmicos borran la cal, destruyen su título. Se alejan. Una mancha gris se expande sobre el centro de la plaza, **han desaparecido las letras.** (emphasis mine, 104)

[They, in turn, begin halting their movements. Their lips murmur the phrase, coming closer and closer to the words, some even tread on them. Finally they cover them completely with their feet. They remain rigid on top. That way nothing is written on the ground, they continue as protagonists occupying the cement. **It's obvious that they feel expelled to the edges of the square like notes in the margin. That's why they cover up the lines. They have understood the aggression.**
They do not look at her and slowly their feet **rub against** the ground. As in an improvised dance, their rhythms rub out the chalk, destroy her title. They move off. A gray stain spreads over the center of the square, **gone are the letters.**] (emphasis mine, 114)

When "los pálidos" view her writing, "dónde vas" [WHERE YOU GOING] (the evocation of future and present, of memory and of history, of opportunities and prohibitions), they respond as if to an aggression. The woman who wrote has spoken for them, has attempted a representation that relegates them (again) to the margins ("como notas" [like notes]). Rather than accept this erasure, they respond in turn by disappearing **her** marks, by physically rubbing themselves against her words and what they represent. The aesthetic of the *frote*, in which the woman confronted both "el luminoso" and literary tradition, has been replaced by the *refrote*, a second rubbing: the historical conditions placed by "los pálidos" on her possibility of writing, or of intervening, in this context. After she attempts once again to write, she finally comprehends their decisive role in this plaza/text: "entiende" (105) [She understands] (115).

E. Luminata's only possible response was submissive deference to the collective of "pálidos," a response reminiscent of CADA member Diamela Eltit's penitential gesture of washing the sidewalk in front of the Maipu brothel. The segment continues:

[L. Iluminada v]uelve con paciencia sus rodillas al suelo y con el borde del vestido comienza a borrar lo escrito, con parsimonia, ordenadamente, sumisa.
Ellos entonces afloran, salen múltiples y con sus pies confirman la borradura. Están una vez más ocupando su espacio en una nueva labor. . . .

5 / THE SOCIAL BODY AND THE REBIRTH OF HISTORY

Este lumperío escribe y borra imaginario, se reparte las palabras, los fragmentos de letras, borran sus supuestos errores, ensayan sus caligrafías, endilgan el pulso, acceden a la imprenta. (105)

[She patiently goes back down on her knees on the ground and with the hem of her dress begins to rub out the writing, calmly, methodically, meek. Then they emerge, come out in numbers and with their feet confirm the rubbing out. Once more they are occupying their space in a new labor. . . . This lumpenpack pretend-writes and rubs out, parcels out the words, the fragments of letters, they rub out their supposed errors, try out their calligraphies, steady the shaking, agree to the printing.] (115–16)

The moment that "los pálidos" become writers, E. Luminata becomes a reader. She is repositioned in the plaza, and ultimately, she is rewritten. As in a baptism,[39] "los pálidos" have marked her body; they have not only confronted her presumptuous narration of them, but also they have narrated her. They have determined the possibilities and the limits of the story. In this way, chapter 5 performs the relationship of (photographic) negativity, the dialectical relationship of power and resistance, whereby center and periphery are **mutually** defining. Joined now with the social body that marks her, E. Luminata "podría acercar por primera vez su rostro hacia ellos" (106) [for the first time . . . {she} could bring her face towards them] (116).

After this definitive chapter, in which Eltit acknowledges how the marginal underclass necessarily conditions—by writing, by reading, and by silence—the possibilities for the female narrator to write, chapters 6 and 7 posit the concomitant impossibility of any univocal truth under these contextual circumstances. Chapter 6 is a set of short poemlike narratives dedicated to exploring and performing the different functions of writing/graffiti in the plaza, juxtaposed with E. Luminata's devotional words; her writing is placed at the bottom of each page, since it has become marginal in its own right. Chapter 7 adds another contradicting element, returning to the scene of police interrogation of witnesses about the filmed scene of E. Luminata's "caída" or "fall" in the plaza. Despite the pressure of the interrogators (whose "truth" is the official script of E. Luminata's "fall"), the interrogated are at a loss for determining what was true or false about the fiction, who had responsibility for intervening in the scene, or how the camera altered the story. In both of these chapters, the central issue is what responsibility to the collective is incumbent on any individual narrator, whether or not s/he chooses to heed that responsibility.

The themes of these two chapters receive their culmination in chapter 8 ("Ensayo General" [Dress Rehearsal]), which begins with the "Maipu" video still photo of Eltit with scarred and burned arms. Taken in dialogue with the text to this point, the photo encapsulates the basic political and aesthetic stance uniting Eltit's work in CADA and in the novel. E. Luminata accedes to the margins in order to gain her memory/scar. Each cut of her arm, like a cinematographic cut (149) and the "cuts" Eltit makes in literary language, is a momentary transgression that prepares her for writing (much as the performance piece provided a kind of dress rehearsal for the novel-in-progress itself). For example, "E.G. 1" consists of the single sliced-up phrase "Muge/r/apa y su mano se nutre final-mente el verde des-ata y maya se erige y vac/a-nal su forma" (142) [D.R. 1: She moo/s/hears and her hand feeds mind-fully the green dis-entangles and maya she erects herself sha/m-an and vac/a-nal her shape] (150). Each violent cut is the "pretext"—"señal" (148) [signal] (156) or "pose" (155)—for her narration. Like Barros's "Foreshadowing of a Trace," Eltit's precarious access to language can only be a preamble, an "Ensayo General" or "Dress Rehearsal," for claiming representational power. Unlike Barros, however, Eltit views her language as fundamentally shaped by the margins (in addition to the cultural exclusion of "woman" by masculine- dominant language, recognized by both authors). According to Eltit, for woman to narrate in this early postcoup context, her body must be inevitably and violently wounded (not sensually traced, as in some of Barros's texts), to reveal the reciprocity of individual and collective bodies, of singular and shared pain.

The final chapter of the text performs (a return to) bourgeois normalcy. Chapter 10 offers a traditional narrative of a woman alone in a Santiago plaza, which empties at nightfall. No lumpen or "pálidos" challenge her, the only "caída" [fall] is of her head in sleep, and the only *(re)frote* that takes place is the rubbing of her hands to stay warm. Nonetheless, she does achieve a way to read and interpret the neon lights differently as she studies them that night. As dawn arrives, she takes a mirror from a paper bag and cuts her hair, "bajo el alero del luminoso" (194) [standing under the eaves of the sign] (201), until she is completely bald, thus eliminating the last trace of "el luminoso's" light in the mirror. The chapter ends at daybreak.

The traditional language and symbolism (mirror, haircut, daybreak) in this chapter provide a pointed juxtaposition to the preceding chapters. Chapter 10 suggests that the female protagonist develops an identity after her transgressive night in the plaza, but the seamless narrative erases the disruptive "lumperío" who in fact made the process possible. Here the woman resists "el luminoso" by marking herself against the traditional univocal and patriarchal codes that would "normally" sexualize her body. Her shaved head disrupts those dominant codes, serves as a small, local gesture of protest. However, what is hidden in this version of the story—and in **any** traditional narrative form, according to *E. Luminata*—is the disturbing effect of the "los pálidos," the photographic negative to this story, the counterpresence (whether silent or voiced) that conditions and limits any possibility of telling this story otherwise. Hence, in response to the question of how one might narrate the marginalized (that is, the literally and/or symbolically disappeared) social body, Eltit responds with a resounding "not with the same traditional discourse that disappeared them in the first place." Instead, by rubbing together competing and conflicting versions of the story, cracks in the narrative might reveal the converging historical forces of "el luminoso" **and** "el lumperío" on every body.

In sum, *E. Luminata*'s syntactic tension and linguistic fragmentation provide the basic thematic support of the novel: the ability to mark and read marginal bodies (to tell the story of the margins) parallels the violently difficult efforts to participate in community-based history after the 1973 coup. *E. Luminata* suggests that only through acceding to the limits of language and society can any small point of resistance—or alternative story—be told. Indicative of the novel's emphasis on the trauma of the early postcoup years, such fleeting opportunities for resistance are seen as ephemeral countergestures with deferred meanings, chalk marks that are erased, or poses that the camera never definitively records. History (and literature) are barely more than a static scene, not a narrative with a large plot, but the performative reinscription of power relations and small resistances, time and again, medium after medium, in seemingly ahistorical repetition.

In parallel fashion to Eltit's literary journey in CADA and this novel, E. Luminata discovers that she must rupture the boundaries of body and text in order to narrate her place in this story. Undoubtedly, this process contains disturbing elements of (self-)destruction, a mutilation of woman's body that parallels the destruction of the feminized social body in the fragmented postcoup context. In so vividly describing this transgression of boundaries, does Eltit ultimately reinscribe violence? Only ambiguously so. Through the *(re)frote*, Eltit suggests that another text might be produced, the ambivalent sound of "el grito" [the cry] that exposes the limits of (dominant) language: this is a sound of survival, if not of much more. In both form and content, *E. Luminata* traces the historical and textual limits placed upon the production and reception of such a cry in the "freeze frame" context of early postcoup society.

Incest, Motherhood, and the Rebirth of History
(From *Por la patria* [For the Fatherland] to
El cuarto mundo [*The Fourth World*])

While Eltit's *E. Luminata* had portrayed the mutilated social body of early postcoup Chile, her next two novels trace the painful process involved in its outward healing. The cry rehearsed by E. Luminata evolves, as Eltit's characters in *Por la patria* and *The Fourth World* discover some bases for telling their own stories. In moving away from the momentary standstill of history shown in *E. Luminata*, Eltit first portrays a collective experience of feminized resistance in *Por la patria*, and finally depicts an imperfectly healed social body/nation, which gives birth to an alternative text/history in *The Fourth World*. While that text is still and always deeply marked by the contaminated interpersonal relations of postcoup society, the trajectory of Eltit's first three novels provides suggestive insights into the difficult and imperfect processes involved in civil society's coming together in Chile by the end of the 1980s.[40]

Por la patria (1986)[41] portrays the fragmented world of Coya/Coa, a marginal female character who, despite her repeated victimization, increasingly claims narrative power over the course of the novel. *Por la patria* was written in the years following the National Protests of 1983–84, and bears out the points that the protests had made public: that oppositional communities were by then not simply surviving (a moment captured by *E. Luminata*), but rather were actively **combating** authoritarianism, and that women had become evident protagonists of that social resistance. As Coya/Coa (and the other *mestizas* of the urban underworld) show, the contested history of resistance lay in the collective hands of those women, marginal and degraded as they were, who attempted to define their place in the radically decentered context of postcoup society.

In direct contrast to the omnipotent presence of "el luminoso" [the lighted sign] in *E. Luminata*, *Por la patria* portrays a world in which the authoritarian, masculinist, military figure is in severe crisis. This crisis is represented by two catalytic events: the death of Coya/Coa's idealized father,[42] and her ambiguous relationship with Juan, the impotent *macho*. Moreover, the crisis of masculinism further provokes ruptures in patriarchal orderings of culture, particularly structures of identity, language, and of course, the concept of *la patria*, the Fatherland, itself. In this context, the novel's epic title and tone are highly parodic, pointing acerbicly to the hollow rhetoric of military discourse and the fervent passions of its mistaken patriotism—a patriotism created by and for the monolithic, official image of a Fatherland that, by the early 1980s, had entered deeply into crisis.

The two parts of the novel ("I. La luz, la luz, la luz, la luz del día" [The light, the light, the light, the light of day], and "II. Se funde, se opaca, se yergue la épica" [The epic goes to ruin, clouds over, and rises again]) narrate this crisis through two parallel journeys: the death of the father(land) and the search for the mother(land) in part I, and the decline of the epic of the father versus the rise of the anti-epic of the mother—as Coya/Coa becomes the "madre de madres" [Mother of Mothers] in part II.[43] Hence, at the same time that *Por la patria* comes to terms with the loss of the idealized father, the novel consists of a massive search for the **mother**, an emergent matrix of language and identity within the feminized oppositional communities of postcoup Chile. This emphasis poses an intriguing contrast between Eltit's second novel (a search for the mother, postcrisis of the father) and Dorfman's *Widows* (as a search for the father, valorized because it is pro-mother). I will return to the contrast between Eltit and Dorfman below.

The two parts of *Por la patria* rest upon a strong referentiality to the postcoup context, an indication that the declining authoritarian figure could be more safely named in public after the National Protests than in the early postcoup years. Part I includes images of a military raid and the destruction of the bar where the characters take refuge, the assassination of the father, and the arrest and torture of the female characters. As the characters face the symbolic and real obstacles impeding their liberation, they discover the importance of narrating what was happening to them (for example, 50–51 and section 5, "Testimonios, parlamentos, documentos, manifiestos" [Testimonies, speeches, documents, manifestos]). This fragmentary literature, created in resistance to their imprisonment, in turn becomes the basis for the (anti-) "épica" [anti-epic] in part II of the novel. It is the violence that the characters withstand throughout their experiences that at once incapacitates any utopian impulse and provides the shaky narrative ground for the transformation of Coya/Coa at the novel's close.

That Coya/Coa's transformation is as much linguistic as historical is implied by her double name. The protagonist of this novel, like her country and her continent, is *mestiza*: daughter of "gringos" or "eslavos" [Slavs] and "indios" (9). She is "Coya," Inca princess and the language of indigenous royalty, and she is (increasingly) "Coa," the contemporary slang of marginal urban Chileans. Djelal Kadir captures this doubleness well: "Whereas Coya signifies institutional decorum and discursive management, Coa is the sign of the indecorous, the haywire, the indeterminate."[44] The challenge for Coya/Coa is to face the complexity of her history, her language, and herself, and to establish (narrate) an identity based on her multiplicity and her marginality. Unlike E. Luminata, Coya/Coa is involved in a collective project to find a voice and a place in postcoup society and in the world. In this regard, Coya/Coa and her cohorts play out in *Por la patria* what E. Luminata could only "rehearse" (the "Ensayo General") in *Lumpérica*: the production of a counter-discourse of resistance.

Both the language and the content of *Por la patria* equate Coya's doubleness with the simultaneously violent, sexual, and forbidden act of incest, the recoupling of certain aspects of feminized, mestizo language, identity, and culture with themselves. In *Por la patria*, univocal, linear, foundational, or "pure" language is associated with the official story, while nonlinear, fractured, ambiguous or "impure" mixtures of language are associated with the emergent "feminine" (matriarchal, androgynous, or incestuous, to use the novel's terms) *memoria* (memoir or memory).[45] Although these two discursive modes in the most general sense also characterize Dorfman's *Widows* (univocality vs. polyvocality), Eltit pushes her language to the outer limits of coherence, fusing poetry's strict economy of emblematic words with prose's more extended length, as she systematically deconstructs any foundational notion of the epic—facets of her work that do not hold for Dorfman's.

Moreover, the seeming dichotomy between official discourse and the polyvocal *memorias* of resistance is not simple in *Por la patria*. On one hand, without patriarchal discourse's absolute centrality, certain limits become permeable, traditional language disintegrates, and other possibilities for ordering language and culture open up. On the other hand, as *Por la patria* shows, a desire for the father figure remains after his death, as do the basic structures of Spanish, despite the context of this collapse: language still conditions any possibility for representation. *Por la patria* plays out the dilemma of how to use language to radically dismantle language, and of how to create a presence for marginals in a literary tradition that bespeaks their absence ("una épica de la marginalidad" [an epic of marginality]).[46] In short, expanding on *E. Luminata*, this novel asks how to create a ground from which to rewrite history from within the precarious and shifting borders of the discursive field (the margins of society).

Given the crisis brought on by the father's death, "la tragedia" (the "tragedy," a cipher for the coup, 21–22), Juan seeks to affirm his own place as father substitute: "—Háblame como si fuera tu papá, me dijo" ["Speak to me as if I were your father," he told me] (45). He allies himself as an informant *(soplón)* with the military regime and against the women of the bar, whom he betrays (24). The women are taken prisoner; Juan becomes their guardian, and he initiates a sexual relationship with Coya. Their encounters illustrate the complete failure of the categories of patriarchal history, portrayed as clichéd, sterile, and impotent. Using very strong language, Coya challenges Juan:

>   —Ponte debajo mío. No, ponte encima, tírame de costado, aplástame, sácame sangre, al menos rebálsame hasta los intestinos.
>   —Cállate, le dice él, cierra la boca que te lo voy a hacer como yo quiera.
>   . . .
>   —¿Qué es lo que estás esperando?
>   —Que me dejes ser hombre a mí y no te muevas tanto.

Coya lo muerde, le clava los dientes en el hombro y él se libra de un tirón.
. . .
Baja las manos y se frota. . . .
—No te metas en esto, me basto sola para mis gustos.
—No, no Coya, dame, déjame que te lo muestre, que te demuestre y te dé muestras de mi valía y corrupción. (62)

["Get under me. No, get on top, throw me on my side, crush me, make me bleed, at least jam yourself up to my intestines."
"Quiet," he tells her, "shut your mouth, I'm going to do it the way I want . . .".
"What are you waiting for then?"
"For you to let me be the man. Stop moving so much."
Coya bites him, she nails her teeth in his shoulder and he gets free in one leap. . . .
She lowers her hands and rubs herself. . . .
"Don't start with that, I can satisfy myself better alone."
"No, Coya, come on, let me, let me show you, let me know you, and you'll see my worth and corruption."]

Coya affronts Juan's sexuality from two angles: either she demonstrates that she does not need him in any way (as in this passage) or she points out his impotence—"Juan, ¿por qué no puedes?" [Juan, why can't you do it?] (64). The power struggle between Juan and Coya entails violent abuse that each directs toward the other in an effort toward self-definition. The fight is sexual (but not sensual), a metaphor for the historical and linguistic struggle to narrate the social body. At this point, however, neither character can quite come to the center stage of history: Juan, because of the crisis of his masculinity; Coya, because of the very instability of her identity. The model that Juan represents has clearly failed, but it is unclear what alternative to it Coya/Coa might discover as she resists her physical and linguistic confines.

Since the death of the father figure and Juan's impotence both signal the disintegration of the patriarchal way of ordering both language and culture, other discursive concepts such as national identity, as well as gender, racial, and sexual identities, therefore also become unstable. Coya/Coa moves within the realm of gender and sexual ambiguity, *mestizaje*, and the urban underworld, and her identity crosses symbolic national borders:

. . . cuando empinamos el vaso y el peso del país se desvaneció en su final y fue argentino quizás y yo también argentina y **perdí nacionalidad** en esa alucinación. . . .

Fuimos la tercera locura en **lo apátrida**.
—No soy, no quiero ser más chilena, le dije. (emphasis mine, 97)

[. . . when we drank down the glass and the weight of the country evaporated in the bottom and it was Argentine perhaps and I too was Argentine and **I lost my nationality** in that hallucination. . . .
We were the third insanity in **our nationlessness.**
"I am not, I no longer wish to be Chilean," I said.]

In their respective testimonies, both Berta and La Rucia echo this fluidity of borders (and lack of grounding: "lo apátrida" [our nationlessness]), as they express antipathy towards the official version of their country. While Berta flatly states that "Ya no somos país, no somos paisanos, no somos paisajes amenos" [we are no longer country, countrymen, pleasant countryside] (129), La Rucia declares:

Para mí el odio, la rabia, la descarga, son lo único que vale para mi estadía chilena y **por eso ser muchacha o muchacho es algo incierto**, insignificante además.
Hace años que no sueño yo. (emphasis mine, 135)

[For me, hate, anger, spouting off, are the only worthwhile aspects of my Chilean status and **therefore being a girl or a boy is something uncertain**, even insignificant.
I haven't dreamed in years.]

Finally, the violation of boundaries expressed in political violence (a biting critique of the postcoup Chilean Fatherland) is linked with a common continental history of *mestizaje* in Coya's words:

Así llevo la cuenta de las personas muertas: uno es mío afirmo [el padre], uno de la lista es don de mí, sin fondo en el calabozo.
¿Quién indemniza a los vivos? . . .
Aquí estamos más muertos que vivos, más asustados que nadie, más inseguros, más animales mestizos. (emphasis mine, 142)

[And so I tally up the dead: one is mine I affirm {the dead father}, one on the list is a gift of mine, of a bottomless prison.
Who indemnifies the living? . . .
Here we are more dead than alive, more scared than anyone, more insecure, more mixed breeds.]

Taken together, these three passages all reveal different consequences of the crisis of representation. In contrast to the seemingly straightforward (and from the dominant perspective, ideologically necessary) boundaries upholding a traditional, masculinist model of history, Eltit's characters resist any fixed categorization of their national, racial, gender, or sexual identities. More subtly, since traditional boundaries have disintegrated, no act is off-limits in this world. Utopian purity is not possible within this "bastardized" context. Here, the characters can only seek a tenuous ground from which to express the complexity of their world. They promiscuously rub together several versions of their story—*E. Luminata*'s aesthetic of the *frote* becomes here the metaphor of incest—in order to represent their precarious and indeterminate sense of themselves.

Coya's own indefinition increasingly causes her to feel aphasic, incapable of expressing her plural linguistic, ethnic, and sexual identities. After her father's death, Coya's ongoing struggle to articulate the word "madre" [mother] becomes part of a larger effort to ally herself with the "mother tongue." As Coya's world becomes increasingly feminized, she turns to her mother's tongue as linguistic tool, but finds instead a sexualized presence. In the section ironically titled "Por la patria" ("For the Fatherland," but dedicated to mothers), Eltit writes the following under the heading "a los pelos de mi abnegada madre" [to the hairs of my abnegated mother]. Coya addresses her mother as follows:

> con la lengua me vas lamiendo y yo desde arriba te miro mamá, te estoy viendo de qué manera la lengua tuya se esgrime, me eleva, me calienta todo el cuerpecito el hueco. Claro que te apuras sí, ya sabes que los chilenitos morenos obedecen a los eslavos y reverencian la masacre, mamá, la sangre que se vulcaniza el alquitrán del hampa en fin mamita
>   tu lengua
>   me lleva
>   al suelo. (89)

> [with your tongue you keep licking me and I from above look at you mama, I see how you brandish your tongue, it makes me rise up, it makes my whole body hot, the heat of my hole. Of course you're hurrying, yes, you know that the little brown Chileans obey the Slavs and revere the massacre, mama, the blood that vulcanizes into the tar of the slums, and finally, dear mommy
>   your tongue
>   takes me
>   to the ground.]

This sexualized image of narrating the body contrasts significantly with the ritual of self-mutilation as self-narration that Eltit had explored in *E. Luminata*, again underscoring the different historical circumstances within which each novel was written. In this scene, reminiscent of Barros's "Foreshadowing of a Trace," Eltit focuses on linguistic/sexual narration of feminized bodies as a narrative response to the context of crisis. However, unlike most other postcoup writers, who stay in the codified realm of heterosexual relations, Eltit explores forbidden sexual relations between women and the doubly forbidden world of incest. Eltit does so in order to graphically posit the mother's tongue—*la lengua materna*—as the literal and figurative matrix for telling Coya/Coa's story, for narrating her body. But the matrix cannot be innocent, since her marginal history is not. Hence, Eltit radically focuses on the incestuous coupling of mother with daughter, of language with marginal language.

In *Por la patria* (and in *The Fourth World*), "mother" is therefore not a singularly moral, maternal, and somewhat asexual or pure figure (as in Dorfman's *Widows*), but rather is a corrupt, contaminated, and decidedly sexual being. She is less the self-abnegating material provider, and more an epitome of insatiable physical need, than the four women in *Tres Marías y una Rosa*. She is both more marginal and more brutal than Barros's protagonist in "Artemisia," since the mothers in *Por la patria* are aggressive to the point of violence (for example, "MI MADRE," 87–94). Eltit further resists gender essentialisms in her depiction of farcical militarized mothers, who both parody the military father and challenge the dominant cultural view of what motherhood should be. Some mothers, such as the "madre general" [Mother General], interrogate Coya as would military men:

> Me pidieron que me definiera. Madre general lo hizo para que escucharan las otras:
> —Defínete, me dijo.
> —No, no puedo. Yo soy mujer cuando me conviene y hombre cuando lo necesito. Me gusta mucho aparentar, les contesté.
> Me quedé callada y antes que se pusieran a hablar, completé mi idea:
> —Yo soy todas las cosas.
> —No seas farsante, me retó furiosa madre general. (149)

> [They asked me to define myself. Mother General did it within earshot of the other women:
> "Define yourself," she said to me.
> "No, I can't. I am a woman when it's convenient and a man when I need to be. I like pretending," I answered them.
> I fell silent but before they could begin talking, I finished my thought: "I am all things."
> "Don't be ridiculous," Mother General scolded me, furious.]

Here, Mother General is clearly aligned with the need for boundaries and clear definition required by military discourse, while Coya/Coa tests the alternative narrative strategy of multiplicity ("Yo soy todas las cosas" [I am all things]). Although it is Mother General who is a farce—she breaks rigid definitions of militarism with her gender transgression—she attributes that quality to Coya, whose lack of definition she finds maddening. It is not surprising that, in order to get those mothers to leave her alone, Coya temporarily fixes her identity: "Irrumpí Coya, reina electa y legítima estéril de esos eriales" [I burst forth as Coya, elected as legitimate queen, sterile, of those wastelands] (149).

However, Coya's identity is not fixed, since military violence not only had provoked the death of her father, but also, following the raid of the bar, stripped Coya of her mother: "No veo a mi mamá" ["I don't see my mama"] (152). Without mother, there could be no language, as this passage illustrates:

> Coya ... gritó sin palabras y a través del tono sostenido apareció la sílaba "ma" que no pudo completar absorbida por los gritos de su madre que también nombró "ma" y parecía en verdad que todos clamaran más.
>   Más guardias, más balas, más instintos.
> Los refugiados gritan "ma" "más." (131)

> [Coya ... cried out without words and through the sustained tone appeared a syllable, "Ma," that she couldn't complete, absorbed by the cries of her mother, who also said "Ma" and it truly seemed that everyone clamored "Ma" more.
>   More guards, more bullets, more instincts.
> The refugees cried out more "Mas."]

After this raid, Coya redoubles her desperate search for the mother tongue *(la lengua materna)*, the mothers ("'ma' 'más'" [more "Mas"]) that will allow her to resist the military violence. As was the case after the raid, the violence of torture in part II repeatedly strips Coya/Coa away from her mother/language/identity ("Una voz que sin ser la mía me habita, le contesta: —nn o ve o aa mm i mm a má" [A voice that was not mine inhabited me, and answered: "I dd do o on nn'tt ss ss ee mm y mm a ma"] 165). Through this violence, any foundational story of self is undermined; Coya is barely coherent. At the end of part I, the refugees' and Coya's search for a voice points symbolically to the crisis of any foundationalist notion of *patria* and to the desired expression of an antifoundationalist notion of *matria* (my term for "motherland") in the novel's second part.

Part II of *Por la patria* outlines this process of death and rebirth, a decline of the masculinist epic that precedes the emergence of a feminized anti-epic. The title of part II underscores this cycle: "Se funde, se opaca, se yergue la épica" [The epic goes to ruin, clouds over, and rises again]. As part I suggested, however, the women's anti-epic continually defines itself against (and in resistance to) the epic, regardless of the epic's precipitous decline. At the same time, the emergent anti- epic resists fixed meaning, for such deferral is the nature of the language of the *matria*, the "give and take away" nature of the antifoundational project. In effect, *Por la patria* constantly works on the edge: its foundation is the destruction of foundations; its epic, rather than consolidating a coherent story, implies constant deconstruction of any basis for univocal Truth. In part II, Coya/Coa's incoherence, her continued search to found an identity in a context that repeatedly deconstructs her efforts, leads to the question: Upon what basis can history be (re)born in this context? In other words, if coherent meaning is constantly deferred, how can another story be told or history be reconceived? Part II of *Por la patria* at once traces the characters' resistance and negates the possibility for their freedom (or transcendence of limits) to take place.

In part II, Coya sets out to be reborn from her mother's womb, to reestablish her own innocence as well as her origins. I am reminded here of the final lines of *Widows*: "Mientras el muerto se mecía entre nuestros brazos como un recién nacido" (187) [While the body {the dead man} was rocked in our arms like a newborn child (146)]. However, the childbirth metaphor in Eltit's *Por la patria* takes a radically different twist. Coya's mother tells her:

>   —Voy a parirte de nuevo.
> Trató de meterme para adentro.
>   Traté de entrar y no cupe.
> No pude el hueco excavar. Yo pujaba y ella contraía;
>   —Métete, me dice, empecemos esto de nuevo.
> Y yo hundiendo la cabeza presionando, haciendo fuerzas para abrir el túnel y sumergirme en la oscuridad cálida del adentro.
> Hablé:
>   —Páreme. Páreme otra vez, guárdame un tiempito.
>   Fue un acto desesperado. . . .
> Cabezazo tras cabezazo me di y el dolor intenso a ella . . . y llorábamos las dos ante lo imposible, ante lo insensible de Dios. (180–81)

>   ["I'm going to give birth to you again."
> She tried to push me inside.
>   I tried to enter but I didn't fit.
> I couldn't excavate the hole. I pushed and she contracted:
> "Come inside," she says to me, "let's start over."
> And I push, burying my head, trying hard to open the tunnel and submerge myself in the warm darkness of her insides.
> I spoke:
> "Give birth to me. Give birth to me again, hold onto me for a little while."
>   It was a desperate act.

I banged my head time and again and her intense pain . . . and the two of us cried, faced with the impossibility, the insensitivity, of God.]

For Coya, any utopian project—a return to the womb, the original prelinguistic matrix—is desperately desired, yet it is also wildly beyond reach, fundamentally inaccessible. Like history and language, Coya cannot be reborn with innocence, but rather must take on her condition as impure, discontinuous, and incestuous. In other words, the impossibility of reentering the womb is the denial of any "large" totalizing narrative (including "God"), and it is precisely this death that gives rise to Coya's anti-epic. The ground of her story is the impossibility of achieving the ground of the womb.

A comparison of Eltit's and Dorfman's childbirth metaphors illustrates just how different the two are. In the context of resistance after the coup, it is no coincidence that the two authors posit woman/mother as generative of the future (historical continuity). However, Dorfman's comparatively more modernist project still allows for the idealization of women, as representatives of the community-based values that the author sees as a source of hope for the future (the widows', Alexis's, and Sofía's symbolic pregnancy). By contrast, Eltit's locally contingent, more postmodern stance precludes any idealization whatsoever, and is only hopeful insofar as it is so graphically placed: the future lies on the threshold of an impossibly closed-off womb in the here and now.

Given these differences, Dorfman's critique of Eltit would be that she offers no communal values and no real basis for hope for the future; Eltit's critique of Dorfman would be that his notion of hope is merely a self-deluding fiction, whose local contingency must be revealed for history to develop differently. This fundamental difference between Dorfman's modernist idealism/utopianism/foundationalism and Eltit's postmodernist radical contingency/anti-utopianism/antifoundationalism is even more clear in their respective next novels. In Dorfman's *La última canción de Manuel Sendero* [*The Last Song of Manuel Sendero*], fetuses refuse to be born until certain changes are made in the world—that is, until the world becomes more ideal like the womb. In Eltit's *The Fourth World*, even the womb has become contaminated by real-world imperfections, as the fetuses begin their incestuous relationship, and struggle over power, before they are even born.

Hence, to return to *Por la patria,* the marginal women's transformation "de vencidas en vencedores," from vanquished to victors, depends first and foremost on revealing their impurity, their unidealized nature, and only when they fully take on their marginal conditions can any change (however subtle) take place. For this reason, there is an increasing premium on Coya's ability to tell her own story, including the violations replete in her past. In other words, Coya/Coa embodies the memory of the community, but she represents history's bastardizations, rather than the ideal possibility of its desire-based continuity. Of her community, represented by the neighborhood bar, Coya states:

> Electa en el erial, adquirí compromiso después de la inmensa burla de mi ma ma mam mamá, cuando ya la pirámide, cuando emerjo **de vencida en vencedora**, presa y desalojada del bar, de mi único barrio.
> Victimada en el soplo: viuda de mi padre, viuda de mi madre, enlutada, me recojo hasta mi propia fundación, anterior al bar, ensañada en la selva oscura de mi madre....
> Para mí que resta poco. **Mi insurrección es total.** Quiero mi casa, mi cama y yacer autóctona con otro nombre y rango.
>   Cedo mi cargo.
>   Ya no Coya incesto e hibridez.
> **Renazco Coa y mi maldad me subyuga**. (emphasis mine, 260)

> [Elected in the wasteland, I became committed after the immense mockery of my ma ma mam mama, after the fire, when I emerge **from defeat to victory**, prisoner and dispossessed of the bar, of my only barrio.
> Victimized by rumors: widow of my father, widow of my mother, grieving, I withdraw to my own foundation, prior to the bar, furious within the dark jungle of my mother....
> For me little remains. **My insurrection is total.** I want my home, my bed, and to lie autochthonous with another name and rank.
>   I cede my position.
>   No longer Coya incest and hybridity.
> **I am reborn Coa and my wickedness subjugates me.**]

For Coya/Coa, rebellion consists of taking on her own disunity using the language of the marginal slum. This transformation is crucial, as "Coa," impure language, is claimed as the basis for narrating the emergent feminine (matriarchal, incestuous) *memoria;* "Coa" undermines the foundation of the epic. Coya's "rebirth" as Coa is, in a basic sense, the rebirth of history, but it is a history that can no longer be transcendent. Because she represents the contaminated tongues of the *hampa*, Coya's transformation into Coa allows her to become the Mother of Mothers—a contaminated matrix of history—by the novel's end.

Since Coya/Coa represents, rather than represses, history's bastardization, the anti-epic emerges. Coya tells Juan:

> Hay una hazaña que no puedes ni podrás con nada desmentir.
> Hay una épica.
> Surgida de la opresión y destello del linchaco.
> Yo para ti madre y padre en cuanto insurgente y diestra, en tanto reina y el poder de resistencia a tu vacío . . .

Olvidé tu cuerpo porque fue mínimo e insuficiente. . . .
De espaldas en la cama, en mi mama, en mi leche me querías: Yo erecta, erguida y doble soy: punzando y recibiendo, mojando y mojada, desmaterna y despaterna, deprendida ya. (273)

[There is a deed that you cannot nor will you ever be able to deny.
There is an epic.
Risen from oppression and sparked by violence.
I, mother and father to you, insurgent and agile, so queenly and resisting your emptiness . . .
I forgot your body because it was minimal and insufficient. . . .
On my back in bed, in my suckling, in my milk you wanted me: I am erect, proud and double: piercing and receiving, moistening and moistened, unmothered and unfathered, unfettered now.]

It is by taking on her incestuous gender, ethnic, and linguistic multiplicity that Coya/Coa triumphs over the failed masculinist model represented by Juan's impotence. Because conventional boundaries had failed, were contaminated, Coa's narrative opportunity became possible—much the same historical circumstances leading real Chilean women (and feminized men) to become the vanguard of postcoup resistance movements. Coya/Coa emerges triumphantly into the street when amnesty is declared, stating that: "Seré de vencida en vencedora especie" [From vanquished, I shall be a victorious species] (275).

The tainted plenitude (or nontranscendent freedom) that the characters reach is based on their facing the contradictions of their past (a process still incomplete in postcoup Chile), including the cultural forms of violence that have always characterized Chilean infrahistory. The struggle of conflicting discourses **composes** these characters' "obstinada resistencia," their obstinate resistance. It is through this multiplicity of discourses that the (impure, nonidealized, and transgendered) mother is found, that the (anti-) epic is founded. The penultimate section reads:

> Me sentí rodeada de un ejército de madres, caminando por calles extrañas. Somos veinte, pensé, veinte rangos en disputa por la carga que ganamos, por esa obstinada resistencia que tuvimos. Somos madre general y madres 1,2,3,4,5,6, al destrone de las viejas y el nuevo símbolo de la parición invertida: la defensa.
> Multiplicadas en veinte coas de raza coya y yo Coya en el incesto total de la patria.
> Libertas hablamos. . . .
> Se apresta el infante:
> Se levanta el coa, el lunfardo, el giria, el pachuco, el caló, caliche, slang, calao, replana. El argot se dispara y yo. (277–78)

[I felt surrounded by an army of mothers, walking on strange streets. There are twenty of us, I thought, twenty ranks in dispute for the position we won, for the obstinate resistance that we put forth. We are Mother General and mothers 1,2,3,4,5,6, dethroning the old ladies and a new symbol of the inverted birth: defense.
Multiplied into twenty coas of the coya race and I Coya in the total incest of the fatherland.
Freed we speak. . . .
The infant is prepared:
The coa, lunfardo, giria, pachuco, caló, caliche, slang, calao, replana rise up. The argot is fired off, as am I.]

While Dorfman's final scene involves the morally grounded collective of mothers joined around the corpse of a community male, here Coya/Coa is herself surrounded by "mothers" in her/their incestuous and conflictual act of resistance. Appropriately, the "infant" in Eltit's experimental novel is language itself, the "bastardized" community-based slang upon which Coya/Coa builds this "yo." The multiple, conflicting, and locally generated versions of Coa thereby undo the repressive order of dominant (masculinist, transcendental) language at the end of the novel. Moreover, this revolutionary process multiplies across the continent, providing a challenge wherever marginal language recouples upon itself: urban Chilean coa, Argentine lunfardo, gypsy caló, Andean caliche, and so on.

Hence, Eltit's "épica" by definition remains profoundly anti-utopian, as seen in the novel's last words:

El fuego, el fuego, el fuego y la épica.
Volví a sentir: volví a sentir sobre el erial,
superpuesta a mi niñez.
Todas soltamos el cuerpo y las manos
móviles y diestras.
Vimos el continente y fuimos otra vez
combatientes y hermanas, humanas, **casi.**
Hablé extenso, feliz, prudente y generosa:
    —Se abre el bar, mujeres. Lo abrimos, lo
administramos con jerarquía.
Y la sed se apoderó de ellas. (emphasis mine, 279)

[The fire, the fire, the fire and the epic.
I began to feel again: again I was able to feel the wasteland,
superimposed on my childhood.
We all loosed our bodies and hands,
swift and agile.
We saw the continent and we were once again
combatants and sisters, human **almost.**

I spoke grandly, happy, prudent and generous:
—The bar is open, ladies. We opened it,
we'll run it hierarchically.
And thirst overcame them.]

The end of the novel is simultaneously hopeful (as the women thirstily return to the bar, leaving behind their imprisonment) and bleak (hierarchies continue, all generative possibilities in the novel are marked by the incestuous intrafamilial, social, and linguistic relationships limiting their historical transcendence). Crucially, though, Coya's conversion to Coa and finally, to the Mother of Mothers, provides a collective narrative ground, however unstable and contested, which is the greatest contrast between *Por la patria*, written after the National Protests, and *E. Luminata*. In order to narrate, the characters in *Por la patria* rely upon an unidealized polyvocality as a narrative strategy—and the combination of multiple formal discourses and slang in language—to represent the unstable discursive field (and marginal subjectivities) upon and through which they might, or must, take a stand. This stand **is** their marginality, which returns us to the problem: can these characters ever take the center stage of history? Eltit's answer in *Por la patria* is "almost." That is, the closest Eltit can come to resolution of this issue is to leave her characters on the threshold of the "casi": almost human, almost coherent, almost narrators of history. This, for me, is one of the most poignant moments in all of postcoup Chilean literature, as it shows where Diamela Eltit's particular, highly contingent sense of hope may lie.

At the same time, it is important that Eltit's characters' "almost" humanity at the end of the novel, like their violent lives throughout the text, seems to preclude any idealized notion of love as the basis for community. This is particularly striking, since some form of love provides the ultimate defining ground for all of the texts I have discussed here. For the two male authors, solidarity is the value that becomes embodied as a sort of maternal love by the women (and in *Widows*, by the feminized men) of the communities. For Barros, in contrast to Dorfman and Benavente/TIT, erotic love is the focus, especially the present or absent desire-based links between people and communities after 1973. Though Eltit, like Barros, reveals the potential for violence in any erotic act (a violence which both writers connect to the postcoup context), it is as if the dictatorship has stripped eroticism of love for the urban marginals in Eltit's first novels. Possibly in response to this, Eltit later explored, with the photographer Paz Errázuriz, the love that was expressed under highly dehumanizing circumstances—those faced by institutionalized mental patients—in their collaborative work *El infarto del alma* [Heart Attack of the Soul], published in 1994.[47]

Although Barros and Eltit both focus on women's (or ambiguously gendered) bodies as the site for narrative struggle in feminized Chilean society, Barros shows that desire-based connections between people—despite authoritarianism—may create imaginary and real points of resistance, however fleeting, for her female narrators. While solitude—a lack of desire-based connections between people—marks many of Barros's characters' lives, she actively posits the expression of desire as an antirepressive strategy. Barros herself creates connections using the aesthetic of the synesthesia, her erotic bending and reshaping of language. Barros seems to say "this is how we can rebuild" Chilean society in the wake of the Pinochet years.

By contrast, Eltit emphasizes just how deeply Chilean society has been marked by various forms of violence. Incest, as an aesthetic practice (the *frote*, fragmentation), disrupts reading by fracturing syntax, exploding recognizable codes, mixing-and-matching discursive strategies. Eltit's work insists that it is a mistake to have language join what history had rendered asunder, because that could foster forms of social amnesia, allowing authoritarian hierarchies and exclusions to persist and reemerge in still more insidious forms over time. For this reason, Eltit aesthetically resists any form of glossing over violence and conflict, especially the superficial reconciliation of opposites that, as it turns out, has largely characterized the first decade of the Chilean transition.

In her first two novels, Eltit's deep interrogation of social structures through both form and content (what I have called a dismantling of the institutions of language itself) also attacks the cultural codes that most readers manage. Hence, the reading experience can feel unsettling, depending on one's allegiances with certain traditional structures. Eltit taps into those historically generated resistances based on the (readers') privilege **not** to see the marginality resulting from traditional forms of power. (I think here of Ignacio Valente's critique of Eltit's "impenetrability," wherein the conservative *padre* sounds like *Por la patria*'s Mother General).[48] In essence, Eltit's protest against authoritarianism is to unmask its ugly and complex underside, just as her critique of narrow, traditional, or seamless literature is to reveal the refractory and multiplicitous character of language. And equally crucial, her resistance to neoliberalism's cultural legacy is to refuse to write anything that could be easily **consumed**. What she risks, however, is not being read, or being read poorly and misunderstood, à la Ignacio Valente. By occupying the literary margins, Eltit's work may remain ghettoized, while the dominant discourses continue to reproduce themselves, fundamentally unchanged. Like the fate after 1990 of some of the most important challenges posed by "new" social actors and movements under Pinochet, Eltit's insightful critiques function within a parallel universe easily excluded from the majority worldview.

Eltit's third novel positions itself somewhat differently vis-à-vis these issues. By the time Eltit finished writing *The Fourth World*,[49] Chile was headed toward the 1989 plebiscite and toward the opportunity to take civilian control of the future. Where *E. Luminata* and *Por la patria* to varying degrees reinscribe marginality as theme and linguistic strategy, *The Fourth World* attempts to find a means of representing both center and margins, to reconceive history from another position. The difference between *The Fourth World* and the earlier novels is therefore how the story is told, with what language and sensibility, with which structures more or less intact and which others in flux. Formally, this means a somewhat more legible language and plot, with a narrative focus on one couple (twins), within one family, who have somewhat coherent (though radically shifting) subjectivities throughout the text.[50] Like *Por la patria*, *The Fourth World* treats the central themes of incest, motherhood, and the rebirth of history, but it does so by closing in on the claustrophobic family home and womb as the sites of contested (social) meaning.[51]

Within this trajectory, *The Fourth World* also subtly marks the substitution of neoliberalism (and its ideological "naturalization") for overt authoritarianism as the predominant cultural coordinate of postcoup Chile at the end of the 1980s. *The Fourth World*'s psychological focus suggests that the market's "invisible hand," perhaps more than the dictator's, conditions even the most intimate of actions and desires. If consumerism (and liberal ideology generally) did eventually provide civil society's "common ground," Eltit narratively reveals the social costs and hidden conflicts involved in this "reconciliation." The contrasting narrative points of view between the first and third novels—especially the camera-like exterior shots in *E. Luminata* versus the two highly interior and subjective first-person narrators in *The Fourth World*—underscores Eltit's view that the real work awaiting civil society after Pinochet lies in exorcising the deep-seated forms of exclusion reproduced independently of the dictator's presence.

Given the novel's content, its title's ambiguous reference to a "Fourth" world—whether the excluded margins of the "Third World," the psychosexual "world" of human relations, or simply the nucleus of the family[52]—emphasizes that the characters' interior lives are intimately conditioned by power structures on the "outside." However, while the novel's reality is highly shaped by economics (everything and everyone has a price, true to neoliberalism's legacy) and by a worldwide hierarchy in which a few nations dominate many others (the First, Second, and Third Worlds to which the title alludes), the global context operates as an absent antagonist present only in the characters' psychosexual longings and conflicts (that is, until the novel's final page). The text never refers to a specific regime or nation or city as a backdrop for the action. All we know is that the novel's characters are "sudacas," a degrading term used by Spaniards for Latin Americans: "a racial mark, an economic stigma, a derogatory political label," in Julio Ortega's words.[53] These characters are children of conquest and of the "new world order," impure, tainted, and invisibly defined both by this outside world's hierarchy and by their own violent history.

The Fourth World is composed of two parts, in which twin siblings trade off as narrators of their life stories. Part I (titled "Será irrevocable la derrota" [Defeat Will Be Irrevocable]) is narrated by the male of the pair, María Chipia, who recounts from the time of his and his sister's conception through their adolescence and the overt sexualization of their long-standing incestuous relationship. His sister narrates from their adolescence to the birth of their child/text in part II (titled "Tengo la mano terriblemente agarrotada" [I Have a Terribly Constrained Hand]). During the first half, María Chipia attempts to understand the relationship of his own body to the bodies of his fellow family members and to the outside world. Fittingly enough, this part ends when the mother commits adultery, violating her domestic and psychological confines, and creating a crisis of (paternal) authority in the family (the catalyst for the feminization of the narrative in the novel's second part). The second half traces the twins' gradual understanding of their place in the sudaca world, and the incestuous creation of their child/story—however degraded and commercialized it may be in this context. It is only in the last line of the novel that the narrator of this second part is named as "diamela eltit" (*sic*), mother and decentered author of this story.

These two first person narratives in *The Fourth World* are pointedly juxtaposed to reveal their differences. María Chipia's style is chronologically linear and rather analytical, somewhat stilted despite the focus on his subjective and emotional reactions to his growth and change. By contrast, the female narrator of the second half speaks fragmentarily and emblematically,[54] using suggestive images and an emphasis on the twins' instinctual actions to portray the bastard child/text's gestation and birth. It is in this way that Eltit questions the concept of authoring as reducible to a centralized authority, and posits tensions and dislocations between masculinist language and feminized language as mutually necessary. The two styles offer different sensibilities, each revealing or concealing distinct psychic impulses. **Both** discourses, and their discrepancies, are the parents of this child/text, which suggests an unidealized coming together not present in the first two novels. If "diamela eltit" thereby acknowledges her debt to her twin brother, the opposite is true as well: María Chipia must embrace the sensibilities of his sister for new narrative possibilities to be "born."

As I stated by way of contrasting this novel to its predecessors and to Dorfman's *The Last Song of Manuel Sendero*, there is no innocence in the womb from which these twins (or the text) emerge. The womb is merely a continuation of the corrupt material world outside, wherein each character's precarious sense of identity develops from constant power struggles against significant others. Just as the mother and father act in stereotypical ways (his authoritarianism, her self-abnegation), so does the pair in the womb (he struggles to maintain his position; she seeks his attention). Both inside and outside of this womb, meaning is made through incest, "el frote permanente de nuestros cuerpos" (20) [the constant rubbing together of our bodies] (translation mine), the increasingly feverish sex acts in which the twins engage over the course of the novel.

In *The Fourth World*, incest is not only the ultimate act defining the narrators' positions vis-à-vis each other, but also it implicitly defines their place in the world. Incest is the past and the future for the sudacas; it is both their heritage and their declaration of identity in this tainted context. The twins decide to have a child (to create a text) in order to acknowledge their position: "—Quiero hacer una obra sudaca terrible y molesta" (88) ["I want to create a creature {or: a work} that is terribly and scandalously sudaca"] (74). Thus, the act of incest is at once sexual and textual, at once highly intimate and exceedingly collective. *The Fourth World* in a large measure is dedicated to the reinscription and reaffirmation of this sudaca history, the basic matrix of the characters' identity in the degraded postcoup (or more generally, postcolonial or peripherally postmodern) world.

That this is a female-centered world (despite the father's illusion of authority) becomes increasingly clear in the text, with "formas femeninas . . . dominantes en la escena" (20) [feminine forms . . . dominant on the scene] (translation mine). María Chipia never achieves the ability to escape self-definition in function of his twin sister:

> [P]ara mí, no había verdaderamente un lugar, que ni siquiera era uno, único, sólo la mitad de otra innaturalmente complementaria y que me empujaba a la hibridez. (25)

> [For me, there really wasn't a single place, nor was I a unique individual; I was simply half of another, unnaturally complementary, person. This forced me to face my own hybridity.] (translation mine)

Not only does she learn to speak before he does (much to the horror of the father, 29–30), but also María Chipia sees his twin as the guarantor of his own (hybrid) "wholeness." At age five, María Chipia enters into crisis, sensing that his body would dis-integrate without his sister's narration of it:

> Empapado en la duda, hasta mi existencia me pareció cuestionable, o bien la prueba más tangible de un mundo oscuramente contrariado. Un mundo caotizado por la ausencia de un forjador. . . . Desde el instante en

que percebí el descabezamiento del mundo sin institución ni norma, choqué con mi momento más oscuro y crítico. . . .

Con el mundo partido en dos, mi única posibilidad de reconstrucción era mi hermana melliza. Junto a ella, solamente, podía alcanzar de nuevo la unidad. . . .

Mi hermana melliza armó pieza por pieza mi identidad. (37–38)

[Shrouded in doubt, even my own existence seemed questionable, or else it was the most tangible proof of an enigmatically vexed world; a world in chaos due to the absence of a guide. . . . From the moment I perceived the unruly world without institutions or norms, I clashed with my most obscure and critical moment. . . .

With the world severed in two, my only path to reconstruction was my twin sister: being next to her would allow me to achieve wholeness again.
. . .

Little by little, my sister reconstructed my identity.] (27)

As in *Por la patria*, the father figure's authority has decayed, and the world is in flux, due to the crumbling of overtly authoritarian, outwardly patriarchal norms ("la ausencia de un forjador," the absence of a "founder" or guide). Lacking boundaries, María Chipia seeks self-definition through his relationship with his sister. Not only does she eventually take over as the narrator of their story—the story of their bodies—but also his feminization (or transgendered identity) becomes steadily more obvious, performed through his cross-dressing throughout their adulthood.

Since the defining act of history was and is incest, the narrators' sexual coupling likewise becomes their sole means of resistance. Incest—the ultimate of inside acts—is their unity in the face of internalized outside forces that seek to divide and conquer. Paradoxically, incest is the "fraternity" or "brotherhood" that gives hope (however tainted) for survival: "Afirmó que sólo la fraternidad podía poner en crisis . . . a la nación más poderosa del mundo" (98) [She asserted that only brotherhood could propel that nation into crisis . . . We had to respond to the most powerful nation in the world] (84). María Chipia's twin tells him:

Soy víctima de un turbulento complot político en contra de nuestra raza. Persiguen aislarnos con la fuerza del deprecio. . . .

Temes a mi hermana y a mi madre, y parece que la multiplicidad de tus sueños te acercara a la nación más famosa y poderosa del mundo.

Pero yo, que leo y traduzco cada movimiento en la genitalidad de la familia, sabía exactamente cuando los miembros hablaban de posesión. . . .

Sólo tú retardaste nuestro encuentro. Porque tú eres yo misma . . . pues ambos sabemos la forma única de frenar nuestra extinción y la humillación de nuestra raza. (103–4)

[I am a victim of a tumultuous political plot against our race. They {attempt to isolate us} with the force of their scorn....
You are afraid of my sister and my mother, and it seems like the multiplicity of your dreams is taking you closer and closer to the most famous and powerful nation in the world.
But it is I, reading and translating {every move in} the sexual activities of this family, who knew exactly when the members would speak of possession....
You were the only one who delayed our encounter. Since you are myself ... we both know which is the only way to delay our extinction and the humiliation of our race.] (89–90)

The only way for these characters to resist the strength of "the most famous and powerful nation in the world"—a cipher for both the dominant capitalist world order and the neoliberal regime that seek to name and narrate their every desire—was to create a text based on the incestuous sexual liaison by which family members could narrate themselves.

The taboo act that would seem to yield self-destruction is seen here as desperately self-affirming, a deeply disturbing confirmation of this "raza's" precarious place in the world:

Fue un homenaje a la especie sudaca. Fue un manifiesto. Fue una celebración dinástica, celebrando la pronta llegada del niño, quien ese día pudo conocer la inmensa fuerza de sus padres. El odio de sus padres. Aislado en un campo netamente orgánico, el niño conoció lo más placentero de sus padres. (122)

[It was a tribute to the sudaca species. It was a manifesto. It was a dynastic celebration of the coming of a child who that day was able to experience the immense power of his or her parents: their hatred. Isolated in a distinctly organic sphere, the child experienced the parents' most charming attributes.] (108)

This repetition of sudaca history through incest reaches (anti-)epic proportions ("una celebración dinástica" [a dynastic celebration]), since such penetration of the womb becomes the principal mechanism for giving the child an identity. Just as the womb itself is not off-limits from this contaminated history, so does that history pose the base for this child/text's precarious sense of self. Woman thereby becomes the unidealized matrix of history; from her body's coupling with the feminized father, María Chipia, the novel is born. For this reason, the narrator reiterates that their future resides with the child/text: "Le hablo, otra vez, del poder de la fraternidad sudaca y de cómo nuestro poder podría destruir a esa nación de muerte. Le hablo del niño" (107) [I talk to him again about the sudaca brotherhood and how our power could destroy that nation of death. I talk to him about the child] (93). The best the child/text can do, then, is to convey the precarious story of its own bastardization.

The last segment of the novel shifts for the first time outside of the psychic world of the characters, to describe the city's corruption, its ruin, and its sterility, despite (or more likely, because of) the erotic promises of consumerism itself. Because the final page serves the crucial role of retroactively reframing the entire novel, I reproduce a substantial portion of it here:

> La ciudad colapsada es ya una ficción nominal. Sólo el nombre de la ciudad permanece, porque todo lo demás ya se ha vendido en el amplio mercado. En la anarquía de la costumbre por la venta se ejecutan los últimos movimientos a viva voz, voceando la venta del vacío.
>
> El dinero que cae del cielo apetece el vacío de la ciudad y cada una de las retóricas del vacío para sembrar el vacío sobre los campos, ya vencidos y definitivamente ajenos. El dinero caído del cielo entra directo por los genitales y las voces ancianas se entregan a un adulterio desenfrenado. El adulterio ha adulterado a la ciudad nominal, que se vende, se vende a los postores a cualquier costo. La transacción está a punto de concluir, y en el dinero caído del cielo está impresa, nítidamente, una sonrisa de menosprecio a la raza sudaca.
>
> Lejos, en una casa abandonada a la fraternidad, entre un 7 y un 8 de abril, diamela eltit [*sic*], asistida por su hermano mellizo, da a luz una niña. La niña sudaca irá a la venta. (127–28)

> [The city, fallen into collapse, is already a fiction. Only the name of the city remains, because everything else has been sold on the open market. Amid the anarchy of supply and demand, the last items are auctioned off, amid accusations of sham and fraud.
>
> The money that falls from the sky stimulates not only urban fraud but also the false rhetoric about planting a hoax in the fields, which is already sold and now belongs to someone else. The money from the sky enters directly through the sex organs, and the ancient voices surrender to wanton adultery. Adultery has perverted the city; the city prostitutes itself, giving itself away at any price to any bidders. The transaction is about to conclude and the contempt for the sudaca race is clearly printed on the money falling from the sky.
>
> Far away, in a house dedicated to brotherhood, between April 7 and 8, diamela eltit {*sic*}, assisted by her twin brother, gives birth to a baby girl. The sudaca baby will go up for sale.] (113–14)

The birth of the child is the birth of the text; however, both are the products of incest. The child is the result of the female narrator's incestuous relationship with her twin brother, while the text, more subtly, is the product of authorial persona diamela eltit's promiscuous *frote* with the dominant language represented by her brother's discourse in the novel's first part. This "baby girl" is irrevocably marked by her sudaca status and by the morally bankrupt neoliberal regime and capitalist world order, in which rabid commercialization and base materialism are the dominant ways of making meaning. She/it (the sudaca child/text), and all sudacas, are imminently prostitute-able, destined to an economic fate they do not own. "La niña/obra sudaca" will be sold to the highest bidder.[55]

At the same time, however, *The Fourth World* itself resists the hegemonic marketplace it describes by linguistically refusing to be an object of facile consumption. This novel/child of incest is ugly, difficult, unwilling to be devoured by readers who reduce its terms; herein lies Eltit's "obstinada resistencia." And yet for this same reason, the challenges the novel offers may remain between the book's covers, boxed away like many of the most challenging social actors from the resistance movements "after" Pinochet.

In the final passages of *The Fourth World*, Eltit again leaves her readers with a double message. Eltit's somewhat "mended" style comes a step closer to the sort of linguistic bending of Barros, or the overcoming of conflict to produce a collective *arpillera* in *Tres Marías y una Rosa*. However, Eltit's anti-utopianism—her view that local postcoup history was perverse, contaminated, and incestuously generated from the social margins—negates any idealism one could feel about this mending. She makes it clear that the authoritarian lives within, that the market drives our desires, that outward healing is only the beginning of a longer, more difficult process of social change. Although history is "reborn" in Eltit's novel, it is done in such a way as to undermine its transcendence, to show the limits of language to convey any truth beyond "verdades sudacas,"[56] sudaca truths, especially within this economic world order. In coming home to the psychological realm as a locus for contested social meaning, Eltit shows how every body, every subjectivity, and every language is implicated in this story of crisis and contamination: no body is innocent. In being the first to name herself as involved, "eltit" implicates herself fully in this social text.

Taken together, Diamela Eltit's first three novels place a premium on local struggle in generating answers to the exclusions created by military authoritarianism, economic neoliberalism, and literary traditionalism. Eltit's is not an idealized world in which a "common ground" is simply established. Instead, grounding is itself a process—radically contested, interrogated, and conflictual—through which another story may be told, and history, reconceived. In this way, history is both challenged and generated from the **photographic negative** of the marginal world that Eltit's characters inhabit—the degraded, commercialized, and incestuous social periphery of postcoup Chile. By keeping her "antennae" sharply attuned to this context, Eltit anticipated that the most insidious obstacles to democracy after Pinochet may lie very close to home: in suppression of conflict and contradiction, hidden forms of violence and exclusion, and in the libidinal promises of consumer culture.

6
Of Bodiless Spirits and the Transition to Democracy

> La realidad es un revoltijo, no alcanzamos a medirla o descifrarla, porque todo ocurre al mismo tiempo.... Yo trato de abrirme camino en este laberinto, de poner un poco de orden en tanto caos, de hacer la existencia más tolerable. Cuando escribo cuento la vida como a mí me gustaría que fuera.
>
> [Reality is a jumble we can't always measure or decipher, because everything is happening at the same time.... I try to open a path through that maze, to put a little order in that chaos, to make life more bearable. When I write, I describe life as I would like it to be.]
> —Isabel Allende, *Eva Luna* (1987)[1]

IN THE PRECEDING PAGES, I HAVE EXPLORED WORKS BY FOUR VERY DIFFERENT authors—Pía Barros, David Benavente and the Taller de Investigación Teatral [Investigative Theater Workshop], Ariel Dorfman, and Diamela Eltit—who struggled, through their literature, to come to terms with the shifting and oftentimes contradictory context of Chilean society since 1973. And yet, it was not the challenging work of these writers who captured the popular imagination during the postcoup years, but the work of Isabel Allende, whose *La casa de los espíritus* [*The House of the Spirits*] (1982)[2] is the second biggest-selling novel ever written in Spanish, following only García Márquez's *Cien años de soledad* [*One Hundred Years of Solitude*], and surpassing Cervantes's *Don Quijote*.[3] The magnitude of Allende's success raises important questions about Chile's cultural and political landscape after this first decade of democracy: who better represents the worldview of a majority of Chileans, Isabel Allende or the other four authors studied here? As Chile moves into the twenty-first century, which cultural tendencies are becoming consolidated, neoliberal individualism or antiauthoritarianism? In order to approach these issues, I believe that the phenomenon of the historical romance merits thought: why have Isabel

Allende's novels been so popular? To what cultural impulses do her texts respond? The answers to these questions hold immense consequences for any view of postcoup resistance culture, and more subtly, for the possibilities for social transformation in Chile after Pinochet.

BODILESS SPIRITS AND THE NEOLIBERAL MARKETPLACE

In considering Chile's future beyond the Pinochet years, two interrelated historical processes cannot be ignored: the country's continuing quest for democracy with justice, and the unwavering hegemony of the neoliberal economic model, in Chile as in many other parts of the world. It is worth remembering the basic interrelationship between the two, namely, that the ideological presuppositions of classical liberalism, inherited from European Enlightenment ideals, fundamentally undergird both political democracy and economic neoliberalism, now coupled together in most late capitalist democracies.[4] A premium on individual freedoms, on rationality over materiality, on self-reliance and equality ("one person, one vote"), underlies the pluralistic ideal behind political democracy, and has been used to justify neoliberalism's faith in the market as a mechanism to bring wealth to all. Of course, history has shown that liberalism's emphasis on the individual at once obfuscates and protects the power structures of capitalism—class, gender, ethnicity, and so forth—structures that make some individuals and groups, and some votes, much more powerful than others. And as discussed in chapter 3, neoliberalism in Chile has led to the rich getting richer, the poor becoming desperate, and the middle class falling into a poverty more severe than at any other time in the country's history.[5] In many respects, then, the historical and ideological underpinnings of liberal democracy **themselves** preclude "justice for all," a tendency exacerbated when the social "safety net" has been shredded by particularly orthodox neoliberal regimes.

Furthermore, we know now that the emergent sectors of resistance under Pinochet have become, to a disappointing degree, the mostly hidden sectors of institutional democracy. The coalition governments of Aylwin and Frei were not comprised of the women of various classes who led the way to *pinochetismo*'s political demise, but rather were formed in a Macondoesque repetition of many of the same names from the same political parties that were in place since before 1973. In fact, the oft-cited smoothness of the Chilean transition may well lie in the fact that it only involved a transfer of authority from the military dictator to civil society's newly restored, but traditionally empowered, political class (Fanon's "pitfall of the national bourgeoisie"),[6] a transition coinciding with the reassuring reinforcement of other dominant hierarchies both societies normally rested upon. And despite their rhetorical emphasis on the need for greater social and economic equity, the Aylwin and Frei governments largely followed the strict neoliberal course originally charted by the military regime—a course which has tended to atomize the collective bodies (new social movements) that had coalesced in opposition to Pinochet.

If nothing else, then, the decade following the 1988 plebiscite has made it evident that one thread of continuity of Chilean history before, during, and after Pinochet has been the hegemony, to varying degrees over time, of exactly those social structures that most concerned Julieta Kirkwood: liberalism (and traditional political parties), (neoliberal) capitalism, and patriarchy.[7] Obviously, recognizing these continuities in recent Chilean history is not meant to gloss over the **overt** violence and authoritarianism of the Pinochet years, nor to assert that nothing has changed for the better in Chile since 1988, but rather to unearth (à la Kirkwood) the **covert** violence that links the basic assumptions of liberal democracy to its more extreme authoritarian and neoliberal incarnations. By the same token, these observations are not intended to negate the achievements of the center-left Concertación coalition,[8] but instead to recognize that its stability has come at a significant cost: the marginalization of many dissenting social actors from the political stage. Only time will tell if Chilean society, in the era of Pinochet's recent legal drama, and with the election of the socialist Ricardo Lagos to the presidency, will consolidate these trends, or open a different path toward greater social inclusiveness and collective memory.

As I turn to Isabel Allende's work within the context of Chile's democratization process, I am reminded of a panel discussion at the 1990 Encuentro Nacional de Arte [National Encounter for the Arts], in which the playwrights Egon Wolff and Ramón Griffero reflected on recent theater and film in Chile. While describing how his own generation of 1950 differed from subsequent generations of writers, Wolff emphasized, somewhat nostalgically, the primacy of storytelling in his day. Contemporary theater, he lamented, had witnessed "la muerte de la fábula":[9] literature no longer told stories. The younger playwright Griffero responded that "la fábula sigue, pero exige otra forma teatral" [storytelling continues, but it requires new theatrical forms].[10] Griffero went on to stress, as I have in the preceding chapters, that the coup created a deep break in the collective faith in utopias, and a profound questioning of language to conceive of transformative historical projects. After 1973, literature, like history itself, could no longer be epic; it would, by necessity, take other more problematized forms.

In contrast to Wolff's nostalgia and Griffero's sense of rupture, Isabel Allende has stated that, "I feel that writing is an act of hope, a sort of communion with our fellow men.... I believe in certain principles and values:

love, generosity, justice. I know that sounds old-fashioned."[11] At a time when much Chilean literature was breaking down under the weight of historical crisis, Isabel Allende had resolved to tell stories. Born in 1942, Allende (whose father was a cousin of the slain president)[12] is chronologically a contemporary of Dorfman and Benavente, and her narrative embraces the "large" qualities of the great Latin American novels of the 1960s. As a woman who began publishing in the 1980s, however, Allende is a peer to Barros and Eltit, and her popularity has made her a unique emblem of the explosion of Latin American women writers that emerged internationally in that decade.[13] At the same time, Allende's emphasis on *la fábula*, captured by her character Eva Luna in the epigraph above, aligns her with the storytelling of Wolff's generation of 1950.[14] Overall, the transgenerational quality of Allende's work gives the sense that it is timeless, even as it could only have been produced during the 1980s (in terms of form and content). But unlike many Chilean authors writing after 1973, Isabel Allende's narrative answers the collective need for assurance that life could go on, that history would continue after Pinochet.

It certainly is not difficult to imagine the attractiveness of such a message, whether from the perspective of the dominant culture—the consumer society's desire to be freed from the fetters of history—or perhaps more significantly, from the viewpoint of resistance cultures experiencing the fatigue of a seventeen-year fight to end the dictatorship. Allende's readers (among whom I of course place myself) are not merely passive or naïve receptors, but active agents who choose to read her novels for their own specific reasons. We must assume that Allende's enormous popularity, especially in the Chilean context, means that her work speaks to real dilemmas in the lives of the nation and of readers themselves. My hypothesis, then, is that reading Allende has continued to accomplish something (or some range of things, albeit often contradictory) for the healing of a country divided and fatigued by the experience of authoritarianism. In my view, Allende's narrative is instructive precisely because it illuminates those deeply entrenched ideologies that unite both the left and the right in Chile's democratization process. Ultimately, what joins these viewpoints are classical liberal assumptions about the individual and a tacit approval of neoliberal capitalism as democratic Chile's economic mode, beyond the Pinochet years. I hope to reveal here that Isabel Allende's popularity, like the stability of the Concertación governments of Aylwin and Frei, rests upon the author's (and the government's) **not** challenging the "self-evident truths" that justify both economic neoliberalism and the social structures of power that support it (especially class and gender). In short, Allende's stories seduce, like liberal democracy itself, because after seventeen years of dictatorship, they give us exactly what we want: a happy ending.

Beginning with *The House of the Spirits* (1982), and continuing with *De amor y de sombra* [*Of Love and Shadows*] (1984) and *Eva Luna* (1987), Isabel Allende embarks on a project to narratively restore *la fábula*, the epic whole, and the possibility for stories to end happily. In her "Writing as an Act of Hope," Allende notes that "maybe, this literature says, it's not true that we are perverse and evil. Maybe the idea of original sin is just a terrible mistake. Maybe we are not here to be punished. . . ."[15] Allende narratively counters the evil in society with a promise of redemption, of restored innocence. The romance formula fits nicely with this vision, since, as Janice Radway has pointed out, such love stories presuppose a happy ending; the variance that stimulates reader interest and pleasure is not this inevitable result, but rather the **process** leading up to it. Although romances are typically told from the female protagonist's point of view, they must, Radway writes, "chronicle not merely the events of a courtship but **what it feels like** to be the **object** of one."[16] As we shall see, the status of women as subjects or objects of the narrative gaze proves a problematic point in Allende's work; not to be questioned, however, is the harmonious resolution each novel assumes from the start.

At the same time, Allende's redemptive authorial stance veils an underlying tension, in that her reassuring narrative gestures require an implicit suppression of the hardship and violence—the historical *crisis de proyecto*, the decidedly **un**happy ending—that the coup meant for opposition communities after 1973. For most Chileans, the struggle for community-based survival during the postcoup years was anything but pleasant or easy; hope was embodied in the many physical, political, and discursive acts of local resistance to the regime's domination. It is because the costs of historical struggle are repressed in her work that Isabel Allende's narrative allows for a collective sigh of relief, a bit of rest, and a dose of pleasure. However, Allende's engaging *fábulas* might well risk marginalizing the very opposition communities she would wish to reassure. In this regard, the tensions in Allende's wishful thinking point toward the thorny paradoxes of Chilean society at large: the need to balance memory and forgetting, past and future, justice and reconciliation. Even as I argue here in favor of the former (i.e., collective memory) as a precondition for progressive social change, I must recognize that there are Chileans who may have very good reasons for wanting to forget.

Allende's tendency to separate her stories from an embodied, material history becomes greater over the course of her literary trajectory. In *The House of the Spirits*, history is represented as a collective process, if localized in an epic tale of a single family. By contrast, *Of Love and Shadows* takes an historical event—the pivotal 1978 discovery of several corpses of the disappeared at Lonquén—and displaces resistance from the actual community-based process to a crossing of middle-class heroism and working-class magic. Eventually, magic,[17] or history as a bodiless spirit, becomes the overarching trope in Allende's work. Although I will limit my remarks to Allende's first two novels, it is worth noting that by the 1987 and 1989 *Eva Luna* diptych, we are left with universalized archetypes acting against a fairy tale backdrop, from which history has completely disappeared.[18]

Within this literary trajectory, Allende's first novel is her most ambitious. Although the country is never named, *The House of the Spirits* traces a century of Chilean history through the tale of the Truebas, a prototypical family of the landowning elite. In addition to linking this family with large events in the nation's history,[19] Allende's insights on gender provide a potentially intriguing connection to the emergent feminism in postcoup culture. Specifically, *The House of the Spirits* locates authoritarian violence in traditional forms of masculinity (as seen especially in the *macho* patriarch, Esteban Trueba), even as it validates the multiple roles women have played in twentieth-century Chile (by emphasizing the family's matrilineage, from the early suffragist Nívea del Valle to the rebellious student Alba Trueba). Allende also attempts to stretch the romance formula to include explicit scenes of the violence ensuing from the 1973 coup, the most significant event in this story: "de una plumada, los militares cambiaron la historia universal" (337) [{w}ith a stroke of the pen, the military changed world history] (383). As a result, at least in the international sphere, *The House of the Spirits* may have spread the word about Chile's recent history to people who otherwise might have known little about it.

Despite these noteworthy aspects, however, *The House of the Spirits* ultimately holds out the promise of collective reconciliation in such a way as to risk undercutting the novel's thematic achievements. If indeed "los militares cambiaron la historia universal" [the military changed world history], how is it that there is no struggle involved in telling this story, that there are no uncomfortable questions engaged by the narrators of this text? In other words, if this is not the same old story of authorial and authoritarian domination, why is it told as if it were? By taking a closer look at *The House of the Spirits*, we find history employed as a trope for creating suspense that, despite promising possibilities, in the end evaporates, for better and for worse, in favor of upholding the hierarchical status quo.

One of the most sweeping reductions of history in *The House of the Spirits* stems from the novel's allegorical structure. Beginning with Esteban Trueba's rebuilding of the countryside ranch "Las Tres Marías" [The Three Marías] in the early chapters, Allende portrays Chilean history as an epic conflict between the oligarchy/landowners and the workers/*campesinos*, between Esteban Trueba and all the Garcías. (This oligarchy/worker conflict also provides the basis for politics in the city later in the novel). Although undoubtedly this is one of the central conflicts in twentieth-century Chile, it is not the only one. Indeed, the mediation of the oligarchy/*campesino* conflict, like mitigation of political tensions between parties of the right and left, had until 1973 been more successful in Chile than in many Latin American countries, due to the strong presence of the political center, and a strong collective belief in liberal democracy itself. This is not to say that Allende's allegory simply needed a Christian Democrat or two to be complete, but that her entire worldview of history as a conflict between political extremes is overly simplistic. It creates a void in the middle into which the author might step with the magic of resolution (the epic sweep of the romance formula), without having to take into account the troublesome, contradictory, and necessary historical agency of the political center, or of the symbolic middle ground. This is particularly ironic given that Allende's own position most closely reflects the political center; but instead of making explicit the tensions in this position, Allende narratively smooths out the wrinkles of difference by keeping conflict safely diffused within the conventions of the historical romance.

Allende's desire to create seamless reconciliation between pairs of political extremes emerges as a pattern as the novel progresses. One example takes place at the moment of Blanca and Pedro Tercero García's post-1973 exile. Decades of the Esteban Trueba/García class conflict—and of father-daughter gender and generational conflict—are magically resolved after Esteban Trueba suddenly asks for his daughter's forgiveness:

> —No he sido un buen padre para usted, hija—dijo—. **¿Cree que podrá perdonarme y olvidar el pasado?**
> —¡Lo quiero mucho, papá! —lloró Blanca echándole los brazos al cuello, estrechándolo con desesperación, cubriéndolo de besos.
> Después el viejo se volvió hacia Pedro Tercero y lo miró a los ojos. Le tendió la mano, pero no supo estrechar la del otro, porque le faltaban algunos dedos. Entonces abrió los brazos y los dos hombres, en un apretado nudo, se despidieron, **libres al fin de los odios y los rencores que por tantos años les habían ensuciado la existencia**. (emphasis mine, 346)

> ["I haven't been a good father to you, my dear," he said. **"Do you think you'll ever be able to forgive me and forget the past?"**
> "I love you so much, Papa!" Blanca wept, throwing her arms around his neck, clasping him to her ardently, and covering his face with kisses.
> After that the old man turned to Pedro Tercero and looked him in the eye. He stretched out his hand, but he did not know how to shake Pedro's hand because it was missing several fingers. Instead, he opened his arms and the two men said goodbye in a tight knot, **free at last of the hatred and rancor that had poisoned their lives for so many years**. (my emphasis.] (emphasis mine, 393–94)

We must remember that, until this point, deep resentment had characterized the relationships shared by these characters: for Esteban, Pedro was the uncivilized peasant who arrogantly stole his daughter's virginity and organized the masses against him; for Blanca, her father was the tyrant who repeatedly thwarted her love affair with Pedro; for García, Esteban represented all that was wrong with the oligarchy, not to mention the reason his fingers were cut off—a bodily reminder of Trueba's violence. Yet these deeper conflicts are never addressed. Instead, love is presumed to conquer all. However, unlike the concept of love in Pía Barros's work, founded on memory and connections with community, love in this scene requires forgetting shared history: "¿Cree que podrá perdonarme y olvidar el pasado?" [Do you think you'll ever be able to forgive me and forget the past?]. The young couple must forget that their exile was required by a regime initially supported by Trueba; they must overlook the fact that he had not modified his worldview, or done anything in particular to merit their forgiveness. They must simply forgive and forget if they are to achieve harmony.

The reader, too, is asked to make a "leap of faith" (in Catherine Boyle's words)[20] about Trueba's goodness in the exile scene. In the chapters leading up to this point, Allende portrays Trueba as the chief representative of a larger culture of authoritarianism that receives its ultimate expression in the military regime—one of the novel's greatest insights. As one of the narrators, Esteban touts his anti-Marxist stance, and places himself in the vanguard of those who provoked the coup. Hence, the seeds are planted in the text to develop connections between the day-to-day authoritarianism of the patriarch Trueba and the eventual military violence. But as Catherine Boyle has pointed out, Esteban instead ceases to believe that the regime is good just at the moment when readers might have to condemn his authoritarian values (after 1973). The "leap of faith" required of readers, then, is to believe Trueba's change of heart about the regime, although his authoritarian attitudes otherwise remain intact.[21]

As a result, Allende also asks her readers to separate Esteban's authoritarianism from that of the authoritarian state, despite her having linked the two earlier in the novel. Boyle rightly asserts that Allende thereby denies the sort of reading she seems to call for in earlier sections of the novel.[22] By ultimately divorcing the two forms of authoritarianism, Allende represses a deeper contemplation of fascism as coming from within patriarchal culture, instead favoring the familiar (and amnesiac) response that authoritarianism in Chile was merely an "aberration."[23] In this way, Allende exempts Trueba (and others like him) from his (their) responsibility in the history of terror that came to pass after 1973. We, as readers, are asked "to forgive and forget" Esteban Trueba's link to the military regime. Allende herself does so, as Trueba's status as a first-person narrator in the novel is never problematized in the text.

Yet it is worth bearing in mind **why** a premium might be placed on harmonious reconciliation, and why this theme might be popular within the Chilean context. In the name of safeguarding institutional stability after Pinochet, previously conflictual factions began in the mid-1980s to take a "kid glove" approach toward one another, suppressing conflicts in order to achieve the unity necessary to defeat the regime. Under the coalition governments of the early 1990s, deeper social demands were voluntarily, and perhaps necessarily, silenced so as to avoid threatening the stability of the nascent democracy. At the most visible level, the Aylwin government's euphemistic response to Commander-in-Chief Pinochet's "military exercises" *(ejercicios de enlace)* in December 1990, the relative lack of protest against neoliberalism's continuing negative impact on the poor, the conciliatory tone of the Commission for Truth and Reconciliation's (Rettig) Report, and the special penal arrangements granted to the former head of secret police, Manuel Contreras, in 1996 are various cases in point.[24] And yet Chile's democracy has paradoxically **not** deepened, writes Manuel Antonio Garretón, precisely because many social demands have gone unexpressed for so long.[25] Although the process of social expression has certainly begun to emerge since 1996 (e.g., student protests against the *ley de modernización* [modernization law] affecting national universities, strikes by teachers and health workers, demands presented by the indigenous populations to government leaders, and most recently, the powerful explosion of protests surrounding Pinochet's eighteen-month house arrest and subsequent return to Chile), the country clearly faces the challenge of achieving a deeper level of political consolidation.

As regards Isabel Allende, then, the author's and readers' desires to produce and consume a nonproblematized sense of reconciliation is at once comprehensible and paradoxical. It is understandable, because Allende's work narratively resolves tensions affecting many Chileans' daily lives, symbolically healing collective pain, and in the process fostering values (e.g., the "forgive and forget" ethos) that in turn make liberal democracy possible. And it is a paradox, since repression of historical conflicts, rather than their resolution, provides a precarious base for moving into the future. Such silences in the end may jeopardize the very process they were supposed to consolidate and deepen, democratization itself.[26]

Returning to the novel, many critics have noted that its magical realism[27] recedes once the specific circumstances of the coup and military terror encroach on the family's lives.[28] This contemporary history emerges strongly in the last three chapters, which mark a move from a period in which spirits reigned to a period in which torturers "become the kings of the new order," as Marjorie Agosín notes.[29] As becomes clear, however, these material agents never quite overtake the text. On the contrary, it is at precisely those novelistic moments in which the sheer violence of postcoup history threatens to overwhelm the idealism of the romance formula, that the formula remains most stubbornly intact. Allende's last three chapters are replete with examples of this dualistic logic (romance over history, idealism over materialism), as character after character comes up against the regime's violence.

The repression of conflict in Blanca's reconciliation with her father finds a strong echo, for example, in her daughter Alba's dissonant response to being released from the concentration camp, where she was tortured at the hand of Trueba's bastard son, Esteban García. Instead of talking about the hardship underlying her survival in the face of pain, Alba blithely notes that: "Lo último que oí al salir fue el coro de mis compañeras. . . . Yo iba llorando. **Allí había sido feliz**" (emphasis mine, 375) [The last thing I heard when I left was the chorus of my friends. . . . I wept as I walked. **I had been happy there**] (emphasis mine, 427). Alba's cellmate also seems untouched by the violent treatment to which she had been subjected, reacting only to her induced abortion to remark: "No importa, algún día tendré otro [hijo]—dijo a Alba cuando volvió a su celda" (361) ["It doesn't matter," she told Alba when she returned to her cell. "Someday I'll have another {child}"] (412). It is important to recognize that these passages do show that the cumulative effect of violence on a society is numbness to terror, a collective dissonance in the face of hardship. We might credit Allende for capturing one of the strongest popular responses to the regime's atrocities, this tendency to distance one's sense of self from violence in order to regain a feeling of normalcy. Again, Allende's implicit fulfillment of this wish, of the desire for stability, might explain why her work was so appealing, and so widely read within Chile (and in other Latin American countries under authoritarianism). After all, in a context of terror, what is wrong with a little rest, with producing and consuming a dose of "normalcy"? We should not sell short the positive impact of such a return to normalcy—including the democratic transition—on many Chileans' lives.

At the same time, I find the placid, almost glib, quality of each character's attitude toward violence in the above passages to be deeply disturbing. In each case, atrocities have occurred which potentially threaten the coherence of both the characters and the text. And yet it is as if history touches no one. Instead, conflict serves here merely to provoke the desire of resolution, and true to the romance genre's conventional fulfillment of such desires, Allende quickly invokes the yearned-for response. Similar to advertising's promises, the fulfillment of desires in Allende's work comes as readily as a hopeful smile or a quick embrace. In final analysis, the romance formula, like the neoliberal marketplace and Chile's democratic consolidation, rely centrally on fleeing from the materiality of violence and from the painfully embodied agency of resistance to achieve their goals.

With these issues in mind, the final passages of the novel are its most unsettling. After Alba has returned from days of rape and torture at the hands of Esteban García, she decides that she must begin writing her story, building upon the family history jotted in Clara's "cuadernos de anotar la vida" (380) [notebooks that bore witness to life] (432). Why does she decide to write? The novel's penultimate passage reveals both Alba's and the author's contradictory answers to that question:

> Escribo, ella escribió, que la memoria es frágil. . . . Por eso mi abuela Clara escribió en sus cuadernos, para ver las cosas en su dimensión real y para burlar la mala memoria. Y ahora yo busco mi odio y no puedo encontrarlo. . . . Me será muy difícil vengar a todos los que tienen que ser vengados, porque mi venganza no sería más que otra parte del mismo rito inexorable. Quiero pensar que mi oficio es la vida y que mi misión no es prolongar el odio, sino sólo llenar estas páginas mientras espero el regreso de Miguel, mientras entierro a mi abuelo . . . , mientras aguardo que lleguen tiempos mejores, gestando la criatura que tengo en el vientre, hija de tantas violaciones, o tal vez hija de Miguel, pero sobre todo, hija mía. (379–80)

> [I write, she wrote, that memory is fragile. . . . That's why my Grandmother Clara wrote in her notebooks, in order to see things in their true dimension and to defy her own poor memory. And now I seek my hatred and cannot seem to find it. . . . {I}t would be very difficult for me to avenge all those who should be avenged, because my revenge would be just another part of the same inexorable rite. . . . I want to think that my task is life and that my mission is not to prolong hatred but simply to fill these pages while I wait for Miguel, while I bury my grandfather . . . , while I wait for better times to come, while I carry this child in my womb, the daughter of so many rapes or perhaps of Miguel, but above all, my own daughter.] (432)

Does Alba write for—or against—memory? Although she says she is doing the former, the subtext of this passage reveals a strong desire for the latter. It seems improbable, no matter how much of a pacifist Alba might be, that she would emerge from torture and rape, with her lover disappeared, and her grandfather freshly deceased, simply to say, "Y ahora yo busco mi odio y no puedo encontrarlo" [And now I seek my hatred and cannot seem to find it].

Most disturbing, it seems to make no difference to Alba whether her pregnancy resulted from rape by the soldiers or from lovemaking with Miguel. In suggesting this, Alba implicitly erases herself and her desires and pain, instead representing her body/womb as a medium for reconciliation between the opposing factions of men (Esteban García versus Miguel, military versus civilians). Paradoxically, then, even as Alba seems to claim agency by becoming a narrator—this is her first first-person interlude in the entire novel—she actually uses her words only to objectify herself, repressing female subjectivity for the men's benefit.[30] Hence, this passage at once reinscribes the dominant, male-centered viewpoint, and suggests that both writing and women provide tools for avoiding the painful parts of the past, instead of for fortifying "fragile" memory. Due to Allende's liberal conception of social reconciliation, Esteban Trueba never loses his narrative power in this text, and Alba never fully gains the ability to tell her own story. Alba's self-effacement shows that being a woman writer does not necessarily make one a feminist.[31]

The final passages of the text also rewrite the status of Trueba's bastard son, Esteban García. Throughout the novel, García subtly replaces the powerful patriarch Trueba as the true villain of the story. It is no coincidence that Trueba's physical stature diminishes as García rises to power.[32] In a sense, however, the villainous García is an easy target, marginal in class and family status, and extreme in his exercise of violence to integrate himself into the power structures that had excluded him. García plays out his desire for power through sexual overtures directed towards Alba, from the time she is a toddler through his eventual rape and torture of her. In Alba's childhood, García "[d]eseaba hacerle daño, destruirla, pero también quería seguir oliéndola ... con un esfuerzo mínimo podía estrangularla.... [T]omó la mano de la criatura y la apoyó en su sexo endurecido" (253–54) [He wanted to hurt her, destroy her, but he also wanted to continue smelling her ... he could strangle her with very little effort.... {He} took her hand and placed it on his stiffened sex] (286). Upon initial reflection, García's sustained efforts to overcome marginality seem to offer an explanation of the working-class rage expressed by police and military men after the 1973 coup. More subtly, however, García's assent to the role of evil authoritarian actually diverts attention—and responsibility for violence—from the traditional patriarch (Trueba) to himself (and the working class/*campesinos*). Held responsible in this way, the illegitimate bastard, not the oligarch, becomes the proper object of our fears; the proletariat is blamed for authoritarian violence, while the owners of Chile are let off the hook. García thus provides the final mechanism for "othering" authoritarianism, and for placing responsibility **away** from those with social privilege.

It is not surprising, then, that García is the last lingering outcast in the novel, even as all other sectors of Chile (incarnate in the Trueba family) reconcile and reunite. Yet there is no way to reconcile García and Alba without indicting the social system that separates them—that is, unless Alba is prepared to forget the past and invite her torturer into the fold. When Alba accepts this solution, she states: "Sospecho que todo lo ocurrido no es fortuito, sino que corresponde a **un destino dibujado** antes de mi nacimiento y Esteban García es parte de ese dibujo" (emphasis mine, 379) [I am beginning to suspect that nothing that happens is fortuitous, that it all corresponds to a **fate laid down** before my birth, and that Esteban García is part of the design] (emphasis mine, 431). History is seen here not as a process that material participation by communities might shape and change, but as an already written story that people simply play out. The circular structure of *The House of the Spirits* likewise reinforces this notion that the story of Chile was merely its fate, its "destino dibujado." Since Alba is bound to this overdetermined (and overdetermining) "cadena de hechos que debían cumplirse" (379) [chain of events that had to complete itself] (431), she reconciles with Esteban García, representing the last of the sectors of Chile and the Trueba family to receive redemption. However, by placing Alba's acceptance of García in these terms, this passage suggests that passive resignation to fate provides the only basis for social "change."

As many critics have noted, *The House of the Spirits* invokes several tropes first employed by García Márquez in his *One Hundred Years of Solitude*, including this circular structure and the attribution of the book's authorship to another source, suggesting that the story had already been written.[33] But while García Márquez employed this mechanism to conduct a deep reading of history in *One Hundred Years of Solitude*, Isabel Allende enacts in *The House of the Spirits* a reading of García Márquez that suppresses the underlying violence that his book reveals. For example, when Alba is taken away by the police, she is described with words parallel (in cadence and verb sequencing) to the opening sentences of *One Hundred Years of Solitude:*

> Alba reconoció sin vacilar la voz de Esteban García y comprendió en ese instante que la había estado esperando desde el día remoto en que la sentó sobre sus rodillas, cuando ella era una criatura. (354)

> [Alba immediately recognized the voice of Esteban García, {and at} that moment she understood that he had been waiting for her ever since the distant day when he had sat her on his knees, when she was just a child.] (404)

The sequence in García Márquez goes on to show how Macondo lost its innocence—an invitation to historical memory—while, as we have seen, this sequence in Allende holds out fictitious innocence as a refuge from violence—an invitation to historical amnesia. Despite their overt stylistic similarities, the philosophical contrast between the two could not be greater.[34]

Perhaps a more suitable comparison to Alba's role in reconciling the nation's disputing factions of men can be found in Ariel Dorfman's drama *La muerte y la doncella* [*Death and the Maiden*], a play written in 1990, which debuted in Santiago in March of 1991. Like Alba, Dorfman's protagonist Paulina is a woman who has been tortured. While Allende's Alba is positioned between Miguel and García (left and right, civilians and military), Paulina is placed between the doctor (her torturer) and her husband (a human rights lawyer on the Truth and Reconciliation Commission). As with Alba, Paulina provides the stage and the story over which the men struggle for control, for the ability to narrate the nation's future. Like Alba, Paulina ultimately has to give up her claim to narrative power, her agency, for the nation to be healed. However, while Allende emphasizes Alba's almost naïve willingness to be the medium for the country's reconciliation, Dorfman posits Paulina's role in Chile's healing as painful, complex, and deeply problematic throughout the entire work. Through Paulina, whose sanity is in question from the very beginning of the play, the tortured female body of the Pinochet years becomes the tortured psyche of the reconciliation (memory posed against forgetting or madness). Only through Paulina's painful exorcism of her torturer's influence can the nation reach consensus, reconcile, and move on. So while both Allende's and Dorfman's female protagonists provide the sites and mediums of Chile's salvation, the two characters' attitudes could not be more different: Alba embraces her role, whereas Paulina seems painfully on the verge of being torn apart by it, even at the play's close. Though Allende and Dorfman both narratively vote for Chile's compromise in the wake of the dictatorship, Dorfman recognizes what Allende does not: that a price will be paid in sustaining this historic compromise, and that that price will not be paid easily.

Another compelling counterpart to Alba's fictitious role may be found in the disconcerting nonfiction work composed by Luz Arce, *El infierno* [*Hell*], published in 1993.[35] Although a full discussion of the *testimonio* genre surpasses the scope of this study, Arce's first-person narrative merits consideration here, as it resonates powerfully with the ideologies undergirding Allende's fiction. *El infierno* traces the onetime leftist militant's descent into the hell of torture at the hand of the DINA during the dictatorship (part 1 of the text), her eventual decision to collaborate with her captors and become one of its most effective female agents for over ten years (part 2), and her eventual confessions to the Truth and Reconciliation Commission about the human rights abuses she witnessed in this capacity (the framing prologues and part 3). This provocative and complex narrative thereby crosses any simple dichotomy of victimizer/victim, traitor/betrayed, subject/object, voice/silence—a crossing crystallized in the meaning of speech itself, as an act with simultaneous potential to redeem or betray within the very different contexts of the torture chamber, the DINA offices, and the witness stand invoked in the narrative's three parts.

In this text, however, Arce operates not within the orality of her implied speech acts in those spaces, but within the terms of literacy, of the written word. *El infierno* thus serves as much to construct (via the narration itself) the author/narrator's redemption, as to form her plea for the reconciliation of society as a whole. Moreover, both of these redemptive acts take place within a traditional Christian framework of forgiveness—Arce's spiritual counterpart to Allende's romance conventions—that eventually diffuses the most complex, ambiguous, and conflictive qualities of author/narrator and society alike by the story's end. In this regard, I should clarify that I do not intend to evaluate the words of any torture victim, or survivor of violence, as an **individual** statement to be praised or condemned. Instead, I only hope to gain some understanding of how Arce's story comes to reflect and represent the dominant values of the society in which it was produced.

From the two prologues forward (one by the priest José Luis de Miguel, the second Arce's "Palabras preliminares" [Preliminary words]), the text links the "poder perdonar y perdonarse" [power to pardon and be pardoned] with Arce's "reencuentro con el Señor" [reencounter with the Lord] (16). Only by writing and by coming to know God can she eventually "recuperar este nombre" (19), save her own name, and "[buscar] el camino que me alejara del infierno" [look for the path that would move me away from hell] (20): the hell of the past, the hell of the sinner. Like Alba, but unlike Paulina, Arce guarantees her own redemption and **inner peace** through this act of pardon, a framework set out from the beginning and reinforced through the text's final part. Thus, Nelly Richard's assertion proves quite apt, namely, that *El infierno* "mixes ... the rhetoric of sincerity ... with the artifice of an 'I' in recomposition ... play[ing] with the [same] codes of simulation and dissimulation of the democratic transition."[36] In both text and context, some bodies become revealed narratively, while others are concealed, in the name of collective reconciliation.

That the lower-middle-class Arce was one of the few female agents in the DINA, having been a female torture victim herself, invites a reading of how Arce's gender and class identities were complicated by her dramatically differing positions within various structures of power. As Diamela Eltit has pointed out, from the time Arce was a Socialist militant working for Popular Unity, she seemed to take part in a dramatic reshaping of her body in the mold of masculinity, rejecting traditional gender norms of femininity, motherhood, and the family as part of her search for gender equality.[37] Early in the text, Arce proudly claims that: "[yo] sería un 'hombre' más de la guarnición" [I would be one more "man" in the garrison] (26).

Later she adds: "Tacho, y . . . ¿yo no soy mujer? Me dio cientos de explicaciones. No me convenció, pero en esos días para mí era todo un halago ser considerada por sobre todo una militante" [Tacho, and . . . aren't I a woman? He gave me hundreds of excuses, none of which convinced me. But to me, in those days, it was a big complement to be considered first and foremost a militant] (51). Arce yearns to gain social prestige through her masculine militancy, a pattern she does not fully sacrifice until the very end of her story.

Once she is arrested, however, this masculinized (or at least de-feminized) militant is subjected to hypersexualized torture methods designed specifically to reinscribe on her body its subordinate (female) position through violence. For Arce, negotiating this violence becomes a process of identity negotiation as well. Of her resistance to torture, Arce recalls a particular moment: "Ya no pensaba en contar ni en mantener activo mi sistema muscular. Estaba entregada, doblegada, quebrada. Aunque no estaba colaborando abiertamente. Defendía muchas cosas aún" [I no longer thought about counting or keeping my muscular system active. I had given in, submitted, been broken. Although I wasn't collaborating openly. I still defended many things] (124). Here Arce narratively (re)positions herself within the process of "breaking," as her body becomes feminized. Yet part of her simultaneously clings to the masculine defense of her former position ("Defendía muchas cosas aún" [I still defended many things]), a position only broken down through the process of her repeated violation and systematic objectification: as the eventual "traidora y puta marxista" [traitor and Marxist whore] (160–61); as part of the "paquete" [package] or unit of the three female agents (196). Forced beyond gender recognition precisely because she was a rebelling woman, Arce comments that: "costaba, al menos a mí me costaba ser mujer" [Being a woman had its costs, at least for me it was costly] (210). And although the objectifying and violent act of torture had erased the possibility for female sexuality (even as it reinscribed her gender submission), Arce later must reenter that explicitly sexual economy to save her own skin: her decision to collaborate is quickly followed with a series of love affairs with her male DINA superiors (part 2). That is, Arce barters for (gender and class) authority, as well as physical salvation, using the terms of a female sexuality at once desired **and** denied by her male captors.[38] Ironically, in this aspect of her narrative self-reconstruction, Arce appears more similar to Esteban García than Alba Trueba, as she climbs into the system that had excluded her based on exaggerated gender behaviors.

In the end, however, the text diffuses these tensions around gender and power through the theme of Christian redemption (part 3). It is no coincidence that Arce's conversion to Christianity, as well as her confession of wrongs and plea for collective reconciliation, take place simultaneous to her acceptance of the traditional gender script from which she had been variously "exiled," as asexual and as hypersexual, as masculinized and superfeminized. Nelly Richard notes of Arce's conversion that

> The reiteration of the trope of obedience within a system of doctrines and commands that goes from the public to the religious . . . only reinforces the ideological convention of a submissive, faithful, and docile femininity. This convention becomes formalized in the readjustment of the sign "woman" to the traditional roles programmed by social morality.[39]

As had been the case for Paulina and Alba, the formerly tortured female body must come back under the terms of the traditional (gendered) script for collective reconciliation to take place. Arce explicitly notes that: "Vivir en Europa . . . me permitió darme cuenta de que necesito a mi familia, a mi esposo, a mis hijos y además sentí que prestar testimonio ante la Comisión 'Rettig' no era suficiente" [Living in Europe . . . permitted me to realize that I need my family, my husband, my children, and I also felt that giving my testimony before the Rettig Commission wasn't sufficient] (351). For these reasons and in this context, Arce decides to write. Thus the triple alliance of traditional Christianity-reconciliation-gender submission provides the moral for (and within and through) Arce's **story**—taking its very shape via the narrative act itself—in a circular structure not unlike that of *The House of the Spirits*. Like Alba's manuscript, Arce's text eventually reinscribes the very terms of silence it proposes to oppose.[40]

Thus Arce's position is finally a docile one, clearly much more akin to Alba's self-sacrifice than to García's dominance or Paulina's anguish. She retroactively accepts her role, and the disciplining of her body (her "domestication"), as positive. Looking back, Arce states:

> Rolf [un amante de la DINA] . . . fue **domesticándome**. Premeditado o no, me mantuvo a salvo de muchas contingencias. Me dio la poca **estabilidad** que tuve en esos años. Mal o bien, y mirada esa relación a través de los años, a pesar de todo fue buena para mí. (emphasis mine, 233)

> [Rolf {one lover in the DINA} . . . slowly **domesticated me**. Whether it was premeditated or not, he kept me safe from various potential risks. He gave me the small bit of **stability** that I had in those years. For better or worse, and looking at that relationship over the years, in spite of everything it was good for me.]

Both Arce and Alba forgive their torturers, submitting themselves—and, ideologically, their stories—to the control of the men who ultimately narrate the nation's future. In this passage, as with the first transition government itself, stability becomes the driving value behind which compromise is forged, and its various repressions are carried out.

Returning to Allende, it is clear, too, that the final resolution of conflict in *The House of the Spirits* reinforces the status quo via the protagonist's passive acceptance.[41] Alba is the female character who, despite her prior political activity, provides the goodwill necessary for salvation. In some senses, the setting aside of differences is precisely what allows the country to move on, to heal old wounds, or at least to move beyond pain as an obstacle to the future. As Alba's name suggests, Chile's "new dawn" could be just around the corner, if we were all to "forgive and forget." Yet it is not merely goodwill—but self-effacement—required of this woman who, instead of confronting her past, must for the good of the nation become the mother of the future: "gestando la criatura que tengo en el vientre, hija de tantas violaciones, o tal vez hija de Miguel, pero sobre todo, hija mía" (380) [carry{ing} this child in my womb, the daughter of so many rapes or perhaps of Miguel, but above all, my own daughter] (432). She must, in short, become the bodiless spirit, the symbolic mother of a fictional Fatherland where history no longer exists. Might something similar not be said of the current status of those female protagonists of resistance during the Pinochet years?

It is important to remember that Alba is not the only female character in *The House of the Spirits* to have rebelled. As I have suggested, each of the Trueba women's protests links her to her era, and to a lineage of Chilean women's challenges to the male dominance of their society.[42] Although Nívea del Valle's suffragists were blind to their own class privilege, they nonetheless did name their society as patriarchal, and provided a legacy of protest for future generations. For her part, Clara discovers the material world after an earthquake at mid-century, for the first time working with others for their collective survival; later, she refuses to speak to Trueba in protest of his violence towards her. Blanca, on the other hand, engages in her own private sexual revolution, through her cross-class affair with Pedro Tercero and her decision to become a single mother. Finally, as we have seen, it is Alba Trueba who becomes the most politicized of all the women; in the aftermath of the coup, she actively works in the opposition, and is imprisoned and tortured for her transgressions. However, with the exception of Alba, who acts publicly and politically and is punished for it, the Trueba women's political actions are exceptional events that break the routine of their lives. Despite their significant rebellions, they never fully challenge the course of a public, male-centered history based (in Allende's terms) on class conflict. Instead, they remain peripheral to that history, marching to the beat of spirits who both empower and limit them to private rebellion, and to ruling their separate sphere.[43]

In fact, by contrast to *El infierno*, Allende relies on the separateness of this world of women as the basis for narratively granting social redemption. Just as Allende resolves differences between oligarchy and *campesinos* through the romance formula, she negotiates gender difference based on an implicit faith in the spiritual superiority of women, who will save the collective from destruction. After all, it was Blanca's immediate goodwill, in the exile scene, that saved the relationships involved. It is telling that the language used in that scene invokes purity, for washing away "los odios y rencores que por tantos años les habían ensuciado la existencia" [the hatred and rancor that had poisoned their lives for so many years]. Indeed, the women's link to restored innocence is underscored by the connotations of all their names: Nívea [snow-white], Clara [clear], Blanca [white], Alba [dawn]. Only because they inhabitant a "pure" separate sphere, outside of (and presumably uncontaminated by) male-centered history, do the women become the sole agents for spiritual cleansing through love. In final analysis, it is clear that Allende's allegorical conception of history as a conflict between Esteban Trueba and all of the García males risks undercutting her overt validation of women as historical agents.[44] It is worth noting, too, that Allende's oppositional logic simultaneously thwarts any reading that would deconstruct the binaries at the center of her work (romance/history; spiritual/material; private/public; feminine/masculine). Not only is Allende not postmodern, but she systematically denies that possibility to her readers as well.

Overall, in *The House of the Spirits*, female spiritual superiority is **not** gained through material and discursive struggle as it is in Dorfman's *Widows*. It is instead simply endowed upon the women as an essential character trait.[45] Allende suggests that the women are simply good, and for that reason alone will save us, despite a postcoup context in which being good provided no guarantee of anything. Hence, it becomes unclear how, exactly, women might intervene in history. In final analysis, it is because Allende nostalgically **desires** that salvation be possible, that she makes it possible, at least in her world of romance. Like her character Eva Luna (cited in my epigraph), Allende recreates life the way she would like it to be.

At the same time, who wouldn't like to believe—as many radical feminists have—that such a female-centered redemption might be possible?[46] Isn't some version of this desire also behind the maternal politics of Women for Life and the Agrupación, despite these groups' decisively public stance? And as for the romance, might not a popular cultural form offer the best vehicle for expanding the base for resistance beyond a politicized vanguard? Finally, why not reaffirm the power of individual actions as society's salvation, particularly at a time when liberal assumptions provided a common language for the rearticulation of a shattered social body? Such desires for safe alternatives to authoritarianism are surely involved in Allende's popularity, and speak to the power of romance to seduce readers and, perhaps, to symbolically heal collective wounds. At the same time, it seems regrettable that Allende narrows the parameters of social change to the comfortable old terms of a liberalism that in final analysis vilifies the proletariat, while also marginalizing the protagonism of the same women whose accomplishments she hopes to validate.

Overall, *The House of the Spirits* suggests that, contrary to Allende's own claim, it is not so crucial that "los militares cambiaron la historia universal" [the military changed world history]. They were merely acting out a story already written, completing their vague fate, their "destino dibujado." And although *The House of the Spirits* might have educated some international readers to recent Chilean history, it more likely just confirmed what the North already desires and "knows" about Latin America: that this Southern "other" is magic and violent, exotic and authoritarian, and condemned not by history but by fate. Readers from **all** contexts are thereby absolved of both historical agency and responsibility for their (our) part of the evil in this story. This is another of the novel's most seductive, and politically problematic, messages.

MIDDLE-CLASS HEROISM, *CAMPESINO* MAGIC

For all of these contradictions, however, *The House of the Spirits* does suggest that there is an interrelationship between the stories of family and nation. By contrast, Allende's second novel, *Of Love and Shadows* (1985),[47] eschews collective history in favor of a focus on individual heroism. Since Allende based this novel on an actual occurrence—the 1978 discovery of fifteen cadavers in a Lonquén mine—*Of Love and Shadows* invites a comparison between the historical event and Allende's popular rewriting of it.[48] However, such a comparison should not be done to advocate a more "accurate" fiction, but rather to unearth the presuppositions about history that the author's text rests upon. This analysis reveals that, unlike Dorfman's *Widows*, *Of Love and Shadows* subtly marginalizes the long community-based struggle for the power to name and narrate disappeared bodies in postcoup Chile. That is, Allende rewrites the Lonquén discovery as an extraordinary achievement by a middle-class couple who neither rely on nor are responsible to the collective historical process. As we shall see, Irene and Francisco effectively subsume history with their own egotism, reinscribing the dominant ideologies in their response to the bodies they find. But like *The House of the Spirits*, this is a love story, so it must end happily.

As I discussed at length in chapter 2, the issue of the disappeared galvanized the Chilean opposition after 1973, led by those predominantly working-class women who had organized themselves to demand accountability of the regime. It is well known that by the 1978 discovery at Lonquén, a groundswell of voices, stories, and denouncements had surfaced, pointing solidarity workers in the direction of this (and other) clandestine tombs. By this time, the Association of Family Members of the Detained-Disappeared had completed several significant public acts, such as hunger strikes and a series of protests, in addition to the less visible grassroots work they had carried out since 1974. A group of predominantly middle-class female journalists had made headway in gaining privileged information from some military officials on the violent tactics they had employed after the coup. For its part, the Vicariate of Solidarity had compiled extensive lists of human rights abuses, and international pressure on Chile was mounting. Just one week before the Lonquén discovery, the Catholic Church had held a ten-day international conference on human rights that further focused negative attention on the Pinochet regime. The conference was still going on when a group consisting of the bishop Enrique Alvear, the vicar Cristián Precht, several church members, and diverse reporters and newswriters followed up on a tip Precht had received. They traveled to the Lonquén mining kilns, and excavated the remains of fifteen *campesinos* who had been arrested, assassinated, and secretly buried there in 1973. This was the first such discovery, and it provided an unflinching public indictment of the regime, in the form of weighty material evidence: fragmented human bodies that could substantiate those stories told and retold about the disappeared. By any measure, the 30 November 1978 discovery at Lonquén represented a culmination of years of collective work and enormous risk-taking, as communities struggled from the bottom up to reclaim their loved ones and to represent themselves.[49]

As Allende tells this story, only one of the historical agents I have mentioned is emphasized: the upper-middle-class female reporter, Irene Beltrán. Throughout the novel, Irene is accompanied by the son of Spanish Civil War exiles, a young photographer named Francisco Leal, with whom she eventually falls in love. Francisco and Irene, privileged couple and the heroes of this romance, are cast as the only active agents in this story. Although Francisco and Irene rely on information from a *campesino* family, the Ranquileos, for discovering a clandestine tomb at "Los Riscos" mine, that family is portrayed as incapable of entering the historical process themselves. Instead, the Ranquileos ask Irene and Francisco to search on their behalf for their disappeared family members. The *campesino* family thus provides a passive foil for the heroism of these middle-class characters.

As the novel progresses, each Ranquileo becomes aligned with hysteria, superstition, or magic, which heightens the difference between our urban heroes and the rural *campesinos*. In fact, Irene and Francisco meet this family precisely because they are so novel. The couple goes to the countryside to interview the daughter, Evangelina, because she is rumored to be "una especie de santa. Dicen que hace milagros . . . quita verrugas, cura el insomnio y el hipo, reconforta la desesperanza y hace llover" (16) [a kind of saint. They say she works miracles . . . removes warts, cures insomnia and hiccups, comforts the forlorn, and makes it rain] (11). Evangelina's visionary seizures occur regularly at noon, drawing miracle seekers from all around. Through this sort of "magical" characterization,[50] Allende makes eccentric, seemingly antiquated practices and desires the province of her *campesino* and working-class characters, and shows them to be marginal to the "progress" of modern history. (Even the Beltrán's maid, Rosa, speaks using mostly proverbs or *refranes*, like a female urban version of Sancho Panza.) By contrast, Irene and Francisco are decidedly contemporary; they share motorcycle rides, wield technology like a second skin (his camera equipment, her tape recorder), and are charmed by their *campesino* and working-class *compatriotas*. Needless to say, as the glamorous protagonists, Irene and Francisco, rugged liberal individualists, seem much more attractive than the medieval "communists" (in the etymological sense), the Ranquileo family. When Allende poses this contrast, she implicitly emphasizes one set of values over the other, and locates history in the hands of the bourgeoisie, eventually erasing the potential for *campesino* and working-class agency in this story.

This core hierarchy of values drives the novel forward. In a suspenseful scene at the end of part 2 (170), Irene and Francisco scale the cordillera in search of Pradelio Ranquileo (who had deserted the Army after his sister Evangelina's disappearance). Pradelio unwittingly blurts out a military secret about the clandestine tomb, his (peasant-class) incompetence thereby fueling our (middle-class) heroes' quest, an adventure that presumably requires Francisco and Irene to face the possibility of death. And yet, when Francisco and Irene subsequently find Evangelina's remains at Los Riscos mine, a moment in which they could no longer be innocent of history's violence, innocence is what they most fervently and nostalgically desire:

Acumularon las mismas piedras en el boquete, trabajando de prisa, atolondrados y nerviosos, como si al clausurarlo pudieran borrar su contenido y retroceder en el tiempo hasta el momento en que aún ignoraban la verdad y podían permanecer inocentes en el lado luminoso de la realidad, lejos de aquel descubrimiento. Francisco tomó a su amiga de la mano y la condujo hacia la choza en ruinas, único refugio visible en la colina. (189)

[They piled up the stones they had removed, and closed the entrance, stunned, nervous, working with frenzy; it was as if in sealing the mine they could erase its contents from their minds and turn time back to the moment before they had known the truth; as if they could again live innocently in a radiant reality, removed from that awful discovery. Francisco took Irene by the hand and led her to the ruined hut, the only visible refuge on the hill.] (193)

As was the case in *The House of the Spirits*, in which conflict emerged merely to inspire resolution, *Of Love and Shadows* reveals the material realities of history only long enough to provoke the desired restoration of innocence. And just as the reconciliation imposed in the first novel left deeper conflicts unresolved, the innocence Allende promises here is based on denial of the material significance of the bodies discovered in the mine. Again Allende captures well the dissonance felt in the face of terror, the desire to quickly regain a sense of normalcy. Yet it is unsettling to see how Allende unites this escape from violence with sensuality, a frequent pairing in this novel; when Francisco takes his friend's hand, seeking refuge from what they have seen, the atmosphere is charged with erotic desire.

In the next scene, Francisco and Irene make love outside the mine shaft, the collective tomb of the missing. This is not the sort of lovemaking that Pía Barros described, in which desire connects to historical solidarity, and female subjectivity is pronounced. Instead, Allende portrays an idealized Eden which suppresses history's challenge, erases community, and objectifies Irene. Francisco is not only able to forget the body in the mine, but also to repress the material circumstances—and human connections—that led him to this place. They become mere pretexts for his amorous conquest:

[T]odas las locuras que lo condujeron a esa caverna eran sólo pretextos para llegar finalmente a ese instante precioso en que la tenía para él, próxima, abandonada, vulnerable. (190)

[{T}he insanity of the events that had led them to this cavern was but an excuse to bring him finally to this precious instant when he had her for himself, close beside him, all her guards lowered, vulnerable.] (194)

Likewise, Allende gives permission to her readers to enjoy the moment, to forget what brought them to this point, and to believe in the redemptive qualities of love. I cannot deny the power of such an invitation; it promises an end to violence, however fictitious, for a society undoubtedly strained by years of terror.

Nonetheless, the love scene reveals the exclusions upon which such redemption has been constructed. Although we might expect Irene's sexual awakening to be the moment at which she becomes a narrator of the text, her incipient subjectivity is quickly engulfed by Francisco's dominant perspective. In this scene, the narrator first identifies with Irene, then with the couple, and then sustains identification with Francisco's viewpoint:

> **Ella notó** el cambio en su respiración, levantó la cara y lo miró. En la tenue claridad de la luna **cada uno adivinó** el amor en los ojos del otro. La tibia proximidad de Irene envolvió a Francisco como un manto misericordioso. **[Francisco c]erró los párpados y la atrajo** buscando sus labios, abriéndolos en un beso absoluto cargado de promesas, síntesis de todas las esperanzas, largo, húmedo, cálido beso, desafío a la muerte, caricia, fuego, suspiro, lamento, sollozo de amor. . . . [A]spiró su aliento, . . . seguro de haber vivido hasta entonces nada más que para esa noche prodigiosa en la cual **se hundiría para siempre en la más profunda intimidad de esa mujer.** (emphasis mine, 190)

> [**Irene sensed** the change in Francisco's breathing, and raised her head to look at him. In the faint light of the moon **each read** the love in the other's eyes. Irene's warm proximity fell over Francisco like a mantle of mercy. **He closed his eyes and drew her to him**, seeking her lips, opening them in an absolute, promise-charged kiss, the synthesis of all hopes, a long, moist, warm kiss, a defiance of death, caress, fire, sigh, lament, sob of love. . . . He . . . inhaled her breath . . . certain that he had lived until then only for this miraculous night **when he would plunge forever into the depths of intimacy with this woman**. (emphasis mine, 195)

Francisco's dominance is narratively reinforced in the rest of this love scene, which describes, part by part, Irene's body. Instead of challenging these male-centered romance conventions, or even allowing Irene's perspective to enter, Allende reproduces the narrative fragmentation of the female body common in male-authored love poetry since Petrarch.[51] In portraying the couple in this way, Allende merely reinscribes the gender norms of the dominant culture (active male, passive female), even as she presumably describes an extraordinary, gender-bending woman in Irene.

Returning to Radway's observation that a romance "must chronicle not merely the events of courtship but **what it feels like** to be the **object** of one" (Radway's emphasis, 64), it seems indeed that Irene's objectification, not her subjectivity, drive forward this scene. And yet, as was the case with Alba in *The House of the Spirits*, it becomes clear that Irene's awakening serves merely to transform her (like Alba) into the means toward restored innocence, as the object of male-centered desire, and not a narrating subject in her own right. In stereotypical fashion, Irene is consistently portrayed as Francisco's muse: most evocative when mute, most desired as a passive beauty. More problematically, Irene's objectification—together with the "othering" of the peasant and working classes I have described—provide the mechanisms by which collective history is repressed. It is therefore difficult for me, despite Radway's sensitive observations, to see transformative potential in these passages of Allende's romance.

As Hernán Vidal has noted, this Eden is for our self-centered heroes only.[52] The novel continues:

> [F]ueron como el primer hombre y la primera mujer antes del secreto original. **No había espacio para otros**, lejos se encontraba la fealdad del mundo o la iminencia del fin, sólo existía la luz de ese encuentro. (emphasis mine, 191)

> [{T}hey were like the first man and the first woman facing the original secret. **There was no room for any{one} else**; the ugliness of the world and the imminence of death were far away; nothing existed but the glow of their encounter.] (emphasis mine, 196)

Although Irene and Francisco have discovered Evangelina's body, all of their subsequent energy goes to making her body (and others like hers) symbolically **disappear**, thus making their own bodies the only ones to exist in their world. Only by excluding history ("la fealdad del mundo" [the ugliness of the world]) can they become "como el primer hombre y la primera mujer antes del secreto original" [like the first man and the first woman facing the original secret].

They perpetuate this exclusion, too, even when they face Digna Ranquileo with the evidence that they have found Evangelina's corpse in the mine. Again the text emphasizes Francisco's perspective:

> Olvidando los muertos que empezaban a brotar del suelo como matas silvestres y el miedo a ser detenidos o asesinados, su mente estaba ocupada en el inagotable afán de hacer el amor. (204)

> [Forgetting the dead who were beginning to spring out of the ground like weeds, and his fear that he and Irene would either be arrested or murdered, he could think of only one thing: his eagerness to make love.] (210)

In short, Irene and Francisco disregard not only the horrors they have witnessed, but also the pain of those most affected by material history. They face Evangelina's body only long enough to pique their desire to be removed from it, to retreat from history before they become dirty, to reaffirm their sense of separateness from horror by making love in their Edenic utopia. Bent on excluding disorder, the heroes rush to restore order.

This need to flee from material history, and from the horrific other, is not so different from the attitude of the military in Chile under Pinochet; neither is it so far removed from the "kid glove" reconciliation fostered by the Concertación since 1990. In fact, this attitude describes not just Francisco and Irene, but also conveys Isabel Allende's principal narrative stance. In its nostalgia for innocence, its fear of impurity and complication, its suppression of material history, its objectification of women and the *campesino* and working classes, and its emphasis on extraordinary individuals over community-based values, Allende's narrative in *Of Love and Shadows* aesthetically replicates the ideological underpinnings—and the material realities—of Chile's neoliberal capitalist "democracy." It is important to notice how this perspective marginalizes the achievements of precisely those men and women who collectively resisted the military regime's domination from 1973 to 1990.[53] And yet Allende risks this no more, and no less, than the Aylwin and Frei governments, whose liberal assumptions about democracy and reconciliation (and implicitly, the market) she shares. But by working within the parameters of this liberal "common ground," perhaps both Isabel Allende and democratic Chile have found the broadest possible formula for their own success.

The final portions of *Of Love and Shadows* deal with Irene's being shot—a reference to the real terror experienced by many reporters during the postcoup years—, followed by her recovery, and the couple's subsequent exile from the country. Given the flight from the painful past that characterizes the novel to this point, it is no wonder that *Of Love and Shadows* ends with the world like new. The text concludes with the confident reassurance that, despite the difficulties involved in exile, everything will be resolved in time. Implicitly, readers seduced to identify with Francisco, and to desire Irene's innocence as well, might also receive the salvation denied them by an historically contingent reality.[54]

And so, Isabel Allende asserts, "I will continue to write." Her "Writing as an Act of Hope" goes on:

> I will continue to write about two lovers embracing in the moonlight, near an abandoned mine where they have found the bodies of fifteen peasants, murdered by the military. Or about raped women and tortured men and families who sell themselves as slaves because they are starving. And also— why not?—about golden sunsets and loving mothers and poets who die of love. I want to tell these stories and say, for example, that I care more for the free man than the free enterprise, more for solidarity than charity. I want to say that it's more important for me to share than to compete. And I want to write about the necessary changes in Latin America that will enable us to rise from our knees after five centuries of humiliation.[55]

It is not for lacking good intentions that Isabel Allende merits critique. Instead, it is because she—like all of us who live in stratified societies, to some degree or other—reproduces the dominant ideologies and structures of social inequality within which our cultures immerse us. There is much to be learned from Allende's political "blind spots."[56] She does not see, for example, that valuing the "free man" stems from the same liberal ideology that upholds and sustains "free enterprise." She does not see that the way she tells the story of "two lovers embracing in the moonlight, near an abandoned mine" can eradicate "the bodies of fifteen peasants, murdered by the military," instead of recuperating their stories. She does not see that her praise of individual heroes overlooks the community-based connections that form the solidarity she expressly desires. And she does not see that a happy ending just might eclipse, at least for some women and the working/peasant classes, the hope it seems to promise. In short, Isabel Allende's narrative is like a neoliberal stick figure in democratic clothes: seductive, because it doesn't **look** authoritarian, and destructive, because it colonizes nonetheless.

There are many reasons Isabel Allende's work has been so popular: its assurance that life could go on despite the dictatorship, its ostensible focus on female characters in a feminist era, and Allende's determination to tell stories (as Eva Luna says) "[para] hacer la existencia más tolerable" [to make life more bearable], when much Chilean literature did not. Allende's popularity is understandable precisely because it rests upon the same profoundly entrenched liberal ideals that shape and limit social transformation in Chile at the beginning of the twenty-first century. In many ways, Allende's popularity signals the triumph of those hidden forms of authoritarianism that, as Julieta Kirkwood repeatedly warned, neither began with Pinochet nor would end with his demise. Hand in hand with those forms of domination goes the seductive neoliberal in democratic disguise. If democratic Chile had been able to resist this tempting seduction, the post-Pinochet period might look very different indeed.

7
Epilogue

THOUGH FUTURE WORK REMAINS TO BE DONE TO ASSESS FULLY THE IMPACT THAT Chile's return to democracy has had on its cultural production, I have already revealed my disappointment that the new social movements of the Pinochet years became marginalized politically and economically under the first two governments of the center-left Concertación coalition. In fact, the first decade of Chile's "incomplete democracy"[1] suggests that it was precisely Isabel Allende, and her hidden narrative ideologies, who best represented the majority of Chileans during this time. While a tacit consensus ostensibly existed about the fact that the dictatorship had ended, large questions remained unasked. These included substantive social concerns about human rights violations and accountability, about the authoritarian enclaves guaranteed by the 1980 Constitution, about the role of the Armed Forces in the new democracy, about the equity and sustainability of the economic model, and about those left on the margins of traditional politics, among other issues. Such questions were avoided precisely because their answers could reveal just how tenuous the democratic "consensus" actually was.[2] Meanwhile, "modernization" remained a linchpin of both the Aylwin and Frei governments, and few of the enormous social costs of the Pinochet years were repaid by these still neoliberal regimes.[3]

At the same time, many grassroots communities that had banded together under the dictatorship dissolved in democracy, and not because all of their needs had been addressed. Instead, many organizations eroded due to a combination of economic pressures and what Tomás Moulian describes as the "sustained attack against the memory of the crimes of the past."[4] Although some voices continued to emphasize the collective need to remember, it was Isabel Allende's "forgive and forget" ethos—or simply a widespread fatigue with human rights issues altogether—that predominated in Chile during these years. Indeed, as recently as 1999, a full 70 percent of Chileans claimed not to care about the former dictator's eventual fate.[5]

And yet Pinochet's dramatic extradition case—which resulted from the Spanish judge Baltasar Garzón's indictment of the ex-dictator for torture and crimes against humanity—has reconfigured the Chilean political landscape, opening possibilities that were literally unthinkable a short time ago. Most remarkably, on 1 August 2000, the Chilean Supreme Court voted 14–6 to strip Pinochet of the immunity from prosecution he had enjoyed as a "Senator for Life" *(senador vitalicio)* under the 1980 Constitution of his own design. That decision, which is binding and cannot be appealed, opened the floodgates to over 200 legal cases filed against Pinochet for the human rights abuses committed under his regime. As a consequence, it appeared that the once seemingly invulnerable retired general would be held accountable for his crimes, and that this process could take place within Chile itself. At present, it is unclear if Pinochet will actually have to stand trial, since a 9 July 2001 Court of Appeals decision suspended legal action against him unless his health improves. Nevertheless, Pinochet's case has awakened passions and unearthed buried tensions around several unresolved social issues, making possible the larger dialogue necessary to deepen and consolidate Chile's democracy overall.

It is worth remembering, however, that during the time of Pinochet's seventeen months of house arrest, the widespread assumption held by international and Chilean human rights advocates alike was that Pinochet could never be tried effectively in the conservative Chilean courts. Responses to Pinochet's arrest had divided the Concertación between those who celebrated the possibilities of legal and moral accountability the case raised, and those in the Frei government who paradoxically joined the right in affirming Pinochet's diplomatic immunity and requesting his release. Pinochet's supporters contended that Chile's national and legal sovereignty had been threatened by this "sudden" globalization of human rights concerns. (That these same center-right players embraced economic globalization, while distancing themselves from its costs, remained an ironic subtext to the extradition drama). In rushing to defend Pinochet, the Chilean government at once embraced and legitimated the arguments of the right **and** gave in to pressure from the military, in effect squelching debate of alternatives and separating itself from prevailing national and international public opinion favoring Pinochet's accountability.[6] In this way, the Frei government reenacted a persistent, decade-long pattern of suppressing conflict, which ultimately favored the right. This pattern was derived from an implicit notion that placating the former dictator was necessary for democratic stability itself. And yet it was exactly this approach that had blocked a deepening of the democratic consolidation. Thus, when the British Home Secretary Jack Straw cleared the way for Pinochet's return to Chile in March 2000 because of his failing health, most observers feared that the ex-dictator would simply return to his former life, safely protected by the institutionalized impunity that had held sway in Chile since he left the presidency. Given that this did not turn out to be the case, what had changed to make it possible to bring Pinochet to justice in his homeland?

First, the Pinochet case was, in fact, much larger than Pinochet. It created an international political climate favoring, at least in theory, the prosecution of state-perpetrated human rights abuses around the globe, and the judgment of an entire cycle of authoritarianism in history.[7] Perhaps the most significant international legacy of Pinochet's case is that British and Spanish courts clearly have established the principle that crimes against humanity may be brought to trial in whatever place an accused despot may find himself. As Ariel Dorfman has pointed out, tyrants everywhere must now consider their steps, must have "their turn to feel fear," knowing that they could face serious legal consequences if they set foot outside their own countries.[8] This international push for accountability also has involved the declassification of CIA documents showing the extent of the DINA's relationship with Pinochet and the CIA, as well as investigations by Argentina and other countries into Pinochet's role in several international conspiracies.[9] Such investigations have only underscored the fact that this dictator's abuses effectively did transcend national borders.

Second, the intense international focus on the Pinochet case resulted in substantial pressure on the Chilean government to support its claims that the ex-dictator could, in fact, receive a fair trial at home. Within this context, several significant changes took place domestically. After a 1997 reform lowered the retirement age for Supreme Court justices, the complexion of the Chilean judiciary changed substantially; nearly all Pinochet appointees had been replaced by reformers by early 1999.[10] The newer judges also began basing decisions on international law, a previously discredited practice in Chile. Within this overall climate, the discourse of the right in turn began to change, as it was no longer tenable simply to deny the fact that human rights abuses had been committed under Pinochet, by labeling them "excesses" to be expected in "wartime."[11] In addition, the growing influence of a new generation of leaders in the Army, the presence of church authorities bringing renewed energy to human rights issues, and the elimination of a national holiday celebrating the 1973 coup, all fostered a domestic climate more favorable to Pinochet's prosecution.[12]

However, perhaps the most significant shift to take place in Chile resulted from Judge Juan Guzmán Tapia's reinterpretation of the 1978 Amnesty Law.[13] In a 1999 case heard in Santiago's Court of Appeals, Guzmán argued that disappearances should be considered ongoing crimes, like kidnappings, until the **bodies** of the victims were found. Only then could the crime be considered complete (in that life or death could be determined definitively) and the applicability of amnesty be assessed. This astute legal position at once kept the cases of the missing alive, a benefit to family members seeking justice, **and** provided incentive to soldiers to produce material evidence about the disappeared, for their own protection. For the first time, both sides shared the same interest: finding and identifying the corpses of the victims.

It seems fitting that Chile's collective debate on human rights should return to that battleground where the national narrative was most powerfully contested during the Pinochet years: the body. Because the issues surrounding the material and symbolic meanings of the disappeared body remain unresolved, it is only by unearthing those real bodies still elusively out of reach, and by determining a common story about the violence done to them, that the collective body might begin the process of its healing, including (rather than glossing over) its scars and disfigurings. In this context of transition, the body becomes a locus for interpretive resolution, without which the national narrative remains inconclusive, suspended, precariously unstable. However, this resolution must **not** be based on the suppression of contradiction, but on its emergence, **not** on the creation of a seamless story, but on the development of a kind of multivocal text in which moral responsibility is assigned and acknowledged. Such a story remains only partially written in Chile today, in the form of the Rettig Report and in the measures of justice established for family members of those victims it identifies. However, since the Rettig Report does not name victimizers, or require their public acknowledgment of responsibility as perpetrators of their crimes, it represents an unequal and unsatisfactory compromise, requiring much more of the victims than of the victimizers.[14] Nor does the Rettig Report take into account the **multiple** forms of violence scarring the Chilean social body during the Pinochet years—violence that may not have resulted in death, but whose effects are still being felt, individually and collectively. Only through garnering the additional material evidence so long suppressed under both the military regime and the Concertación, and with a more full recognition by the Armed Forces of their own role in committing human rights abuses, can the process of "Facing History"[15] advance, and democracy deepen.

Most recently, it is not only the bodies of the victims that have been subjects of debate, but also the body—and mind—of Pinochet himself. Santiago courts have revisited the same questions about Pinochet's fitness to stand trial first considered by Jack Straw in early 2000. At that time, the trilateral tug-of-war surrounding Pinochet—a legal contest about the effects of authoritarian violence on the bodies of others—found its displaced conclusion through a reading of Pinochet's **own** body as decrepit, frail, and unfit. Though Straw's "humanitarian" argument physically freed the former dictator to return home— where, as many cynically predicted, he "miraculously" leapt from his wheelchair into the arms of his supporters—it involved an additional irony. As scans of Pinochet's brain circulated on the internet,[16] inviting interpretation by amateurs and experts alike, it became clear that Pinochet not only had lost the hegemonic ability to narrate "other" bodies, but that he could no longer even make a unitary claim to his own. In this dramatic inversion, the dictator had been made vulnerable, even if he was not literally unfit.

In Chile, the wrangling between Pinochet's defense team, which insisted that only physical exams be admitted to assess his capacity to stand trial, and the prosecution, which insisted that only psychiatric evidence would allow the case to be dismissed, reached a compromise, in that both sets of exams were conducted and the evidence assessed. On 9 July 2001, the Santiago Court of Appeals voted 2–1 to suspend legal action against Pinochet, declaring him mentally and physically unfit to stand trial. In theory, a trial could take place if his condition improves, though this seems unlikely. In the meantime, the retired general (like seven other ex-military officials) has been banned legally from leaving his country, under an *orden de arraigo* issued by the Chilean Supreme Court. Thus, his body must remain "rooted" in Chile, the one place he never thought he would face constraints. Whether Pinochet's body and mind eventually will have to be made present in court—or are allowed to remain "missing"—it seems clear that the dictator/patriarch, and all he represents, will not escape the judgment of history. Ultimately, his regime did fail to eradicate those fragments of stories and bodies that are now being legally exhumed.

And yet this current moment in Chilean history has emerged out of more than a decade of discouraging trends. We must assess those aspects of the transition in order to situate the present moment in its complexity, in order to see what has changed in Chile, and what (as yet) has not. Clearly, the first decade after Pinochet was one in which many remained on the margins of democracy's rewards and of economic "success," while others consolidated their privilege. At the same time, this decade witnessed a progressive dismembering and atomization of many of those collective bodies that had formed under Pinochet.

In fact, within the first few years of the transition, the dissolution of grassroots organizations began to occur at an astonishing rate. Elizabeth, one *arpillerista* whom I quoted in chapter 3, wrote to me in June 1994 that:

> We women disbanded the workshop because each one of us had to look for a job in order to subsist, since crafts don't sell like they used to internationally. People think that the dictatorship ended and that democracy has arrived, but there's nothing democratic about it [se piensa que se terminó la dictadura y llegó la democracia, que de democracia no tiene nada].[17]

According to Marjorie Agosín, Elizabeth's case was not unique: only about 13 of an initial group of 200 *arpilleristas* in the greater Santiago area remained active by mid-1994.[18] Paradoxically, for these *pobladoras*, the end of the dictatorship brought a double bind: although on one hand the democratic governments of Aylwin and Frei had not done much to repay the social debt of the Pinochet years, the old subsistence strategies of selling handicrafts abroad no longer worked. This was because, as Elizabeth suggests, the *arpilleras* no longer represented denouncement of the atrocities of an undemocratic regime in the eyes of a potential foreign buyer: "people think that the dictatorship ended and that democracy had arrived."

Yet the democracy Elizabeth fought for was one which questioned the liberal assumptions that only became reaffirmed during the first two Concertación governments. In this context, Elizabeth's words offer a powerful critique both of market forces, which tend to diffuse social action, and of the shortcomings of democracy in Chile since 1990. Far from having assimilated the lessons generated in a postcoup culture critical of liberal democracy, Chile's first decade of democracy "after" Pinochet replicated the same economic and gender inequalities inherited from the past. But, in contrast to the Pinochet years, there was insufficient denouncement of these unjust realities. The poignant words of Agosín say it all: "Democracy has not improved their [the *arpilleristas*'] standard of living, and has subjected them [instead] to the deep oblivion of a nation that prefers not to speak about its past."[19] Although Chilean society may now be making a move toward recuperating the past, economic pressures have only further marginalized and isolated people like Elizabeth and Tomás, her husband. When I last visited them in June 1998, Elizabeth was doing hosiery piecework in her home for a few cents per dozen and had long abandoned feminist organizing; she and Tomás, now a taxi driver, harbor dreams of moving to Cuba.

It is particularly telling, too, with relation to those left on democracy's margins, that in 1999–2000, the popular Socialist Ricardo Lagos, a cabinet member under Aylwin and Frei and the presidential candidate for the Concertación, found himself locked in such a tight presidential race against Joaquín Lavín, the candidate for the right-wing Alliance for Chile. (Lavín, the unabashedly neoliberal former mayor of Las Condes, is a member of the ultraconservative Opus Dei, and a long-standing political ally of Pinochet's.) For Peter Winn, the favorable public response to Lavín's recasting of himself as a populist—as an "apolitical pragmatist whose sole interest was in solving the concrete problems of the people"[20]—reveals important dimensions of the political landscape in Chile today. According to Winn, Lavín's populism and his distance from the Concertación struck a strong chord with the Chilean poor precisely because they felt left out of both the country's economic prosperity and traditional party politics. Lagos, by contrast, was perceived as the candidate of continuity *(continuismo)*, and so the debilities of the Frei government became his own. In addition, Winn states that "the repression and stress on individualism during the Pinochet years" had led to an erosion of "the strong and stable [political] identifications that used to characterize Chilean society"[21]—a tendency only reinforced by neoliberalism's continuing hegemony. In this context, as in the U.S., electoral decisions have become more like consumer choices, conditioned at least as much by marketing and style (where the telegenic publicist Lavín easily surpassed the academic statesman Lagos) as by the content of the candidates' messages. Though Lagos did "win by a thread," if he winds up continuing, rather than challenging, past Concertación relations with the poor, this may well become, as Winn warns, "the Concertación's last hurrah."[22] However, Lagos's strong leadership on human rights, and his clear stand in support of Pinochet's being tried in the country, offered an early indication that this Concertación president may well lead in a more inclusive direction.

Since 1990, coeval with the fragmentation of *arpillerista* workshops and of other grassroots organizations, the larger Chilean women's movement has entered a period of crisis. In the absence of a clear common referent around which to rally, previously embodied in the authoritarian figure of Pinochet, the differences between women's organizations have proliferated. This has been positive, in terms of creating a heightened awareness among women of the many threads of difference they represent—age, class, sexual orientation, political party affiliation, and so forth. But the experience also has been negative, insofar as it has fostered not dialogue but insularity, a sort of clique orientation to activism that has proven highly destructive of the ties fostered by hardship during the Pinochet years. The conflicts I witnessed among the Chilean feminists who attended the 1990 Encuentro Feminista Latinoamericano y del Caribe [Latin American and Caribbean Feminist Meeting] in San Bernardo, Argentina, provided an early indication of the factionalism that has only grown deeper in recent years.

Since democracy's return, the tensions between *políticas* (women active through political parties) and *feministas* (women active through independent organizations), first analyzed by Julieta Kirkwood in 1982,[23] have become exacerbated as well. In effect, the return of political parties as the chief means of political expression in Chile has marginalized the very women who had been at the forefront of resistance during the Pinochet years. The return of the same set of male leaders to the political scene in the late 1980s, who provided the public voice for their parties, suggested that very little really had changed since the early 1970s. There were fewer women in Aylwin's cabinet than had been in Pinochet's, and only one female mayor (María Antonieta Saa) was appointed after the 1989 elections.

Although the tide appeared to be turning since 1993—with the creation of the Servicio Nacional de la Mujer [National Service for Women] or SERNAM, and the parties' adoption of a quota system whereby no more than 60 percent of candidates may be of the same sex[24]—many grassroots demands were not represented through these official structures.

Teresa Valdés and Marisa Weinstein provide a pithy summary of the various contextual factors that have fueled divisions within the women's movement:

> [The disarticulation of the movement] has been explained . . . as a consequence of the negotiated character of the transition, which privileged the protagonism of specialized and select political actors . . . ; as a characteristic of market democracies at the end of the century, which foster consumerism as an individual identity, relegating to the background ties of social solidarity; as a product of the fatigue engendered by the fight against the dictatorship . . . ; as a result of early frustration at the lack of participation that characterizes our democracy of spectators; or, finally, as the result of the State's 'co-optation' of important leaders of the women's movement, who saw the opportunity for action in a space where only exclusion and the reproduction of inequality existed before.[25]

So in addition to the context of fragmentation impacting social organizing overall, the women's movement faced new tensions stemming from the State's institutionalization of a feminist agenda. While feminist issues did gain increased public visibility and legitimacy through SERNAM and the political parties' quotas, the very process of governmental involvement redefined and narrowed the movement's focus. As Verónica Schild has persuasively argued, this institutionalization within Chile's neoliberal democracy has reduced feminism to a reformist "set of policy options," "technical tasks," and "market-based solutions," thereby diluting the more radical movement demands for social justice.[26] Meanwhile, as the case of Elizabeth illustrates, women figure more and more prominently among the poorly paid, underemployed, and highly exploited workers at the margins of the formal sector, whose needs are not being addressed by SERNAM or elsewhere.[27] This has only increased the feelings of alienation among working-class women vis-à-vis the democratic transition process. The government incorporation of a gender equity agenda has paradoxically exacerbated tensions between those working inside versus outside of political institutions to effect social change, and between middle-class professionals and working-class feminist activists themselves.

Thus, previous conflicts between *políticas* and *feministas* have been reinscribed along the lines of *feministas autónomas* versus *feministas institucionales*: those working independently versus those "institutionalized" in governmental or nongovernmental organizations (the so-called *femócratas* or "femocrats"). This schism became painfully obvious during the November 1996 Encuentro Feminista Latinoamericano y del Caribe [Latin American and Caribbean Feminist Meeting], held in Santiago. According to Marysa Navarro, this 1996 conference manifested in the form of personal attacks and defensive postures several underlying sources of division. First, international funding was directed toward select feminist NGOs only, which made the development of a collective local agenda more difficult (e.g., in preparation for, and in the aftermath of, the 1995 U.N.-sponsored Fourth World Conference on Women in Beijing). Second, conflicts stemmed from the incapacity of any group of women to represent the diversity of the movement. And third, the tensions reflected an inadequate rearticulation of the movement for the context of democracy.[28] Given the ongoing hegemony of market-based neoliberalism and its individualizing ethos, it is unclear how (or if) the legacy of cross-class organizing of the 1970s and 1980s—with its **simultaneous** questioning of capitalist exploitation and gender oppression—might be recuperated in Chile today.[29] Needless to say, the deep conflicts in the women's movement, posed as competing "brands" of activism (I use the metaphor intentionally), mark an impasse that has prevented a feminist common ground from being reestablished since democracy's return.

As for the official gender scripts offered by the new democratic governments, two incidents from 1994–95 prove particularly revealing of just how little had changed relative to Pinochet's emphasis on the traditional, patriarchal family as a vital ideological pillar for his regime and for society. The first of these events took place in August 1994, when a scandal surged in the media and the legislature alike, about the circulation of a postcard reproduction of a Juan Dávila painting of Simón Bolívar provocatively portrayed as a transvestite. The Venezuelan Embassy immediately expressed its disapproval of the image (as "an aggression to our national honor")[30] to the Chilean Ministry of Foreign Relations. It further criticized the fact that Dávila's work had been financed by the Chilean Ministry of Education. For his part, Ñuñoa's mayor, Juan Castillo Soto, denounced the work as an "affront" to "the fundamental values of democracy and liberty," while the Chilean ambassador Aniceto Rodríguez called it a "gratuitous insult to the great American statesman [*prócer*]."[31] This exaggerated response by public figures in both countries unmasked, in Nelly Richard's view, a previously hidden set of "nationalist histories and hysterias, ideologies of (good) taste in art, sexual repressions, Latin American mythologies, official political [scripts], and the bureaucracies [underlying] national culture."[32]

Specifically, Dávila's work provoked such a scandal because it brazenly transgressed the ideologically constructed "purities" of the nationalist (Independence) tale and its prevailing gender, ethnic, and class categories. As Richard points out, the masculine, white, oligarchical *prócer* was contaminated and confused in Dávila's painting through several "indecorous" signs: (1) of the **feminine** (gaps in Bolívar's uniform expose his breasts, ambiguous genitals, pantyhose, earrings and rouge); (2) of the **indigenous** (his darkened ethnic identity is clearly mestizo); and (3) of the **popular classes** (his obscene, streetwise, middle-finger gesture reinforces the sexualization of the image overall).[33] As the Santiago artists explained: "Dávila's postcard is not, then, a representation of Bolívar, but an essay on identity itself."[34] Stylistically, the work's combination of realistic and abstract elements, of "avant-garde modernity—and its cosmopolitan quotations—with popular realism and folklore,"[35] served to emphasize the *prócer*'s hybridity. The work also resisted standard codification by the museum, through its extraofficial circulation as a postcard, thereby "proliferating the transgressive virtuality of the image [and] disseminating its readings outside of institutional mechanisms of control."[36]

Although the transgressive quality of Dávila's work clearly struck a nerve in Venezuela (and elsewhere in Latin America), it took on a special meaning within the context of postcoup Chile. The fact that public, governmental figures rushed to restore the *prócer* (and the larger narrative of nationalism) to a "purified" state reveals the ideological continuities between Chile's dictatorship and its democracy. Both the official discourse under Pinochet and the democratic "consensus" had been constructed and consolidated by containing and reducing ambiguities, and by marginalizing transgressive stories, bodies, and identities (expressed only indirectly through denouncement of this art as in poor taste). Both governments, in effect, had relied on a "sanitized" official story. It is important to recognize, however, that the overt violence employed by the military state to these ends is subterfuged and avoided within the new democracy itself. Diamela Eltit hypothesizes that the hysteria surrounding this representation of Bolívar's body enacted a displaced exorcism of those other bodies most obviously forgotten by Chileans at that time: bodies disappeared, tortured, and humiliated by the military regime.[37]

The second event occurred in June 1995, at SERNAM's presentation to the Chilean Senate of materials prepared for the Beijing Conference on Women. After much debate, the response to SERNAM's quite moderate gender proposals was to veto the use of the concept of gender itself, which senators concluded was essentially "anti-Chilean." Kemy Oyarzún cites Gonzalo Vial:

Why use such an unusual word to refer to the sexes? Could it be to introduce . . . the notion that there are not only two [sexes], but several, [that they are] not sharply defined [*tajantes*], but with **diffuse and uncertain limits** [de límites difusos e inciertos]?[38]

In the Senate discussion, Gabriel Valdés argued that "any sort of semantic ambiguity or free interpretation" around issues affecting sex roles and the family undermined national tradition,[39] by potentially introducing and legitimating such social "aberrations" as homosexual families, sexual relations not geared toward procreation, and abortion.[40] And so the contested cultural construct of gender found an orthodox "end" in the Chilean Senate, the "authorized and legitimate territory of the Father, the site capable of containing the paradoxes and heterodoxies of marginal voices."[41]

As Oyarzún rightly holds, this Senate veto of gender discourse and its ambiguities

> not only stemmed from profound national disagreements, but also from old suspicions and fears. [It represented] the not-so-subtle rattling of certain paranoid mechanisms of the dictatorship right in the heart of this transition's consensus [en el seno consensuado de esta transición].[42]

This episode suggested that the traditional family, in its strict triadic configuration (father-mother-children), proved to be as strong an ideological support of the current political discourse as it had been under Pinochet. And yet one important difference lay in the fact that, with democracy, alternative spaces could, and had, opened up to question gender orthodoxies from within **other** public institutions (with resultant opportunities and potential contradictions). For example, in 1995, the same year as these Senate debates, the new gender studies program at the University of Chile also opened its doors.[43]

Likewise, we must not forget that at the same time as grassroots social movements faded and traditional gender scripts predominated in official discourse, some groups nevertheless were able to gain public space and to express their demands within Chile's limited democracy of the 1990s. Gays and lesbians have become more visible, starting with their presence at Aylwin's inauguration and the founding of Chile's first major gay political organization, el Movimiento de Liberación Homosexual [Homosexual Liberation Movement] (MOVILH), formed in 1991 to defend human rights and to combat discrimination in Chilean society at large. Although 1993–96 witnessed several episodes of antigay violence, as well as the internal fragmentation of MOVILH itself, gay and lesbian issues have become part of public discussion in Chile for the first time in the country's history. Publication of literature by openly gay writers like Pedro Lemebel, the ongoing radio program Triángulo Abierto [Open Triangle], and the candidacy of a few gay politicians for public office demonstrate this broadening of the discourse overall—despite the reactionary backlash illustrated in the Dávila and SERNAM incidents.[44]

Chilean students also have organized nationwide in protest of the government's continuing the neoliberal policies of "self-financing" of the public universities. The Concertación was forced to negotiate with student organizers, and to provide some partial financial concessions, in mid-1997. The May 1999 protest by some 40,000 students demanding increased funding of higher education, which resulted in the shooting death by police of one protester in Arica, drew international attention to the students' demands.[45] While we must also remember Patricio Guzmán's moving documentary portrait of Chilean students' short historical memory, and their conflicted emotional responses to confronting the recent past in *Chile: Obstinada Memoria* [*Chile: Obstinate Memory*] (1997),[46] this recent activism does suggest a political coming of age of some of those Chileans born after 1973.

Finally, the protests in 1998–99 by the long-marginal indigenous populations of Chile, who have demanded rights to their ancestral lands, also resulted in a conversation with the government—if not much else.[47] As has become clear in the case of these indigenous groups, but was also present with gays/lesbians and with the students, the Concertación governments of Aylwin and especially Frei proved adept at diffusing most social demands and at stalling long enough for many groups to dissolve under the weight of their own internal divisions. Only time will tell if any of these social issues will be more effectively addressed through policy and social changes in the context of Lagos's presidency.

As for the authors studied in these pages, many are still coping with the fact that some of their best work was done during the horrific Pinochet years. In the last chapter, I discussed Dorfman's first literary effort after the return of democracy, *La muerte y la doncella* (1991),[48] which portrayed a female torture survivor, and focused centrally on the disturbing links between traditional gender roles and authoritarian violence. This play was rejected by Santiago audiences primarily for its historical contingency—for dwelling on the painful past—as if democracy were a sufficient guarantor against the need to remember. At the same time, the lukewarm reception of both the play and its author in Santiago may have been fueled by a kind of resentment directed toward "those who left" the country by "those who stayed" during the dictatorship—a resentment aimed at exiles seen as returning in better times to "explain" pain to those who experienced it. That the play debuted in such close proximity in time to the release of the Rettig Report did not help diminish the perception of its discursiveness or increase public receptivity to the issues it raised.

By contrast, produced at a distance from its historical referents, the

English-language version of the play, *Death and the Maiden*, won major acclaim in London and on Broadway, and later became a feature film in English directed by Roman Polanski. The play has been heralded in South Africa and elsewhere for its meaningful examination of the marks of terror on victimizers and victims, as well as on those who were merely there, as active or passive witnesses. Among his subsequent works, Dorfman has published two thrillers (*Konfidenz* and *Terapia* [*Blake's Therapy*]), a personal memoir reflecting on his own biculturalism (*Rumbo al sur, deseando al norte* [*Heading South, Looking North*]), and has made a film with his son, Rodrigo, paralleling immigrant children's fears of the U.S. Immigration and Naturalization Service to the kinds of terror experienced during the Pinochet years.[49] All of this points to a heightened internationalization of this formally-exiled author's work. Perhaps history has made Dorfman realize that, despite his inevitably complex sense of who he is, "home" may be where his body has been all of these years: in the United States.

At the same time, Chilean theater inside the country has entered into a new *crisis de proyecto*. The playwright Ramón Griffero describes his own sense of uncertainty:

> Having directed all of my creative energy against a dictatorship, the change to democracy has produced in me an almost existential crisis. I've had to make the transition to a world beyond social commitment. Moreover, democracy is not the awaited sleeping beauty; it has come with the wrinkles brought on by the passage of time, and accompanied by the laws of the market.[50]

After having played such a central role in the country under Pinochet, theater groups are now experiencing a lack of collective purpose, and playwrights such as David Benavente and Ramón Griffero are facing a changed context for the production and reception of their work. In Griffero's view, the continuing neoliberalism of democratic Chile, and its concomitant consumer culture, have nourished a collective desire for pleasurable entertainment, in theater as in other cultural venues. Stated plainly, Griffero suggests that "complacent" art sells, a "law of the market" very much at odds with the socially committed work produced during the dictatorship. Although these large trends are happening at a global level as well, it is no wonder that Griffero stresses democracy's "wrinkles" after the specific experiences of creating art during the Pinochet years.

As for Pía Barros, known for her rejection of "large" narrative forms and her eschewal of the public sphere: she published a novel, entitled *El tono menor del deseo* [*The Lesser Tone of Desire*] in 1991,[51] a sign of the more solid narrative ground available to her upon democracy's return. However, in more recent years, she has published much less. Though she continues to pursue the themes of eroticism and violence in her writing, the majority of her energy has been directed towards the literary workshops that she now runs out of her home. Although she has inspired an entire new generation of writers, Barros herself seems to have retreated into this somewhat more private realm. By contrast, Diamela Eltit has launched an international literary career, teaching courses in the U.S., Europe, and Chile, after fulfilling her post as Cultural Attaché for Chile in Mexico (1990–94). Among other works, she has published the novels *Vaca sagrada* [*Sacred Cow*] (1991), *Los vigilantes* [The Nightwatchmen] (1994), and *Los trabajadores de la muerte* [Workers of Death] (1998), and continues to probe the issues of increasingly internalized forms of power operant in Chilean society today.[52] Having consolidated themselves as important, but very different sorts of literary figures, both Barros and Eltit have differently reinvented what, exactly, they are writing **for**, now that the referents they wrote **against** during the Pinochet years have become less imposing. While Eltit refuses to water down her discourse, and speaks against the complacent character of consumer culture, Barros has saved her words, for now, for other writers-in-the-making.

And what of Isabel Allende? Ironically, it took a personal tragedy—the long-term illness and death of her daughter, Paula—to lead her from the *fábula* back into her own history. In *Paula* (1995),[53] Allende has written an autobiography of surprising scope, in which she admits at least some of the painful aspects of both her life and that of her country, difficulties previously excluded from her fictional narratives. In that work, she even asserted that this personal crisis may prevent her from writing fiction again. And yet, this crisis is exactly what kept her writing. In *Paula*, one senses that Allende's self-construction feeds on her daughter's absent subjectivity, that Allende's sense of self is bolstered to a disturbing degree by her daughter's inability to act. Although this situation potentially exploits both Paula and the reader's emotions to the author's own ends, it is nonetheless significant that *Paula* marks Allende's first admitted *crisis de proyecto*, the first moment death had struck so personally as to make the author question her narrative ground—however briefly. Not even the military coup managed that. In the wake of Pinochet's 1998 arrest, Allende has taken a public stand requesting the dictator to "recogni[ze] past errors" so that "a true reconciliation among Chileans [may] begin."[54] Although Allende still takes this position within a classical liberal frame, never problematizing her own relationship to the notion of reconciliation itself, at least she has used her international popularity to stand in solidarity with the victims of the Pinochet years. And like Dorfman, Allende most recently has come full circle in her work, linking her past in Chile to the many years she has spent in the U.S. It seems fitting that her *Hija de la fortuna* [*Daughter of Fortune*] (1999),[55] about Chileans' participation in the 1848 California Gold Rush, received the ultimate popular consecration offered in the U.S.: being chosen as a selection for Oprah Winfrey's Book Club.

Finally, I come back to Julieta Kirkwood, who pointed out before her death in 1985 that authoritarianism in Chile had not begun with Pinochet, nor would it necessarily end with his demise. The return of the familiar "old" structures of liberal democracy, coupled with a continuation of free market economic policies, has meant, true to Kirkwood's warning, that patriarchy and its traditional gender scripts are alive and well and operative in Chilean society after the dictatorship. Moreover, the increased gap between economic classes inherited from the military regime has not narrowed enough for Elizabeth and many others to call this truly *una democracia*. Of course, no one involved in the resistance movement would advocate a return of the military regime in any form whatsoever. But it certainly has proven far from easy to assimilate the lessons of the Pinochet years, taking into account women's protagonism during the crisis, and the critique from many "feminized" civilian sources of the deeply ingrained forms of authoritarianism operating culturally.

As some progressive Chileans continue to struggle to "write" a more just future, the dilemmas faced during the postcoup years by Pía Barros, David Benavente and the Investigative Theater Workshop, Ariel Dorfman, and Diamela Eltit, and the thousands of other men and women struggling for "democracy in the country and in the home" provide a model for facing historical contradiction just when circumstances most seemed to demand retreat. And yet current trends suggest that it is Isabel Allende's nostalgic erasure of history's materiality, and neoliberal individualism, that in fact triumphed in the Chilean society of the 1990s. It appears that Diamela Eltit was right: history provides both possibilities and limits for social transformation. And so we are left with a paradox, an aptly postmodern conclusion to this historical *coyuntura*. As much as Chileans must continue to struggle for authoritarianism's demise, it may never truly become a thing of the past.

Notes

PROLOGUE

1. Tomás Moulian, *Chile Actual: Anatomía de un mito* [Chile Today: Anatomy of a Myth] (Santiago: LOM Ediciones, 1997), 31–37.
2. Brian Loveman writes of Chile's "democracy on a tether" in "The Transition to Civilian Government in Chile, 1990–1994," in *The Struggle for Democracy in Chile*, ed. Paul W. Drake and Iván Jaksić, revised edition (Lincoln: University of Nebraska Press, 1995), 309.
3. For excellent work on Latin American new social movements, see Arturo Escobar and Sonia E. Alvarez, eds., *The Making of Social Movements in Latin America: Identity, Strategy, and Democracy* (Boulder, Colo.: Westview Press, 1992); and Sonia E. Alvarez, Evelina Dagnino, and Arturo Escobar, eds., *Cultures of Politics/Politics of Cultures: Re-visioning Latin American Social Movements* (Boulder, Colo.: Westview Press, 1998).
4. Jean Franco, *Plotting Women: Gender and Representation in Mexico* (New York: Columbia University Press, 1989), xi.
5. See, for example, Carlos Olivárez, ed., *Nueva narrativa chilena* [New Chilean Narrative] (Santiago: LOM Ediciones, 1997); and Rodrigo Cánovas, *Novela chilena. Nuevas generaciones. El abordaje de los náufragos* [The Chilean Novel. New Generations. The Boarding of the Shipwrecked Ones] (Santiago: Editorial de la Universidad Católica, 1997).
6. Clifford Geertz, *The Interpretation of Cultures* (New York: Basic Books, 1973), 266.

CHAPTER 1: INTRODUCTION

1. In *El último día de Salvador Allende* [Salvador Allende's Last Day] (Santiago: Aguilar, 1999), Oscar Soto, Allende's physician, offers a stirring account of what happened inside La Moneda during the coup, including the circumstances of the Chilean president's death.
2. In addition to engaging Jean Franco's notion of "interpretive power" in *Plotting Women*, cited previously, I build upon Barbara Harlow's definition of "resistance narrative," as developed in her *Resistance Literature* (London: Methuen, 1987):

> Resistance narratives, embedded as they are in the historical and material conditions of their production and given furthermore the allegiances and active participation of their authors . . . in the political events of their countries, testify to the nature of the

struggle for liberation as it is enacted behind the dissembling statistics of western media coverage and official government reports. The polyphony of these novels . . . betrays their manifold role as historical documents, ideological analyses and visions of future possibilities produced out of the contemporary struggle against oppression. (98)

I will use the term "resistance culture" to embrace all those cultural forms in Chile—including, but not limited to, narrative—produced to contest the hegemony of the dominant regime since 1973.

3. Cary Nelson, Paula A. Treichler, and Lawrence Grossberg, "Cultural Studies: An Introduction,'" in *Cultural Studies,* ed. Lawrence Grossberg, Cary Nelson, and Paula A. Treichler (New York: Routledge, 1992), 2.

4. Nelson, Treichler, and Grossberg cite Tony Bennett (ibid., 3).

5. In addition to my debt to countless Chilean activists and thinkers whose work I will discuss at length in this book, and without creating an endless litany, I think that works by the following North American feminist scholars have been especially important for my trajectory: Susan Bordo, Jean Franco, Teresa DeLauretis, Barbara Christian, Barbara Johnson, bell hooks, Tania Modleski, Audre Lorde, Gloria Anzaldúa, and Joan Wallach Scott.

6. Fredric Jameson, *Postmodernism, or, The Cultural Logic of Late Capitalism* (Durham, N.C.: Duke University Press, 1991); and idem, "Third World Literature in the Era of Multinational Capitalism," *Social Text* 15 (1986): 65–88.

7. Fortunately, this tide is turning. In his "Truth Claims, Postmodernism, and the Latin American Novel," in *Profession 92* (New York: Modern Language Association, 1992), Raymond L. Williams makes an important distinction: "Latin American postmoderns, like Latin American moderns but unlike many of their Anglo-American counterparts, have generally refused to lose a sense of history" (8). An insistence on historical specificity is evident, for example, in George Yúdice, Jean Franco and Juan Flores, eds., *On Edge: The Crisis of Contemporary Latin American Culture* (Minneapolis: University of Minnesota Press, 1992); and John Beverley and José Oviedo, eds., *The Postmodernism Debate in Latin America,* a special issue of *boundary 2* 20, no. 3 (Fall 1993).

8. From an interview with Régis Debray, in his *The Chilean Revolution: Conversations with Allende* (New York: Random House Vintage Books, 1971), 95.

9. David Benavente, "Ave Félix" [Bird of Happiness], in *Pedro, Juan y Diego/Tres Marías y una Rosa,* by ICTUS, David Benavente, and TIT, prologue by María de la Luz Hurtado (Santiago: CESOC Ediciones ChileAmérica, 1989), 282.

10. The following texts were especially important in shaping my understanding of the period: Federico Gil, Ricardo Lagos, and Henry Landsberger, eds., *Chile at the Turning Point: Lessons of the Socialist Years, 1970–1973* (Philadelphia: Institute for the Study of Human Issues, 1979); Peter Winn, *Weavers of Revolution* (New York: Oxford University Press, 1986); Joan E. Garcés, *Allende y la experiencia chilena: Las armas de la política* [Allende and the Chilean Experience: The Arms of Politics] (Santiago: Ediciones BAT, 1990); Carlos Huneeus, *Los chilenos y la política: Cambio y continuidad bajo el autoritarismo* [Chileans and Politics: Change and Continuity under Authoritarianism] (Santiago: CERC/ICHEH, 1987); and finally, Manuel Antonio Garretón, *Dictaduras y democratización* [Dictatorships and Democratization] (Santiago: FLACSO, 1984), and his *The Chilean Political Process* (Boston: Unwin Hyman, 1989), especially chapter 2, "A People's Project, 1970–1973: Its Meaning and Defeat."

11. U.S. Senate Staff Report of the Select Committee to Study Governmental Operations with Respect to Intelligence Activities, *Covert Action in Chile, 1963–1973* (Washington, D.C.: U.S. Government Printing Office, 1975), 1. Paul E. Sigmund analyzes the role of the U.S. government, the CIA, and the ITT during the 1960s through 1976 in *The Over-*

throw of Allende and the Politics of Chile, 1964–1976 (Pittsburgh, Pa.: University of Pittsburgh Press, 1977) and in *The United States and Democracy in Chile* (Baltimore: The Johns Hopkins University Press, 1993), especially chapters 3 and 9.

12. U.S. Senate Staff Report, *Covert Action in Chile*, 33.

13. Ibid., 32. The text quotes the U.S. ambassador telling Frei's defense minister that "not a nut or bolt would be allowed to reach Chile under Allende."

14. Ibid., 36–39.

15. Ibid., 11.

16. See, for example, Peter Kornbluh, "Declassifying U.S. Intervention in Chile," *NACLA Report on the Americas* 32, no. 6 (May/June 1999): 36–42; idem, "CIA Outrages in Chile," *Nation* 271, no. 11 (16 October 2000), 4–5; and Christopher Hitchens, "The Case against Henry Kissinger," part 1, *Harper's Magazine* 302, no. 1809 (February 2001): 33–58, and part 2, *Harper's Magazine* 302, no. 1810 (March 2001): 49–74.

17. Garretón, *The Chilean Political Process*, 25–26. Unlike Garretón's coalition-building impulse, Gabriel Smirnow takes a harder leftist line in *The Revolution Disarmed: Chile, 1970–1973* (New York: Monthly Review Press, 1979). Smirnow argues that the Popular Unity's emphasis on constitutional legality "became the main source of weakness for the whole revolutionary process and, at a given moment, hobbled the constitutional regime and undermined its authority" (12).

18. Garretón, *The Chilean Political Process*, 25.

19. In *El peso de la noche, nuestra frágil fortaleza histórica* [The Weight of Night: Our Fragile Historical Fortress] (Santiago: Planeta, 1997), Alfredo Jocelyn-Holt Letelier argues that the myth of Chile's "unique" democratic tradition was useful in constructing national identity in the nineteenth and twentieth centuries, but that the reality was much more fragile and contradictory. Moulian's *Chile actual* also emphasizes the threads of continuity across the radically different governments in Chile from the 1960s to today.

20. See Michelle Mattelart's "Chile: El golpe de estado en femenino o cuando las mujeres de la burguesía salen a la calle" [Chile: The Female Coup, or When Bourgeois Women Take to the Streets], *Casa de las Américas* 88 (January/February 1975): 75–90. The *cacerola* protests offer a clear example of what Sonia Montecino calls "maternal politics" in *Madres y huachos: Alegorías del mestizaje chileno* [Mothers and *Huachos*: Allegories of Chilean *Mestizaje*] (Santiago: Editorial Cuarto Propio-CEDEM, 1991, 101), that is, political actions by women who claim moral superiority as mothers. However, while Montecino's study strikes me as an impressive attempt to understand the intersection of gender and indigenous culture for a "Chilean subjectivity," the author frequently makes insufficiently historicized leaps in her argument for the sake of establishing her model. For example, she equates these mobilizations of right-wing women who protested Popular Unity with the protests of the Association of Family Members of the Detained-Disappeared during the Pinochet period. I think it is an error to minimize the fundamental difference between the two groups' uses of their respective roles as mothers: on the right, an emphasis on motherhood meant an antifeminist desire for strict patriarchy, while on the left, it became a vehicle for challenging traditional gender hierarchies and military authoritarianism.

21. Montecino, *Madres y huachos*, 103.

22. María Elena Valenzuela, *Todas íbamos a ser reinas: La mujer en el Chile militar* [All of Us Were Going to Be Queens: Women in Military Chile] (Santiago: ACHIP/CESOC Ediciones ChileAmérica, 1987), 95.

23. Julieta Kirkwood, *Feminarios* [Feminars] (Santiago: Ediciones Documentas, 1987), 116–19. Although I focus on the women and men who contested that official definition of gender roles, it is important to recognize that in a mid-1980s survey, José Joaquín Brunner found that the highest level of complicity with the military regime was among wealthy housewives. María Elena Valenzuela attributes this dedicated female following of Pinochet's

to the women's contentment to exchange any potential for public influence for total control over domestic life (69). Whatever its cause, this conservative female support for Pinochet underscores the fact that, because a traditional conception of gender was already powerfully operative in Chilean culture throughout its modern history, the military regime could capitalize very effectively on its terms. See also Eugenia Hola, "Mujer, dominación y crisis" [Women, Domination, and Crisis], in *Mundo de mujer: Continuidad y cambio* [Women's Worlds: Continuity and Change], ed. Centro de Estudios de la Mujer (Santiago: Ediciones CEM, 1988), 13–50.

24. I thank an anonymous reviewer of this manuscript for highlighting this image of Allende as exemplary of contested gender ideologies played out during the military coup.

25. According to the *Summary of the Truth and Reconciliation Commission Report* (Santiago: Chilean Human Rights Commission and Centro IDEAS, 1991, 58), 1,213 (about 53 percent) of the total 2,279 victims of death or disappearance from 1973 to 1990 occurred during the period between 11 September 1973 and 31 December 1973. Samuel Chavkin provides Joan Jara's account of her husband's death in *Storm over Chile: The Junta under Siege* (Westport, Conn.: Lawrence Hill and Company, 1985), chapter 8.

26. Giselle Munizaga and Carlos Ochensius describe the elements of this *gran familia chilena* in their "El discurso público de Pinochet (1973–1976)" [The Public Discourse of Pinochet (1973–1976)], reprinted in *The Discourse of Power: Culture, Hegemony and the Authoritarian State*, ed. Neil Larsen (Minneapolis, Minn.: Institute for the Study of Ideologies and Literature, 1983), 81. Munizaga continues this analysis in her study of official publications (including those of the Mothers' Centers and the National Secretariat of Women), in *Vecino, mujer y deportista: Micromedios de gobierno* [Neighbor, Woman, Athlete: The Local Spheres of Government] (Santiago: CENECA, 1983).

27. Valenzuela, *Todas íbamos a ser reinas*, 178.

28. See Norbert Lechner and Susana Levy, "Notas sobre la vida cotidiana III: El disciplinamiento de la mujer" [Notes on Daily Life III: The Disciplining of Women] (Santiago: FLACSO Material de discusión, 1984). Like many nongovernmental organizations of the period, FLACSO (Facultad Latinoamericana de Ciencias Sociales, a social sciences think tank in Santiago), was composed mostly of those intellectuals who had been "relieved" of their regular university positions by the military regime.

29. Valenzuela, *Todas íbamos a ser reinas*, 85. Valenzuela further explains that the governmental organizations overseen by Lucía Hiriart de Pinochet were staffed by over twenty thousand women from upper-middle-class homes, serving an estimate of over one million working-class women (110). The organizations stressed class differences between women, and were geared toward reinforcing the roles of housewife and mother, and toward encouraging poor women to adapt individually to economic difficulty. The organizations thereby reinforced and diffused the ideology of the regime (113). Since benefits such as social security could only be gotten through the Mothers' Centers, many poor women had to join, for lack of other options.

30. See Ana María Arteaga, "Politización de lo privado y subversión de lo cotidiano" [Politization of the Private and the Subversion of Daily Life], in Centro de Estudios de la Mujer, *Mundo de mujer*, 565–92. In addition, sociologists at FLACSO produced a number of essays rethinking the public-private split during the 1980s. See, for example, Norbert Lechner, "Vida cotidiana y ámbito público en Chile" [Daily Life and the Public Sphere in Chile] (4 papers) (Santiago: FLACSO, 1980) and his later collection *Los patios interiores de la democracia: Subjetividad y política* [The Interior Patios of Democracy: Subjectivity and Politics] (Santiago: FLACSO, 1988); Ximena Barraza, "Notas sobre la vida cotidiana en un orden autoritario" [Notes on Daily Life in an Authoritarian Order] *Araucaria* 11 (1980): 53–72; Hernán Pozo, "Espacio cotidiano y poder" [Space and Power in Daily Life] (Santiago: FLACSO Material de Discusión no. 113, 1988); José Joaquín Brunner, "La mujer

y lo privado en la comunicación social" [Women and Private Life in Social Communication] (Santiago: FLACSO Material de Discusión, 1983); and Manuel Antonio Garretón, "La herencia de los autoritarismos" [The Legacy of Authoritarianisms] (Santiago: FLACSO, Documento de Trabajo no. 237, 1984).

31. "Democracia en el país y en la casa" [Democracy in the country and in the home] was one slogan used in the December 1983 mobilization of twelve thousand women in the Caupolicán Theater in Santiago. This public gathering crossed class lines, as women came together in organizations ranging from the grassroots and human rights groups so prevalent in the late 1970s, to the feminist organizations that became particularly visible after the National Protests of 1983–84. See my discussion of these events in chapter 4.

32. For Garretón, see especially "La herencia de los autoritarismos" and *Dictaduras y democratización*. Julieta Kirkwood, a sociologist with FLACSO and a catalyst for the Feminist Movement, died prematurely in 1985. Her numerous articles have been reedited in the volumes *Feminarios* and *Ser política en Chile: Los nudos de la sabiduría feminista* [Being a Political Woman in Chile: The Knots of Feminist Knowledge], 2d ed. (Santiago: Editorial Cuarto Propio, 1990).

33. Kirkwood, *Ser política en Chile*, 35.

34. See Luis Albala-Bertrand, coordinator, *Democratic Culture and Governance: Latin America on the Threshold of the Third Millennium* (Buenos Aires: UNESCO, Hispamérica, 1992); and José Joaquín Brunner, Alicia Barrios, and Carlos Catalán, *Chile: Transformaciones culturales y modernidad* [Chile: Cultural Transformation and Modernity] (Santiago: FLACSO, 1989).

35. For a general assessment of the generation of 1950, see Fernando Alegría, *La literatura chilena del siglo XX* [Chilean Literature of the Twentieth Century] (Santiago: Zig-Zag, 1970).

36. In *Casa de campo* [*A House in the Country*] (1978; reprint, Barcelona: Seix Barral, 1987), Donoso questions his ability as "author" to avoid the traps of an "authoritarian" in narrating his story. *El jardín de al lado* [*The Garden Next Door*] (Barcelona: Seix Barral, 1981) treats an exiled couple's struggle to understand the troubled history of their country. The last chapter reveals that the narrator of the couple's story is not the male author/character, but his wife. While Donoso's own wife, Pilar Serrano, became a feminist during the Pinochet years and undoubtedly influenced her husband's worldview, the trajectory of Donoso's work (and of Serrano's) most broadly reflects the changes of historical events in Chile under Pinochet.

37. Mercedes Valdivieso, *Maldita yo entre las mujeres* [I, Cursed Among Women] (Santiago: Planeta Biblioteca del Sur, 1991).

38. Roberto Parra, *"La negra Ester,"* *Apuntes* 98 (1989): 33–54.

39. This refers to Donoso's 1986 novel, *La desesperanza* [*Curfew*] (Barcelona: Seix Barral, 1986).

40. For a synthesis of this trajectory of recent Chilean literature, see Juan Armando Epple, "La narrativa chilena: Historia y reformulación estética" [Chilean Narrative: History and Aesthetic Reformulation], in *Tradición y marginalidad en la literatura chilena del siglo XX* [Tradition and Marginality in Chilean Literature of the Twentieth Century], ed. Lucía Guerra-Cunningham and Juan Villegas (Los Angeles, Calif.: Ediciones de la frontera, 1984).

41. See Raúl Silva-Cáceres, "Un viaje de Cortázar a Skármeta y Dorfman: La difícil esperanza en el Cono Sur" [A Journey from Cortázar to Skármeta and Dorfman: Difficult Hope in the Southern Cone], *Les cahiers* 1 (1983): 81–91.

42. Antonio Skármeta, *Soñé que la nieve ardía* [*I Dreamt the Snow Was Burning*] (Barcelona: Plaza y Janés, 1985).

43. See Ernesto Laclau, "Fascism and Ideology," in *Politics and Ideology in Marxist Theory* (New York: Verso, 1977); and Klaus Theweleit, *Women, Floods, Bodies, History,*

trans. Stephen Conway with Erica Carter and Chris Turner, vol. 1 of *Male Fantasies*, foreword by Barbara Ehrenreich (Minneapolis: University of Minnesota Press, 1987).

44. Although I can certainly think of Argentine and Uruguayan women writers who do this, a nontraditional focus on gender is much less common among male writers in militarized Argentina and Uruguay than in Chile. For exemplary scholarly work on literature and repression in those countries, see Daniel Balderston et al., *Ficción y política: La narrativa durante el proceso militar* [Fiction and Politics: Narrative during the Argentine Military Dictatorship] (Buenos Aires: Alianza Editorial/University of Minnesota, 1987); and Saúl Sosnowski and Louise B. Popkin, eds., *Repression, Exile, and Democracy: Uruguayan Culture*, trans. Louise B. Popkin (Durham, N.C.: Duke University Press, 1993).

45. Diego Muñoz Valenzuela and Ramón Díaz Eterovic, "La joven narrativa chilena: Seis años después" [Work by Young Chilean Prose Writers: Six Years Later], introduction to *Andar con cuentos: Nueva narrativa chilena* [Walking with Stories: New Chilean Narrative] (Santiago: Mosquito Editores, 1992), 8. See also Soledad Bianchi's valuable "Where to Begin to Grasp This Land? (Reflections on Culture and Authoritarianism in Chile: 1973–1986)," in *Chile: Dictatorship and the Struggle for Democracy*, ed. Grinor Rojo and John J. Hassett (Gaithersburg, Md.: Ediciones Hispamérica, 1988).

46. Pía Barros, "La seducción de Pía Barros" [The Seduction of Pía Barros], interview by Faride Zerán, *La Epoca, Literatura y Libros*, año 3, no. 138 (2 December 1990): 4–5.

47. Beverley and Oviedo, *The Postmodernism Debate in Latin America*, 8.

48. Representative of the social science view of Chile's emergent feminism is the excellent work of Patricia Chuchryk, for example, her "Feminist Anti-Authoritarian Politics: The Role of Women's Organizations in the Chilean Transition to Democracy," in *The Women's Movement in Latin America*, ed. Jane Jacquette (Boston: Unwin Hyman, 1989); the genre-oriented studies include Soledad Bianchi's *Poesía Chilena (Miradas-Enfoques-Apuntes)* [Chilean Poetry (Approaches, Readings, Notes)] (Santiago: CESOC/Ediciones Documentas, 1990); the work on women writers in postcoup society includes Barbara Lee Loach, "Power and Women's Writing in Chile 1973–1988" (Ph.D. diss., Ohio State University, 1991).

49. Cited by René Jara, "Arqueología de un paradigma de negación: El discurso del Jefe de Estado" [An Archeology of a Paradigm of Negation: Discourse of the Head of State], in Larsen, *The Discourse of Power*, 25–26.

50. Susan R. Bordo, *Unbearable Weight: Feminism, Western Culture, and the Body* (Berkeley: University of California Press, 1993), 289.

51. Susan R. Bordo, "The Body and the Reproduction of Femininity: A Feminist Appropriation of Foucault," in *Gender/ Body/ Knowledge: Feminist Reconstructions of Being and Knowing*, ed. Alison M. Jaggar and Susan R. Bordo (New Brunswick, N.J.: Rutgers University Press, 1989), 13.

52. Ibid., 13 (original emphasis).

53. Michel Foucault, *Discipline and Punish*, trans. Alan Sheridan (New York: Vintage Books, 1979), 91.

54. As is well known, Bentham's Panopticon was a prison with cells organized around, and open toward, a central surveillance tower. Because the tower's windows were covered with Venetian blinds, prisoners could not tell whether they were actually being watched or not, and internalized the observer's "gaze." That is, they behaved as if they were being watched whether or not they literally were.

55. Michel Foucault, *Power/Knowledge: Selected Interviews and Other Writings, 1972–1977*, ed. Colin Gordon, trans. Colin Gordon, Leo Marshall, John Mepham, and Kate Sopen (New York: Pantheon, 1980), 155.

56. Michel Foucault, *A History of Sexuality*, vol. 1, *An Introduction*, trans. Robert Hurley (New York: Vintage Books, 1980), 94–96.

57. Ibid., 95.
58. Bordo, *Unbearable Weight*, 17 (original emphasis).
59. Ibid., 21.
60. Bordo, "The Body," 14.
61. I am thinking here of Leila Ahmed, *Women and Gender in Islam* (New Haven: Yale University Press, 1992); Molara Ogundipe-Leslie, *Re-creating Ourselves: African Women and Critical Transformations* (Trenton, N.J.: Africa World Press, 1994); and Kwok Pui-Lan, "The Future of Feminist Theology: An Asian Perspective," in *Feminist Theology from the Third World: A Reader*, ed. Ursula King (Maryknoll, N.Y.: Orbis, 1994). Other useful anthologies include Miranda Davies, comp., *Third World-Second Sex: Women's Struggles and National Liberation* (London: Zed Books, 1983); and Eugenia Delamotte, Natania Meeker, and Jean O'Barr, eds., *Women Imagining Change: A Global Anthology of Women's Resistance* (New York: Routledge, 1997).
62. Bordo, *Unbearable Weight*, 21.
63. Ibid., 21 (original emphasis).
64. Ibid., 33 (original emphasis).
65. Ibid., 33.
66. Ibid., 15.
67. Ibid., 294.
68. Hernán Vidal, "La Declaración de Principios de la Junta Militar chilena como sistema literario: La lucha antifascista y el cuerpo humano" [The Chilean Military Junta's Declaration of Principles as a Literary System: Antifascist Struggle and the Human Body], in Larsen, *The Discourse of Power*, 47.
69. Ibid., 48–53.
70. Ibid., 48.
71. Jara, "Arqueología," 34.
72. Hernán Vidal, *Dar la Vida por la Vida: La Agrupación Chilena de Familiares de Detenidos Desaparecidos (Ensayo de antropología simbólica)* [Giving Life for Life: The Chilean Association of Family Members of the Detained-Disappeared (An Essay on Symbolic Anthropology)] (Minneapolis, Minn.: Institute for the Study of Ideologies and Literature, 1982), 57.
73. Ibid., 57.
74. Hernán Vidal, "Postmodernism, Postleftism, Neo-Avant-Gardism: The Case of Chile's *Revista de Crítica Cultural*," in Beverley and Oviedo, *The Postmodernism Debate*, 219.
75. Ibid., 221.
76. Hernán Vidal, "Para una definición culturalista de la crítica literaria latinoamericana" [Toward a Culturalist Definition of Latin American Literary Criticism], in *La cultura nacional chilena, crítica literaria y derechos humanos* [Chilean National Culture, Literary Criticism, and Human Rights], vol. 5 of *Literature and Human Rights*, ed. Hernán Vidal (Minneapolis, Minn.: Institute for the Study of Ideologies and Literature, 1989), 11–12.
77. Ibid., 13.
78. Vidal, "Postmodernism, Postleftism, Neo-Avant-Gardism," 220.
79. Mary Beth Tierney-Tello makes this point in her excellent article, "Testimony, Ethics, and the Aesthetic in Diamela Eltit," *PMLA* 144, no. 1 (January 1999): 80.
80. Nelly Richard, "Reply to Vidal (from Chile)," in Beverley and Oviedo, *The Postmodernism Debate*, 231 (original emphasis).
81. Ibid., 231.
82. Bordo, *Unbearable Weight*, 294.
83. Eugenia Brito, *Campos minados (Literatura post-golpe en Chile)* [Mined Fields: Postcoup Chilean Literature] (Santiago: Editorial Cuarto Propio, 1990), 11.

84. Ibid., 18–19.
85. Vidal, "Declaración de Principios," 47.
86. Ariel Dorfman, "Political Code and Literary Code: The Testimonial Genre in Chile Today," in *Some Write to the Future* (Durham, N.C.: Duke University Press, 1991), 141.
87. Cited in Cristina Larraín, *Catastro de organizaciones femeninas del gobierno* [Survey of Governmental Women's Organizations] (Santiago: Instituto Chileno de Estudios Humanísticos, 1982), 93.
88. Ibid., 69.
89. Terry Lovell, *Consuming Fiction* (London: Verso, 1987), 71.
90. I adopt this phrase from Benedict Anderson's outstanding study of nationalism, *Imagined Communities* (1983; reprint, London: Verso, 1991), in which he defines the nation as "an imagined political community" (6). I have made use here of the metaphor in its broadest sense, to suggest that local communities and families, as well as the Chilean nation, were in effect constantly imagined, constructed, or narrated in the context of groups telling their own stories, in an effort to rewrite the dominant national narrative offered by the military regime.

CHAPTER 2: THE DISAPPEARED BODY AND THE EXILED VOICE: DISPLACEMENT AND THE STRUGGLE FOR NARRATIVE POWER

1. Information from Adriana, a member of the Association of Family Members of the Detained-Disappeared, interview by author, 24 October 1990, Santiago, Chile, tape recording.
2. According to the *Summary of the Truth and Reconciliation Commission Report*, 1,828 (about 80 percent) of the total 2,279 victims from 1973 to 1990 died or disappeared during 1973–76 (93).

By far the fiercest period of this repression began in the days immediately after the coup, and continued through the creation of the Dirección Nacional de Inteligencia [National Intelligence Directorate], or DINA, in June 1974 *(Statute of the Military Junta)*. According to George Gelber, M. Amelia de Sosa, and Juan Caveda's *Evaluación de FASIC* [Evaluation of FASIC] (Santiago: FASIC Estudios y Publicaciones, 1988), this initial period was characterized by massive executions under the pretext of the *ley de fuga* (a law justifying the shooting of fleeing criminals) and/or labeled as "wartime" casualties; collective executions of peasants and workers (Lonquén, Yumbel, Mulchén); incarcerations in numerous concentration camps; torture; and a widespread use of disappearance. These actions were geared toward the military regime's consolidation and toward "extermination of the enemy" (Gelber, Sosa, and Caveda, *Evaluación de FASIC,* 7).

During the period of the DINA (1974–77), the practice of repression changed, as torture and disappearance were used more selectively, and were directed toward specific political actors on the left. The DINA operated as secret police (using unmarked cars and civilian clothes), and functioned as part of a global strategy to consolidate political power into the hands of Pinochet and an omnipotent police apparatus, and to control social discontent through multiple covert strategies of terror and violence. As I discuss in chapter 3, this period also coincided with the "shock treatment" of orthodox monetarist policies implemented by the government's economic team, known as the "Chicago Boys."

When the DINA was replaced by the Central Nacional de Informaciones [National Information Office], or CNI, in August 1977, disappearance was employed extremely selectively, and the years 1977 and 1978 mark a period of diminished repression, followed by isolated cases of disappearance after 1979. No women disappeared after the CNI's creation.

3. One of the most elaborate instances of the regime's denial of the disappeared took

place in 1975. On 7 November of that year, the Chilean delegate to the U.N., Sergio Diez, stated before the United Nations that the problem of disappearance **itself** did not exist, since (he claimed) 64 of the disappeared had been declared legally dead in Chile, 153 never had existed, and 119 had reappeared in Argentina. See Patricia Verdugo's *Tiempo de días claros* [Time of Clear Days] (Santiago: CESOC Ediciones ChileAmérica, 1990), chapter 2, n. 9, for a fragment of Diez's U.N. speech. In the case of the 119 missing MIRists (members of the Revolutionary Leftist Movement) said by Diez to be alive in Argentina, the regime's whitewashing maneuvers were quite complex. They involved an operation engineered by the DINA, in which fabricated news items were published in three Chilean newspapers *(La Segunda, La Tercera,* and *El Mercurio),* in Brazil's *O'Dia* (the only number of this paper ever published), and in Argentina's *Lea* (likewise a single edition). These articles all declared that the 119 had been discovered training in paramilitary techniques in Argentina (Eugenio Ahumada et al., "La Operación Colombo" [Operation Colombo], *Chile: La memoria prohibida* [Chile: Prohibited Memory] [Santiago: Pehuén, 1990], 2:101–40). Ahumada et al. hold that the work of human rights organizations, which struggled to make visible the problem of the disappeared, had unsettled the military enough to require such involved measures for discrediting the problem.

4. The *Summary of the Truth and Reconciliation Commission Report* states that 2,153 (94.5 percent) of the total 2,279 victims of death or disappearance from 1973 to 1990 were men; the majority (1,356, or 59.5 percent) were between 20 and 35 years of age at the time of their death or disappearance (92). It is important to recognize that these figures depend on each victim's having been survived by someone who could describe or recount the person's story, which was surely not the case for all the disappeared. Vicariate of Solidarity, information from interviews by author, Santiago, Chile, 8 and 11 October 1990.

5. According to the *Summary of the Truth and Reconciliation Commission Report* (94), the number of victims according to their work activities is as follows:

Disappeared, by Employment Type	*Number*
Professionals	207
Administrators, Managers, High Officials	45
Office Workers	305
Workers and *Campesinos.*	686
Self-Employed (Artisans, Farmers, Sales, etc.)	314
Students	324
Armed Forces and Security Services	132
Other (Housewife, Retired, Unemployed, etc.)	226
Unknown (No information)	40
TOTAL:	2,279

6. Hannah Arendt, *Origins of Totalitarianism* (1948, reprint, New York: Harcourt Brace Jovanovich, 1979), 478.

7. Many became aware that the problem of the disappeared extended beyond their personal cases because they crossed paths with others searching for missing family members at police commissaries and morgues. Others met when presenting their cases to the Committee for Peace in Chile, an organization created under the auspices of the Catholic Church to document human rights violations committed during the time of the Pinochet regime. These factors motivated family members to support one another in their common situation, and led to the collective organizations described here. Information from members of the Association of Family Members of the Detained-Disappeared, interview by author, 24 October 1990, Santiago, Chile, tape recording.

8. Groups organized at the national level included: the previously mentioned Vicariate of Solidarity (1976, formerly Committee for Peace in Chile, created in 1974), the Association of Family Members of the Detained-Disappeared (1974), the Fundación de Ayuda Social de las Iglesias Cristianas [Foundation for Social Work by Christian Churches, FASIC] (1975), the Comisión Chilena de Derechos Humanos [Chilean Human Rights Commission] (1978), Mujeres por la Vida [Women for Life] (1983), and the Movimiento contra la tortura Sebastián Acevedo [Anti-Torture Movement "Sebastián Acevedo"] (1983).

9. Since its beginning, the Agrupación has been composed of roughly 97 percent women. Information from the Association of Family Members of the Detained-Disappeared, interviews by author, 17 and 21 October 1990, Santiago, Chile, and 24 October 1990, Paine, Chile, tape recordings.

10. Hernán Vidal, *Dar la vida por la vida*, chapters 1 and 3, the latter reprinted in *La cultura nacional chilena*.

11. Vidal, *La cultura nacional chilena*, 81.

12. Foucault, *Discipline and Punish*, 135–41.

13. Patricia Verdugo's five book-length reports (*libros-reportajes*) are exemplary, and perhaps the best-known, efforts to recuperate the prohibited memory of political violence of the Pinochet years. They include: *Detenidos-desaparecidos: Una herida abierta* [The Detained-Disappeared: An Open Wound] (Santiago: Editorial Aconcagua, 1980), *André de La Victoria* [Andre from La Victoria] (Santiago: Editorial Aconcagua, 1985), *Rodrigo y Carmen Gloria: Quemados vivos* [Rodrigo and Carmen Gloria: Burned Alive] (Santiago: Editorial Aconcagua, 1986), *Los zarpazos del Puma* [Slashes of the Puma] (Santiago: CESOC, Ediciones ChileAmérica, 1989), and the previously mentioned *Tiempo de días claros: Los desaparecidos*.

14. Mónica González, interview by author, 23 July 1991, Santiago, Chile, tape recording. See also Ximena Bunster-Barotto, "Surviving Beyond Fear: Women and Torture in Latin America," in *Women and Change in Latin America*, by June Nash, Helen Safa and contributors (South Hadley, Mass.: Bergin and Garvey Publishers, 1985), 297–325.

15. Since women journalists gained some advantage both because and in spite of the regime's stereotypical discourse on women, the degree to which their activities could transform these stereotypes remains a complex question, as I will discuss further. Comments by Pía Barros, Carla Grandi, Sergio Marras, and Jaime Valdivieso (Encuentro de Narradores Chilenos [Chilean Writers' Conference], 3 November 1990, Valdivia, Chile).

16. In the interview, González repeatedly insisted that her story was not extraordinary: every situation she described could be retold through analogous stories of the many women who devised strategies to survive repression on a day-to-day basis.

17. According to figures published by the Chilean Human Rights Commission in their *Informe Mensual* [Monthly Report] (Santiago), no. 73–74 (January–February, 1988): 13, Chileans known to be prevented from living in their country (11 September–31 January 1988) gave the following official reasons for their exile:

Exile, by Explanation	*Number*
Administrative expulsions	0
Prohibitions of entrance	589
Asylum	(no information)
Political refugees	(no information)

The gaps in this very partial data set are its most interesting feature. Ostensibly, the official story of exile had less to do with expulsion and more to do with the regime's strategy of prohibiting the return of those who left, thereby ensuring their prolonged exile. It is hardly surprising that little information was recorded about the situations of those exiled for explicitly political reasons.

18. *Incilio,* or "incile," as a middle term between actual imprisonment and exile, serves here to describe the condition of those people in opposition to the regime who spent the entire Pinochet period within the country. A term employed by Mario Benedetti, this expression was first brought to my attention by the Uruguayan film critic Alicia Migdal, in an interview by author, 23 May 1989, Montevideo, Uruguay.

19. Ariel Dorfman, *Viudas,* 2d ed. (Buenos Aires: Siglo XXI, 1985). Translated as *Widows,* trans. Stephen Kessler (New York: Vintage, 1984). All textual citations will be given parenthetically, and unless noted otherwise, refer to these editions. When only one citation is provided, it refers to the Spanish original.

Widows contrasts enormously with Dorfman's prior novel, *Moros en la costa* [*Hard Rain*] (Santiago: Editorial Universitaria, 1973), which exuded the effervescence and neobaroque excess directly related to Dorfman's experience of the Popular Unity period (1970–73). After his exile, Dorfman faced a tremendous difficulty in continuing to write, as all the structures used to describe reality before the coup seemed to fall along with the utopian impulse of the Allende years (information from interview by author, 15 September 1990, Santiago, Chile). However, Dorfman began to search for a language capable of representing the horror of the postcoup context by writing poems—an excerpt of which appears as this chapter's epigraph. The poem sequence comprising "Desaparecer" [Disappear] was composed between 1976 and 1978, and first appeared in 1978 in the German bilingual edition *Desaparecer/Aus der Augen verlieren* (Bornheim-Merten: Lamuv Verlag, 1979). The bare atmosphere and indeterminate poetic voices of this work opened the path that Dorfman pursued in subsequent narrative efforts leading up to *Widows.* For example, his short story "Travesía" [Crossing], from *Cría ojos* [roughly, Keep Your Eyes Peeled] (Mexico, D.F.: Editorial Nueva Imagen, 1979), demonstrated a search for language, while also exploring the connections of gender, power, and authoritarianism that Dorfman later developed in *Widows.*

20. Dorfman has brought to my attention that this prologue was in fact written in 1979, but that the publishers asked that he change the date because they had taken so long to bring the book out. Given the difficulty of publishing this novel, these material conditions required that even the date of the prologue be temporally displaced.

21. In his own highly ironic and political prologue, Cervantes describes authorship and paternity in parallel terms, as would Dorfman after him. However, Cervantes writes of his text, conceived in prison, as "un hijo seco, avellanado, antojadizo" [a sniveling child, withered, whining], of whom "aunque parezco padre, soy padrastro" (19) [I'm only his stepfather . . . though I may seem to be {his} parent] (7). Cervantes thus anticipates the displaced structures of authorship defining his own text: as is well known, *Don Quijote* was ostensibly written in Arabic by the Moorish chronicler Sidi Hamid Benengeli, who had pieced it together from various fragments and original testimonies gathered in La Mancha. The work was later discovered by an unnamed "editor" in a Toledo market, who had it "faithfully" translated into Spanish by a *morisco* (Christianized Arab). Through these structures, and despite his having written under very different (though perhaps not so distant) historical circumstances, Cervantes questions univocal truth and its authority, providing a touchstone for Dorfman in *Widows.* See Miguel de Cervantes, *Don Quijote de la Mancha,* ed. Martín de Riquer (Barcelona: Editorial Juventud, 1985), 19. Translated as *Don Quijote,* ed. Diana de Armas Wilson, trans. Burton Raffel (New York: W. W. Norton, 1999), 7.

22. The term is Dorfman's. See "Entre el subte y la esperanza: ¿Tenemos quién nos escriba?" [Between the Subway and Hope: Does Anyone Write to Us?] *Página 30,* February 1991, 40–42 and *Some Write to the Future.* For his earlier work on these themes, see *Imaginación y violencia* [Imagination and Violence] (Santiago: Editorial Universitaria, 1970).

23. Theweleit, *Male Fantasies*, vol. 1.

24. This is a moment of transition after the ferocity of Gheorghakis's rule in the post. Dorfman implicitly evokes the distinction between *dictadura*, or hard-core dictatorship, and *dictablanda*, or soft-core dictatorship.

25. Dorfman has worked extensively on the notion of infantalization and politics in his essays. See, for example, *The Empire's Old Clothes* (New York: Pantheon Books, 1983).

26. In his dissertation on Dorfman's work ("Aproximación crítica a la obra de Ariel Dorfman: Ficción y crítica cultural" [Critical Approximation to Ariel Dorfman's Oeuvre: Fiction and Cultural Criticism] [Ph.D. diss., Arizona State University, 1990]), Salvador Antonio Oropesa fails to situate *Widows* within the sociopolitical context informing the author's position vis-à-vis the narrator and the characters in the novel. Oropesa states:

> This flight from man—as macho—by the author is not easy to explain. Neither is his choice of a heroine. Only one explanation occurs to me: that ethics at this point in the twentieth century functions desperately, because values no longer receive their justification in God, nor in Reason, nor in the State. As in any other modern work, one finds in *Widows* the death of God. . . . (translation mine, 61)

Because Oropesa does not examine the ways that gender identity is destabilized in this (con)text, he is perplexed. Instead of analyzing the ways in which this dilemma operates in the novel, he resolves the problem with an appeal to metatextual answers, which I believe miss the point of the novel's specificity as a product fundamentally shaped by the circumstances of its production.

27. This position resembles that of the Chilean Association of Family Members of the Detained-Disappeared, who refuse to call themselves "Widows," for the reasons Alejandra outlines in the novel. They maintain that they are not, and cannot be, widows, until all the bodies of the disappeared are returned, alive or dead. Information from an interview by author, 24 October 1990, Santiago, Chile, tape recording.

28. I am reminded here of Raúl Zurita's *Canto a su amor desaparecido* [Song to Her Disappeared Love] (Santiago: Editorial Universitaria, 1987), a text narrated from the position of a female subject as poetic "yo." This voice emerges through the initial framing moment of the collection. In his epigraph, Zurita establishes his double authorial position as one of power and of impotence, privilege and exclusion, for he is simultaneously placed outside and inside the widows' position: "Ahora Zurita—me largó—ya que de puro verso y desgarro pudiste entrar aquí, en nuestras pesadillas; ¿tú puedes decirme dónde está mi hijo?" [Now, Zurita—she jabbed—now that you got in here through poetry and impudence, into our worst nightmares, tell me: where can I find my son?] (translation mine).

29. Barbara Johnson makes a similar point in her "Gender and Poetry: Charles Baudelaire and Marceline Desbordes-Valmore," in *Displacements: Women, Tradition, Literatures in French*, ed. Joan de Jean and Nancy K. Miller (Baltimore: The Johns Hopkins University Press, 1991), 178.

30. The most useful analyses of fascism, like Ernesto Laclau's "Fascism and Ideology," cited previously, work against such a concept of "aberration."

31. The first break between the two threads illustrates the back-and-forth movement of this segment and the interplay of naming and unnaming:

> —Bien. ¿Y fuiste solo hasta la casa o llevaste a tu novia?
> No, señor. Ella se había quedado esperando en el yip.
> —¿Y cuánto duró la conversación con don Felipe?
> Tres horas. /
> Cuando Emmanuel se subió al yip, ella no quiso quejarse ni preguntarle nada de

inmediato. El tampoco hizo ningún comentario, pese a que aquí adentro hacía un calor insoportable. . . . (126)

["Fine. And did you go to the house alone or did you take your girl friend along?"
No, sir. She'd stayed waiting in the jeep.
"And how long did your conversation with Mr. Kastoria last?
Three hours. /
When Emmanuel climbed back into the jeep, she didn't want to complain or ask him anything right away. He didn't say anything either, despite the fact that it was baking hot inside. . . .] (95–96)

Obviously, I have had to treat the threads in a more linear fashion than they appear in the novel. To conserve a sense of the movement between the threads composing this segment, however, I have noted the narrative breaks in the citations used here.

32. The debate between David and Felipe in Dorfman's *La última canción de Manuel Sendero* [*The Last Song of Manuel Sendero*], 2d ed. (Santiago: Editorial Planeta, 1990) parallels the dilemma of Alexis and Sofía expressed in this segment.

33. Diana Taylor, *Disappearing Acts: Spectacles of Gender and Nationalism in Argentina's "Dirty War"* (Durham, N.C.: Duke University Press, 1997), 20.

34. Omar Cabezas's *testimonio* was published in 1982, *La montaña es algo más que una inmensa estepa verde* [*Fire From the Mountain*], 6th ed. (México, D.F.: Siglo XXI, 1987). See also Margaret Randall's incisive feminist critique *Gathering Rage: The Failure of Twentieth Century Revolutions to Develop a Feminist Agenda* (New York: Monthly Review Press, 1992).

35. James C. Scott, *Domination and the Arts of Resistance: Hidden Transcripts* (New Haven: Yale University Press, 1990), xiii.

36. Ibid., 166 n. 70.

Chapter 3: The Hungry Body and Patchwork Histories

1. From an interview conducted by Gloria Angelo, included in her *Pero ellas son imprescindibles* [But They Are Essential] (Santiago: Biblioteca de la Mujer, Centro de Estudios de la Mujer, 1987), 44.

2. María de la Luz Hurtado and Carlos Ochensius, researchers at the Centro de Indagación y Expresión Cultural y Artística [Center for Research on Cultural and Artistic Expression], or CENECA, use the term *obras alternativas-críticas* (alternative-critical plays) to refer to **professionally** produced plays that critically examine the social contingencies of the country. Examples include *Bienaventurados los pobres* [Blessed Are the Poor] (Vadell, Salcedo, Benavente, 1977), *¿Cuántos años tiene un día?* [How Many Years in a Day?] (ICTUS/ Vodanovic, 1978), Radrigán's *Hechos consumados* [Consummate Facts] (1981), the plays I analyze here, and many others. I have adopted this definition, and use interchangeably the terms "independent theater" and "alternative theater" to refer to works with this orientation. Like Hurtado and Ochensius, I exclude from this definition the production of Golden Age or other classics, cabaret shows, and nonprofessional theater. It is important to remember, however, that the concentration camps, as well as the *poblaciones* themselves, were crucial nonprofessional loci for the survival and transformation of Chilean theater on the whole after the coup. See María de la Luz Hurtado and Carlos Ochensius, "Nómina de obras teatrales montadas entre 1968 y 1980 por compañías profesionales y aficionadas en salas comerciales" [List of Plays Performed Between 1968 and 1980 by Professional Companies in Commercial Theaters], Publicaciones CENECA no. 16, 1980; and idem, "Transformaciones del teatro chileno en la década del '70" [Transformations in Chilean Theater during

the 1970s], introduction to *Teatro Chileno de la Crisis Institucional 1973–1980 (Antología Crítica)* [Chilean Theater of the Institutional Crisis, 1973–1980 (Critical Anthology)], ed. María de la Luz Hurtado, Carlos Ochensius, and Hernán Vidal (Minneapolis and Santiago: University of Minnesota Latin American Series and CENECA, 1982).

3. For an overview of the regime's process of political and economic consolidation, see Manuel Antonio Garretón's "The Political Evolution of the Chilean Military Regime and Problems in the Transition to Democracy," in *Transitions from Authoritarian Rule: Latin America*, ed. Guillermo O'Donnell, Philippe C. Schmitter, and Lawrence Whitehead, foreword by Abraham F. Lowenthal (Baltimore: The Johns Hopkins University Press, 1986), 95–122. See also my discussion of the regime's trajectory in chapter 2, note 2.

4. Walden Bello's forward to Joseph Collins and John Lear's *Chile's Free-Market Miracle: A Second Look* (Oakland, Calif.: The Institute for Food and Development Policy, 1995) notes that "enthusiasts like the World Bank and the International Monetary Fund" have held out the Chilean neoliberal experiment as a model not only for Latin America and much of the South, but also as an answer to the postsocialist crisis of the former Soviet Union (ix–x).

5. Cited in Manuel Délano and Hugo Traslaviña, *La herencia de los Chicago Boys* [The Legacy of the Chicago Boys] (Santiago: Ediciones del Ornitorrinco, 1989), 47 (translation and emphasis mine).

6. In fact, from 1976 to 1982, a record 30.3 percent of Chileans lived in "extreme poverty." The most wealthy 10 percent of Chileans controlled 46.1 percent of the country's economic resources, while the most impoverished 20 percent earned only 3.3 percent of the total (ibid., 70).

7. See Eduardo Morales and Sergio Rojas's study "Relocalización socio-espacial de la pobreza. Política estatal y presión popular, 1979–1985" [Socio-spacial Relocation of Poverty: State Policy and Popular Pressure, 1979–1985], in *Espacio y poder: Los pobladores* [Space and Power: Shantytown Dwellers], ed. Hernán Pozo (Santiago: FLACSO, 1987), 75–121.

8. The following table shows the unemployment rate in Chile from 1970 to 1989, according to data compiled by the National Institute for Statistics (INE, information from interview by author, 10 July 1991, Santiago, Chile). The first number corresponds to the official unemployment rate, while the second, after the development of the governmental minimal work programs PEM and POJH, includes workers involved in those programs. I have included a third figure in brackets, which indicates the unemployment rate, including PEM and POJH, as calculated by the nongovernmental organization Programa de Economía del Trabajo [Program on Labor Economics], or PET, published in Délano and Traslaviña, *Chicago Boys*, 195. The difference between the second and third figures clearly reflects the political discrepancies between official and unofficial criteria for inclusion among the unemployed. To my knowledge, neither the INE nor the PET completed statistical calculations of unemployment by year and sex for this period.

Percentage Unemployment by Year (1970–1989)

Year	Official	(PEM/POJH)	[PET]	Year	Official	(PEM/POJH)	[PET]
1970	5.7%			1980	10.4%	(15.7%)	[17.2%]
1971	3.8%			1981	11.2%	(16.1%)	[16.3%]
1972	3.1%			1982	19.4%	(26.4%)	[27.4%]
1973	4.8%			1983	15.0%	(28.5%)	[34.6%]
1974	9.2%			1984	15.5%	(24.6%)	[26.9%]
1975	14.5%	(16.8%)	[16.4%]	1985	12.2%	(21.0%)	[23.9%]
1976	12.9%	(17.8%)	[19.9%]	1986	8.8%	(13.9%)	[19.0%]
1977	11.8%	(17.7%)	[18.6%]	1987	7.9%	(10.8%)	[15.5%]
1978	14.1%	(18.3%)	[17.9%]	1988	6.3%	(7.0%)	[8.9%]
1979	13.6%	(17.5%)	[17.7%]	1989	5.3%	(5.3%)	[6.6%]

9. In *Entre la sobrevivencia y la acción política: Las organizaciones de pobladores en Santiago* [Between Survival and Political Action: Shantytown Organizations in Santiago] (Santiago: ILET, 1987), Guillermo Campero maintains that 64.5 percent of those working in artisans' workshops in Conchalí in 1986 were women, while 75 percent of the directors of neighborhood soup kitchens *(ollas comunes)* were women. In terms of those staffing the *ollas*, however, a striking 95 percent were women (71).

It is also important to remember that the *ollas* have a long history in Chile. Ana María Medioli notes in her article "Ollas comunes en Chile" [Soup Kitchens in Chile], *Trabajo Social,* no. 6 (1984): 5–14, that the existence of the *poblaciones* in Santiago, as well as the development of soup kitchens in Chile, began in the 1930s, with the crisis of the saltpeter industry in the north. Though the economic problems in the periphery of the city were greatly alleviated during the 1960s and early 1970s, governmental support of the *pobladores* ended with the military coup. While *comedores infantiles* had reemerged after 1973—in 1975, there were approximately three hundred, serving forty-five thousand children—it was only in the winter of 1982 that *ollas comunes* had reappeared on a broad scale. This happened after a severe flood in the greater Santiago area, which made it clear that children were no longer the only people affected by the severe economic conditions. By July 1984, in the Santiago *población* La Florida alone, there were 414 families served by some twelve *ollas*, all supported by the Vicariate of Solidarity. By 1988, some five hundred soup kitchens operated in the Santiago area, serving approximately fifty thousand people (information from Mirta Osandún and Ana María Medioli, interviews by the author at the Vicariate of Solidarity, 24 October 1990, Santiago, Chile, and with representatives of Compartiendo la Mesa [Sharing the Table], 31 October 1990, Santiago, Chile, tape recordings). The experience of organization in the *ollas*, particularly in terms of development of organizational skills among the women participants, leads Graciela Ortega to conclude that "Poverty and need are still the same, but the women are very different." From "Ollas comunes: Mucho más que un plato de comida" [Soup Kitchens: Much More Than a Plate of Food], *El canelo (Revista chilena de desarrollo local)* [Chilean Magazine on Local Development] 42, no. 14 (October 1989): 3.

10. See Bernarda Gallardo, "El redescubrimiento del carácter social del hambre: Las ollas comunes" [Rediscovery of the Social Nature of Hunger: The Soup Kitchens], in Pozo, *Espacio y poder: Los pobladores,* 171–202.

11. Information from Winnie Lira of the workshops section of the Vicariate of Solidarity, interview by author, 24 October 1990, Santiago, Chile, tape recording. It is important to note that the Vicariate's support of these groups was both material and organizational; the groups therefore depended upon an outside source at the same time as they sought autonomous control of their situations. This proved to be a central tension for most of the organizations from their beginnings, and continued to be an issue after the Vicariate withdrew material aid from subsistence organizations in 1989 (at the outset of the democratic transition).

12. Benavente, "Ave Félix," 282 (translation mine).

13. Ibid., 284 (translation mine).

14. Cathy Lisa Schneider's *Shantytown Protest in Pinochet's Chile* (Philadelphia: Temple University Press, 1995) shows not only artisan's networks, but also those of political parties, labor, students, and others that took part in the slow process of reestablishing social networks in the shantytowns. These networks gained momentum and became visible in the 1983–84 National Protests, discussed at length by Schneider. I address this trajectory in chapter 4.

15. This information is from interviews I conducted with artisans. For quoted material, I have relied upon taped collective interviews: (1) with *dirigentes* (leaders) of *arpillera* workshops (La Morada, 29 October 1990, Santiago, Chile, tape recording); (2) with the

Taller "Los Almendros" (6 February 1991, Puente Alto, Chile, tape recording); and (3) with the Taller "Sector Sur" (5 February 1991, Santiago, Chile, tape recording). Elizabeth and Yolanda were *dirigentes* present at these meetings.

16. Marjorie Agosín, *Scraps of Life: Chilean Arpilleras*, trans. Cola Franzen (London: Zed Books, 1987), 84. Agosín's book gives particular attention to the explicit political content of the *arpilleras* made by members of the Association of Family Members of the Detained-Disappeared. By choosing this focus, however, Agosín conflates the *arpillera* organizations with the activities of the Agrupación, two distinct phenomena that did overlap at their inception, but that took very different trajectories over time. The phenomenon that draws my own attention is the broadly based network of artisans' workshops that developed throughout the Santiago shantytowns during the 1970s and 1980s.

17. Ibid., 84. See also Agosín's *Literatura y derechos humanos: Aproximaciones, lecturas y encuentros* [Literature and Human Rights: Approaches, Readings, Encounters] (San José, Costa Rica: Editorial Universitaria Centroamericana, 1989), 177–83.

18. Gradually, a range of community-based art forms, including written *testimonios*, denunciatory songs, poems, and theater pieces, many of them produced by people who had not previously pursued these modes of expression, began to be produced during the second half of the 1970s. For an overview of this production, see Manuel Alcides Jofré, "Culture, Art, and Literature in Chile: 1973–1985," *Latin American Perspectives* 16, no. 2 (Spring 1989): 70–95.

19. Of the many attempts by journalists and social scientists to narrate the officially hidden pockets of local resistance after the coup, many took as their focus the activities of working-class women. Among the abundance of *testimonios*, sociological analyses, and interviews on shantytown women published after 1973 are the particularly notable studies by: M. Angélica Meza, ed., *La otra mitad de Chile* [The Other Half of Chile] (Santiago: CESOC Ediciones Chile y América, 1986); Dagmar Raczynski and Claudia Serrano, *Vivir la pobreza, Testimonios de mujeres* [Living in Poverty: Testimonies by Women] (Santiago: CIEPLAN, 1985); Teresa Valdés, *Venid, benditas de mi Padre (Las pobladoras, sus rutinas y sus sueños)* [Come, My Father's Blessed Ones (Shantytown Women, Their Routines and Their Dreams)] (Santiago: FLACSO, 1988); and the previously cited works by Gloria Angelo and Guillermo Campero.

20. Unlike the experiences of neighboring Argentina and Uruguay, where theater was virtually eliminated by military governments, alternative theater groups in Chile created a niche where they could both survive and critique the sociopolitical context. In his essay on postcoup Chilean theater, David Benavente likens the Chilean case to those of Poland and South Africa, where revitalized theater movements bloomed in the face of repressive regimes (Benavente, "Ave Félix," 279).

21. Because of the inflation and unemployment culminating in the first severe economic recession of the dictatorship (1975), the military government created the Programa de Empleo Mínimo (PEM), a program in which the unemployed could work in government-sponsored projects for a salary well below the minimum wage at the time. *Pedro, Juan y Diego* relies on audience recognition of this referent, as Benavente acknowledges: "They are in the PEM [Minimum Employment Program], although these words are never mentioned in the play" ("Ave Félix," 302).

22. David Benavente and the Taller de Investigación Teatral, *Tres Marías y una Rosa*, in ICTUS, David Benavente, and TIT, *Pedro, Juan y Diego/ Tres Marías y una Rosa*, prol. María de la Luz Hurtado (Santiago: CESOC Ediciones ChileAmérica, 1989). All page citations for both plays will be included parenthetically in the text, and refer to this edition. All translations are my own.

23. By November 1980, sixty thousand people had attended the play since its opening night. See "Las Tres Marías Hacen Las Maletas (La Rosa, También)" [The Three Marías

Pack Their Bags (And Rosa, Too)], *Las últimas noticias,* 3 November 1980, 64. It is important to note that by 1979, the regime realized that the IVA tax (an economic measure geared toward dissuading attendance at plays by making them more expensive) had actually sparked interest in some "alternative" plays, and therefore had had the undesirable effect of drawing larger audiences to them. That year, *Tres Marías y una Rosa* stimulated debates within the Ministry of Education about how to incapacitate its production without drawing either international criticism or heightened local interest. Benavente publishes the memorandum directed from the Ministry to the secret police (CNI) stating that the most effective strategy to those ends would be to allow the play to go on without the IVA tax ("Ave Félix," 313–16). This document illustrates how a confluence of factors created the possibility for *Tres Marías y una Rosa* to be produced without the IVA, undoubtedly connected, at least in part, to the play's popularity. The IVA polemic is also discussed in Hans Ehrmann's "Teatro Postgolpe: Pedro, Juan, María y Rosa" [Postcoup Theater: Pedro, Juan, María and Rosa] *Gestos: Teoría y práctica del teatro hispánico* [Gestures: Theory and Practice of Hispanic Theater] 4, no. 8 (November 1989): 155–61.

24. Based on the research by Hurtado and Ochensius cited in note 2 above, Benavente lists thirty-one "alternative-critical" plays written and staged in Santiago by independent playwrights and theater groups between 1974 and 1981 ("Ave Félix," 320–21).

25. For example, one month after its debut in October 1974, the first play produced professionally after the coup was closed down by the military government. *Al principio existía la vida* [In the Beginning, There Was Life] had been written by the independent theater company directed by Oscar Castro, El Aleph, and its members were incarcerated in diverse concentration camps in Chile, to be exiled two years later. Castro later wrote a play about creating theater pieces in prison, which I was able to see in Santiago in October 1990. Titled *Casimiro Peñafleta, prisionero político* [Casimiro Peñafleta, Political Prisoner], the play humorously portrays political prisoners' ability to trick prison authorities, by asking for permission to stage "classic" theater pieces by "well-known" authors, an ostensibly harmless activity to which the authorities would agree, though the pieces were in fact created by the prisoners themselves. While such activity was certainly not possible in all Chilean concentration camps, Castro's experience illustrates the prisoners' ability to take advantage of small gaps in prison vigilance to piece together a collective, imaginative project, an activity seen by many as essential to their survival. See Benavente, "Ave Félix," 293.

26. Military intervention in the universities, a principal center of Chilean theater since the 1940s, posed another obstacle to the development of postcoup theater. Because the universities, as well as independent theater groups, lost the State support that they had received throughout this century, virtually all alternative theater projects verged on bankruptcy by the mid-1970s. Of course, several independent professional theater companies had already broken from the institutional structures of the university before 1973 and did not, therefore, miss state support. Such independent groups included ICTUS (from the theater group Teatro de Ensayo at the Catholic University), "La Compañía de los Cuatro" [The Company of Four] (from the Experimental Theater group at the University of Chile), and "El Cabildo" [Town Hall] (from the University of Concepción), among others (Benavente, "Ave Félix," 286). Rodrigo Cánovas insightfully explores the trajectory of ICTUS from the late 1950s through the dictatorship in his *Lihn, Zurita, ICTUS, Radrigán: Literatura chilena y experiencia autoritaria* [Lihn, Zurita, ICTUS, Radrigán: Chilean Literature and the Authoritarian Experience] (Santiago: FLACSO, 1986), chapter 3.

27. I use the term "domestication" to include the phenomenon that the literary critic Catherine Boyle has called the "feminization" of Chilean theater after the military coup. In her "El espacio escénico, O cómo el teatro chileno se hizo femenino" [Theater Space, or How Chilean Theater Became Feminine] (photocopy), a paper presented at the International Symposium on Iberoamerican Theater: History, Theory, Methodology (Catholic

University, 17 May 1991, Santiago, Chile), Boyle limits her remarks to the politics of the theater spaces themselves, always maintaining a dichotomy between the interior (indoor, domestic, "feminine") spaces characteristic of early postcoup theater, versus the exterior (or outdoor, political, "masculine") spaces occupied in the late 1980s. Boyle maintains that the intimate character of Chilean theater of the 1970s was a "feminine" structure broken by the 1988 production of Roberto Parra's *La Negra Ester* in public spaces such as the Santa Lucía Hill in downtown Santiago. While I believe that the public-private split was itself becoming effaced because of the postcoup crisis, I find Boyle's observation of a spacial shift in postcoup theater quite useful.

28. Manuel Antonio Garretón, "En torno a algunas funciones sociales del teatro chileno actual" [On Some Social Functions of Theater in Chile Today], in *Seminario "Teatro chileno en la década del 80"* [Seminar "Chilean Theater in the 1980s"], ed. Hurtado and Ochensius (Santiago: CENECA, serie documentos no. 11, 1980), 160.

29. María de la Luz Hurtado and Carlos Ochensius, *Serie testimonio (Maneras de hacer y pensar el teatro en el Chile actual)* [Ways of Creating and Thinking about Theater in Chile Today], vol. 3: *TIT, Taller de Investigación Teatral* [Investigative Theater Workshop] (Santiago: CENECA, n.d. [1980?]), 4–5. All translations from this work are my own.

30. For Vidal's important discussion of sociology of theater as an emergent discipline, see his *Dictadura militar, trauma social e inauguración de la sociología del teatro en Chile* [Military Dictatorship, Social Trauma, and the Inauguration of Sociology of Theater in Chile], vol. 8 of *Literature and Human Rights*, ed. Hernán Vidal (Minneapolis, Minn.: Institute for the Study of Ideologies and Literature, 1991).

31. Hurtado and Ochensius, *TIT,* 4–5.

32. The work of the Brazilian theater artist and director Augusto Boal in turn builds on work by Paolo Freire. Like Freire's work, Boal's *Theater of the Oppressed* (1974), trans. Charles A. and Maria-Odilia Leal McBride (New York: Theater Communications Group, 1985) was highly influential in Chile during the 1970s.

33. Hurtado and Ochensius, *TIT,* 4.

34. Ibid., 7.

35. Ibid., 6.

36. Ibid., 10. This strategy reflects the Brechtian approach influencing both TIT members and Benavente, namely creation based on developing a basic *gestus* of a story, involving all physical elements of the theater in its evolution. However, the TIT differs with Brecht's notion of the "alienation effect," for TIT actors claim to "be" their characters (rather than to "demonstrate" them in the Brechtian tradition). See Karl-Heinz Schops's discussion of Brecht's essay "On Experimental Theater" (1939) in *Bertolt Brecht: Life, Work and Criticism* (Fredericton, N.B.: York Press Ltd., 1989), chapter 2, as well as Boal's discussion of Hegel and Brecht in chapter 3 of *Theater of the Oppressed*.

37. Hurtado and Ochensius, *TIT,* 8.

38. Ibid., 61.

39. Ibid.

40. Ibid., 45–46.

41. Ibid., 35.

42. Ibid., 50.

43. Ibid., 53 (emphasis mine).

44. Ibid., 54–55.

45. Ibid., 69.

46. Ibid., 64.

47. Ibid., 57.

48. Ibid., 64.

49. Ibid., 63.

50. María de la Luz Hurtado describes this self-reflexivity in her introduction to this edition of the play, 15.

51. I was particularly struck by this when I saw the 1981 videotape of the production, thanks to David Benavente's generosity. The video version greatly informs my analysis, though textual citations necessarily come from the written version. See David Benavente and the Taller de Investigación Teatral, *Chilean Drama: Tres Marías y una Rosa*, produced by the York University Department of Instructional Aid Resources, directed by Raúl Osorio (stage director), David A. Homer and Robert Myles McKenzie (video directors), 122 min., York University, 1981, videocassette.

52. Negro's whereabouts, and the potential for him to interrupt at any moment, are signaled by the presence of his bicycle at the opening of scenes 1 and 3, and conversely, by its absence in scenes 2, 4, 5, and 6.

53. In *El discurso sobre el trabajador y el poblador en "El Mercurio" y "La Tercera" (1973–1983)* [Newspaper Discourse on Workers and Shantytown Dwellers, "El Mercurio" and "La Tercera" (1973–1983)] (Santiago: Documentos CENECA no. 62, 1986), Paulina Gutiérrez and Cristián Warnken hold that a nearly religious discourse underscoring the need for suffering by the popular sectors and workers, as well as "faith" in the future, "for the common good" and the success of the economic model, were the dominant messages in journalism dealing with those groups from 1973 to 1983.

54. See Kirkwood's *Feminarios*, particularly part I "Sexo-Género" ("personhood" is discussed on page 19), and "El feminismo como negación del autoritarismo" [Feminism as a Negation of Authoritarianism] (Santiago: FLACSO, Materia de Discusión no.32, 1983).

55. In the production of the play, a actual *arpillera* sewn by an artisans' workshop in Lo Hermida was used on stage, again reinforcing the impulse toward a faithful representation of the situation of the women observed by the TIT.

56. The play invokes the working-class neighborhood food and drink stands customary for celebrating Chilean Independence Day on 18 September.

57. The style of their song is typical of Chilean *payadores*, popular musicians (usually working-class or *campesino* men) who improvise lyrics for *cuecas* and many other traditional styles of Chilean folk music.

58. In *Tres Marías y una Rosa*, the audience learns in the wedding scene that Maruja had been widowed after her first marriage, and in this final scene, she dances the *cueca* alone in front of the wall hanging, clearly invoking the dance of the members of the Association of Family Members of the Detained-Disappeared.

CHAPTER 4. EROTIC DESIRE AND BODILY VIOLENCE

1. Julieta Kirkwood, "Feminismo y participación política en Chile" [Feminism and Political Participation in Chile] (1982), reproduced as chapter 5, "Tiempos difíciles" [Hard Times], in *Ser política en Chile*, 186–87.

2. Pía Barros, interview with Faride Zerán, 4–5.

3. Of course, Benavente was not, strictly speaking, the single author of *Tres Marías y una Rosa*, which was based on improvisations by the actresses of the TIT, as discussed in chapter 3.

4. Additional prose writers of this generation include Sonia González, Diego Muñoz Valenzuela, Leandro Urbina, Jaime Collyer, Antonio Ostornol, and others. See prologue, note 5, for texts on the "new Chilean narrative."

5. In viewing the cultural transition from the late 1970s to the early 1980s, it is important to consider that one of the primary ways that literary activity continued after the coup was through the proliferation of *talleres literarios*, which provided a collective space

for both the defense and the development of literary craftspeople (predominantly in poetry and narrative). For example, Pía Barros attended Enrique Lafourcade's workshop at the University of Chile (which in 1976 became the first "legal" postcoup *taller*); a few years later Ana María del Río in turn attended Barros's (by then established) workshop; Sonia Montecino attended José Donoso's narrative workshop, while Ramón Díaz Eterovic and Diego Muñoz worked with Poli Délano; Diamela Eltit formed part of the Colectivo de Acciones de Arte [Collective for Art Actions, CADA] with the poet Raúl Zurita, the video artist Lotty Rosenfeld, and others (as I discuss in chapter 5).

Typically, people with varying degrees of literary experience joined these workshops, which normally consisted of about ten members, one of whom would guide the group as its *monitor/a* (the person with the longest literary trajectory). Many people came to workshops seeking a forum for exchanging their opinions about daily life in militarized society; some sought to express themselves more effectively using the creative "distance" afforded them in literary writing. For others, mostly young middle-class students or experienced older writers, the workshop fulfilled some of the former functions of the university. Workshop members usually met weekly to complete creative writing exercises, and to give and receive opinions about works-in-progress.

Because publication was prohibitively expensive and books were censored (until 1983), many workshops developed alternative ways to produce and distribute literature collectively, through handcrafted magazines, photocopied editions, and leaflets. Even after censorship was lifted, small editorial houses, which would publish work with the aid of the author's or an institution's financial backing, provided a base for literary publication. In these ways, literature became a more collective enterprise because of (and despite) the pressures of postcoup Chilean society.

My participant observation in a few Santiago *talleres* taught me the value of this work for creating community ties. I thank members of Pía Barros's workshop at Ergo Sum; La Morada women's reading group "Lectura de Mujeres"; Edmundo Herrera's workshop at the Sociedad de Escritores de Chile [The Chilean Writers' Society], SECh; and Pedro Araucana's workshop in the *población* Lo Hermida. I also found useful Carlos Mellado's unpublished papers "Los talleres literarios en el período 1973–1983" [Literary Workshops, 1973–1983] and "Los talleres en los últimos 10 años" [Literary Workshops in the Last Ten Years], and his audiocassette recording of a 1983 meeting on *talleres* at the SECh in Santiago, with participation by Pía Barros, Erwin Díaz, Carlos Mellado and Bruno Serrano, for which Mellado's first paper was prepared.

6. I borrow these terms from Josefina Muñoz, Soledad Bianchi, Rodrigo Cánovas, Erwin Díaz, and Eugenia Brito, respectively. See Josefina Muñoz, "Reflexiones acerca de algunas huellas del poder en la narrativa de la generación del 80" [Reflections on Some Marks of Power on the Narrative of the Generation of 1980], in *Escribir en los bordes: Congreso Internacional de Literatura Femenina Latinoamericana, 1987* [Writing in the Margins: International Congress on Latin American Literature by Women], ed. Carmen Berenguer et al. (Santiago: Editorial Cuarto Propio, Colección Bajo Palabra, 1990), 259–71; Soledad Bianchi, "Una generación dispersa" [A Disperse Generation], in *Poesía chilena (Miradas-enfoques-apuntes)*, 20–36; Rodrigo Cánovas, *Novela chilena. Nuevas generaciones* and "La novela de la orfandad" [The Novel of Orphanhood], in Olivárez, *Nueva narrativa chilena*, 21–28; Erwin Díaz, "Algunas consideraciones" [Some Considerations], prologue to his anthology *Poesía chilena de hoy, de Parra a nuestros días* [Recent Chilean Poetry: From Parra to Today], 4th ed. (Santiago: Ediciones Documentas, 1991), 5–8; Eugenia Brito, introduction to *Campos minados*, 7–26.

7. I discuss these generational differences in chapter 1. See also Carlos Olivárez's introductory essay in *Los veteranos del 70* [Veterans of the 1970s] (Santiago: Ediciones Melquíades, 1988), 7–13; and José Promís, "Programas narrativas en la novela chilena del

siglo XX" [Narrative Programs in the Twentieth Century Chilean Novel], *Revista Iberoamericana* 168–69 (Julio–Diciembre 1994): 925–33.

8. Barros, interview with Faride Zerán, 5.

9. Foucault, *The History of Sexuality*, 94–96.

10. Pía Barros, *Miedos transitorios (de a uno, de a dos, de a todos)* (Santiago: Ergo Sum, 1986).

11. Josefina Muñoz cites this as a generational characteristic, "Reflexiones," 263. For her part, Barros refers to the contradiction of writing "pamphlets," of simplifying history and art rather than showing complexity, a strategy that, in its reductiveness, risked similarity to the official discourse. In her interview with Zerán, Barros commented:

> I remember a time when I was writing more pamphlets than stories. And it wasn't just me. Our literature [that of my generation] is the evidence of a constant contradiction, and of being a living witness to that contradiction [es la muestra de una contradicción constante, y de vivenciar esa contradicción]. (translation mine, 5)

Barros maintains that this writing was necessary precisely because the regime had excluded or denied the experiences of so many people. Hence, the most necessary **initial** response was the contestatory or confrontational one, in order to open up space for more complex discursive struggle. As Barros stressed in an interview I conducted with her in Santiago (19 December 1990): "la cosa contestataria era un error que había que cometer" [the contestatory stance was a mistake that we needed to make].

12. These brief political actions were "staged" in the center of Santiago, usually lasted from five to ten minutes, and dispersed just before the police would arrive. See Muñoz, "Reflexiones," 265.

13. The *microcuento* "Golpe" in *Miedos transitorios* presents a particularly transparent example of such references. It reads as follows:

> —Mamá, dijo el niño, ¿qué es un golpe?
> —Algo que duele muchísimo y deja amoratado el lugar donde te dio.
> El niño fue hasta la puerta de la casa. Todo el país que le cupo en la mirada tenía un tinte violáceo. (39)

> ["Mama," said the child, "what is a *golpe* {in Spanish, a coup d'état or a physical blow}?"
> "Something that hurts a lot and leaves a bruise in the place where it hit you."
> The child went to the door of the house. All of the country within his gaze had a violet tint.] (translation mine)

14. Pía Barros, *A horcajadas* (Santiago: Mosquito Editores, 1990). All Spanish language citations refer to this edition. All page citations for the English translations refer to the subsequent Spanish-English edition titled *A horcajadas/Astride*, trans. and ed. Analisa Taylor, with translations by Amanda Powell, Stephen F. White, Alice A. Nelson, and Kathryn Kruger-Hickman (Santiago: Editorial Asterión, 1992). Where only one citation is given, it refers to the first Spanish edition.

15. The beginning of the United Nations Decade for Women in 1975 legitimized international discussion of gender issues and allocated financial resources for that purpose. This funding eventually supported several nongovernmental organizations in Santiago. Rosa Bravo and Rosalba Todaro ("Chilean Women and the UN Decade for Women," trans. Patricia Chuchryk, *Women's Studies International Forum* 8, no. 2 [1985]: 111–16) discuss the increased political organization of women in Chile, and their higher participation in the labor

force, during the UN Decade. They also note that in 1975 the Pinochet regime institutionalized its policies toward women (using the rhetoric/ideology of volunteerism, e.g., women as "servants to the Fatherland"), by creating the National Secretariat for Women and by allocating additional resources to CEMAs-Chile, the right-wing volunteer organizations for women led by Lucía Hiriart de Pinochet.

16. My understanding of the reemergence of feminism in postcoup Chile has been immeasurably enriched by interviews with some of the women involved in early groups, including Margarita Pisano (at La Morada, 12 June 1989, 19 and 24 November 1990, and informal conversations subsequent to her departure from La Morada, June 1998), María Antonieta Saa (at ISIS, 7 and 9 June 1989, and later, as mayor of Conchalí under Aylwin, 27 October 1990), Coti Silva (of MOMUPO, 8 June 1989 and 27 October 1990), and Adriana Santa Cruz (at *Fempress*, 9 June 1989). All of these interviews took place in Santiago, Chile.

17. The most thorough investigation of the reemergence of feminism in Chile is Patricia Marie Chuchryk's fascinating doctoral thesis, "Protest, Politics and Personal Life: The Emergence of Feminism in a Military Dictatorship, Chile 1973–1983" (Ph.D. diss., York University [Toronto], 1984). The term "feminist awakening" is hers (317).

Many groups contributed to this feminist presence. I have discussed some cases of the working-class women's resistance in the previous chapters. In addition, a small group of leftist middle-class women, including some who had recently returned from exile (with access to funding from international feminist agencies), began to meet in the "safe space" afforded them within the Academia de Humanismo Cristiano [Academy for Christian Humanism], or AHC, in 1977. This group, initially called the Asociación para la Unidad de las Mujeres [Association for the Unity of Women], or ASUMA, strategically decided that each of its members would form another group dedicated to discussion of the situation of women in militarized Chile. By 1979, the original members had formed several new nongovernmental organizations, and ASUMA became the Círculo de Estudios de la Mujer [Circle on Women's Studies], a group committed to generating systematic information and discussion of gender issues.

Gradually, a number of groups concerned with distinct visions of gender and class oppression also formed. In 1978, for example, the Women's Department of the Coordinadora Nacional Sindical (CNS, a new organization that in effect replaced the former CUT, a major labor union that became illegal after the coup) organized an extraordinary public meeting attended by some seven thousand women in the Caupolicán Theater in Santiago, for discussion among women workers about general labor issues. By the early 1980s, many women's departments and new feminist NGOs had likewise formed, including the Women's Section of the Chilean Human Rights Commission, 1979; the Comité de Defensa de los Derechos de la Mujer [Committee in Defense of Women's Rights], or CODEM, 1980; the Programa de Estudios y Capacitación de la Mujer Campesina e Indígena [Program for Research and Empowerment of Peasant and Indigenous Women], or PEMCI, 1981; Mujeres de Chile [Women of Chile], or MUDECHI, 1981; and the Movimiento de Mujeres Pobladoras [Shantytown Women's Movement], or MOMUPO, 1982; and others. The emergence of these groups was accompanied by a flourishing of small magazines that they produced, including *Vamos mujer* [Let's Go Women] by working-class women in subsistence organizations, 1980]; *Furia* [Fury], by middle-class socialist women, 1981; *Ormiga* [Ant], by university women with a Christian and feminist focus, 1981; and *Hojita* [Leaflet], coedited by MOMUPO and CDM for a primarily working-class audience, 1982.

By November 1982, all of these groups came together, crossing class lines, for the first "Jornada de la Mujer" [Woman's Day], sponsored by the Círculo, a meeting which led to the founding of two umbrella groups: the Centro de Estudios de la Mujer [Center for Women's Studies], for feminist research, and the Movimiento Feminista [Feminist Movement], dedicated to political activism. See Chuchryk, "Protest, Politics, and Personal Life," 352; and Natacha Molina, "Cronología" (Appendix), in *Lo femenino y lo democrático en el Chile de hoy* [Feminism and Democracy in Chile Today] (Santiago: Ediciones Documentas/VECTOR, 1986), for more on this history.

18. Members of MEMCh'83 worked to compile a written history of women's political work in Chile. Among the published titles are: Olga Poblete et al., *Antología del MEMCh* [MEMCh Anthology] (Santiago: Editorial MEMCh, 1984); Edda Gaviola et al., *Queremos votar en las próximas elecciones* [We Want to Vote in the Next Election] (Santiago: Coedición Centro de análisis y difusión de la condición de la mujer, "La Morada", *Fempress*, ILET, ISIS, Librería Lila, PEMCI, CEM, 1986); and Kirkwood, *Ser política en Chile*.

19. This slogan appeared on many pamphlets distributed during the first National Protest, preceding its role in the December 1983 mobilization in the Caupolicán Theater in Santiago.

20. Chuchryk, "Protest, Politics, and Personal Life," 334.

21. Ibid., 355.

22. My understanding of the protests relies on Gonzalo de la Maza and Mario Garcés, *La explosión de las mayorías: Protesta Nacional 1983–1984* [The Explosion of the Majority: National Protests, 1983–1984] (Santiago: ECO Educación y comunicaciones, 1985); Cathy Lisa Schneider, *Shantytown Protest in Pinochet's Chile;* and Tomás Moulian, *Chile actual*, "Tercera Parte: Mirando hacia atrás II. La dictadura constitucional" [Part 3: Looking Back II: The Constitutional Dictatorship]. Genaro Arriagada interprets these events from a more centrist perspective in *Pinochet: Politics of Power* (Boston: Unwin Hyman, 1988), chapter 6.

23. These factors were of course on top of the generalized repression that the population had endured. The years 1981–82 marked the end of the so-called "economic miracle," as unemployment rates soared, wages dropped, businesses and banks which had been riding on credit faced bankruptcy, and poverty extended beyond the working class to become a middle-class reality. This followed the 11 September 1980 "plebiscite" staged by the regime for pubic approval of the military government's constitution of 1980. This document, drafted by Pinochet's ideologues to replace Chile's 1925 constitution, guaranteed that the regime would remain in power for a minimum of eight more years, with a vote on its continuation in power to take place in 1989. This 1980 plebiscite proved to be a democratic farce, in which voting was restricted and results fabricated to meet the regime's need for institutional legitimacy. At the same time, the constitution established mechanisms for ensuring the military's institutional transcendence well beyond 1989, as I discuss in the epilogue. See Eugenio Ahumada et al., *La memoria prohibida*, vol. 3, chapter 10, "¿Algo nuevo bajo el sol?" [Something New Under the Sun?] and Tomás Moulian, *Chile actual*, "Tercera Parte," chapter 2.

24. See my discussion of James C. Scott's notion of "disguised ideological insubordination" in chapter 2.

25. The first protest was called by the Confederación de Trabajadores del Cobre [Copper Workers Federation]. By the third and fourth protests (12 July 1983 and 11 August 1983), the oppositional leadership role had shifted from labor to the reconstituted political parties, joined together as the Alianza Democrática [Democratic Alliance].

26. Julieta Kirkwood's work, particularly *Ser política en Chile*, emphasizes this historic relationship between feminism and leftist political parties in Chile. This relationship is reminiscent (despite crucial contextual differences) of tensions that emerged within the New Left in the United States during the 1960s and 1970s; see, for example, Sara Evans's engaging book *Personal Politics: The Roots of Women's Liberation in the Civil Rights Movement and the New Left* (New York: Vintage Books, 1980).

27. In appendix 4 of "Protest, Politics, and Personal Life," Chuchryk includes an

English translation of the 18 August statement. The concluding paragraphs make explicit the link between traditional gender politics and the military regime: "we know that all this [repression] is a product of the ruling authoritarian culture that is inspired by a *machista* conception of society." The text also pointed to the need to reestablish what I have called desire-based links with community: "We stand for a society which does not deny feeling and emotion as essential to human relations and organizations and which does not continue to exclude that participation of women in all instances of decision-making" (488).

28. De la Maza and Garcés, *La explosión de las mayorías*, 108 (translation and emphasis mine).

29. After the first four protests, the Pinochet government realized that it faced the real threat of a maturing civil society. It responded with the most brutal repression it had exercised since the early months after the coup. De la Maza and Garcés describe the military response to the fourth protest as a "massacre" (99): the eighteen thousand troops unleashed in Santiago alone resulted in twenty-seven deaths and twenty-six hundred arrests. However, the regime was forced to make some political concessions, allowing the return of some exiles and announcing the government's "willingness" to dialogue with the opposition. This last concession was actually the government's astute political strategy to show its own "openness" while attempting to disable the protests by dividing the opposition. This strategy worked, for the opposition became divided between those who would consider negotiation with the government and those who thought that such dialogue conceded legitimacy to the regime, and that popular struggle was the only answer. See de la Maza and Garcés, *La explosión de las mayorías*, 98–102.

30. Chuchryk ("Protest, Politics, and Personal Life," 348) gives UPI's figure of four hundred thousand, citing *Hoy* 331 (1983): 7.

31. De la Maza and Garcés, *La explosión de las mayorías*, 48–49.

32. Ibid., part 5, especially 126–34; see also my epilogue.

33. Though the perception of authors and publishers alike is that the number of books published dramatically increased by the years 1985–86, no figures are available to substantiate this claim. The lack of data shows how disarticulated literary production had become after the coup. Even after the lifting of prior censorship, many authors continued to publish using alternative channels, for economic reasons. At the same time, the increasing importance of television and other media led to a decrease in the number of books purchased by Chileans during the entire Pinochet period. See Bernardo Subercaseaux, ed., *El libro en Chile (su presente y su futuro)* [Books in Chile: Their Present and Future] (Santiago: CENECA, Cámara chilena del libro, CED, 1986); and Brunner, Barrios, and Catalán, *Chile*, 137–41.

34. This perception among writers and publishers is substantiated by a number of newspaper articles which speak of a wave of "new women writers" producing during the 1980s. See, for example: Claudia Donoso, "Para reconocerse mejor" [Recognizing Oneself Better], *APSI*, 27 April–3 May 1987, 44–45; Luisa Ulibarri, "Cien mujeres y cinco días de preguntas" [One Hundred Women and Five Days of Questions], *La Epoca*, 15 August 1987, 24; Poli Délano, "La irrupción de las novelistas" [The Eruption of Women Novelists], *Fortín Mapocho*, 3 November 1987, 9; Ana María Foxley, "Literatura de mujeres: ¿una palabra sospechosa?" [Women's Literature: A Suspicious Phrase?], *Literatura y libros*, supplement in *La Epoca*, 15 May 1988, 1–2; Rosario Guzmán Bravo, "Se desplegaron las letras femeninas" [Women's Writing Takes Off], *Ya (Revista Femenina de El Mercurio)* 336 (20 February 1990): 8–9; "Congreso Internacional de Literatura Femenina Latinoamericana: Una forma de transgresión" [International Congress on Latin American Literature by Women: A Form of Transgression], *Revista VIVA* (Lima, Peru), November 1987, 50–52.

Though any anthology is a subjective measure of literary production, it nonetheless seems significant that many anthologies produced in the 1980s either approached a gender balance or explicitly focused on women writers. See Jorge Calvo et al., *Cuento aparte* [Separate Story] (Santiago: Ediciones Cerro Huelén, 1986); Fempress, ed., *El cuento feminista latinoamericano* [Latin American Feminist Stories] (Santiago: ILET, 1988); Juan Villegas, ed., *Antología de la nueva poesía femenina chilena* [Anthology of New Poetry by Chilean Women] (Santiago: Editorial La Noria, 1985); Inge Corssen, ed., *La mujer en la poesía chilena de los '80* [Women in Chilean Poetry of the 1980s] (Santiago: Ediciones INCOR Ltda., 1987). Two points of comparison with the previous generation: in a conference of the generation of 1970—Antonio Avaria, Poli Délano, Fernando Jeréz, Ernesto Malbrán, Ramiro Rivas, and Antonio Skármeta, "Los novísimos, veinte años después" [The Newest Writers, Twenty Years Later], a panel discussion at the SECh [Chilean Writers' Society], Santiago, Chile, 25–26 June 1991—panelists could only name one woman prose writer who was their contemporary (Eugenia Echeverría). Likewise, only two women (Echeverría and the poet Cecilia Vicuña) are included in Carlos Olivarez's anthology of poetry and prose, *Los veteranos del 70*. It must be remembered, however, that the generation of 1950 had several important women writers (Mercedes Valdivieso, Isidora Aguirre, and others).

35. In her introductory remarks to the collected proceedings of the Congreso (Carmen Berenguer et al., *Escribir en los bordes*), Eugenia Brito states that:

> It was no coincidence that a body of thought on the relationship between women, writing, and power had emerged precisely in a country dominated by tyranny. To create implies reclaiming [reconquering] one's own body and one's own history. (translation mine, 7–8)

It is also significant that much of the criticism written about this production was written by women involved directly or indirectly in the feminist movement (e.g., Raquel Olea, Eliana Ortega, Soledad Bianchi, Adriana Valdés, Nelly Richard, Lucía Guerra, among others).

36. As discussed in the Introduction, I have found enabling Foucault's analysis of the ways in which culturally produced discourses codify bodies, especially his notion of "discipline" in part 3 of *Discipline and Punish* (1975). I also build upon his notion of sexual "boundaries" (and "regulation" of pleasure) in *The History of Sexuality*, vol. 1 (1976), especially chapter 3 ("Domain"). See also my discussion of Susan Bordo's work on feminism and Foucault in the Introduction.

37. Juan Carlos Lértora, introduction to the Spanish edition, 7.

38. Foucault, *The History of Sexuality*, 95.

39. See Hélène Cixous, "The Laugh of the Medusa," in *New French Feminisms*, ed. Elaine Marks and Isabelle Courtivron (New York: Schocken Books, 1981), 245–64.

40. The idea of different "sides" of reality evokes Julio Cortázar's work, particularly *Rayuela*. Since Cortázar was read widely (though clandestinely) by prose writers of Barros's generation, her use of this structure would be easily recognized in that community.

41. See María Luisa Bombal, *La última niebla/La amortajada* [*The House of Mist and The Shrouded Woman*] (Barcelona: Seix Barral Biblioteca Breve, 1984).

42. It is no coincidence that Ismael, one of the few named characters in this collection, should have that unusual Biblical name. In the Judeo-Christian tradition, Ismael was the son of Abraham and Hagar, a slave bought by Sara to serve as the progenitor of Abraham's offspring, due to Sara's own infertility. Later, after the birth of Isaac to Abraham and Sara, Ismael was blessed by God, and became the founder and patriarch of the twelve lost tribes of Israel, or the Ismaelites. According to this foundational fable, Ismael, as a bastard son, established his sense of identity by exercising patriarchal power as a warrior and social leader. Barros's Ismael unwittingly has inherited both a "bastard" status (in a mestizo culture) as well as his role as "patriarch" within the domestic space.

43. This interrelationship between repression and obsession experienced by the *ama de casa*, who is closed in by her husband's (culturally generated) expectations, is treated especially strongly in the collection's tenth story, "Lo había odiado con pulcritud" ["He Had Hated It with Pulchritude"]. This thematic focus not only invokes Barros's connection to Bombal's *La última niebla*, as mentioned above, but also brings to mind the work of the nineteenth-century U.S. feminist Charlotte Perkins Gilman, specifically *The Yellow Wallpaper* (1899). See the edition with an afterword by Elaine R. Hedges (New York: The Feminist Press, 1973).

44. Foucault, *Discipline and Punish*, 138.

45. Octavio Paz, *El laberinto de la soledad* [*Labyrinth of Solitude*] (Mexico, D.F.: Fondo de Cultura Económica, 1984), 59–80.

46. See Montecino's "La 'política maternal' y la palabra disociada de las prácticas" [Maternal Politics and the Word Disassociated from Practice], in *Madres y huachos*, 95–120. See also chapter 1, n. 20.

47. See, for example, Marta Brunet, *Aguas abajo: Cuentos* [*Downstream: Stories*] (1943; reprint, with a prologue by Kemy Oyarzún, Santiago: Cuarto Propio, 1997).

CHAPTER 5: THE SOCIAL BODY AND THE REBIRTH OF HISTORY

1. Brito, *Campos minados*, 11.

2. Diamela Eltit, *Por la patria* [*For the Fatherland*] (Santiago: Las Ediciones del Ornitorrinco, 1986), 180 (translation mine).

3. Eltit's exploration of this increasingly subjective reproduction of power reaches its most interiorized expression in *Los vigilantes* [*The Nightwatchmen*] (Santiago: Editorial Sudamericana, 1994).

4. Diamela Eltit, introduction to *El padre mío* [*Father of Mine*] (Santiago: Francisco Zegers Editor, 1989), 11 (translation and emphasis mine). Theodor W. Adorno would call this a negative dialectical relationship. See *Negative Dialectics*, trans. E. B. Ashton (New York: Continuum, 1973).

5. Insofar as Eltit views public history as being contested within the social margins, I am reminded of Benavente's focus on the shantytown women's resistance in *Tres Marías y una Rosa*, although the two works are markedly different in aesthetic approach. Among postcoup writers, theater written by the working-class playwright Juan Radrigán perhaps comes closest to Eltit's vision of marginals as the degraded protagonists of authoritarian society. See his *teatro de juan radrigán (sic)* [Theater by Juan Radrigán] (Santiago: CENECA, 1984) and chapter 3 of Rodrigo Cánovas's *Lihn, Zurita, ICTUS, Radrigán*, cited previously. Eltit's radically fragmented language distinguishes her work from Radrigán's and from the older generations of Chilean writers who treated the theme of marginality before her, including Carlos Droguett, Marta Brunet, Manuel Rojas, Acevedo Hernández, José Donoso, and others.

6. I am indebted to Brito's discussion of the "sistema del frote" [system of the rub], *Campos minados*, 185.

7. Brito points out how the press created a "bad boy" persona of Zurita, despite hailing him as the "next Neruda" (ibid., 174). A similar pattern occurred with Eltit in the years following *E. Luminata*'s publication—which may (or may not) be due to her link with Zurita (they were married until 1985). Ignacio Valente, the conservative priest of *El Mercurio*'s literary column who launched Zurita's career, did recognize Eltit's work, but gave it increasingly negative attention over time. His first piece was a structural analysis of *E. Luminata* that separated the text from any political ramifications by emphasizing its hermetic language, an "accusation" that has plagued the reception of Eltit's work since that

time. See Ignacio Valente, "Diamela Eltit: Una novela experimental" [Diamela Eltit: An Experimental Novel] *El Mercurio,* 25 March 1984, E3; and Manuel Espinosa Orellana, *Aproximaciones a cuatro mundos de la poesía chilena actual* [Approaches to Four Worlds of Chilean Poetry Today] (Quilpué: Ediciones Altazor, Quincena Crítica, 1984).

8. Since, with the Guggenheim, Eltit was sanctioned from outside of Chile as a novelist of exceptional merit, the Chilean media, little accustomed to nonpaternalistic reception of women writers, finally set about reviewing her work. Although *E. Luminata* had been published two years earlier, much of the critical attention it received was in August 1985, probably a direct result of Eltit's Guggenheim; a majority of the articles were written by women. See A.M.F. [Ana María Foxley?], "Diamela Eltit: Acoplamiento incestuoso" [Diamela Eltit: Incestuous Coupling] *Hoy,* no. 421 (12–18 August 1985): 41; Carmen Ortúzar "Una escritora chilena obsesiva de la realidad" [A Chilean Woman Writer Obsessed with Reality], *El Mercurio* (Antofagasta-Calama, 21 August 1985), suplemento *Arte y Cultura,* 4; María Eugenia Brito, "Entrevista a Diamela Eltit: Desde la mujer a la androginía" [Interview of Diamela Eltit: From Woman to Androgyny], *Pluma y pincel,* no. 17 (August 1985): 42–43; and *"Lumpérica* de Diamela Eltit, Una novela que traza su propio horizonte" [*E. Luminata* by Diamela Eltit: A Novel That Invents Its Own Horizon], *Pluma y pincel,* no. 17 (August 1985): 43–45. Eltit's growing status within the U.S. academy was confirmed only a few years later, including the analysis of her work presented by a speaker at the President's Forum during the December 1991 Modern Language Association Annual Conference in San Francisco, California (see Raymond L. Williams's "Truth Claims, Postmodernism, and the Latin American Novel").

9. Brito comments on these three elements of the title (*Campos minados,* 187).

10. Nelly Richard examines the intergenerational aspects of CADA and the *avanzada* in her "Una cita limítrofe entre neovanguardia y postvanguardia" [Border Citation Between Neo- and Post-Avant-Garde] in *La insubordinación de los signos (cambio político, transformaciones culturales y poéticas de la crisis)* [The Insubordination of Signs (Political Change, Cultural Transformation, and Poetics of Crisis)] (Santiago: Cuarto Propio, 1994), 37–54. She discusses the utopian/modernist impulse behind some of CADA's statements in tension with the more postmodern polyvalence of its practices.

11. Here I am thinking of Zurita's Dantean *Purgatorio* [Purgatory] (Santiago: Editorial Universitaria, 1979) and *Anteparaíso* [Anteparadise] (Santiago: Editores Asociados, 1982); Fariña's *El primer libro* [The First Book] (Santiago: Ediciones Amaranto, 1985) and *Albricia* [Good News] (Santiago: Ediciones Archivo, 1988); Maqueira's *La tirana* [Female Tyrant] poems (Santiago: Edición Tempus Tacendi, 1983); and Martínez's *La nueva novela* [The New Novel] (Santiago: Ediciones Archivo, 1977). Brito seems to agree with this point, since Eltit is the only novelist she includes in her study of postcoup poetry, *Campos minados.* See also chapter 2, note 28, with reference to Zurita's foundationalism vis-à-vis Dorfman's *Widows.*

12. See chapter 4, note 5.

13. Diamela Eltit, interview by the author, 14 August 1990, Santiago, Chile, tape recording.

14. See Nelly Richard, *Margins and Institutions: Art in Chile Since 1973,* a special issue of *Art & Text* 21 (1986), especially the chapter "The Rhetoric of the Body," 65–73; and Brito, *Campos minados,* 176.

15. Richard compares what she terms Carlos Leppe's aesthetic of the "sexualized body" with CADA's aesthetic of the "stigmatized body"; she claims that these two aesthetics form the main framework for visually representing the body in postcoup Chile. According to Richard, Leppe's 1975 art installation at the Gallery "Módulos y Formas," *El perchero* [The Clothes Rack] was "the first photographic treatment of the male nude disguised as a woman in Chilean Art" (*Margins and Institutions,* 65–66). Though I have chosen to limit

my own remarks to CADA, Leppe's work provides an interesting early example of the feminized social body in art after the coup.

16. These terms come from the essays by Brito and Richard cited in note 14.

17. In *Margins and Institutions* (152 n. 4), Richard cites "Una ponencia del CADA" [A paper by CADA], *Ruptura* [Rupture] (Santiago: Ediciones CADA, 1982). Emphasis and translation are mine.

18. Eltit emphasized the symbolism of this art action at length in the interview with me. In *La insubordinación de los signos*, Richard mentions the full page text CADA placed in *Hoy* [Today] magazine to coincide with this act: "imaginar esta página completamente blanca / imaginar esta página blanca como la leche diaria a consumir / imaginar cada rincón de Chile privado del consumo diario de leche como páginas blancas para llenar" [Imagine this page completely blank / imagine this blank page as white as milk for everyday consumption / imagine all corners of Chile deprived of the everyday consumption of milk as blank pages to fill up] (39, translation mine). CADA simultaneously played a recorded text read in five languages denouncing poverty in Chile at the United Nations building.

19. Richard, *Margins and Institutions*, 138 (emphasis mine).

20. Tierney-Tello, "Testimony," 80.

21. Richard, *Margins and Institutions*, 68.

22. This notion also motivated Raúl Zurita's 1975 burning part of his face (to show how each body is scarred by collective suffering) and his 1980 attempt to blind himself. However, these acts were taken up by the press as evidence of Zurita's "bad boy" tendencies, and were not therefore generally understood as challenging the dominant order.

23. Richard, *Margins and Institutions*, 55.

24. Eltit, interview by author.

25. In *Margins and Institutions*, Richard provides further evidence of the restricted public reception of CADA's work. She cites two 1975 events—Leppe's *Perchera* and Zurita's burning of his cheek—as the first *acciones de arte*. Yet these "art actions" took place, respectively, in a small Santiago art gallery (Módulos y Formas) and in Zurita's private home (though his face was photographed, to become part of his 1979 poetry collection *Purgatorio*). In *Chile: Transformaciones culturales y modernidad*, Brunner, Barrios, and Catalán critique this aspect of the "new art scene," describing it ultimately as a "ghetto experience" (155).

26. Richard shows that CADA did connect, however, with some modernist work:

> At this time [September 1983], collective works emerged in which the artists "chose to address the walls of the city and voice their protest with the brief and simple cry, *No +*, which encouraged others to fill in the missing word: for instance, no more hunger, no more pain, no more death" (*Hoy*, Sept. 1983). The walls, whose use was forbidden throughout the regime, were reconquered by the CADA artists as places for a popularly committed art, but in a way that linked up with the earlier . . . Brigadas Muralistas, thus eradicating the difference between the two. (*Margins and Institutions*, 57)

27. In forging this path, the avanzada occupied a border zone between neo- and post-avante-garde, as Richard points out in *La insubordinación de los signos*, 37–54.

28. Richard, "Reply to Vidal," 231 (discussed in my introduction).

29. Eltit, interview with Brito, 42–43.

30. Diamela Eltit, *Lumpérica* (Santiago: Las Ediciones del Ornitorrinco, 1983). Published in English as *E. Luminata*, translated and with an afterword by Ronald Christ (Santa Fe, N.Mex.: Lumen, 1997). Citations in Spanish refer to the original edition, while those in English refer to the Christ translation. Where only one work is cited, the reference is to the Spanish original.

31. Eltit, interview with Brito, 43.

32. Given this context, it is no coincidence that there was a video boom in Chile during the late 1970s and early 1980s. Video was relatively easy to use and could be as private or as public as circumstances required; it was also easily hidden and could be easily shown, two advantages in a repressive context.

33. Brito also describes the novel as performance, *Campos minados*, 168–69.

34. This image bears a striking resemblance to the totalizing "gaze" of surveillance from an indefinite source, discussed by Foucault in *Discipline and Punish*, especially part 3, chapter 3.

35. Each of these elements has its echo in different segments of other chapters. For example, the issue of resistance symbolized by the *contraluz* of chapter 1 evolves into the darkness of the next chapter's interrogation scene, and later, into the act of the light's "condensation," as rendered in the old Spanish of chapter 3: "Porque si la luz se condensara sobre su cuerpo, cualquier forma tomaría entonces, la más vil; dejaría sus ancares o la fortaleza del mugido hasta reducido aspecto . . ." (59) [Because if the light condensed on her body, then she could take any form, the vilest; it could leave her haunches or the strength of the moo diminished in presence] (69).

36. See note 9.

37. The reversal of the Chilean Nobel Prize–winning poet Pablo Neruda's names is particularly pointed here. Eltit's irreverence in this passage reminds me of Nicanor Parra's antipoems, for example, his "Manifiesto" [Manifesto], in which Parra ironically proclaims that "Los poetas bajaron del Olimpo" [The poets descended from Olympus]. In *Obra gruesa* [Collected Works] (Santiago: Andrés Bello, 1983), 153.

38. Brito offers her meditation on these two key words in *Campos minados*, chapter 5, especially 187–88.

39. In *Campos minados*, Brito describes *E. Luminata* as a ritual of baptism by E. Luminata of "los pálidos" (169). In what is otherwise an insightful essay that shares several points of agreement with the present chapter, Brito miscasts the place of "los pálidos" in marking E.'s body (rather than, as she has it, the other way around). It is crucial that "los pálidos" reject E.'s naming of them, an affront to their own significant (if ephemeral) narrative power.

40. In her dissertation ("Power and Women's Writing in Chile: 1973–1988," mentioned in the introduction), Barbara Lee Loach makes some interesting observations on Eltit's work, but fails to make adequate connections between the sociopolitical context and the changes in Eltit's style. For example, she observes that the trajectory of Eltit's first three novels is one of "destruction" *(E. Luminata),* to "reconstruction" *(Por la patria),* to "creation" *(The Fourth World),* but she does not interpret this trajectory in any historicized way. Instead, Loach generically states: "Eltit's language demonstrates resistance to traditional discourse through the disruption and negation of conventional language and the inclusion of experimental techniques associated with the *nouveau roman*" (250). Although this is formally true, Loach fails to see this as a specific aesthetic response to the context of the Pinochet regime (which she had taken care to describe in her opening chapters). I see this as a significant gap if text and context are to be read together meaningfully.

41. All page citations of the novel will be included parenthetically in the text, and refer to the Spanish language edition cited in note 2. All translations are my own.

42. The death of the father also had biographical significance for Eltit. In her "Experiencia literaria y palabra en duelo" [Literary Experience and the Word in Mourning], in *Duelo y creatividad (Seminario: Literatura, sicoanálisis, enfoque sistémico)* [Mourning and Creativity (Seminar: Literature, Psychoanalysis, Systemic Focus)] (Santiago: Editorial Cuarto Propio, Cuaderno "Mujer y Límites," Serie Ensayo no. 1, 1989), Eltit states that she began writing *Por la patria* after the violent death of her own father in 1983, and that the novel's

title responded to her own double sense of loss in the postcoup context. The title *Por la patria* was for Eltit "an encoded epitaph to my father and a social epitaph in solidarity with the numerous deaths that have taken place in the country due to the violence of the system, which has instilled a clandestine grief throughout the land" (27, translation mine). In another interview—Patricio Ríos S., "Chile: ni deprecio ni puro amor" [Chile: Neither Contempt Nor True Love], *Cauce* 100 (23 March 1987): 30—Eltit elaborates the title's denunciatory aspect: "Nos hemos hecho polvo en este país, por este país, por la patria" [We've destroyed ourselves in this country, for this country, for the Fatherland {during these years of dictatorship}].

43. Brito analyzes the importance of this conversion to "Mother of Mothers" in "El doble relato en la novela *Por la patria* de Diamela Eltit" [The Double Tale in the Novel *Por la patria* by Diamela Eltit], in Berenguer et al., *Escribir en los bordes*, 243–58.

44. Djelal Kadir, *The Other Writing: Postcolonial Essays in Latin America's Writing Culture* (West Lafayette, Ind.: Purdue University Press, 1993), 196.

45. An obvious example of this contrast appears in chapter 5. One subsection begins with a clichéd line attributed to Juan, "HABLA JUAN—Por aire, por mar, por tierra" [JUAN SAYS: "By air, by sea, by land"], before continuing with a very complex narration attributed to Coya for the next few pages (141–43).

46. This is the phrase that Eltit used to characterize *Por la patria* in her 1987 interview with Patricio Ríos S., "Chile: ni desprecio ni puro amor." For reception of *Por la patria*, see Rodrigo Cánovas, "Para leer" [To Read], *Análisis,* no. 159 (27 January 1987): 43; and Marta Contreras, "*Por la patria:* Una novela femenina de vanguardia" [*Por la patria:* An Avant-garde Novel Written by a Woman], *El Sur,* 7 June 1987, supplement *Arte y cultura,* vii.

47. Paz Errázuriz and Diamela Eltit, *El infarto del alma* [Heart Attack of the Soul] (Santiago: Francisco Zegers, 1994). See also Tierney-Tello's "Testimony," 78–96.

48. True to his increasingly negative attitude toward Eltit's work, Valente concludes, "I have no idea if anyone will understand the febrile writing in the second part of *The Fourth World*." See Valente's "El cuerpo es un horror y es una gloria" [The Body in Horror and Glory] *Revista de libros de "El Mercurio,"* 21 May 1989, 1 and 4.

49. Diamela Eltit, *El cuarto mundo* (Santiago: Editorial Planeta Biblioteca del Sur, 1988). Published in English as *The Fourth World*, translated and with a foreword by Dick Gerdes (Lincoln: University of Nebraska Press, 1995). Citations in Spanish refer to the original edition, while those in English refer to the Gerdes translation, unless otherwise noted. Where only one work is cited, the reference is to the Spanish original.

50. Given Eltit's reputation (as fostered by Valente), Planeta significantly chose to highlight *El cuarto mundo*'s accessibility on its back cover, which reads: "Con un estilo depurado, despojado de toda retórica vacía, Diamela Eltit alcanza en *El cuarto mundo* una comunicación plena con el lector" [With a bare, lean style, stripped of all empty rhetoric, Diamela Eltit achieves in *The Fourth World* ample communication with her readers] (translation mine). Perhaps also due to the novel's language, or to its author's growing public recognition, it received more reviews than had *Por la patria* after its publication. See Agata Gligo, "'El Cuarto Mundo' de Diamela Eltit" [Diamela Eltit's *The Fourth World*], *Mensaje* 377 (March–April 1989): 110–11; Fernando Jeréz, "'El cuarto mundo,' Novela de Diamela Eltit" [*The Fourth World*, a novel by Diamela Eltit], *Fortín Diario,* 23 April 1989, 21; and Ana María Larraín "Diamela Eltit: El trabajo es la vida y mi vida" [Diamela Eltit: Work Is Life, and Is My Life], *Revista de Libros de EL MERCURIO,* 21 May 1989, 1, 4–5.

51. In *Lengua víbora: Producciones de lo femenino de la escritura de mujeres chilenas* [Viper Tongue: Producciones of the Feminine in Writing by Chilean Women] (Santiago: Cuarto Propio, 1998), Raquel Olea explores these spaces as metaphors of "encierro" or confinement (63).

52. Raymond L. Williams ascribes to the first theory: *"The Fourth World*, from the French *le quart monde*, can be postulated as a space consisting of a periphery of a periphery, that is, as a marginal space in an already peripheral Third World nation" (8).

53. Julio Ortega, "Diamela Eltit y el imaginario de la virtualidad" [Diamela Eltit and the Virtual Imaginary] in the very important critical anthology on Eltit's work, edited by Juan Carlos Lértora, *Una poética de literatura menor: La narrativa de Diamela Eltit* [A Poetics of "Small" Literature: The Narrative of Diamela Eltit] (Santiago: Editorial Cuarto Propio, 1993), 79.

54. Here I use terms emphasized by Eltit in an interview with Radomiro Spotorno, "Diamela Eltit, escritora: 'Debemos ser más emblemáticos y menos analíticos'" [The Writer Diamela Eltit: "We Should Be More Emblematic and Less Analytical"], *Página abierta*, no. 12 (16 April 1990): 34–35. In it, Eltit describes how the dictatorship affected bodies and discourses:

> During the dictatorship, bodies were lost, entire marginal groups were lost. . . . There is a whole mass of people that was lost, in one form or another, during these years, millions of lost people. What are you going to say to those people? You have to offer them a discourse other than analysis; we need to be more emblematic and less analytical. (35, translation mine)

55. Olea, *Lengua víbora*, 62.
56. Williams, "Truth Claims," 7.

Chapter 6: Of Bodiless Spirits and the Transition to Democracy

1. Isabel Allende, *Eva Luna* (Barcelona: Plaza y Janés, 1987), 276. Translated as *Eva Luna*, trans. Margaret Sayers Peden (New York: Bantam, 1989), 300–301.

2. Isabel Allende, *La casa de los espíritus* (Barcelona: Plaza y Janés, 1987). Translated as *The House of the Spirits*, trans. Magda Bogin (New York: Bantam, 1986). All citations will be included parenthetically in the text, and refer to these editions. Where only one citation is offered, it refers to the original Spanish.

3. As I will discuss further, Allende's success in translation has also been phenomenal. Nora Erro-Peralta and Caridad Silva-Núñez, eds., state in *Beyond the Border: A New Age in Latin American Women's Fiction* (San Francisco, Calif.: Cleis Press, 1991) that *The House of the Spirits* "became an instant best-seller in Spain, France, Germany, Japan, and the United States. This novel alone makes her the most widely read Latin American woman of all time" (23).

4. I take the term "late capitalist" from Ernest Mandel, *Late Capitalism*, trans. Joris DeBres (London: Verso, 1987).

5. Collins and Lear state: "[B]etween 1978 and 1988 the richest 10 percent increased their share of national income from 37 to 47 percent, while the next 30 percent saw their share shrink from 23 to 18 percent. Poverty widened dramatically: from 17 percent of Chileans in 1973 to 45 percent in 1990. Among the impoverished, the percentage forced to live in extreme poverty more than doubled" (*Chile's Free-Market Miracle*, 243).

6. Frantz Fanon, *The Wretched of the Earth*, trans. Constance Farrington, preface by Jean-Paul Sartre (New York: Grove Press, 1963), 148–205.

7. See Julieta Kirkwood, *Ser política en Chile*, particularly chapters 2 and 3.

8. In fact, this political alliance between the Christian Democrats and the Socialists, together with smaller parties of the center and left—but excluding the Communist Party—

has been able to stay in power since 1990 precisely due to its clear majority, in contrast to the factionalist tendencies of previous democratic periods in the country's history. This is perhaps the greatest compromise in Chilean politics during the twentieth century.

9. Egon Wolff, Ramón Griffero, and Ignacio Agüero, "Teatro y cine en Chile" [Theater and Film in Chile], roundtable discussion at the Encuentro Nacional de Arte [National Encounter for the Arts], or ENART, Catholic University, Santiago, Chile, 11 August 1990.

10. Ibid.

11. Isabel Allende, "Writing As An Act of Hope," in *Paths of Resistance: The Art and Craft of the Political Novel*, ed. William Zinsser (Boston: Houghton Mifflin Company, 1989), 48–49. Allende continues: "In literature we have been told, optimism is dangerous; it flirts with simplicity and is an insurrection against the sacred laws of reason and good taste. But I don't belong to that group of desperate intellectuals" (49–50).

12. Much has been made of this relationship, since the author's name, her subject matter, and her commercial success all call attention to it. However, according to Marcelo Coddou, although Salvador's and Isabel's fathers grew up together, Allende and her mother were estranged from that side of the family after her parents' separation in her early youth. Salvador became the only representative of Isabel's father's family that they continued to see from time to time during Isabel's childhood. See Coddou's "Para leer a Isabel Allende: Su vida en su obra" [For Reading Isabel Allende: Her Life in Her Work], *Araucaria de Chile* 38 (1987): 127.

13. It is important to note that Allende was the first of several Chilean women writers to achieve recent commercial success based on the primacy of telling a good story: Elena Castedo and Marcela Serrano, among others, also come to mind here.

14. As we have seen, however, Donoso, Mercedes Valdivieso, and others of their generation did experience crises in their literature after 1973, unlike Allende.

15. Allende, "Writing As An Act of Hope," 55.

16. Janice Radway, *Reading the Romance: Women, Patriarchy, and Popular Literature* (Chapel Hill: University of North Carolina Press, 1984), 64 (original emphasis).

17. Any discussion of magic in Allende's work must take into account Patricia Hart's *Narrative Magic in the Fiction of Isabel Allende* (Toronto: Associated University Presses, 1989). In this book (based on the author's doctoral thesis), Hart coins the term "magical feminism" as a category for considering Allende's work in terms both of "magical realism" and of its particular feminist content. Hart defines the term as "magical realism used in a femino-centric novel, or to make an authentic observation about the behavior and condition of women in the sociohistoric conditions depicted in the novel" (174). Hart makes a particularly well-developed case for the relationship between magic and Chilean history in *The House of the Spirits* in her first eight chapters, but finds *Of Love and Shadows* less successful as a novel, with magic employed mostly as a characterization device there. Of *Eva Luna*, Hart writes that

> The strictly 'magical' events . . . are few, but the sense of wonder, hyperbole, and the uncommon are strong enough to put the text into the 'marvelous' category for me, just as the femino-centric descriptions of women finding new ways to live their lives and deal with their problems puts it into the feminist category. (176)

Hart works within a very general liberal feminist tradition without acknowledging it as such, for she insists that she does not want to make "invidious value judgements about the 'correctness' of woman A's feminism over women B's brand" (31). Even as Hart clearly values Allende's dialogue with history in her first novel, Hart's liberalism (like Allende's) leads her to value uncritically the sorts of compromises Allende's female characters make in these novels, as I will discuss further.

18. The sequel to *Eva Luna*, titled *Cuentos de Eva Luna* [*Stories of Eva Luna*] (Buenos Aires: Editorial Sudamericana, 1989), provided the public with the fairy tales that Eva Luna was noted for telling in the 1987 novel.

19. The novel paints contemporary history with large strokes, beginning with the turn of the century suffrage movements, the northern mining boom and the agrarian south, World War II, an earthquake at midcentury, party politics into the 1960s, the hopes and fears expressed during the Allende period, and finally, the military coup and its violent aftermath.

20. Catherine Boyle uses this phrase in her "Frameworks and Contexts in *La casa de los espíritus:* A Chronicle of Teaching," *Journal of Latin American Cultural Studies* 4, no. 1 (1995): 110.

21. Ibid., 110–11.

22. Ibid., 105.

23. Allende has shown a surprising degree of political naïveté in interviews, suggesting that she herself believed that the coup was a brief aberration, soon to be resolved. In an exchange with Magdalena García Pinto, *Women Writers of Latin America: Intimate Histories*, trans. Trudy Balch and Magdalena García Pinto (Austin: University of Texas Press, 1991), Allende stated:

> In my case, I was deeply affected because my family was particularly involved [in the coup]. Nonetheless, I didn't leave Chile immediately after the coup, partly because I didn't understand what was going on and partly because I didn't have enough information. (26–27)

Rather than reaffirm her proximity to the Salvador Allende family, this quote suggests that Isabel was somehow sheltered from the political battlefield of the early 1970s.

24. This assessment is informed particularly by Rafael Otano's *Crónica de la transición* [Chronicle of the Transition] (Santiago: Editorial Planeta, 1995); and FLACSO Chile's *Chile 96: Análisis y opiniones* [Chile 96: Analysis and Opinions] (Santiago: FLACSO, 1997), *Chile 97: Análisis y opiniones* [Chile 97: Analysis and Opinions] (Santiago: FLACSO, 1998), and *Chile 98: Entre la II Cumbre y la detención de Pinochet* [Chile 98: From the II Summit to Pinochet's Arrest] (Santiago: FLACSO, 1999).

25. Manuel Antonio Garretón, "Los desafíos de la profundización democrática" [The Challenges of Deepening Democracy] in FLACSO Chile, *Chile 96*, 33–40, and "Chile 1997–98: Las revanchas de la democratización incompleta," [The Revenge of an Incomplete Democracy] in FLACSO Chile, *Chile 98*, 153–66.

26. Obviously, I point here to the term "democracy" as contested in the two directions I have discussed: traditional liberal democracy versus "democracy with justice," a concept advocated à la Kirkwood by the more radical sectors of the opposition under Pinochet.

27. Although I generally prefer Alejo Carpentier's term "lo real maravilloso" [the marvelous real], I have chosen to employ "magical realism" here, since it is the term used to market Allende's work internationally.

28. Among the critics who mention this change in tone, see Mario A. Rojas, "*La casa de los espíritus* de Isabel Allende: Un caleidoscopio de espejos desordenados" [Isabel Allende's *The House of the Spirits*: A Kaleidoscope of Chaotic Mirrors], in *Los libros tienen sus propios espíritus: Estudios sobre Isabel Allende* [Books Have Their Own Spirits: Studies About Isabel Allende], ed. Marcelo Coddou (Veracruz: Universidad Veracruzana, Cuadernos del Centro de Investigaciones Lingüístico-Literarias, 1986), 83–90.

29. Agosín, "*La casa de los espíritus:* historia, ficción y mujeres" [*The House of the Spirits:* History, Fiction, and Women], in *La literatura y los derechos humanos*, 129.

30. In my view, Marcelo Coddou misses the mark when he holds that Alba's narration at the novel's end shows how the Trueba women eventually "exercise the right to be sub-

jects of the discourse that, until then, has been enunciated against them" (31, translation mine). See his "Dimensión del feminismo en Isabel Allende" [Dimensions of Feminism in Isabel Allende], in Coddou, *Los libros tienen sus propios espíritus*, 29–53.

31. Linda Gould Levine replicates Allende's ideological stance in her article "A Passage to Androgyny: Isabel Allende's *La casa de los espíritus*," in *In the Feminine Mode: Essays on Hispanic Women Writers*, ed. Noël Valis and Carol Maier (Lewisburg, Pa.: Bucknell University Press, 1990). She states:

> While Alba's forgiveness of Esteban García may evoke a feminist or political response of anger or confusion, it is the only conclusion that seems harmonious with the rest of the novel and with Alba's optimistic personality. It also exemplifies Allende's implicit desire to rewrite traditional literary and historical patterns, even one as highly charged as a woman's attitude toward rape. (169)

This particular eschewal of violence and history around the issue of rape strikes me as regrettable.

32. Hart overlooks this connection in her chapter "The Incredible Shrinking Man" (*Narrative Magic*, 125–35).

33. One of Hart's more intriguing insights is to point out the aptness of the determinism in the novel for communicating the idea that the Chilean coup was inevitable, under the historical circumstances (ibid., 69). I appreciate this point, even as I have a different take on the political consequences of the novel's determinism.

34. For comments on the connections between Allende's and García Márquez's novels, see Rodrigo Cánovas, "Los espíritus literarios y políticos de Isabel Allende" [The Literary and Political Spirits of Isabel Allende], in *Critical Approaches to Isabel Allende's Novels*, ed. Sonia Riquelme Rojas and Edna Aguirre Rehbein (New York: Peter Lang, 1991), 37–45. For other intertextual studies see Juan Manuel Marcos and Teresa Méndez-Faith, "Multiplicidad, dialéctica y reconciliación del discurso en *La casa de los espíritus*" [Multiplicity, Dialectics, and Reconciliation in the Discourse of *The House of the Spirits*]; Marcelo Coddou, "*La casa de los espíritus:* De la historia a la Historia" [*The House of the Spirits:* From history to History]; and Mario Rodríguez, "García Márquez/Isabel Allende: Relocación textual" [García Márquez/Isabel Allende: Textual Relocation], in Coddou, *Los libros tienen sus propios espíritus* (62–70, 7–14, and 79–82, respectively).

35. Luz Arce, *El infierno* [Hell] (Santiago: Planeta, 1993). All citations will be included parenthetically in the text, and refer to this edition. All translations are my own.

36. Nelly Richard, *Residuos y metáforas (Ensayos de crítica cultural sobre el Chile de la transición)* (Santiago: Cuarto propio, 1998), 52.

37. Diamela Eltit, "Nomadic Bodies," *Review: Latin American Literature and Arts* 54 (Spring 1997): 43.

38. Eltit writes: "[T]o become part of the military system, [Arce] made use of the most classical space in the meeting of masculine and feminine, sexuality" (ibid., 46).

39. Richard, *Residuos y metáforas*, 62.

40. See also Eltit, "Nomadic Bodies," 48.

41. In her "Ruptura y preseverancia de estereotipos en *La casa de los espíritus*" [Rupture and Perseverance of Stereotypes in *The House of the Spirits*], Gabriela Mora comments on the strange move toward passivity in Alba's character at the novel's end: "Alba—spokesperson for the central ideology—suddenly changes from a women who risked her life for helping victims of the dictatorship, into a figure happy with her maternity (individual pleasure) and with waiting for things to happen (passive)" (Coddou, *Los libros tienen sus propios espíritus*, 78, my translation).

42. Nora Glickman outlines this progression of the female characters in "Los personajes

femeninos en *La casa de los espíritus*" [Female Characters in *The House of the Spirits*], in Coddou, *Los libros tienen sus propios espíritus*, 54–60. Richard McCallister shows how the women are narratively bound together in his "Nomenklatura in *La casa de los espíritus*" [Nomenclature in *The House of the Spirits*], in Riquelme Rojas and Aguirre Rehbein, *Critical Approaches*, 21–33. For his part, Mario Rojas praises the women in exaggerated terms as "the centers of the pulsing and propulsing energy of the narrative dynamism, gynoforces that challenge patriarchal despotism, sexual prejudices, dictatorship, and political repression" ("Caleidoscopio," in Coddou, *Los libros tienen sus propios espíritus*, 85, translation mine).

43. In his "*La casa de los espíritus*: Mirada, espacio, discurso de la otra historia" [*The House of the Spirits*: Gaze, Space, Discourse of the Other Story], René Campos holds that the novel provides an alternative to official discourse (Coddou, *Los libros tienen sus propios espíritus*, 21–28). I see the women's world more as a parallel universe, overly romanticized by both Rojas and Campos, than a fully articulated challenge to the structure of gendered separate spheres. That is, the counterhistory that the Trueba women offer remains "other" (as even Campos's title suggests) throughout the novel.

44. Patricia Hart uncritically defends Allende's passive female characters, as she writes: "The fact that Blanca and Clara are unable to liberate themselves from passivity and manipulation is hardly a criticism of Allende's own feminism; rather it is a tribute to her honesty as a novelist" (*Narrative Magic*, 54). At the same time as Hart sees this female passivity as realistic, as an implicit critique of "women's condition" offered by Allende, she rightly emphasizes Alba's possibilities as an alternative to this pattern. At different moments in her work, Hart contends that "It is up to Alba to break the chain of passivity that has kept the women in the family from meeting life fully for so long" (54), and that "The chain of hatred cannot be broken until a character like Alba, who bears the scars of conflict in her own flesh, has the magnitude of spirit to consciously put her past behind her and not exact an eye for an eye, a finger for a finger" (110). Like Hart, Norma Helper praises Alba's role as Chile's healer in her "Binding the Wounds of the Body Politic: Nation as Family in *La casa de los espíritus*," in Riquelme Rojas and Aguirre Rehbein, *Critical Approaches*, 49–56. However, neither of these critics addresses as problematic the fact that Alba happily effaces her own agency in reconciling the conflicting factions of Chile's men as Allende's solution to deep historical conflict.

45. While it appears that this trait is shared across social classes, Esteban Trueba's classism leads him to wish to forget, for example, the prostitute Tránsito Soto's role in Alba's release from the concentration camp. Yet he admits that "this story could not have been written if she hadn't intervened to rescue us and, in the process, our memories" (119). If, as Alba later suggests, it would actually be such women who would defeat the regime, why do working-class women appear only briefly, as romanticized types, "like so many others" (429), rather than being more fully characterized or included more centrally in this story? Kavita Panjabi offers a more optimistic view about Soto as a character; see her "*The House of the Spirits*, Tránsito Soto: From Periphery to Power," in Riquelme Rojas and Aguirre Rehbein, *Critical Approaches*, 11–19.

46. The most famous analysis of female superiority for the context of Latin America is Evelyn P. Stevens, "*Marianismo*: The Other Face of *Machismo* in Latin America," in *Female and Male in Latin America*, ed. Ann Pescatello (Pittsburgh: University of Pittsburgh Press, 1973), in which Stevens defines *marianismo* as the empowering "cult of feminine spiritual superiority, which teaches that women are semi-divine, morally superior to and spiritually stronger than men" (71). In the North American context, Mary Daly's *Gyn/Ecology: The Metaethics of Radical Feminism* (Boston: Beacon Press, 1978) is one defining text; Adrienne Rich's *Of Woman Born* (New York: W. W. Norton, 1979) is another. Of course, radical Anglo-American feminist perspectives have been amply critiqued as

Eurocentric by feminists of color, on one hand, and as essentialist by postmodern feminists, on the other. See, for example, Audre Lorde's reply to Mary Daly in *Sister Outsider* (Trumansburg, N.Y.: Crossing Press, 1984) and Denise Riley's antiessentialist *"Am I That Name?": Feminism and the Category of 'Women' in History* (Minneapolis: University of Minnesota Press, 1988).

    47. Isabel Allende, *De amor y de sombra* (Buenos Aires: Editorial Sudamericana, 1985). Translated as *Of Love and Shadows*, trans. Margaret Sayers Peden (New York: Bantam Books, 1988). All textual citations will appear parenthetically in the text, and refer to these editions.

    48. As Allende reports to Magdalena García Pinto in *Women Writers of Latin America*, *Of Love and Shadows* became a huge best-seller:

> My second novel got a terrific reception from the Chilean public, bad reviews from *El Mercurio*, silence from the official media, and excellent reviews from professors, intellectuals, and literary journals. They say it's more well written than the first one. ... I've been lucky with all my translations [of this novel]. ... In Norway, they sold forty thousand copies in a few weeks, and that's a country with four million people. In Germany I was at the top of the best-seller list for almost a year. In France the Club du Livre alone published 350,000 copies. It seems vain to talk about all this, but that's how it's been. And I don't look at it as a personal success, but as more recognition for Latin American literature. (39)

    49. In his excellent "En torno a *De amor y de sombra* de Isabel Allende: Una apreciación socio-histórica" [On *Of Love and Shadows* by Isabel Allende: A Sociohistorical Assessment] (in *La cultura nacional chilena*, 185–96), Hernán Vidal cites these events, and states that, due to the Lonquén discovery, the regime had to recognize the problem of the disappeared for the first time. He calls 1978 the Year of Human Rights in Chile (189). Patricia Verdugo ("Lonquén: un horno para quince" [Lonquén: An Oven for Fifteen], chapter 6 in *Tiempo de días claros*) and Eugenio Ahumada et al. ("Le conté que me habían fusilado" [I Told Him They Shot Me], in chapter 11 of vol. 1 of *La memoria prohibida*) provide journalistic accounts of the events leading to the Lonquén discovery, and emphasize its importance as a benchmark in the opposition's early struggle for human rights. For other perspectives on the relationship between fiction and history in *Of Love and Shadows*, see Elías Miguel Muñoz, "La voz testimonial de Isabel Allende en *De amor y de sombra*" [The Testimonial Voice of Isabel Allende in *Of Love and Shadows*], in Riquelme Rojas and Aguirre Rehbein, *Critical Approaches*, 61–72; and Wesley J. Weaver III, "La frontera que se esfuma: Testimonio y ficción en *De amor y de sombra*" [The Border that Evaporates: Testimony and Fiction in *Of Love and Shadows*], in Riquelme Rojas and Aguirre Rehbein, *Critical Approaches*, 73–82.

    50. The other Ranquileos also have quirks reminiscent of García Márquez: the father is a melancholy circus clown, and the mother consults priests, midwifes, and witches in search of a cure for her daughter's condition. The son, Pradelio, joins the army to quell his incestuous desire for his sister. And like the two Buendía twins in *One Hundred Years of Solitude*, Evangelina was supposedly switched at birth with another Evangelina, the daughter of a cursed family, the Flores, which started all their troubles in the first place.

    51. See Nancy J. Vickers, "Diana Described: Scattered Woman and Scattered Rhyme," *Critical Inquiry* 8, no. 2 (1982): 265–79.

    52. In his "En torno a *De amor y de sombra*," Vidal likewise highlights Allende's "radical narrowing" of the widespread social defense of human rights in postcoup Chile. Vidal notes that society is reduced to Irene and Francisco, who act "according to a marked individualistic hedonism" (194, translation mine). He also observes that the entire women's

movement becomes subsumed as the exclusive privilege of Irene Beltrán. While my own argument clearly agrees with these assertions about the novel's emphasis on individualism, Vidal does not link this point to the gender and class issues underlying Allende's narrative strategies. Exclusions based on gender and class provide interrelated cornerstones both of official discourse, and of Allende's replication of its ideologies.

53. In another reduction of an actual event, Sebastián Acevedo's suicide in Santiago's Plaza de Armas, Allende suggests that Francisco's father might have done the same thing (202). This painful episode in postcoup history is evoked not to point out Leal's relationship to it, but as a mere trope used to characterize the professor as naïve and a bit crazy. This revision of history risks disregarding the pain of those involved in the actual, historical event.

54. In the final words of her "A Passage to Androgyny," Linda Gould Levine shows just how seductive Allende's promises can be, for many types of readers, including literary critics:

There may pass another sixty or one hundred years of solitude before this union of different spheres is realized. Until then, might we not follow Allendè's footsteps and bequeath this entrancing dream to be told and retold to our children as their bedtime draws near? (in Valis and Maier, *In the Feminine Mode,* 177)

I was the target of reactions similarly protective of Allende (and her popularity) when I read a portion of this chapter at a Latin American Studies conference. I discovered that my readings aroused passions in the audience, both adamant agreement and ardent critiques of my work as "not about literature." I also received the relativistic (liberal) comment that, as feminist critics, we need to appreciate and affirm *all* women writers. For me, the experience confirmed that I was questioning several "sacred cows" at once—including the boundaries of liberalism and literary criticism themselves—while offering this feminist critique of a woman writer.

55. Allende, "Writing As An Act of Hope," 56.
56. I use this term in the same sense as does bell hooks in her *Outlaw Culture: Resisting Representation* (New York: Routledge, 1994).

Chapter 7: Epilogue

1. The phrase is Garretón's. See "Chile 1997–98. Las revanchas de la democratización incompleta" [Chile 1997–98. The Revenge of an Incomplete Democracy], in FLACSO Chile, *Chile 98,* 153–66.
2. Ibid., 154.
3. Rodrigo Baño has pointed out that the Chilean press began to speak not of the "Chicago Boys" but of the "Frei Boys," thereby highlighting the technocratic, presidentialist, and neoliberal orientation of the government of (the former businessman) Eduardo Frei. Rodrigo Baño Ahumada, "La tranquilidad de un gobierno que descansa en la economía" [The Tranquility of a Government that Rests on the Economy], in FLACSO Chile, *Chile 96,* 20.
4. Tomás Moulian, "A Time of Forgetting: Myths of the Chilean Transition," *NACLA Report on the Americas* 32, no. 2 (September/October 1998): 16.
5. Soledad Bianchi told me this was widely cited in the Chilean media; I later saw the figure published in Isabel Allende, "Pinochet Without Hatred," *The New York Times Magazine,* 17 January 1999, 27. In addition, a study of public opinion in seventeen Latin American countries showed that, while 65 percent of Chileans preferred democracy as their

system of government in 1990, only 53 percent preferred democracy by 1998. (The rest were split between those preferring a military regime and those that didn't care.) Perhaps most revealing, only 27 percent of Chileans stated that they were satisfied with their democracy in 1998. Data from Marta Lagos, "Visiones latinoamericanas: Latinobarómetro 1998" [Latin American Visions: Latin Barometer 1998], in FLACSO Chile, *Chile 98*, 29–30.

6. Garretón, "Chile 97–98," 163.

7. I paraphrase Detlef Nolte, "El juicio de la historia: Espectros del pasado en América Latina" [The Judgment of History: Specters of the Past in Latin America], in FLACSO Chile, *Chile 98*, 115. For more on the case's international impact, see Jorge Mario Eastman, ed., *Pinochet: El déspota que revolucionó el derecho internacional (Documentos y opiniones)* [Pinochet: The Despot Who Revolutionized International Law (Documents and Opinions)] (Santafé de Bogotá: Tercer Mundo, 2000); and Paz Rojas et al., *Tarde pero llega: Pinochet ante la justicia española* [The Moment Arrives, If Late: Pinochet Before the Spanish Courts] (Santiago: LOM, 1998).

8. Ariel Dorfman, "Pinochet's Mind," *NACLA Report on the Americas* 34, no. 1 (July/August 2000): 50.

9. See Sebastian Brett, "Impunity on Trial in Chile," *NACLA Report on the Americas* 34, no. 1 (July/August 2000): 34–36; and Peter Kornbluh, "CIA Outrage in Chile," *Nation* 271, no. 11 (16 October 2000): 4–5.

10. Brett, "Impunity on Trial," 35. A note (errata) in *NACLA Report on the Americas* 34, no. 2 (September/October 2000) clarifies that four Pinochet appointees were left by early 1999, and that the January 2000 death of one of them leaves only three on the bench (4).

11. Brett, "Impunity on Trial," 35.

12. Garretón, "Chile 97–98," 162.

13. Discussed in Brett, "Impunity on Trial"; in Garretón, "Chile 97–87"; and in Rogelio Pérez, "Pinochet y la justicia: Una reflexión sobre los cambios en el derecho" [Pinochet and Justice: Reflections on Changes in the Law], in FLACSO Chile, *Chile 98*, 99–111.

14. Nolte, "El juicio de la historia," 122.

15. I borrow the phrase from Martha Minow's insightful book, *Between Vengeance and Forgiveness: Facing History after Genocide and Mass Violence* (Boston: Beacon Press, 1998). On this issue, see also José Zalaquett, "Balance de la política de derechos humanos en la transición chilena a la democracia" [An Assessment of Human Rights Politics in the Chilean Transition to Democracy], in FLACSO Chile, *Chile 98*, 87–98.

16. One site displaying Pinochet's brain scan in early 2000: http://news.bbc.co.uk/hi/english/health/newsid_645000/645043.stm

17. Letter from Elizabeth (of the former "Taller 'Los Almendros'"), Puente Alto, Chile, to the author, 15 June 1994 (translation mine).

18. Marjorie Agosín, "Patchwork of Memory," *NACLA Report on the Americas* 27, no. 6 (May/June 1994): 13.

19. Ibid., 14.

20. Peter Winn, "Lagos Defeats the Right—By a Thread," *NACLA Report on the Americas* 33, no. 5 (March/April 2000): 7.

21. Ibid., 10.

22. Ibid.

23. See Kirkwood's "Feministas y políticas," in *Ser política en Chile*, 218–33.

24. Teresa Valdés and Marisa Weinstein, "Corriendo y descorriendo túpidos velos" [Opening and Closing Thick Curtains], in FLACSO Chile, *Chile 96*, 72.

25. Ibid., 69 (translation mine).

26. Verónica Schild, "'Gender Equity' Without Social Justice: Women's Rights in the Neoliberal Age," *NACLA Report on the Americas* 34, no. 1 (July/August 2000): 25–28.

27. Ibid., 27.

28. Marysa Navarro, comments on the panel "Latin American Feminist NGOs and Global Society: Critical Perspectives" at the XX International Conference of the Latin American Studies Association, Guadalajara, Mexico, April 17–19, 1997.

29. Schild, "'Gender Equity,'" 27–28.

30. Kemy Oyarzún, "Prólogo: El escándalo como modo de recepción" [Prologue: Scandal as a Mode of Reception], in Brunet, *Aguas abajo,* 10. All translations are my own.

31. Ibid., 10. See also "El caso 'Simón Bolívar' y la polémica del Fondart, Dossier de prensa" [The 'Simón Bolívar' Case and the FONDART Polemic, Press Dossier], in the *Revista de crítica cultural* [Magazine of Cultural Criticism], no. 9 (November 1994): 25–36.

32. Richard, *Residuos y metáforas,* 180. All translations are my own.

33. Ibid., 187.

34. Ibid., 188.

35. Ibid.

36. Ibid., 184.

37. Ibid., 192–93.

38. Kemy Oyarzún, "Saberes críticos y estudios de género" [Critical Disciplines and Gender Studies], *Revista Nomadías* 1, no. 1 (December 1996): 20. All translations are my own.

39. Ibid., 20.

40. Ibid., 22.

41. Ibid.

42. Ibid., 20.

43. Richard calls this a "contra-escena," a "scene" (space, discourse) counter to the one that developed in the Chilean Senate debate on gender (*Residuos y metáforas,* 218).

44. Víctor Hugo Robles, "History in the Making: The Homosexual Liberation Movement in Chile," *NACLA Report on the Americas* 31, no. 4 (January/February 1998): 36–43. For literary pieces by Pedro Lemebel, see *La esquina es mi corazón: Crónica urbana* [The Streetcorner Is My Heart: Urban Chronicle] (Santiago: Editorial Cuarto Propio, 1995) and *Loco afán: Crónicas de Sidario* [Crazy Ardor: AIDSary Chronicles] (Santiago: Ediciones LOM, 1996).

45. Antonio Prieto, "Students Organize Across Latin America," *NACLA Report on the Americas* 33, no. 1 (July/August 1999): 52.

46. *Chile: Obstinada Memoria* [*Chile: Obstinate Memory*], dir. Patricio Guzmán, 58 min., First Run/Icarus Films, 1997, videocassette.

47. In "La problemática indígena en el Chile actual" [Indigenous Issues in Chile Today], in FLACSO Chile, *Chile 98,* 229–53, Gerardo Zúñiga contends that the positive steps made under Aylwin toward achieving a consensus-based set of legal mechanisms to ensure indigenous participation in decisions affecting them were in effect undone by the Frei government's autocratic decision to build an hydroelectric complex that would displace Pehuenche families permanently from their lands.

48. My impressions are shaped by having seen Dorfman's *La muerte y la doncella* [*Death and the Maiden*] in its debut run at the Teatro de la Esquina, Santiago, Chile, 15 March 1991.

49. Ariel Dorfman, *Konfidenz* [*Konfidenz*] (New York: Vintage Español, 1995), *Terapia* [*Blake's Therapy*] (New York: Siete Cuentos, 2001), and *Rumbo al sur, deseando al norte*

[*Heading South, Looking North*] (Buenos Aires: Planeta, 1999). For the film, see Rodrigo and Ariel Dorfman, *My House Is on Fire*, 19 min., First Run/Icarus Films, 1997, videocassette.

50. Griffero's statement appears in Isidora Aguirre et al., "Chilean Theater, 1973–1993: Statements by Isidora Aguirre, Gregory Cohen, Ramón Griffero, and Egon Wolff," *Review: Latin American Literature and the Arts* 49 (Fall 1994): 87.

51. Pía Barros, *El tono menor del deseo* [The Lesser Tone of Desire] (Santiago: Editorial Cuarto Propio, 1991).

52. Diamela Eltit, *Vaca sagrada* [*Sacred Cow*] (Santiago: Planeta, 1991), *Los vigilantes* [The Nightwatchmen] (Santiago: Editorial Sudamericana, 1994), and *Los trabajadores de la muerte* [Workers of Death] (Barcelona: Seix Barral, 1998).

53. Isabel Allende, *Paula* [*Paula*] (New York: Harper Collins [Spanish edition], 1996).

54. Allende, "Pinochet Without Hatred," 27.

55. Isabel Allende, *Hija de la fortuna* (New York: Harperperennial [Spanish edition], 2000).

Bibliography

Adorno, Theodor W. *Negative Dialectics*. Translated by E. B. Ashton. New York: Continuum, 1973.

Agosín, Marjorie. *Scraps of Life: Chilean Arpilleras*. Translated by Cola Franzen. London: Zed Books, 1987.

———. "Los collages del espíritu" and "*La casa de los espíritus*: historia, ficción y mujeres." In *Literatura y derechos humanos: Aproximaciones, lecturas y encuentros*. San José, Costa Rica: Editorial Universitaria Centroamericana, 1989.

———. "Patchwork of Memory." *NACLA Report on the Americas* 27, no. 6 (May/June 1994): 13–16.

Agrupación de Familiares de Detenidos-Desaparecidos. Interviews by author. Tape recordings. Santiago, Chile, 17, 21, 24 October 1990, and Paine, Chile, 24 October 1990.

Aguirre, Isidora, Gregory Cohen, Ramón Griffero, and Egon Wolff. "Chilean Theater, 1973–1993: Statements by Isidora Aguirre, Gregory Cohen, Ramón Griffero, and Egon Wolff." *Review: Latin American Literature and the Arts* 49 (fall 1994): 84–89.

Ahmed, Leila. *Women and Gender in Islam*. New Haven: Yale University Press, 1992.

Ahumada, Eugenio, Rodrigo Atria, Javier Luis Egaña, Augusto Góngora, Carmen Quesney, Gustavo Saball, and Gustavo Villalobos. *Chile: La memoria prohibida*. 4th ed. Vols. 1 and 2. Santiago: Pehuén, 1990.

Albala-Bertrand, Luis, coordinator. *Democratic Culture and Governance: Latin America on the Threshold of the Third Millennium*. Buenos Aires: UNESCO, Hispamérica, 1992.

Alegría, Fernando. *La literatura chilena del siglo XX*. Santiago: Zig-Zag, 1970.

Allende, Isabel. *La casa de los espíritus*. 24th ed. Barcelona: Plaza y Janés, 1987. Originally published in 1982.

———. *The House of the Spirits*. Translated by Magda Bogin. 1985. Reprint, New York: Bantam, 1986.

———. *De amor y de sombra*. Buenos Aires: Editorial Sudamericana, 1985.

———. *Eva Luna*. Barcelona: Plaza y Janés, 1987.

———. *Of Love and Shadows*. Translated by Margaret Sayers Peden. New York: Bantam Books, 1988.

———. *Eva Luna*. Translated by Margaret Sayers Peden. New York: Bantam, 1989.

———. "Writing as an Act of Hope." In *Paths of Resistance: The Art and Craft of the Political Novel*, edited by William Zinsser. Boston: Houghton Mifflin Company, 1989.

———. *Cuentos de Eva Luna*. Buenos Aires: Editorial Sudamericana, 1989.

———. *Stories of Eva Luna*. Translated by Margaret Sayers Peden. New York: Atheneum, 1991.

———. *Paula*. New York: Harper Collins [Spanish edition], 1996.

———. *Paula*. Translated by Margaret Sayers Peden. New York: Harper Collins, 1996.

———. *Hija de la fortuna*. 1998. Reprint, New York: Harper Perennial, 2000.

———. *Daughter of Fortune*. Translated by Margaret Sayers Peden. New York: Harper Collins, 1999.

———. "Pinochet Without Hatred." *The New York Times Magazine,* 17 January 1999, 24–27.

Alvarez, Sonia E., Evelina Dagnino, and Arturo Escobar, eds. *Cultures of Politics/Politics of Cultures: Re-visioning Latin American Social Movements*. Boulder, Colo.: Westview Press, 1998.

A. M. F. [Foxley, Ana María?]. "Diamela Eltit: Acoplamiento incestuoso" *Hoy,* no.421 (12–18 August 1985): 41.

Anderson, Benedict. *Imagined Communities*. 1983. Reprint, London: Verso, 1991.

Angelo, Gloria. *Pero ellas son imprescindibles*. Santiago: Biblioteca de la Mujer, Centro de Estudios de la Mujer, 1987.

Arce, Luz. *El infierno*. Santiago: Planeta, 1993.

Arendt, Hannah. *Origins of Totalitarianism*. 1948. Reprint, New York: Harcourt Brace Jovanovich, 1979.

Arriagada, Genaro. *Pinochet: The Politics of Power*. Boston: Unwin Hyman, 1988.

Arteaga, Ana María. "Politización de lo privado y subversión de lo cotidiano." In *Mundo de mujer: Continuidad y cambio*, edited by Centro de Estudios de la Mujer (CEM). Santiago: Ediciones CEM, 1988.

Avaria, Antonio, Poli Délano, Fernando Jeréz, Ernesto Malbrán, Ramiro Rivas, and Antonio Skármeta. "Los novísimos, veinte años después." Panel discussion at the Sociedad de Escritores de Chile. Santiago, Chile, 25–26 June 1991.

Balderston, Daniel, David William Foster, Tulio Halperín Donghi, Francine Masiello, Marta Morello-Frosch, and Beatriz Sarlo. *Ficción y política: La narrativa argentina durante el proceso militar*. Buenos Aires: Alianza Editorial/University of Minnesota, 1987.

Baño Ahumada, Rodrigo. "La tranquilidad de un gobierno que descansa en la economía." In *Chile 96: Análisis y opiniones*, edited by FLACSO Chile. Santiago: Nueva Serie Flacso, 1997.

Barraza, Ximena. "Notas sobre la vida cotidiana en un orden autoritario." *Araucaria* 11 (1980): 53–72.

Barros, Pía. *Miedos transitorios (de a uno, de a dos, de a todos)*. Santiago: Ergo Sum, 1986.

———. *A horcajadas*. Prologue by Juan Carlos Lértora. Santiago: Mosquito Editores, 1990.

———. *El tono menor del deseo*. Santiago: Editorial Cuarto Propio, 1991.

———. *A horcajadas/Astride*. Translated and edited by Analisa Taylor, with translations by Amanda Powell, Stephen F. White, Alice A. Nelson, and Kathryn Kruger-Hickman. Santiago: Editorial Asterión, 1992.

———. "La seducción de Pía Barros." Interview with Faride Zerán. *La Epoca,* supplement *Literatura y libros* año 3, no. 138 (2 December 1990): 4–5.

———. Interviews by author. Tape recordings. Santiago, Chile, 19–20 December 1990.

Barros, Pía, Erwin Díaz, Carlos Mellado, and Bruno Serrano. "Los talleres literarios." Panel discussion at the Sociedad de Escritores de Chile. Santiago, Chile. Audiocassette [1983].

Barros, Pía, Carla Grandi, Sergio Marras and Jaime Valdivieso. Working group discussion. Encuentro de narradores chilenos, PRED. Valdivia, Chile, 3 November 1990.

Benavente, David. "Ave Félix." In *Pedro, Juan y Diego/Tres Marías y una Rosa*, by ICTUS, David Benavente, and TIT. Prologue by María de la Luz Hurtado. Santiago: CESOC Ediciones ChileAmérica, 1989.

Benavente, David, and the Taller de Investigación Teatral. *Chilean Drama: Tres Marías y una Rosa*. Directed by Raúl Osorio (stage director), David A. Homer, and Robert Myles McKenzie (video directors). Produced by the York University Department of Instructional Aid Resources. 122 min. York University, 1981. Videocassette.

Berenguer, Carmen, Eugenia Brito, Diamela Eltit, Raquel Olea, Eliana Ortega, and Nelly Richard, eds. *Escribir en los bordes: Congreso Internacional de Literatura Femenina Latinoamericana 1987*. Santiago: Editorial Cuarto Propio, Colección Bajo Palabra, 1990.

Beverley, John and José Oviedo, eds. *boundary 2* 20, no. 3 (1993).

———. *The Postmodernism Debate in Latin America*. Durham, N.C.: Duke University Press, 1993.

Bianchi, Soledad. "El movimiento artístico chileno en el conflicto político actual." *Casa de las Américas* 130 (1982): 146–54.

———. "Where to Begin to Grasp This Land? (Reflections on Culture and Authoritarianism in Chile: 1973–1986)." In *Chile: Dictatorship and the Struggle for Democracy*, edited by Grinor Rojo and John J. Hassett. Gaithersburg, Md.: Ediciones Hispamérica, 1988.

———. *Poesía Chilena (Miradas-Enfoques-Apuntes)*. Santiago: CESOC Ediciones Documentas, 1990.

Boal, Augusto. *Theater of the Oppressed*. Translated by Charles A. and Maria-Odilia Leal McBride. 1974. Reprint, New York: Theater Communications Group, 1985.

Bombal, María Luisa. *La última niebla/La amortajada*. 1948. Reprint, Barcelona: Seix Barral Biblioteca Breve, 1984.

———. *The House of Mist and The Shrouded Woman*. Translated by Naomi Lindstrom. Austin: University of Texas Press, 1995.

Bordo, Susan. "The Body and the Reproduction of Femininity: A Feminist Appropriation of Foucault." In *Gender/Body/Knowledge: Feminist Reconstructions of Being and Knowing*, edited by Alison M. Jaggar and Susan R. Bordo. New Brunswick, N.J.: Rutgers University Press, 1989.

———. *Unbearable Weight: Feminism, Western Culture, and the Body*. Berkeley: University of California Press, 1993.

Boyle, Catherine. "El espacio escénico. O cómo el teatro chileno se hizo femenino." Unpublished paper, presented at the Simposium Internacional de Teatro Iberoamericano (Historia, Teoría, Metodología). Universidad Católica, Santiago de Chile, 17 May 1991.

———. "Frameworks and Contexts in *La casa de los espíritus:* A Chronicle of Teaching." *Journal of Latin American Cultural Studies* 4, no. 1 (1995): 105–12.

Bravo, Rosa, and Rosalba Todaro. "Chilean Women and the UN Decade for Women." Translated by Patricia Chuchryk. *Women's Studies International Forum* 8, no. 2 (1985): 111–16.

Brett, Sebastian. "Impunity on Trial in Chile." *NACLA Report on the Americas* 34, no. 1 (July/August 2000): 34–36, and errata *NACLA Report on the Americas* 34, no. 2 (September/October 2000): 4.

British Broadcasting Corporation. Augusto Pinochet's Brain Scan. Available at http://news.bbc.co.uk/hi/english/health/newsid_645000/645043.stm

Brito, Eugenia. "Entrevista a Diamela Eltit: Desde la mujer a la androginía." *Pluma y pincel,* no. 17 (August 1985): 42–43.

———. "*Lumpérica* de Diamela Eltit, Una novela que traza su propio horizonte." *Pluma y pincel,* no. 17 (August 1985): 43–45.

———. *Campos minados (Literatura post-golpe en Chile).* Santiago: Editorial Cuarto Propio, 1990.

———. "Introducción" and "El doble relato en la novela *Por la patria* de Diamela Eltit." In *Escribir en los bordes: Congreso Internacional de Literatura Femenina Latinoamericana 1987,* edited by Carmen Berenguer, Eugenia Brito, Diamela Eltit, Raquel Olea, Eliana Ortega, and Nelly Richard. Santiago: Editorial Cuarto Propio, Colección Bajo Palabra, 1990.

Brunet, Marta. *Aguas abajo: Cuentos.* 1943. Reprint, with a prologue by Kemy Oyarzún, Santiago: Cuarto Propio, 1997.

Brunner, José Joaquín. "La mujer y lo privado en la comunicación social." Santiago: FLACSO Material de Discusión, 1983.

Brunner, José Joaquín, Alicia Barrios, and Carlos Catalán. *Chile: Transformaciones culturales y modernidad.* Santiago: FLACSO, 1989.

Bunster-Burotto, Ximena. "Surviving Beyond Fear: Women and Torture in Latin America." In *Women and Change in Latin America,* by June Nash, Helen Safa, and contributors. South Hadley, Mass.: Bergin and Garvey, 1985.

Cabezas, Omar. *La montaña es algo más que una inmensa estepa verde.* 6th ed. México, D.F.: Siglo XXI, 1987. Originally published in 1982.

———. *Fire from the Mountain.* Translated by Kathleen Weaver. Foreword by Carlos Fuentes. Afterword by Walter LaFeber. New York: Plume, 1985.

Calvo, Jorge, Alejandra Basualto, Alvaro Cuadra, Gabriela Boza, Poli Délano, Lilian Elphick, Jaime Hagel, Carmen Oviedo, Jorge Marchant, Gabriela Soto, Reinaldo Martínez, Yolanda Venturini, José Luis Rosasco. *Cuento aparte.* Santiago: Ediciones Cerro Huelén, 1986.

Campero, Guillermo. *Entre la sobrevivencia y la acción política: Las organizaciones de pobladores en Santiago.* Santiago: ILET, 1987.

Campos, René. "*La casa de los espíritus*: Mirada, espacio, discurso de la otra historia." In *Los libros tienen sus propios espíritus: Estudios sobre Isabel Allende,* edited by Marcelo Coddou. Veracruz: Universidad Veracruzana, Cuadernos del Centro de Investigaciones Lingüístico-Literarias, 1986.

Cánovas, Rodrigo. *Lihn, Zurita, ICTUS, Radrigán: Literatura chilena y experiencia autoritaria.* Santiago: FLACSO, 1986.

———. "Para leer." *Análisis,* no. 159 (27 January 1987): 43.

———. "Los espíritus literarios y políticos de Isabel Allende." In *Critical Approaches to Isabel Allende's Novels,* edited by Sonia Riquelme Rojas and Edna Aguirre Rehbein. New York: Peter Lang, 1991.

———. *Novela chilena. Nuevas generaciones. El abordaje de los naúfragos.* Santiago: Ediciones de la Universidad Católica, 1997.

Casa de la Mujer "La Morada." Interview by author with directors of artisan's workshops. Tape recording. Santiago, Chile, 29 October 1990.

Castro, Oscar. *Casimiro Peñafleta.* Teatro del Cerro, Santiago, Chile, 15 October 1990.

Centro de Estudios de la Mujer (CEM), eds. *Mundo de mujer: Continuidad y cambio.* Santiago: CEM, 1988.

Cervantes, Miguel de. *Don Quijote de la Mancha*, Part I. 1605. Reprint, edition and notes by Martín de Riquer, Barcelona: Editorial Juventud, 1985.

———. *Don Quijote*. Edited by Diana de Armas Wilson. Translated by Burton Raffel. New York: W. W. Norton, 1999.

Chavkin, Samuel. *Storm over Chile: The Junta under Siege*. Westport, Conn.: Lawrence Hill and Company, 1985.

Chuchryk, Patricia Marie. "Protest, Politics, and Personal Life: The Emergence of Feminism in a Military Dictatorship, Chile, 1973–1983." Ph.D. diss., York University (Toronto), 1984.

———. "Feminist Anti-Authoritarian Politics: The Role of Women's Organizations in the Chilean Transition to Democracy." In *The Women's Movement in Latin America*, edited by Jane S. Jacquette. Boston: Unwin Hyman, 1989.

Cixous, Hélène. "The Laugh of the Medusa." In *New French Feminisms*, edited and with introductions by Elaine Marks and Isabelle Courtivron. New York: Schocken Books, 1981.

Coddou, Marcelo. "Dimensión del feminismo en Isabel Allende" and "*La casa de los espíritus*: De la historia a la Historia." In *Los libros tienen sus propios espíritus: Estudios sobre Isabel Allende*, edited by Marcelo Coddou. Veracruz: Universidad Veracruzana, Cuadernos del Centro de Investigaciones Lingüístico-Literarias, 1986.

———. "Para leer a Isabel Allende: Su vida en su obra." *Araucaria de Chile* 38 (1987): 127.

Collins, Joseph, and John Lear. *Chile's Free Market Miracle: A Second Look*. Foreword by Walden Bello. Epilogue by Stephanie Rosenfeld. Oakland, Calif.: A Food First Book, The Institute for Food and Development Policy, 1995.

Comisión Chilena de Derechos Humanos. "Situación de los Derechos Humanos en Chile." *Informe Mensual*, no. 73–74 (January–February 1988): 13.

Compartiendo La Mesa. Interview by author. Santiago, Chile, 31 October 1990.

"Congreso Internacional de Literatura Femenina Latinoamericana: Una forma de transgresión." *Revista VIVA* (November 1987): 50–52.

Contreras, Marta. "*Por la patria*: Una novela femenina de vanguardia." *El Sur* (7 June 1987): supplement *Arte y cultura*, vii.

Corssen, Inge, ed. *La mujer en la poesía chilena de los '80*. Santiago: Ediciones INCOR, 1987.

Cortázar, Julio. *Rayuela*. 9th ed. Buenos Aires: Editorial Sudamericana, 1968. Originally published in 1963.

———. *Hopscotch*. Translated by Gregory Rabassa. New York: Avon Books, 1966.

Daly, Mary. *Gyn/Ecology: The Metaethics of Radical Feminism*. Boston: Beacon Press, 1978.

Davies, Miranda, comp. *Third World-Second Sex: Women's Struggles and National Liberation*. London: Zed Books, 1983.

Debray, Régis. *The Chilean Revolution: Conversations with Allende*. New York: Vintage, 1971.

de la Maza, Gonzalo, and Mario Garcés. *La explosión de las mayorías: Protesta Nacional, 1983–1984*. Santiago: ECO Educación y comunicaciones, 1985.

Delamotte, Eugenia, Natania Meeker, Jean O'Barr, eds. *Women Imagining Change: A Global Anthology of Women's Resistance*. New York: Routledge, 1997.

Délano, Manuel, and Hugo Traslaviña. *La herencia de los Chicago Boys.* Santiago: Ediciones del Ornitorrinco, 1989.

Délano, Poli. "La irrupción de las novelistas." *Fortín Mapocho,* 3 November 1987, 9.

Díaz, Erwin. "Algunas consideraciones." Prologue to *Poesía chilena de hoy, de Parra a nuestros días,* 4th ed., edited by Erwin Díaz. Santiago: Ediciones Documentas, 1991.

Donoso, Claudia. "Para reconocerse mejor." *APSI,* 27 April–3 May 1987, 44–45.

Donoso, José. *El obsceno pájaro de la noche.* 1970. Reprint, Barcelona: Seix Barral, 1985.

———. *The Obscene Bird of Night.* Translated by Hardie St. Martin and Leonard Mades. New York: Knopf/Random House, 1973.

———. *Casa de campo.* 1978. Reprint, Barcelona: Seix Barral, 1987.

———. *El jardín de al lado.* Barcelona: Seix Barral, 1981.

———. *A House in the Country.* Translated by David Pritchard with Suzanne Jill Levine. New York: Knopf/Random House, 1984.

———. *La desesperanza.* Barcelona: Seix Barral, 1986.

———. *Curfew.* Translated by Alfred MacAdam. New York: Weidenfeld and Nicholson, 1988.

———. *The Garden Next Door.* Translated by Hardie St. Martin. New York: Grove Press, 1992.

Dorfman, Ariel. *Imaginación y violencia.* Santiago: Editorial Universitaria, 1970.

———. *Moros en la costa.* Santiago: Editorial Universitaria, 1973.

———. *Desaparecer/Aus der Augen verlieren.* Bornheim-Merten: Lamuv Verlag, 1979.

———. *Cría ojos.* Mexico, D.F.: Editorial Nueva Imagen, 1979.

———. *Viudas.* 2d ed. Buenos Aires: Siglo XXI, 1985. Originally published in 1981.

———. *La última canción de Manuel Sendero.* 1982. Reprint, Santiago: Editorial Planeta, 1990.

———. *The Empire's Old Clothes.* New York: Pantheon Books, 1983.

———. *Widows.* Translated by Stephen Kessler. New York: Vintage, 1984.

———. *The Last Song of Manuel Sendero.* New York: Penguin, 1988.

———. *Hard Rain.* Translated by George Shivers with the author. Columbia, La.: Readers International, 1990.

———. "Entre el subte y la esperanza: ¿Tenemos quién nos escriba?" *Página 30,* February 1991, 40–42.

———. "Political Code and Literary Code: The Testimonial Genre in Chile Today." *Some Write to the Future.* Durham, N.C.: Duke University Press, 1991.

———. *La muerte y la doncella.* Performed at the Teatro de la Esquina, Santiago, Chile, 15 March 1991.

———. *Death and the Maiden.* New York: Penguin, 1992.

———. *Konfidenz.* New York: Vintage Español, 1995.

———. *Heading South, Looking North.* New York: Penguin, 1998.

———. *Rumbo al sur, deseando al norte.* Buenos Aires: Planeta, 1999.

———. "Pinochet's Mind." *NACLA Report on the Americas* 34, no. 1 (July/August 2000): 4, 50.

———. Interview with Oscar Castro. "Theater and Social Action in the Concentration Camps of Chile." *Canadian Theater Review,* n.d. [1970s?].

———. *Blake's Therapy.* New York: Seven Stories Press, 2000.

———. *Terapia.* New York: Siete Cuentos, 2001.

Dorfman, Rodrigo, and Ariel Dorfman. *My House Is On Fire.* Directed by Rodrigo and Ariel Dorfman. 19 min. First Run/Icarus Films, 1997. Videocassette.

Drake, Paul W., and Iván Jaksić, eds. *The Struggle for Democracy in Chile.* Revised edition. Lincoln: University of Nebraska Press, 1995.

Eastman, Jorge Mario, ed. *Pinochet: El déspota que revoluncionó el derecho internacional (Documentos y opiniones).* Santafé de Bogotá: Tercer Mundo, 2000.

Ehrmann, Hans. "Teatro Postgolpe: Pedro, Juan, María y Rosa." *Gestos: Teoría y práctica del teatro hispánico* 4, no. 8 (November 1989): 155–61.

Elizabeth (of the former "Taller 'Los Almendros'"). Letter from Puente Alto, Chile, to the author, 15 June 1994.

Eltit, Diamela. *Lumpérica.* Santiago: Las Ediciones del Ornitorrinco, 1983.

———. *Por la patria.* Santiago: Las Ediciones del Ornitorrinco, 1986.

———. *El cuarto mundo.* Santiago: Editorial Planeta Biblioteca del Sur, 1988.

———. *El padre mío.* Santiago: Francisco Zegers Editor, 1989.

———. "Experiencia literaria y palabra en duelo." In *Duelo y creatividad (Seminario: literatura, sicoanálisis, enfoque sistémico),* by Eleonora Casaula, Edmundo Covarrubias, and Diamela Eltit. Santiago: Editorial Cuarto Propio, Cuaderno "Mujer y Límites," Serie Ensayo no. 1, 1989.

———. *Vaca sagrada.* Santiago: Planeta, 1991.

———. *Los vigilantes.* Santiago: Editorial Sudamericana, 1994.

———. *The Fourth World.* Translation and foreword by Dick Gerdes. Lincoln: University of Nebraska Press, 1995.

———. *Sacred Cow.* Translated by Amanda Hopkinson. New York: Serpent's Tail, 1995.

———. *E. Luminata.* Translation and afterword by Ronald Christ. Santa Fe, N.M.: Lumen, 1997.

———. "Nomadic Bodies." *Review: Latin American Literature and Arts* 54 (Spring 1997): 43–50.

———. *Los trabajadores de la muerte.* Barcelona: Seix Barral, 1998.

———. "Entrevista a Diamela Eltit: Desde la mujer a la androginía." Interview with Eugenia Brito. *Pluma y pincel,* no. 17 (August 1985): 42–43.

———. "Chile: ni desprecio ni puro amor." Interview with Patricio Ríos S. *Cauce* 100 (23 March 1987): 30–31.

———. Interview by author. Tape recording. Santiago, Chile, 14 August 1990.

Epple, Juan Armando. "La narrativa chilena: Historia y reformulación estética." In *Tradición y marginalidad en la literatura chilena del siglo XX,* edited by Lucía Guerra-Cunningham and Juan Villegas. Los Angeles, Calif.: Ediciones de la frontera, 1984.

Errázuriz, Paz, and Diamela Eltit. *El infarto del alma.* Santiago: Francisco Zegers, 1994.

Erro-Peralta, Nora, and Caridad Silva-Núñez, eds. *Beyond the Border: A New Age in Latin American Women's Fiction.* San Francisco, Calif.: Cleis Press, 1991.

Escobar, Arturo, and Sonia E. Alvarez, eds. *The Making of Social Movements in Latin America: Identity, Strategy, and Democracy.* Boulder, Colo.: Westview Press, 1992.

Espinoza Orellana, Manuel. *Aproximaciones a cuatro mundos de la poesía chilena actual.* Quilpué: Ediciones Altazor, Quincena Crítica, 1984.

Evans, Sara. *Personal Politics: The Roots of Women's Liberation in the Civil Rights Movement and the New Left.* New York: Vintage Books, 1980.

Fanon, Frantz. *The Wretched of the Earth*. Translated by Constance Farrington. Preface by Jean-Paul Sartre. New York: Grove Press, 1963.

Fariña, Soledad. *El primer libro*. Santiago: Ediciones Amaranto, 1985.

———. *Albricia*. Santiago: Ediciones Archivo, 1988.

Fempress, ed. *El cuento feminista latinoamericano*. Santiago: ILET, 1988.

Feria del Libro Latinoamericano (FELL). Special session entitled "Los talleres literarios en los '80." Concepción, Chile, 20 April 1991.

FLACSO Chile, eds. *Chile 96: Análisis y opiniones*. Santiago: FLACSO, 1997.

———. *Chile 97: Análisis y opiniones*. Santiago: FLACSO, 1998.

———. *Chile 98: Entre la II Cumbre y la detención de Pinochet*. Santiago: FLACSO, 1999.

Foucault, Michel. *Discipline and Punish*. Translated by Alan Sheridan. 1977. Reprint, New York: Vintage, 1979.

———. *A History of Sexuality*. Vol. 1, *An Introduction*. Translated by Robert Hurley. 1976. Reprint, New York: Vintage Books, 1980.

———. *Power/Knowledge: Selected Interviews and Other Writings, 1972–1977*. Edited by Colin Gordon. Translated by Colin Gordon, Len Marshall, John Mepham, and Kate Soper. New York: Pantheon, 1980.

Foxley, Ana María. "Literatura de mujeres: ¿una palabra sospechosa?" *La Epoca*, supplement *Literatura y libros*, año 1, no. 5 (15 May 1988): 1–2.

Franco, Jean. *Plotting Women: Gender and Representation in Mexico*. New York: Columbia University Press, 1989.

Gallardo, Bernarda. "El redescubrimiento del carácter social del hambre: Las ollas comunes." In *Espacio y poder: Los pobladores*, edited by Hernán Pozo. Santiago: FLACSO, 1987.

Garcés, Joan E. *Allende y la experiencia chilena: Las armas de la política*. 1976. Reprint, Santiago: Ediciones BAT, 1990.

García Márquez, Gabriel. *Cien años de soledad*. 1967. Reprint, Madrid: Selecciones Austral, 1982.

———. *One Hundred Years of Solitude*. Translated by Gregory Rabassa. New York: Harper and Row, 1970.

García Pinto, Magdalena. Interview with Isabel Allende. *Women Writers of Latin America: Intimate Histories*. Translated by Trudy Balch and Magdalena García Pinto. Austin: University of Texas Press, 1991.

Garretón, Manuel Antonio. "En torno a algunas funciones sociales del teatro chileno actual." In *Seminario "Teatro chileno en la década del 80"*, edited by María de la Luz Hurtado and Carlos Ochensius. Santiago: CENECA, serie documentos no.11, 1980.

———. *Dictaduras y democratización*. Santiago: FLACSO, 1984.

———. "La herencia de los autoritarismos." Santiago: FLACSO, Documento de Trabajo no. 237, 1984.

———. "The Political Evolution of the Chilean Military Regime and Problems in the Transition to Democracy." In *Transitions from Authoritarian Rule: Latin America*, edited by Guillermo O'Donnell, Philippe C. Schmitter, and Lawrence Whitehead. Foreword by Abraham F. Lowenthal. Baltimore: The Johns Hopkins University Press, 1986.

———. *The Chilean Political Process*. Boston: Unwin Hyman, 1989.

———. "Los desafíos de la profundización democrática." In *Chile 96: Análisis y opiniones*, edited by FLACSO Chile. Santiago: FLACSO, 1997.

———. "Chile 1997–98. Las revanchas de la democractización incompleta." In *Chile 98: Entre la II Cumbre y la detención de Pinochet*, edited by FLACSO Chile. Santiago: FLACSO, 1999.

Gaviola, Edda, Ximena Jiles, Lorella Lopresti, and Claudia Rojas. *Queremos votar en las próximas elecciones: Historia del movimiento femenino chileno, 1913–1952*. Santiago: Coedición Centro de análisis y difusión de la condición de la mujer, "La Morada", Fempress, ILET, ISIS, Librería Lila, PEMCI, CEM, 1986.

Geertz, Clifford. *The Interpretation of Cultures*. New York: Basic Books, 1973.

Gelber, George, M. Amelia de Sosa, and Juan Caveda. *Evaluación de FASIC*. Santiago: Estudios y Publicaciones FASIC, 1988.

Gil, Federico, Ricardo Lagos, and Henry Landsberger, eds. *Chile at the Turning Point: Lessons of the Socialist Years, 1970–1973*. Philadelphia: Institute for the Study of Human Issues, 1979.

Gilman, Charlotte Perkins. *The Yellow Wallpaper*. 1899. Reprint, with an afterword by Elaine R. Hedges, New York: The Feminist Press, 1973.

Glickman, Nora. "Los personajes femeninos en *La casa de los espíritus*." In *Los libros tienen sus propios espíritus: Estudios sobre Isabel Allende*, edited by Marcelo Coddou. Veracruz: Universidad Veracruzana, Cuadernos del Centro de Investigaciones Lingüístico-Literarias, 1986.

Gligo, Agata. "'El Cuarto Mundo' de Diamela Eltit." *Mensaje* 377 (March–April 1989): 110–11.

González, Mónica. Interview by author. Tape recording. Santiago, Chile, 23 July 1991.

Gutiérrez, Paulina, and Cristián Warnken. *El discurso sobre el trabajador y el poblador en "El Mercurio" y "La Tercera" (1973–1983)*. Santiago: Documentos CENECA no. 62, 1986.

Guzmán, Patricio. *Chile: Obstinada Memoria*. Directed by Patricio Guzmán. A coproduction of the National Film Board of Canada and Les Films d'Ici (Paris). 58 min. First Run/Icarus Films, 1997. Videocassette.

Guzmán Bravo, Rosario. "Se desplegaron las letras femeninas." *Ya (Revista Femenina de El Mercurio)* 336 (20 February 1990): 8–9.

Harlow, Barbara. *Resistance Literature*. London: Methuen, 1987.

Hart, Patricia. *Narrative Magic in the Fiction of Isabel Allende*. Toronto: Associated University Presses, 1989.

Helper, Norma. "Binding the Wounds of the Body Politic: Nation as Family in *La casa de los espíritus*." In *Critical Approaches to Isabel Allende's Novels*, edited by Sonia Riquelme Rojas and Edna Aguirre Rehbein. New York: Peter Lang, 1991.

Herrera, Bernal. "Reseña de *Por la patria*, de Diamela Eltit" *Plaza*, no. 14–15 (spring–fall 1988): 81–82.

Hitchens, Christopher. "The Case against Pinochet." Part 1. *Harper's Magazine* 302, no. 1809 (February 2001): 33–58.

———. "The Case against Pinochet." Part 2. *Harper's Magazine* 302, no. 1810 (March 2001): 49–74.

Hola, Eugenia. "Mujer, dominacion y crisis." In *Mundo de mujer: Continuidad y cambio*, edited by Centro de Estudios de la Mujer (CEM). Santiago: CEM, 1988.

hooks, bell. *Outlaw Culture: Resisting Representation*. New York: Routledge, 1994.

Huneeus, Carlos. *Los chilenos y la política: Cambio y continuidad bajo el autoritarismo*. Santiago: CERC/ICHEH, 1987.

Hurtado, María de la Luz, and Carlos Ochensius. "Nómina de obras teatrales montadas entre 1968 y 1980 por compañías profesionales y aficionadas en salas comerciales." Publicaciones CENECA no. 16, 1980.

———. *TIT, Taller de Investigación Teatral.* Vol. 3 of *Serie Testimonio (maneras de hacer y pensar el teatro en el Chile actual).* Santiago: CENECA, n.d. [1980?].

———. "Transformaciones del teatro chileno en la década del 70." In *Teatro Chileno de la Crisis Institucional 1973–1980 (Antología Crítica)*, edited by María de la Luz Hurtado, Carlos Ochensius, and Hernán Vidal. Minneapolis and Santiago: University of Minnesota Latin American Series and the Centro de Indagación y Expresión Cultural y Artística (CENECA), 1982.

ICTUS, David Benavente, and TIT. *Pedro, Juan y Diego/Tres Marías y una Rosa.* Prologue by María de la Luz Hurtado. Santiago: CESOC Ediciones ChileAmérica, 1989.

Instituto Nacional de Estadísticas. Unemployment Rate by Year in Chile, 1970–89. Information gathered 10 July 1991.

Jameson, Fredric. *The Political Unconscious: Narrative as a Socially Symbolic Act.* Ithaca, N.Y.: Cornell University Press, 1981.

———. "Postmodernism, or, The Cultural Logic of Late Capitalism." *New Left Review* 146 (1984): 53–92.

———. "Third World Literature in the Era of Multi-national Capitalism." *Social Text* 15 (1986): 65–88.

———. *Postmodernism, or, The Cultural Logic of Late Capitalism.* Durham, N.C.: Duke University Press, 1991.

Jara, René. "Arqueología de un paradigma de negación: el discurso del Jefe de Estado." In *The Discourse of Power: Culture, Hegemony, and the Authoritarian State*, edited by Neil Larsen. Minneapolis, Minn.: Institute for the Study of Ideologies and Literature, 1983.

Jeréz, Fernando. "'El cuarto mundo,' Novela de Diamela Eltit." *Fortín Diario*, 23 April 1989, 21.

Jocelyn-Holt Letelier, Alfredo. *El peso de la noche, nuestra frágil fortaleza histórica.* Santiago: Planeta, 1997.

Jofré, Manuel Alcides. "Culture, Art, and Literature in Chile: 1973–1985." *Latin American Perspectives* 16, no. 2 (Spring 1989): 70–95.

Johnson, Barbara. "Gender and Poetry: Charles Baudelaire and Marceline Desbordes-Valmore." In *Displacements: Women, Tradition, Literatures in French*, edited by Joan de Jean and Nancy K. Miller. Baltimore: The Johns Hopkins University Press, 1991.

Kadir, Djelal. *The Other Writing: Postcolonial Essays in Latin America's Writing Culture.* West Lafayette, Ind.: Purdue University Press, 1993.

Kirkwood, Julieta. *Ser política en Chile: Las feministas y los partidos.* Santiago: FLACSO, 1982.

———. "El feminismo como negación del autoritarismo." Santiago: FLACSO, Material de Discusión no. 32, 1983.

———. *Feminarios.* Santiago: Ediciones Documentas/Mujer, 1987.

———. *Ser política en Chile: Los nudos de la sabiduría feminista.* 2d ed. Santiago: Editorial Cuarto Propio, 1990.

Kornbluh, Peter. "Declassifying U.S. Intervention in Chile," *NACLA Report on the Americas* 32, no. 6 (May/June 1999): 36–42.

———. "CIA Outrage in Chile." *The Nation* 271, no. 11 (16 October 2000): 4–5.
Kwok Pui-Lan. "The Future of Feminist Theology: An Asian Perspective." In *Feminist Theology from the Third World: A Reader*, edited by Ursula King. Maryknoll, N.Y.: Orbis, 1994.
Laclau, Ernesto. "Fascism and Ideology." In *Politics and Ideology in Marxist Theory*. New York: Verso, 1977.
Lagos, Marta. "Visiones latinoamericanas: Latinobarómetro 1998." In *Chile 98: Entre la II Cumbre y la detención de Pinochet*, edited by FLACSO Chile. Santiago: FLACSO, 1999.
Larraín, Ana María. "Diamela Eltit: El trabajo es la vida y mi vida." *Revista de Libros de El Mercurio* (21 May 1989): 1, 4–5.
Larraín, Cristina. *Catastro de organizaciones femeninas del gobierno*. Santiago: Instituto Chileno de Estudios Humanísticos, 1982.
Larsen, Neil, ed. *The Discourse of Power: Culture, Hegemony, and the Authoritarian State*. Minneapolis, Minn.: Institute for the Study of Ideologies and Literature, 1983.
"Las tres Marías Hacen Las Maletas (La Rosa, También)." *Las Ultimas Noticias*, 3 November 1980, 64.
Lechner, Norbert. "Vida cotidiana y ámbito público en Chile." (4 papers.) Santiago: FLACSO, 1980.
———. *Los patios interiores de la democracia: Subjectividad y política*. Santiago: FLACSO, 1988.
Lechner, Norbert, and Susana Levy. "Notas sobre la vida cotidiana III: El disciplinamiento de la mujer." Santiago: FLACSO Material de discusión, 1984.
Lemebel, Pedro. *La esquina es mi corazón: Crónica urbana*. Santiago: Editorial Cuarto Propio, 1995.
———. *Loco afán: Crónicas de Sidario*. Santiago: Ediciones LOM, 1996.
Lertora, Juan Carlos. "Prólogo: Escritura/Erotismo/Violencia." In *A horcajadas*, by Pía Barros. Santiago: Mosquito Editores, 1990.
———, ed. *Una poética de literatura menor: La narrativa de Diamela Eltit*. Santiago: Editorial Cuarto Propio, 1993.
Levine, Linda Gould. "A Passage to Androgyny: Isabel Allende's *La casa de los espíritus*." In *In the Feminine Mode: Essays on Hispanic Women Writers*, edited by Noël Valis and Carol Maier. Lewisburg, Pa.: Bucknell University Press, 1990.
Lira, Winnie. Personal interview about the Workshops section of the Vicariate of Solidarity. Tape recording. Santiago, Chile, 24 October 1990.
Loach, Barbara Lee. "Power and Women's Writing in Chile: 1973–1988." Ph.D. diss., Ohio State University, 1991.
Lorde, Audre. *Sister Outsider*. Trumansburg, N.Y.: Crossing Press, 1984.
Lovell, Terry. *Consuming Fiction*. London: Verso, 1987.
Loveman, Brian. "The Transition to Civilian Government in Chile, 1990–1994." In *The Struggle for Democracy in Chile*, edited by Paul W. Drake and Iván Jaksić. Revised edition. Lincoln: University of Nebraska Press, 1995.
Mandel, Ernest. *Late Capitalism*. Translated by Joris DeBres. 1975. Reprint, London: Verso, 1987.
Maqueira, Diego. *La tirana*. Santiago: Edición Tempus Tacendi, 1983.

Marcos, Juan Manuel, and Teresa Méndez-Faith. "Multiplicidad, dialéctica y reconciliación del discurso en *La casa de los espíritus*." In *Los libros tienen sus propios espíritus: Estudios sobre Isabel Allende*, edited by Marcelo Coddou. Veracruz: Universidad Veracruzana, Cuadernos del Centro de Investigaciones Lingüístico-Literarias, 1986.

Martínez, Juan Luis. *La nueva novela*. Santiago: Ediciones Archivo, 1977.

Mattelart, Michelle. "Chile: El golpe de estado en femenino o cuando las mujeres de la burguesía salen a la calle." *Casa de las Américas* 88 (January–February 1975): 75–90.

McCallister, Richard. "Nomenklatura in *La casa de los espíritus*." In *Critical Approaches to Isabel Allende's Novels*, edited by Sonia Riquelme Rojas and Edna Aguirre Rehbein. New York: Peter Lang, 1991.

Medioli, Ana María. "Ollas comunes en Chile, Organización para la sobrevivencia: Una experiencia de trabajo poblacional." *Trabajo Social* (1984): 5–14.

Mellado, Carlos. "Los talleres literarios en el período [1973–1983]." Unpublished paper.

———. "Los talleres en los últimos 10 años." Unpublished paper.

Meza, M. Angélica, ed. *La otra mitad de Chile*. Santiago: CESOC Ediciones ChileAmérica, 1986.

Migdal, Alicia. Interview by author. Montevideo, Uruguay, 23 May 1989.

Minow, Martha. *Between Vengeance and Forgiveness: Facing History after Genocide and Mass Violence*. Boston: Beacon Press, 1998.

Molina, Natacha. *Lo femenino y lo democrático en el Chile de hoy*. Santiago: Ediciones Documentas/VECTOR, 1986.

Montecino, Sonia. *Madres y huachos: Alegorías del mestizaje chileno*. Santiago: Editorial Cuarto Propio-CEDEM, 1991.

Mora, Gabriela. "Ruptura y preservancia de estereotipos en *La casa de los espíritus*." In *Los libros tienen sus propios espíritus: Estudios sobre Isabel Allende*, edited by Marcelo Coddou. Veracruz: Universidad Veracruzana, Cuadernos del Centro de Investigaciones Lingüístico-Literarias, 1986.

Morales, Eduardo and Sergio Rojas. "Relocalización socio-espacial de la pobreza. Política estatal y presión popular, 1979–1985." In *Espacio y poder: Los pobladores*, edited by Hernán Pozo. Santiago: FLACSO, 1987.

Moulian, Tomás. *Chile actual: anatomía de un mito*. Santiago: LOM Ediciones, 1997.

———. "A Time of Forgetting: Myths of the Chilean Transition." *NACLA Report on the Americas* 32, no. 2 (September/October 1998): 16–22.

Munizaga, Giselle. *Vecino, mujer y deportista: Micromedios de gobierno*. Santiago: CENECA, 1983.

Munizaga, Giselle, and Carlos Ochensius. "El discurso público de Pinochet (1973–1976)." In *The Discourse of Power: Culture, Hegemony and the Authoritarian State*, edited by Neil Larsen. Minneapolis, Minn.: Institute for the Study of Ideologies and Literature, 1983.

Muñoz, Elías Miguel. "La voz testimonial de Isabel Allende en *De amor y de sombra*." In *Critical Approaches to Isabel Allende's Novels*, edited by Sonia Riquelme Rojas and Edna Aguirre Rehbein. New York: Peter Lang, 1991.

Muñoz, Josefina. "Reflexiones acerca de algunas huellas del poder en la narrativa de la generación del 80." In *Escribir en los bordes: Congreso Internacional de Literatura Femenina Latinoamericana 1987*, edited by Carmen Berenguer, Eugenia Brito, Diamela Eltit, Raquel Olea, Eliana Ortega, and Nelly Richard. Santiago: Editorial Cuarto Propio, Colección Bajo Palabra, 1990.

Muñoz Valenzuela, Diego, and Ramón Díaz Eterovic. "La joven narrativa chilena: Seis años después." Introduction to *Andar con cuentos: Nueva narrativa chilena*. Santiago: Mosquito Editores, 1992.

Navarro, Marysa. Comments on the panel "Latin American Feminist NGOs and Global Society: Critical Perspectives" at the Twentieth International Conference of the Latin American Studies Association. Guadalajara, Mexico, 17–19 April 1997.

Nelson, Cary, Paula A. Treichler, and Lawrence Grossberg. "Cultural Studies: An Introduction." In *Cultural Studies*, edited by Lawrence Grossberg, Cary Nelson, and Paula A. Treichler. New York: Routledge, 1992.

Nolte, Detlef. "El juicio de la historia: Espectros del pasado en América Latina." In *Chile 98: Entre la II Cumbre y la detención de Pinochet*, edited by FLACSO Chile. Santiago: FLACSO, 1999.

Ogundipe-Leslie, Molara. *Re-creating Ourselves: African Women and Critical Transformations*. Trenton, N.J.: Africa World Press, 1994.

Olea, Raquel. *Lengua víbora: Producciones de lo femenino de la escritura de mujeres chilenas*. Santiago: Cuarto Propio, 1998.

Olivárez, Carlos, ed. *Los veteranos del 70*. Santiago: Ediciones Melquíades, 1988.

———, ed. *Nueva narrativa chilena*. Santiago: LOM Ediciones, 1997.

Oropesa, Salvador Antonio. "Aproximación crítica a la obra de Ariel Dorfman: Ficción y crítica cultural." Ph.D. diss., Arizona State University, 1990.

Ortega, Graciela. "Ollas comunes: Mucho más que un plato de comida." *El canelo (Revista chilena de desarrollo local)* 4, no. 14 (October 1989): 3–5.

Ortega, Julio. "Diamela Eltit y el imaginario de la virtualidad." In *Una poética de literatura menor: La narrativa de Diamela Eltit*, edited by Juan Carlos Lértora. Santiago: Editorial Cuarto Propio, 1993.

Ortúzar, Carmen. "Una escritora chilena obsesiva de la realidad." *El Mercurio*, 21 August 1985, supplement *Arte y Cultura*: 4.

Osandún, Mirta, and Ana María Medioli. Interview by author about the "Ollas Comunes" section of the Vicariate of Solidarity. Tape recording. Santiago, Chile, 24 October 1990.

Otano, Rafael. *Crónica de la transición*. Santiago: Editorial Planeta, 1995.

Oyarzún, Kemy. "Saberes críticos y estudios de género." *Revista Nomadías* 1, no. 1 (December 1996): 11–23.

———. "Prólogo: El escándalo como modo de recepción." In *Aguas abajo: Cuentos,* by Marta Brunet. Santiago: Cuarto Propio, 1997.

Panjabi, Kavita. "*The House of the Spirits*, Tránsito Soto: From Periphery to Power." In *Critical Approaches to Isabel Allende's Novels*, edited by Sonia Riquelme Rojas and Edna Aguirre Rehbein. New York: Peter Lang, 1991.

Parra, Nicanor. *Obra gruesa*. Santiago: Andrés Bello, 1983.

Parra, Roberto. *"La negra Ester."* *Apuntes* 98 (1989): 33–54.

Paz, Octavio. *El laberinto de la soledad*. 1950. Reprint, Mexico, D.F.: Fondo de Cultura Económica, 1984.

———. *The Labyrinth of Solitude: Life and Thought in Mexico*. Translated by Lysander Kemp. New York: Grove Press, 1961.

Pérez, Rogelio. "Pinochet y la justicia: Una reflexión sobre los cambios en el derecho." In *Chile 98: Entre la II Cumbre y la detención de Pinochet*, edited by FLACSO Chile. Santiago: FLACSO, 1999.

Piglia, Ricardo. *Respiración artificial.* 2d ed. Buenos Aires: Editorial Sudamericana, 1988.

———. *Artificial Respiration.* Translated by Daniel Balderston. Durham, N.C.: Duke University Press, 1994.

Pisano, Margarita. Interviews by author. Santiago, Chile, 12 June 1989 and 27 June 1998, and San Bernardo, Argentina, 19 and 24 November 1990.

Poblete, Olga, ed. *Antología del MEMCh.* Santiago: Editorial MEMCh, 1984.

Pozo, Hernán. "Espacio cotidiano y poder." Santiago: FLACSO Material de Discusión no. 113, 1988.

Prieto, Antonio. "Students Organize Across Latin America." *NACLA Report on the Americas* 33, no. 1 (July/August 1999): 51–52.

Promís, José. "Programas narrativos en la novela chilena del siglo XX." *Revista Iberoamericana* 168–169 (July–December 1994), 925–33.

Raczynski, Dagmar, and Claudia Serrano. *Vivir la pobreza, Testimonios de mujeres.* Santiago: CIEPLAN, 1985.

Radrigán, Juan. *teatro de juan radrigán* [sic]. Santiago: CENECA, 1984.

Radway, Janice. *Reading the Romance: Women, Patriarchy, and Popular Literature.* Chapel Hill: University of North Carolina Press, 1984.

Randall, Margaret. *Gathering Rage: The Failure of Twentieth-Century Revolutions to Develop a Feminist Agenda.* New York: Monthly Review Press, 1992.

Rettig Guissen, Raúl (president of the commission); Jaime Castillo Velasco, José Luis Cea Egaña, Mónica Jiménez de La Jara, Ricardo Martin Díaz, Laura Novoa Vásquez, Gonzalo Vial Correa, José Luis Zalaquett Daher (members of the commission); Jorge Correa Sutil (secretary of the commission). *Informe Rettig (Informe de la Comisión Nacional de Verdad y Reconciliación).* Santiago: La Nación and Ediciones del Ornitorrinco, 1991.

Rich, Adrienne. *Of Woman Born.* New York: W. W. Norton, 1979.

Richard, Nelly. *Margins and Institutions: Art in Chile Since 1973..* Special Issue of *Art & Text* 21 (1986).

———. "Reply to Vidal (from Chile)." In *The Postmodernism Debate in Latin America*, edited by John Beverley and José Oviedo. Durham, N.C.: Duke University Press, 1993.

———. *La insubordinación de los signos (cambio político, transformaciones culturales y poéticas de la crisis).* Santiago: Editorial Cuarto Propio, 1994.

———. *Residuos y metáforas (Ensayos de crítica cultural sobre el Chile de la transición).* Santiago: Cuarto propio, 1998.

———, ed. "El caso 'Simón Bolívar' y la polémica del Fondart, Dossier de prensa." *Revista de crítica cultural,* no. 9 (November 1994): 25–36.

Riley, Denise. *"Am I That Name?": Feminism and the Category of 'Women' in History.* Minneapolis: University of Minnesota Press, 1988.

Ríos S., Patricio. "Chile: ni desprecio ni puro amor." Interview of Diamela Eltit. *Cauce* 100 (23 March 1987): 30–31.

Riquelme Rojas, Sonia, and Edna Aguirre Rehbein, eds. *Critical Approaches to Isabel Allende's Novels.* New York: Peter Lang, 1991.

Robles, Víctor Hugo. "History in the Making: The Homosexual Liberation Movement in Chile." *NACLA Report on the Americas* 31, no. 4 (January/February 1998): 36–43.

Rodríguez, Mario. "García Márquez/Isabel Allende: Relocación textual." In *Los libros tienen sus propios espíritus: Estudios sobre Isabel Allende*, edited by Marcelo Coddou. Veracruz: Universidad Veracruzana, Cuadernos del Centro de Investigaciones Lingüístico-Literarias, 1986.

Rojas, Mario A. "*La casa de los espíritus* de Isabel Allende: Un caleidoscopio de espejos desordenados." In *Los libros tienen sus propios espíritus: Estudios sobre Isabel Allende*, edited by Marcelo Coddou. Veracruz: Universidad Veracruzana, Cuadernos del Centro de Investigaciones Lingüístico-Literarias, 1986.

Rojas, Paz, Víctor Espinoza, Julia Urquieta, and Hernán Soto. *Tarde pero llega: Pinochet ante la justicia española*. Santiago: LOM, 1998.

Saa, María Antonieta. Interviews by author. Santiago, Chile, 7 and 9 June 1989, 27 October 1990.

Santa Cruz, Adriana. Interview by author. Santiago, Chile, 9 June 1989.

Schild, Verónica. "'Gender Equity' without Social Justice: Women's Rights in the Neoliberal Age." *NACLA Report on the Americas* 34, no. 1 (July/August 2000): 25–28.

Schneider, Cathy Lisa. *Shantytown Protest in Pinochet's Chile*. Philadelphia: Temple University Press, 1995.

Schops, Karl-Heinz. *Bertolt Brecht: Life, Work and Criticism*. Fredericton, N.B.: York Press, 1989.

Scott, James C. *Domination and the Arts of Resistance: Hidden Transcripts*. New Haven: Yale University Press, 1990.

Sigmund, Paul E. *The Overthrow of Allende and the Politics of Chile, 1964–1976*. Pittsburgh, Pa.: University of Pittsburgh Press, 1977.

———. *The United States and Democracy in Chile*. Baltimore: The Johns Hopkins University Press, 1993.

Silva, Coti. Interviews by author. Santiago, Chile, 8 June 1989 and 27 October 1990.

Silva-Cáceres, Raúl. "Un viaje de Cortázar a Skármeta y Dorfman: La difícil esperanza en el Cono Sur." *Les cahiers* 1 (1983): 81–91.

Skármeta, Antonio. *Soñé que la nieve ardía*. 1975. Reprint, Barcelona: Plaza y Janés, 1985.

———. *I Dreamt the Snow Was Burning*. Translated by Malcolm Coad. New York: Readers International, 1985.

Smirnow, Gabriel. *The Revolution Disarmed: Chile, 1970–1973*. New York: Monthly Review Press, 1979.

Sosnowski, Saúl, and Louise B. Popkin, eds. *Repression, Exile, and Democracy: Uruguayan Culture*. Translated by Louise B. Popkin. Durham, N.C.: Duke University Press, 1993.

Soto, Oscar. *El último día de Salvador Allende*. Santiago: Aguilar, 1999.

Spivak, Gayatri Chakravorty. "French Feminism in an International Frame." In *In Other Worlds: Essays in Cultural Politics*. New York: Routledge, 1987.

———. "Can the Subaltern Speak?" In *Marxism and the Interpretation of Culture*, edited by Cary Nelson and Lawrence Grossberg. Chicago: University of Illinois Press, 1988.

Spotorno, Radomiro. "Diamela Eltit, escritora: 'Debemos ser más emblemáticos y menos analíticos.'" *Página abierta*, no. 12 (16 April 1990): 34–35.

Stevens, Evelyn P. "*Marianismo:* The Other Face of *Machismo* in Latin America." In *Female and Male in Latin America*, edited by Ann Pescatello. Pittsburgh, Pa.: University of Pittsburgh Press, 1973.

Subercaseaux, Bernardo, ed. *El libro en Chile (su presente y su futuro)*. Santiago: CENECA, Cámara chilena del libro, CED, n.d. [1980s?].

Summary of the Truth and Reconciliation Commission Report. Santiago: Chilean Human Rights Commission and Centro IDEAS, 1991.

Sweezy, Paul M., and Harry Magdoff, eds. *Revolution and Counter-Revolution in Chile.* New York: Monthly Review Press, 1974.

Taller "Los Almendros" (*Arpilleristas* from Puente Alto). Interview by author. Tape recording. Puente Alto, Chile, 6 February 1991.

Taller "Sector Sur" (*Arpilleristas* from south Santiago). Interview by author. Tape recording. Santiago, Chile, 5 February 1991.

Taylor, Diana. *Disappearing Acts: Spectacles of Gender and Nationalism in Argentina's "Dirty War."* Durham, N.C.: Duke University Press, 1997.

Theweleit, Klaus. *Women, Floods, Bodies, History.* Vol. 1 of *Male Fantasies.* Translated by Stephen Conway with Erica Carter and Chris Turner. Foreword by Barbara Ehrenreich. Minneapolis, Minn.: University of Minnesota Press, 1987.

Tierney-Tello, Mary Beth. "Testimony, Ethics, and the Aesthetic of Diamela Eltit." *PMLA* 144, no. 1 (January 1999): 78–96.

Ulibarri, Luisa. "Cien mujeres y cinco días de preguntas." *La Epoca,* 15 August 1987, 24.

U. S. Senate. *Covert Action in Chile, 1963–1973.* Staff Report of the Select Committee to Study Governmental Operations with Respect to Intelligence Activities. Washington, D.C.: U.S. Government Printing Office, 1975.

Valdés, Teresa. *Venid, benitas de mi Padre (Las pobladoras, sus rutinas y sus sueños).* Santiago: FLACSO, 1988.

Valdés, Teresa, and Marisa Weinstein. "Corriendo y descorriendo túpidos velos." In *Chile 96: Análisis y opiniones,* edited by FLACSO Chile. Santiago: Nueva Serie Flacso, 1997.

Valdivieso, Mercedes. *Maldita yo entre las mujeres.* Santiago: Planeta Biblioteca del Sur, 1991.

Valente, Ignacio. "Diamela Eltit: Una novela experimental." *El Mercurio,* 25 March 1984, E3.

———. "El cuerpo es un horror y es una gloria." *Revista de Libros de El Mercurio,* 21 May 1989, 1, 4.

Valenzuela, María Elena. *Todas íbamos a ser reinas: La mujer en el Chile militar.* Santiago: ACHIP/CESOC Ediciones Chile y América, 1987.

Verdugo, Patricia. *Detenidos-desaparecidos: Una herida abierta.* Santiago: Editorial Aconcagua, 1980.

———. *André de la Victoria.* Santiago: Editorial Aconcagua, 1985.

———. *Rodrigo y Carmen Gloria: Quemados vivos.* Santiago: Editorial Aconcagua, 1986.

———. *Los zarpazos del Puma.* Santiago: CESOC Ediciones ChileAmérica, 1989.

———. *Tiempo de días claros: Los desaparecidos.* Santiago: CESOC Ediciones ChileAmérica, 1990.

Vicaría de la Solidaridad. Interviews by author with directors of "Zonas," "Ollas Comunes," and "Talleres." Tape recordings. Santiago, Chile, 8, 11, and 23–24 October 1990.

Vickers, Nancy J. "Diana Described: Scattered Woman and Scattered Rhyme." *Critical Inquiry* 8, no. 2 (1982): 265–79.

Vidal, Hernán. *Dar la Vida por la Vida: La Agrupación Chilena de Familiares de Detenidos-Desaparecidos (Ensayo de antropología Simbólica).* Minneapolis, Minn.: Institute for the Study of Ideologies and Literature, 1982.

———. "La Declaración de Principios de la Junta Militar chilena como sistema literario: La lucha antifascista y el cuerpo humano." In *The Discourse of Power: Culture, Hegemony, and the Authoritarian State,* edited by Neil Larsen. Minneapolis, Minn.: Institute for the Study of Ideologies and Literature, 1983.

———. "En torno a *De amor y de sombra* de Isabel Allende: Una apreciación socio-histórica." In *La cultura nacional chilena, crítica literaria y derechos humanos*, vol. 5 of *Literature and Human Rights*, edited by Hernán Vidal. Minneapolis, Minn.: Institute for the Study of Ideologies and Literature, 1989.

———. "La Agrupación de Familiares de Detenidos-Desaparecidos: Metáforas de vida." In *La cultura nacional chilena, crítica literaria y derechos humanos*, vol. 5 of *Literature and Human Rights*, edited by Hernán Vidal. Minneapolis, Minn.: Institute for the Study of Ideologies and Literature, 1989.

———. "Para una definición culturalista de la crítica literaria latinoamericana." In *La cultura nacional chilena, crítica literaria y derechos humanos*, vol. 5 of *Literature and Human Rights*, edited by Hernán Vidal. Minneapolis, Minn.: Institute for the Study of Ideologies and Literature, 1989.

———. *Dictadura militar, trauma social e inauguración de la sociología del teatro en Chile*. Vol. 8 of *Literature and Human Rights,* edited by Hernán Vidal. Minneapolis, Minn.: Institute for the Study of Ideologies and Literature, 1991.

———. "Postmodernism, Postleftism, Neo-Avant-Gardism: The Case of Chile's *Revista de Crítica Cultural.*" In *The Postmodernism Debate in Latin America*, edited by John Beverley and José Oviedo. Durham, N.C.: Duke University Press, 1993.

Villegas, Juan, ed. *Antología de la nueva poesía femenina chilena*. Santiago: Editorial La Noria, 1985.

Weaver, Wesley J., III. "La frontera que se esfuma: Testimonio y ficción en *De amor y de sombra.*" In *Critical Approaches to Isabel Allende's Novels*, edited by Sonia Riquelme Rojas and Edna Aguirre Rehbein. New York: Peter Lang, 1991.

Williams, Raymond L. "Truth Claims, Postmodernism, and the Latin American Novel." *Profession 92* (1992): 6–9.

Winn, Peter. *Weavers of Revolution*. New York: Oxford University Press, 1986.

———. "Lagos Defeats the Right—By a Thread." *NACLA Report on the Americas* 33, no. 5 (March/April 2000): 6–10.

Wolff, Egon, Ramón Griffero, and Ignacio Agüero, "Teatro y cine en Chile." Roundtable discussion at ENART (Encuentro Nacional de Arte), Universidad Católica, Santiago de Chile, 11 August 1990.

Yúdice, George, Jean Franco, and Juan Flores, eds. *On Edge: The Crisis of Contemporary Latin American Culture*. Minneapolis: University of Minnesota Press, 1992.

Zalaquett, José. "Balance de la política de derechos humanos en la transición chilena a la democracia." In *Chile 98: Entre la II Cumbre y la detención de Pinochet*, edited by FLACSO Chile. Santiago: FLACSO, 1999.

Zerán, Faride. "La seducción de Pía Barros." *La Epoca,* supplement *Literatura y libros,* año 3, no. 138 (2 December 1990): 4–5.

Zúñiga, Gerardo. "La problemática indígena en el Chile actual." In *Chile 98: Entre la II Cumbre y la detención de Pinochet*, edited by FLACSO Chile. Santiago: FLACSO, 1999.

Zurita, Raul. *Purgatorio*. Santiago: Editorial Universitaria, 1979.

———. *Anteparaíso*. Santiago: Editores Asociados, 1982.

———. *Canto a su amor desaparecido*. Santiago: Editorial Universitaria, 1987.

Index

Abortion, 230
Academy for Christian Humanism, 256 n. 17
Acciones de arte. *See* Art actions
Acevedo, Sebastián, 271 n. 53
Adorno, Theodor W., 260 n. 4
Africa, 123
Agosín, Marjorie, 86, 202, 225, 250 n. 16
Agrupación Cultural Universitaria. *See* University Cultural Association
Agrupación de Familiares de Detenidos-Desaparecidos. *See* Association of Family Members of the Detained-Disappeared
Aguirre, Isidora, 31, 259 n. 34
Aguirre Rehbein, Edna, 269 n. 44
Ahmed, Leila, 37
A horcajadas. See *Astride* (Barros)
Ahumada, Eugenio, 270 n. 49
Ahumada, Rodrigo Baño, 271 n. 3
Aleph, El (theater collective), 251 n. 25
Alianza Democrática. *See* Democratic Alliance
Alienation, 121
Allende, Isabel: and Barros, 196, 200, 215; and Benavente, 196; and Chilean literature, 11, 30, 47, 193, 195–96; and democratic transition, 193, 195–96, 220, 233–34; and Dorfman, 196, 206; and Eltit, 104, 196; and happy endings, 196–97; and hope, 195–96, 218, 266 n. 11; and *la fábula*, 195–97; and magic, 198, 199, 212–19, 266 n. 17; political naïveté of, 267 n. 23; popularity of, 193–94, 196, 202, 212, 219, 220, 265 n. 3, 266 n. 13, 270 n. 48; relationship with Salvador Allende, 196, 266 n. 11, 267 n. 23; and romance conventions, 199, 202, 207, 216–17; treatment of violence, 203–5; on writing, 195–97. *See also specific works of Allende*
Allende, Salvador: election of, 25; feminization of, 28, 31, 140; funeral of, 21–22, 34; and government spending, 83; and human rights, 270–71 n. 52; and hunger, 154; and Marxism, 50; political obstacles of, 26; and Popular Unity, 21, 25, 78, 118, 245 n. 19; relationship with Isabel Allende, 196, 266 n. 11, 267 n. 23
Alliance for Chile, 225
Alonso, Soledad, 94, 95, 103
Alternative theater: and Chilean literature, 11, 30; definition of, 247 n. 2; in democracy, 232; and domestication, 89–90, 251 n. 27; and market, 93–95; productivity of, 251 n. 24; repression of, 82, 89, 251 n. 26; and social rearticulation, 83, 90, 106, 114; statistics on, 88, 251 n. 4; and tax on theater tickets, 89, 251; and working class, 87–89. *See also* Investigative Theater Workshop
Alvear, Enrique, 213
Amnesty International, 22
Amnesty Law, 222
Anderson, Benedict, 242 n. 90
Angelo, Gloria, 250 n. 19
Araucana, Pedro, 254 n. 5
"árbol, El" (Bombal), 132
Arce, Luz, 206–11

Arendt, Hannah, 50
Argentina, 50, 78, 79, 182, 222, 240 n. 44, 243 n. 3, 250 n. 20
Aristotle, 38
Arpilleras: and alternative theater, 90, 93–106, 253 n. 55; and democratic transition, 224–26; and market, 117; as political, 250 n. 16; storytelling with, 85–87
Arriagada, Genaro, 257 n. 22
Art actions, 120, 153, 262 n. 18. *See also* Collective for Art Actions (CADA)
"Artemesia" (Barros), 143–45
Artisan's workshops, 84–86, 91, 95, 249 n. 9, 250 n. 16
Asia, 123
Asociación para la Unidad de las Mujeres (ASUMA). *See* Association for the Unity of Women
Assassinations. *See* Executions
Association for the Unity of Women (ASUMA), 256 n. 17
Association of Family Members of the Detained-Disappeared: and *arpilleras*, 85–89, 250 n. 16; and art actions, 153–54; and *cueca sola*, 10, 51, 253 n. 58; formation of, 51, 243 n. 7; and infrapolitics of power, 79; members of, 49; and political redemption, 211; protests of, 51–53, 213, 237 n. 20; and stories of disappeared, 153; symbolic analysis of, 41, 51; and widowhood, 256 n. 27
Astride (Barros), 45, 117–18; and alienation, 121; and erotic desire, 128–47; and feminism, 122, 128; and maternal love, 143–45; and power systems, 120, 128; and synesthesia, 121, 137, 141, 147; and utopian purity, 131; and violence, 121, 130, 133, 136–43; and working class, 134, 135
ASUMA. *See* Association for the Unity of Women (ASUMA)
Authoritarianism: as "aberration," 70, 120, 200, 246 n. 30; beginnings of, 234; and Chilean "exceptionalism," 27; crisis of, 170–83; cultural authoritarianism, 36, 124, 258 n. 27; and democracy, 9, 47, 124–25, 235; and economic experiments, 83–89; effects of, 30, 120, 196; and family, 29, 122, 124;

and "feminine" concept, 128–29; and language, 149; military authoritarianism, 36, 124, 128, 129, 150, 222; "othering" authoritarianism, 204; and patriarchy, 200; and politics of literature, 153, 157–59; as self-generated, 35–36, 46, 78–79, 81, 99, 120, 149–50; and sexuality, 129, 132, 146, 155; and totalizing narratives, 42, 66, 70, 119, 147; and violence, 198. *See also* Masculine culture; Military
Auto-ediciones. See Self-financed editions
Avanzada. See Neo-avant-garde
Avaria, Antonio, 259 n. 34
"Ave Félix" (Benavente), 85
Aylwin, Patricio, 194–96, 201, 218, 220, 225, 226, 231, 273 n. 47

Balcells, Fernando, 153
Balch, Trudy, 267 n. 23
Barros, Pía, 121, 137, 141, 147, 151; and aesthetic of synesthesia, 151; and Isabel Allende, 196, 200, 215; and Benavente, 56, 117–18, 143, 151, 183; and body metaphor, 117, 151; and Chilean literature, 11, 30; contemporaries of, 32, 118–19, 196, 253 n. 4; in democracy, 232–33; and disenchantment, 33, 119, 144; and Dorfman, 56, 117–18, 143, 183; and Eltit, 56, 150–53, 156, 168, 175, 176, 183–84; and erotic desire, 45, 46, 93, 128–47, 183, 215; and feminism, 120, 128; and language, 129, 131, 142; and literary workshops, 118, 152–53, 233, 254 n. 5; and maternal love, 143–45; and *microcuentos*, 153; and middle class, 122, 145; and "pamphlets," 255 n. 11; and sexuality, 45, 116, 117–18, 121–22; writing style of, 56, 151. *See also specific works of Barros*
Battle of Algiers (Pontecorvo), 50
Beijing. *See* World Conference on Women in Beijing (Fourth)
Bello, Walden, 248 n. 4
Benavente, David: and Isabel Allende, 196; and alternative theater, 87–89, 94–95, 250 n. 20, 251 n. 24; and Barros, 56, 117–18, 143, 151, 183; and body metaphor, 117; and Chilean literature, 11, 30, 151, 152; contemporaries of,

Benavente, David *(continued)*
118, 195; and disenchantment, 119; and Dorfman, 56, 78, 112, 116–17, 151, 183; and Eltit, 56, 151, 183, 260 n. 5; and motherhood, 143; and "tower of silence," 25, 85, 92, 146; and working class, 116–17, 122, 145. *See also specific works of Benavente*
Benedetti, Mario, 245 n. 18
Benengeli, Sidi Hamid, 245 n. 21
Bentham, Jeremy, 35, 240 n. 54
Berenguer, Carmen, 44
Beverley, John, 33
Bianchi, Soledad, 240 n. 48, 259 n. 35
Blake's Therapy (Dorfman), 232
Boal, Augusto, 91
Bodiless spirits, 193–212
Body: and *arpilleras*, 86; bodiless spirits, 193–212; collective bodies, 22, 34, 51, 53–54, 87, 113, 117, 145, 153–56, 168; and colonization, 37, 139–43; and cultural norms, 35; as cultural space, 46, 223; and Dávila scandal, 228–29; and democracy, 223; and "discipline," 72, 140, 259 n. 36; as evil, 39–40; and feminism, 35, 37–39; and hunger, 154–55; and labor, 96–97; and literary narrative, 184, 187–88; and marginalization, 148–92; market value of, 159; and power, 128–47, 148; reclamation of dead bodies, 21–22, 34, 67, 67–68; and religious metaphor, 39–40; scarring of, 161; and self-definition, 173–75; and self-directed violence, 155–56, 160–61, 167–69, 262 n. 25; sexualized body, 168–69, 261–62 n. 15; as site of historical struggle, 22, 23, 50–51; social control and, 34–36, 153, 223, 261–62 n. 15; "stigmatized body," 261–62 n. 15; traumatized social body, 149; and value of life, 51; virginity, 106; women's bodies, 96–99, 106–7, 110, 113, 128–29, 146, 150–51, 158–69, 206. *See also* Disappeared bodies
Body metaphor: and *Astride*, 128–47; for Chilean society, 34, 41, 44, 259 n. 35; and disappearance, 44–45, 53–54; and *E. Luminata*, 157–69; Junta's Declaration of Principles, 39–40; and literary narrative, 161–69; and military authoritarianism, 36, 150; and military patriarchy, 40; and national body, 44–45; and neoliberalism, 45, 83; and Pinochet regime, 34–40, 45; and politics, 34–40; and torture, 34–35; and value of life, 51. *See also* Disappeared bodies
Bolívar, Simón, 228–29
Bombal, María Luisa, 132
Bordo, Susan, 35, 37–39, 42
Boyle, Catherine, 200, 251–52 n. 27
Bravo, Rosa, 255–56 n. 15
Brazil, 243 n. 3
Breast-feeding, 143–45
Brecht, Bertolt, 252 n. 36
Brito, Eugenia, 44, 148, 155–56, 259 n. 35, 260 n. 7, 263 n. 39
Brunet, Marta, 143, 260 n. 5
Brunner, José Joaquín, 237 n. 23
Butler, Judith, 39

Cabezas, Omar, 78
"Cabildo, El." *See* Town Hall (theater collective)
CADA. *See* Collective for Art Actions (CADA)
Campero, Guillermo, 250 n. 19
Campos, René, 269 n. 43
Campos minados (Brito), 44, 263 nn. 38 and 39
Cánovas, Rodrigo, 251 n. 26
Capitalism, 30, 40, 189, 191, 194, 195, 196. *See also* Consumer culture; Democracy; Neoliberalism
Carpentier, Alejo, 267 n. 27
Casa de campo. *See House in the Country* (Donoso)
casa de los espíritus, La. *See House of the Spirits* (Allende)
Casimiro Peñafleta, prisionero político (Castro), 251 n. 25
Castedo, Elena, 266 n. 13
Castillo, Juan, 153
Castillo Soto, Juan, 228
Castro, Oscar, 251 n. 25
Catholic Church, 63, 107, 213, 243 n. 7. *See also* Christianity
Catholic University of Santiago, 91
Caupolicán Theater, 126, 256 n. 17, 257 n. 19
CEM. *See* Center for Women's Studies

CEMAs-Chile. *See* Mothers' Centers
CENECA. *See* Center for Research on Cultural and Artistic Expressions (CENECA)
Censorship, 31, 85, 89, 121, 127, 153, 254n. 5, 258n. 33
Center for Research on Cultural and Artistic Expressions (CENECA), 90–91, 95, 247n. 2
Center for Women's Studies (CEM), 256 n. 17
Central Nacional de Informaciones (CNI). *See* National Information Office (CNI)
Centro de Estudios de la Mujer (CEM). *See* Center for Women's Studies
Centro de Indagación y Expresión Cultural (CENECA). *See* Center for Research on Cultural and Artistic Expressions (CENECA)
Centros de Madre (CEMAs-Chile). *See* Mothers' Centers
Cervantes, Miguel de, 58, 193, 245n. 21
Chavkin, Samuel, 238n. 25
"Chicago Boys," 83–84, 242n. 2, 248n. 8, 271n. 3. *See also* Neoliberalism
Childbirth metaphor, 70–81, 178–79
Chile: Obstinate Memory (Guzmán), 231
Chilean "exceptionalism," 27, 237n. 19
Chilean Human Rights Commission, 256 n. 17
Chilean Independence Day, 253n. 56
Chilean narrative. *See* Narrative
Chilean theater. *See* Alternative theater; Investigative Theater Workshop (TIT); *and specific theater collectives*
Chilean Writers' Society (SECh), 259n. 34
Christian Democratic Party, 25–26, 199, 265n. 8
Christianity, 207–9. *See also* Catholic Church
Christianized Arabs, 245n. 21
Chuchryk, Patricia, 124, 240n. 48, 256 n. 17, 257n. 17
CIA, 25–26, 222, 236–37n. 11
Cicero, 38
Circle on Women's Studies, 256n. 17
Cixous, Hélène, 131
Class. *See* Socioeconomic class
CNI. *See* National Information Office (CNI)
CNS. *See* Women's Department of the Coordinadora Nacional Sindical (CNS)
Coddou, Marcelo, 266n. 12
CODEM. *See* Committee in Defense of Women's Rights (CODEM)
Colectivo de acciones de arte (CADA). *See* Collective for Art Actions (CADA)
Colectivo de Escritores Jóvenes. *See* Young Writers' Collective
Collective for Art Actions (CADA), 46, 153–58, 168, 169, 254n. 5, 261n. 10, 262nn. 18 and 26
Collins, Joseph, 248n. 4
Collyer, Patricia, 52
Comisíon Chilena de Derechos Humanos. *See* Chilean Human Rights Commission
Comité de Defensa de los Derechos de la Mujer (CODEM). *See* Committee in Defense of Women's Rights (CODEM)
Comité Pro Paz in Chile. *See* Committee for Peace in Chile
"Commiseration" (Barros), 131, 145
Committee for Peace in Chile, 84–85, 243n. 7
Committee for Truth and Reconciliation, 22, 201, 206–9. *See also* Rettig Commission
Committee in Defense of Women's Rights (CODEM), 256n. 17
Communist Party, 22. *See also* Leftists; Socialism
Community-based values, 71–80
Company of Four (theater collective), 251n. 26
Compartiendo la Mesa. *See* Sharing the Table
Comprando juntos. *See* Cooperative shopping
Concentration camps, 85, 247n. 2, 251n. 25
Concertación coalition, 11, 195, 196, 218, 220, 221, 223, 225–26, 231, 265–66 n. 8
Confederación de Trabajadores del Cobre. *See* Copper Workers Federation
Congress on Latin American Literature by Women, 127, 259n. 35
Constitution of 1980, 125, 192, 220, 221, 257n. 23

Consumer culture, 9, 45, 185, 196, 227. *See also* Capitalism; Democracy; Neoliberalism
Consuming Fiction (Lovell), 47
Contreras, Manuel, 201
Cooperative shopping, 84
Copper Workers Federation, 257 n. 25
Correa, Raquel, 52
Cortázar, Julio, 32, 118, 259 n. 40
Cortés, Hernán, 140–42
Coup d'état of 11 September 1973: and crisis of language and history, 27, 195; holiday celebration of, 222; long-term effects of, 9; and military junta, 28; traumatic impact of, 24–25; and unhappy endings, 197. *See also* Military; Pinochet regime
Covert Action in Chile, 1963–1973, 25, 237 n. 13
cuarto mundo, El. See *Fourth World* (Eltit)
Cuba, 32, 118, 153
Cueca sola. See Association of Family Members of the Detained-Disappeared
Cultural anthropology, 24, 35
Cultural resistance, 11
Cultural studies, 23

Daly, Mary, 269–70 n. 46
Dar la vida por la vida (Vidal), 41
Daughter of Fortune (Allende), 233–34
Dávila, Juan, 228–29
De amor y de sombra. See *Of Love and Shadows* (Allende)
Death and the Maiden (Dorfman), 206, 231–32
Decade for Women, 122, 255 n. 15
De la Maza, Gonzalo, 126, 257 n. 22, 258 n. 29
Délano, Manuel, 248 n. 8
Délano, Poli, 32, 254 n. 5, 258 n. 34, 259 n. 34
Del Río, Ana María, 32, 118, 254 n. 5
Democracy: and authoritarianism, 9, 47, 124–25, 235; and bodiless spirits, 193–219; Chilean attitudes toward, 271–72 n. 5; and Chilean "exceptionalism," 27, 237 n. 19; and Chilean literature, 23, 34; and covert violence, 195; and cultural production, 220; democratic transition, 9–11, 23, 34, 114, 192, 194–95, 201, 220–34, 267 n. 26; and exclusion, 145, 224–26; and fatigue, 196, 227; and gay rights, 220; and gender scripts, 228–30, 234; and happy endings, 196; and home life, 147; and indigenous groups, 231; and individualism, 196; and liberalism, 194–96; and MEMCh'83, 124; and Morandé 80, 23; obstacles to, 192; and resistance movements, 194; and social expression, 201; and students, 231; types of democracy, 267 n. 26; and violence, 223; and women's movement, 226–30; and working–class women, 225. See also *Arpilleras;* Historical memory; Neoliberalism; Reconciliation
Democratic Alliance, 257 n. 25
Derridian thought, 35
"Desfiladero de iguanas." *See* "Procession of Iguanas" (Barros)
"Deshabitados and la ventana." *See* "Desolate Before the Window" (Barros)
"Desolate Before the Window" (Barros), 146
Díaz, Erwin, 254 n. 5
Díaz Eterovic, Ramón, 32, 118, 254 n. 5
"Dictionaries" (Barros), 131
Diez, Sergio, 243 n. 3
DINA. *See* National Intelligence Directorate (DINA)
Dirección Nacional de Inteligencia (DINA). *See* National Intelligence Directorate (DINA)
Disappeared bodies: and activist movements, 243 n. 3; and community connection, 76; denial of existence of, 30, 242–43 n. 3, 270 n. 49; disappearance as ongoing crime, 222–23; and displacement, 55–60; and employment, 97–98; and feminization, 54; frequency of, 49–50; and gender, 50, 72, 243 n. 4; and Lonquén mine, 212–13; and masculine culture, 72–80; and National Intelligence Directorate, 242 n. 2; and Pinochet regime, 9, 45, 49; and reclamation of dead bodies, 21–22, 34, 67, 67–68; statistics on, 238 n. 25, 242 n. 2, 243 nn. 4 and 5; stories of, 22; and struggles for narrative power, 50, 54–55; and

working-class women, 97–98, 103. *See also* Body; Body metaphor
Discipline and Punish (Foucault), 35–36, 140, 259n. 34
Disenchantment, 33, 119, 150
Displacement, 55–60, 118–19
Dittborn, Eugenio, 44, 153
Doctrine for National Security, 41
Domestic violence, 98–99, 105. *See also* Violence
Domination and the Arts of Resistance (Scott), 79
Donoso, Claudia, 258n. 34
Donoso, José, 31, 42, 239n. 36, 254n. 5, 260n. 5
Don Quijote (Cervantes), 193, 245n. 21
Dorfman, Ariel: and Isabel Allende, 196, 206; and Barros, 56, 117–18, 143, 183; and Benavente, 56, 78, 112, 116–17, 151, 183; and body metaphor, 44–45, 117; and Chilean literature, 11, 30, 151, 152; contemporaries of, 32, 118, 196; and democracy, 231–32; and disappeared bodies, 116; and disenchantment, 119; and displacement, 55–60, 119; early postcoup writings of, 245n. 21; and Eltit, 56, 151–52, 171, 172, 176, 179, 183, 186–87; and exile, 56–57, 82, 90, 245n. 19; feminization of, 57; and hope, 179; and military authoritarianism, 120, 124; and motherhood, 143, 144, 171; poetry of, 49; and social privilege, 69, 77–78, 112; on tyrants, 222; and working class, 122, 145. *See also* Disappeared bodies; *and specific works of Dorfman*
Douglas, Mary, 35
Droguett, Carlos, 260n. 5
"Duerme." *See* "Go to Sleep" (Barros)

Echeverría, Eugenia, 259n. 34
Economic crisis of 1981–82, 125
"Economic miracle," 257n. 23
Economic violence, 45, 242n. 2
Edwards, Jorge, 31
Ehrmann, Hans, 251n. 23
"Elizabeth" *(arpillerista)*, 86, 224–25, 227. See also *Arpilleras*
El Salvador, 50
Eltit, Diamela: and Isabel Allende, 104, 196; on Arce, 207, 268n. 38; and Barros, 56, 150–53, 168, 175, 176, 183–84; and Benavente, 56, 151, 183, 260n. 5; and body metaphor, 44, 46, 148, 153; career initiation of, 32, 118, 150; and Chilean literature, 11, 30, 153; contemporaries of, 32, 196; critical attention to works of, 184, 260–61n. 7, 261n. 8, 264nn. 48 and 50; as cultural attaché in Mexico, 233; and Dávila scandal, 229; in democracy, 233; and Dorfman, 56, 151–52, 171, 172, 176, 179, 183, 186–87; on being emblematic, 265n. 54; father's death, 263–64n. 42; and Guggenheim Award, 152, 261n. 8; on her own work, 157–58; and hope, 183; and internalized authoritarianism, 46, 149; intervention style of, 56; and language, 121, 151–52, 168, 260n. 5, 263n. 40; and literary establishment, 152; and literary workshops, 152–53, 254n. 5; and "Maipu," 155, 166; and "marginal zones," 150; and narrative fragmentation, 148–50, 157, 169, 185; and neoliberalism, 159–60, 184–92; as postmodernist, 43; and repression, 165; and social privilege, 155–56; on social transformation, 234. *See also* Collective for Art Actions (CADA); *and specific works of Eltit*
E. Luminata (Eltit): aesthetic of *frote* in, 151, 158, 162–69, 175, 260n. 6; and exclusion, 151–52, 158–59, 162; language usage in, 148–49, 157–69; and "Maipu," 155, 158, 166, 167; and neoliberalism, 159–60; and self-directed violence, 155, 158, 160–61, 167–69; and traumatized social body, 149
Employment. *See* Labor
Encuentro Feminista Latinoamericano y del Caribe. *See* Latin American and Caribbean Feminist Meetings
Encuentro Nacional de Arte. *See* National Encounter for the Arts
Erotic desire, 45, 46, 116–47, 183, 183–84, 215
Errázuriz, Paz, 183
"Esperanza" (Dorfman), 49
Estado de Derecho, El (Ibáñez), 34
European Enlightenment, 194

298 INDEX

Eva Luna (Allende), 193, 196, 197, 211, 219, 267n. 18
Exclusion, 70, 125, 145, 158–59, 162, 184, 224–26
Executions, 28, 50, 242n. 2, 263–64n. 42
Exile: and alternative theater, 251n. 25; of authors, 82, 90, 245n. 19; and feminization, 57; and Pinochet regime, 9; reasons for, 244–45n. 17; resentment of exiles, 231; return from, 256n. 17, 258n. 29; and women, 256n. 17

fábula, La, 195–97, 233
Facultad Latinoamericano de Ciencias Sociales. *See* FLACSO
Family, 28, 29, 65, 73, 122, 124, 129, 228. *See also* Authoritarianism; Military; Motherhood; Patriarchy
Fanon, Frantz, 194
Fariña, Soledad, 152
Fatherland, 41, 47, 54, 61, 71, 169–84, 210, 256n. 15, 264n. 42
Fatherland and Liberty (paramilitary group), 26
Fatigue, 196, 227
Female Power (organization), 28
Feminine values, 28, 60–70
Feminism: and authoritarianism, 124, 128; and bodies, 35, 37–39; and democracy, 226–30; and female spiritual superiority, 211, 269–70n. 46; and "femocrats," 228; and international context, 122–23; and leftist political parties, 125–26, 257n. 26; "magical feminism," 266n. 17; and male authors, 32; and military authoritarianism, 128; and narrative power, 24; and National Protests and Strikes of 1983–84, 122, 125–27, 239n. 31; reemergence in Chile, 29–30, 118, 120, 122–23, 198, 256nn. 16 and 17; and resistance cultures, 33; and slogans, 29, 124, 239n. 31; and socioeconomic class, 122, 123; State's institutionalization of, 227; and women writers, 127, 259n. 35
Feminization: of Salvador Allende, 28, 31, 140; of Chilean theater, 251–52n. 27; definition of, 32; and disappeared bodies, 54; of Dorfman, 57; of language, 171–72; reaction to, 98–99; and *Widows* (Dorfman), 54–70

"Femocrats," 228
Feria, La (theater collective), 90
Fire from the Mountain (Cabezas), 78
First Congress on Latin American Literature by Women, 127, 152, 259 n. 35
FLACSO, 238nn. 28 and 30, 239n. 32
"Foreshadowing of a Trace" (Barros), 129–34, 168, 175–76
Forgiveness, 207–9
Foucault, Michel, 35–36, 37–39, 119, 140, 259n. 36, 263n. 34
Fourth World (Eltit): and civil society, 148; and crisis of authority, 186–91; and families, 46; and incest metaphor, 186–92; and internalized authoritarianism, 149–50, 185, 191; and language, 151, 185; and marginality, 186–91; and motherhood, 185; and neoliberalism, 185–92; and reconciliation, 185
Foxley, Ana María, 258n. 34
France, 265n. 3
Franco, Jean, 10, 235n. 2
Franz, Carlos, 118
Frei, Eduardo, 26, 194–96, 220, 225, 231, 271n. 3, 273n. 47
"Frei Boys," 271n. 3
Freire, Paolo, 252n. 32
Friedman, Milton, 83
Frote aesthetic, 151, 158, 162–69, 175, 260n. 6

Garcés, Mario, 126, 257n. 22, 258n. 29
García Márquez, Gabriel, 118, 193, 205, 270n. 50
García Pinto, Magdalena, 267n. 23, 270 n. 48
Garden Next Door (Donoso), 31, 239n. 36
Garretón, Manuel Antonio, 26, 30, 89–90, 201, 236n. 10, 237n. 17, 248n. 3, 271n. 1
Garzón, Baltasar, 221
Gaviola, Edda, 257n. 18
Geertz, Clifford, 11
Gender: and bonding, 106–10; and democratic transition, 228–30, 234; and disappeared bodies, 50, 72, 243 n. 4; gender balance in publishing, 258–59n. 34; gender boundaries, 60–70; gender identity, 246n. 26; gender

scripts, 28–30, 45, 46, 65, 134–40, 207, 228, 234; and historical context, 23–34, 41, 70; and male writers, 240 n. 44; and national narrative, 27, 60–70; and National Protests, 125; and politics, 23–34, 54, 129; and sexual humiliation, 52; and sexualized slogans, 27; and social class, 38–39; and traditional roles, 27–28; veto on use of concept of, 229–30; and violence, 98–99, 105, 120, 125, 130–31, 136–43, 206–9. *See also* Sexuality
Germany, 265n. 3
Gilman, Charlotte Perkins, 260n. 43
Glickman, Nora, 268–69n. 42
González, Mónica, 52, 244n. 16
"Go to Sleep" (Barros), 145
Greece, 56
Griffero, Ramón, 195, 232
Grossberg, Lawrence, 23
Guatemala, 50
Guerra, Lucía, 259n. 35
Guggenheim Award, 152, 261n. 8
Gutiérrez, Paulina, 253n. 53
Guzmán, Patricio, 231
Guzmán Bravo, Rosario, 258n. 34
Guzmán Tapia, Juan, 222–23

Harlow, Barbara, 235n. 2
Hart, Patricia, 266n. 17, 268nn. 32 and 33, 269n. 44
Heading South, Looking North (Dorfman), 232
"He Had Hated It with Pulchritude" (Barros), 146, 260n. 43
Helper, Norma, 269n. 44
herencia de los Chicago Boys, La (Délano and Traslaviña), 83–84
Hernández, Acevedo, 260n. 5
Hija de la fortuna. *See Daughter of Fortune* (Allende)
Hiriart de Pinochet, Lucía 45–46, 238 n. 29, 256n. 15
Historical memory, 9, 59, 100, 149–50, 158, 161, 166, 180, 223; and forgetting, 11, 22, 47, 140–41, 195, 197, 200, 203–5, 214–18, 220, 225
History of Sexuality (Foucault), 35–36
Hitler, Adolph, 21, 61
Hobbes, Thomas, 38
Hojas de Parra (Valdell and Salcedo), 89

Homosexuality, 60, 63, 65, 176, 230–31
Homosexual Liberation Movement (MOVILH), 230
hooks, bell, 271n. 56
Hope, 179, 183, 195–96, 218
"Hope" (Dorfman), 49
House in the Country (Donoso), 31, 42
House of Mist (Bombal), 132
House of the Spirits (Allende): allegorical structure of, 198–99, 204–5; circular structure of, 205, 209; class conflict in, 198–205; conflict resolution in, 215; and *Death and the Maiden* (Dorfman), 206, 209; and female spiritual superiority, 211; as *la fábula*, 197; and *El infierno* (Arce), 206–10; and *One Hundred Years of Solitude* (García Márquez), 205; and passivity, 268 n. 41, 269n. 44; and political reconciliation, 198–212; popularity of, 193–94; and romantic conventions, 199, 202
Human rights: human rights abuses, 213, 220, 222; material human rights, 47; spiritual human rights, 47; and working-class women, 10, 29; Year of Human Rights in Chile, 270n. 49. *See also* Disappeared bodies; Torture; Violence
Humiliation, 52
Humor, 100, 101, 110
Hunger, 84, 96, 96–105, 154–55
Hunger strikes, 213
Hurtado, María de la Luz, 90, 247–48 n. 2

Ibánez, G., 34
ICTUS (theater collective), 87, 90, 251 n. 26
I Dreamt the Snow Was Burning (Skármeta), 32
Imagen (theater collective), 90
"Imagined communities," 47, 242n. 90
IMF. *See* International Monetary Fund (IMF)
Imprisonment: and handicrafts, 84–85; of literary writers, 32; and National Intelligence Directorate (CNI), 242 n. 2; and women, 53
Incest metaphor, 151, 169–84, 186–92
"Incile," 54, 120, 245n. 18

Individualism, 9, 99, 102, 194, 196. *See also* Consumer culture; Democracy; Neoliberalism
infarto del alma, El (Errázuriz and Eltit), 183
infierno, El (Arce), 206–9, 211
Inflation, 250 n. 21
"Initiations" (Barros), 131, 144
International Congress on Latin American Literature by Women, 152
International Monetary Fund (IMF), 9, 248 n. 4
International Telephone and Telegraph, Inc. (ITT), 25, 236–37 n. 11
"Interpretative power," 235 n. 2
Investigative Theater Workshop (TIT): and Barros, 93; and Benavente, 94–95; and CENECA, 95; and Chilean literature, 11, 30; creation of, 91; in democracy, 234; and emotion, 92; and *gestus* of stories, 252 n. 36; and human body, 45; and *memorias*, 91–92; move to Santiago's center, 93–94, 117; and neoliberal capitalism, 103; and participatory observation, 91–92; philosophical contradictions in, 94–96; repression of, 89; split of, 93; and *teatro de servicio*, 91, 93; and *Tres Marías y una Rosa*, 45, 82, 87, 88, 96–115
ITT. *See* International Telephone and Telegraph, Inc. (ITT)
IVA tax, 89, 121, 251 n. 23

Jacquette, Jane, 240 n. 48
Jameson, Fredric, 24
Japan, 265 n. 3
Jara, Joan, 238 n. 25
Jara, Víctor, 28
jardín de al lado, El. See Garden Next Door (Donoso)
Jeréz, Fernando, 32, 259 n. 34
Jiménez, Luz, 92
Jocelyn-Holt Letelier, Alfredo, 27, 237 n. 19
Journalists, 52–53, 213, 244 n. 15, 250 n. 19, 253 n. 53, 270 n. 49
Junta's Declaration of Principles, 39–40

Kadir, Djelal, 171
Kidnapping, 222–23

Kirkwood, Julieta: on authoritarianism, 36, 116, 124, 219, 234; death of, 239 n. 32; and democracy, 47, 195, 267 n. 26; and political parties, 226, 257 n. 26; research studies of, 30; and women's political organizations, 226
Konfidenz (Dorfman), 232
Kwok Pui-Lan, 37

Labor: government-sponsored projects, 250 n. 21; importance of work, 96–97; labor unions, 125; and oppositional leadership, 257 n. 25; and unemployment, 84, 87, 238 n. 28, 248 n. 8, 250 n. 21, 257 n. 23; women in labor force, 255–56 n. 15
Laclau, Ernesto, 32, 70
Lafourcade, Enrique, 31, 153, 254 n. 5
Lagos, Ricardo, 195, 225–26, 231
Land reform, 25
Language: of *arpilleristas*, 87–89; and exclusion, 129, 131; feminized language, 171–72; hybrid language, 151; as literary device, 148–49, 151–52, 168, 169, 172, 260 n. 5; and masculine culture, 172; and military authoritarianism, 149; and resistance, 169; slang, 158, 171, 180, 182; and social experiences, 70; and socioeconomic class, 180; suppression of, 85; and synesthesia, 121, 137, 141, 147, 151; traditional language, 168; and violence, 129–31; visual language, 86–87
Last Song of Manuel Sendero (Dorfman), 179, 186, 247 n. 32
Latin America: and Dávila scandal, 229; and gender scripts, 139–40; neoliberal model for, 248 n. 4; North American conceptions of, 212; postmodernism in, 24, 34, 236 n. 7; and sense of history, 236 n. 7; and "structural adjustment" packages, 9; and women's movements, 78
Latin American and Caribbean Feminist Meetings, 226, 228
Lavín, Joaquín, 225–26
Lear, John, 248 n. 4
Leftists, 9, 28, 29, 42–43, 125–26, 243 n. 3, 256 n. 17, 257 n. 26. *See also* Communist Party; Marxism; Socialism

Lemebel, Pedro, 230
Leppe, Carlos, 44, 153, 261–62n. 15, 262n. 25
Lértora, Juan Carlos, 130
Levine, Linda Gould, 268n. 31, 271n. 54
Liberalism, 30, 111, 194, 195. *See also* Neoliberalism
"Lightning fast" protests, 120, 255n. 12
Lira, Winnie, 249n. 11
Literary workshops, 118, 127, 152–53, 233, 253–54n. 5
Loach, Barbara Lee, 263n. 40
"Lo había odiado con pulcritud." *See* "He Had Hated It with Pulchritude" (Barros)
Lohmann, Eric, 58–59
Lohmann, Sirgud, 55, 58–59, 70
Lonquén mine, 197, 212–13, 270n. 49
Lorde, Audre, 269–70n. 46
Lovell, Terry, 47
Loveman, Brian, 235n. 2
Lumpérica. See *E. Luminata* (Eltit)

Machiavelli, Niccolò, 38
Madres de la Plaza de Mayo, 79
Magic, 198, 199, 212–19, 266n. 17
"Magical feminism," 266n. 17
"Magical realism," 201, 266n. 17, 267n. 27
"Maipu" (CADA), 155, 158, 166, 167–69
Malbrán, Ernesto, 259n. 34
Maldita yo entre las mujeres (Valdivieso), 31
Malinche, 140–43
Mandel, Ernest, 255n. 4
Manifestaciones-relámpago. *See* "Lightning fast" protests
"Manifesto" (Parra), 263n. 37
Maqueira, Diego, 78, 152
Martínez, Juan Luis, 44, 152
Martyrdom, 155–56
Marxism, 38, 40, 42, 50. *See also* Communist Party; Leftists; Socialism
Masculine culture: in alternative theater, 94–96; community–based values and, 71–80; crisis in, 170–83; and disappeared bodies, 72–80; and domestic control, 98–99; and historical model, 175; and language, 172; male alliances, 71–72; revision of, 111; and sexualization of women's bodies, 168–69; traditional forms of masculinity, 198
Material human rights, 47
McCallister, Richard, 269n. 42
Medioli, Ana María, 249n. 9
Mellado, Carlos, 254n. 5
MEMCh'83, 123–24, 125, 147, 257n. 18
Memorias, 91–92, 172, 180
Memory. *See* Historical memory
Mercurio, El, 25
Meza, M. Angélica, 250n. 19
Microcuentos, 153
Middle class, 29, 256n. 17, 257n. 23
Miedos transitorios (De a uno, de a dos, de a todos) (Barros), 120, 255n. 13
Migdal, Alicia, 245n. 18
Military: and Salvador Allende's death, 21; and childbirth metaphor, 70–81; and family, 28, 29, 65, 72; and gender scripts, 45; and homophobia, 60, 63, 65; and "ladies," 52–53; and language, 149; and masculinity, 71–72, 198; military authoritarianism, 124, 129; military patriarch, 40; and misogyny, 60, 65, 74, 78, 124–25; and unemployment, 238n. 28; and universities, 251n. 26; and violence, 28, 60; and women writers, 52–53, 149, 244n. 15; working class as enemy of, 84. *See also* Authoritarianism; Coup d'état of 11 September 1973; Pinochet regime
"Military exercises," 201
Ministry of Education, 228, 251n. 23
Ministry of Foreign Relations, 228
Misogyny, 60, 65, 74, 78, 124–25
Modernization law, 201
Molina, Natacha, 257n. 17
MOMUPO. *See* Shantytown Women's Movement (MOMUPO)
moñtana es algo más que una inmensa estepa verde, La. *See* *Fire from the Mountain* (Cabezas)
Montecino, Sonia, 118, 143, 237n. 20
Mora, Gabriela, 268n. 41
Morandé 80, 21, 23
"Mordaza." *See* "Muzzle" (Barros)
Moriscos, 245n. 21
Motherhood: and *Astride* (Barros), 143–45; childbirth metaphor, 70–81; and erotic desire, 144; and incest, 169–92; and masculinist discourse, 79;

Motherhood *(continued)*
    maternal solidarity, 143; militarized mothers, 176–77; and military authoritarianism, 65, 237n. 20, 237–38n. 23; and moral superiority, 51, 65, 237n. 20; and Pinochet regime, 51, 65, 176–77, 237n. 20, 237–38n. 23; and violence, 143–45. *See also* Women
Mothers' Centers (CEMAS-Chile), 28, 45–46, 238nn. 26 and 29, 265n. 15
Moulian, Tomás, 10, 220, 237n. 19, 257n. 22
Movement for the Emancipation of Chilean Women. *See* MEMCh'83
Movimiento de Liberación Homosexual (MOVILH). *See* Homosexual Liberation Movement (MOVILH)
Movimiento de Mujeres Pobladoras. *See* Shantytown Women's Movement (MOMUPO)
Movimiento Pro Emancipación de las Mujeres de Chile. *See* MEMCh'83
MUDECHI. *See* Women of Chile (MUDECHI)
muerte y la doncella, La. See *Death and the Maiden* (Dorfman)
Mujeres de Chile (MUDECHI). *See* Women of Chile (MUDECHI)
Mujeres por la vida. *See* Women for Life
Munizaga, Giselle, 238n. 26
Muñoz, Diego, 32, 254
Muñoz, Josefina, 255
Murder. *See* Executions
Museo Abierto. *See* Open Museum
Museum of Fine Arts, 154
Muslims, 50
"Muzzle" (Barros), 139–43, 151

Narrative: and community-based values, 71–80; and cultural anthropology, 24; of death, 61; disappearance narratives, 55–60; and feminism, 24; and gender, 27, 60–70; national narrative, 10–11, 23, 28, 41, 54, 71, 87, 110, 206, 223; and poststructuralism, 24; "resistance narratives," 235n. 2; and social change, 71–80; struggles for narrative power, 10, 22–23, 27, 53–54, 70–71, 129–30, 163–69. *See also specific narratives*
National Congress, 51
National Encounter for the Arts, 22, 195
National Information Office (CNI), 52, 242n. 2
National Institute for Statistics, 248n. 8
National Intelligence Directorate (DINA), 52, 206–9, 222, 242–43nn. 2 and 3
National narrative. *See* Narrative
National Protests and Strikes of 1983–84: assessment of, 125–27, 257n. 23; combating authoritarianism, 170–71; and Eltit, 149, 170; and feminism, 10, 122, 125–27, 239n. 31; and gender, 125, 149, 183; and repression, 258n. 29; and slogans, 124, 257n. 19; and state of siege, 126; and women writers, 45, 127, 149, 183, 258–59n. 34, 259n. 35; and working-class women, 249n. 14
National Secretariat for Women, 28, 45–46, 238n. 26, 256n. 15
National Service for Women (SERNAM), 227, 229
National Stadium, 22, 28
Navarro, Marysa, 228
Nazis, 58, 60
negra Ester, La (Parra), 31
Nelson, Cary, 23
Neo-avant-garde, 41–43, 153, 156–57, 261n. 10, 262n. 27
Neoliberalism: and authoritarianism, 83–84; and capitalism, 189, 191; and Chilean history, 195; and entertainment, 232; and European Enlightenment, 194; and individualism, 196, 228; and "modernization," 220; neoliberal economic model, 9, 82–84, 194; and political reconciliation, 185; and representational power, 95; and violence, 203; and working-class women, 102–3. *See also* "Chicago Boys"; Consumer culture; Democracy; "Economic miracle"; Individualism
Neruda, Pablo, 263n. 37
New Chilean narrative, 10–11, 235n. 5
New social movements, 10, 184, 220, 235n. 3. *See also* Feminism
NGOs, 228, 256n. 17
Nicaragua, 78
Nixon administration, 25–26
novísimos, Los, 31–32
Nueva narrativa chilena. *See* New Chilean narrative

INDEX   303

Ochensius, Carlos, 90, 238n. 26, 247–48 n. 2
Of Love and Shadows (Allende): conflict resolution in, 215; and individual heroism, 212–19; and *la fábula*, 197; and neoliberal capitalist democracy, 218–19; and *One Hundred Years of Solitude* (García Márquez), 270n. 50; and romance convention, 216–17; and social classes, 213–14, 218–19
Ogundipe-Leslie, Molara, 37
Olea, Raquel, 259n. 35, 264n. 51
Olivárez, Carlos, 259n. 34
Ollas communes. See Soup kitchens
"Olor a madera y a silencio." *See* "Scents of Wood and Silence" (Barros)
One Hundred Years of Solitude (García Márquez), 193, 205
Open Museum, 22
Open Triangle, 230
Oprah Winfrey Book Club, 234
Opus Dei, 225
Origins of Totalitarianism (Arendt), 50
Oropesa, Salvador Antonio, 246n. 26
Ortega, Eliana, 259n. 35
Ortega, Graciela, 249n. 9
Ortega, Julio, 186
Osandún, Mirta, 249n. 9
Osorio, Raúl, 91, 93, 95
Oviedo, José, 33
Oyarzún, Kemy, 229–30

padre mío, El (Eltit), 150
Panama, 26
Panjabi, Kavita, 269n. 44
Panopticon, 35, 240n. 54
Panza, Sancho, 214
Parra, Nicanor, 263n. 37
Parra, Roberto, 31, 252n. 27
Paso de dos (Pavlovsky), 78
Patriarchy, 30, 40, 168, 195, 200, 228, 259n. 42. *See also* Authoritarianism; Fatherland; Masculine culture; Military
Patria y Libertad. *See* Fatherland and Liberty
Paula (Allende), 233
Pavlovsky, Eduardo, 78
payasos de la esperanza, Los (Investigative Theater Workshop), 93
Paz, Octavio, 140

Pedro, Juan y Diego (ICTUS/Benavente), 87–88, 96–97
Petrarch, 216
Pinochet, Augusto: arrest of, 10, 201, 221, 233; and CIA, 222; Constitution of 1980, 125, 220, 221, 257n. 23; demise of, 122–27, 194, 201, 219, 258n. 29; extradition of, 195, 220–21; health of, 221–24; and human rights abuses, 222; and immunity from prosecution, 221; and "kid glove" reconciliation, 217–18; "military exercises" of, 201; on neoliberal Chile, 45; trial of, 221–24, 226
Pinochet regime: and authoritarianism, 9, 27, 78–79, 81; and body metaphor, 34–40, 45; and "Chicago Boys," 83–84; and CIA, 25–26, 222, 236–37 n. 11; cultural forms of resistance to, 11; and cultural production, 220; daily life under, 150–51; and democratic transition, 114, 192, 194, 267n. 26; and disenchantment, 119; economic plan of, 83–84; and elimination of political left, 9; exposé of violence under, 22; and family model, 28, 29, 228; and feminine values, 28, 60–70, 128–47; and gender politics, 125–26, 258n. 27; and human rights abuses, 213, 242n. 2; and hunger, 154–55; and imprisonment of literary writers, 32; long-term effects on Chile, 9; and motherhood, 51, 65, 176–77, 237 n. 20, 237–38n. 23; and neo-avant-garde, 41–42; and neoliberalism, 45; and "new" social movements, 184; and political reconciliation, 217–18; and public/private spheres, 29; and "sanitized" official stories, 229; and social representation, 47, 53–54, 129; and theater repression, 82, 89, 251 n. 26; and upper-class women, 27–28, 237n. 20; and violence, 9, 26, 28, 32, 36; and women as "servants to Fatherland," 256n. 15; women in cabinet of, 226. *See also* Authoritarianism; Coup d'état of 11 September 1973; Disappeared bodies; Military; Neoliberalism; Violence
Pisano, Margarita, 256n. 16
Plato, 38

Poblete, Olga, 257 n. 18
Poder Femenino. *See* Female Power (organization)
Poland, 250 n. 20
Polanski, Roman, 232
Politzer, Patricia, 52
Popular Unity coalition: and Salvador Allende, 21, 25, 78, 118, 245 n. 19; assessment of, 25–27; and constitutional legality, 237 n. 17; defeat of, 32–33, 78; and hunger, 154; influence of, 32; and literary writers, 11, 31–32, 118–19, 151; and militants, 207; opposition to, 26, 27, 237 n. 20; and optimism, 245 n. 19; and younger generation, 119. *See also* Pinochet regime
Por la Patria (Eltit): childbirth metaphor in, 178–79; and crisis in authoritarianism, 170–83; and hope, 179, 183; and incest metaphor, 169–84; language usage in, 148–49, 151–52, 157, 172, 180, 182, 183; and National Protests and Strikes of 1983–84, 170, 171, 183; and resistance to authoritarianism, 170–71; and self-directed violence, 175–76
Portales, Diego, 27
Postcoup Chile, and narrative power, 24
Postmodernism in Latin America, 24, 34, 236 n. 7
Poststructuralism, 24, 35, 39
Poverty, 82–84, 194, 248 n. 6, 249 n. 9, 257 n. 23, 265 n. 5
Precht, Cristián, 213
"Prefiguracíon de una huella." *See* "Foreshadowing of a Trace" (Barros)
Primer Congreso de Literatura Femenina Latinoamericana. *See* First Congress on Latin American Literature by Women
"Procession of Iguanas" (Barros), 146
Programa de Empleo Mínimo (PEM). *See* Program for Minimum Employment (PEM)
Programa de Estudios y Capacitación de la Mujer Campesina e Indígena (PEMCHI). *See* Program for Research and Empowerment of Peasant and Indigenous Women

Program for Minimum Employment (PEM), 87
Program for Research and Empowerment of Peasant and Indigenous Women (PEMCHI), 256 n. 17
Program on Labor Economics (PET), 248 n. 8
Publishers, 57, 151, 258 n. 33, 258–59 n. 34

Race, 38–39
Raczynski, Dagmar, 250 n. 19
Radrigán, Juan, 260 n. 5
Radway, Janice, 197, 216
Randall, Margaret, 247 n. 34
Rape, 268 n. 31
Reconciliation: 9, 184, 185, 233; and female self-effacement, 203–12; and *House of the Spirits* (Allende), 197–212; "kid glove" reconciliation, 217–18; and memory, 206; and violence, 184
Religion, 63, 107, 207–9, 213, 243 n. 7
Resistance culture, 11, 236 n. 2
"Resistance narratives," 235 n. 2
Rettig Commission, 22, 201, 209, 223, 231. *See also* Committee for Truth and Reconciliation
Revista de crítica cultural, 43
Revolutionary Leftist Movement, 243 n. 3
Rich, Adrienne, 269 n. 46
Richard, Nelly, 43–44, 155–57, 207, 209, 228–29, 259 n. 35, 261 nn. 10 and 15, 262 nn. 18, 25, 26, and 27
Riquelme Rojas, Sonia, 269 n. 44
Rivas, Ramiro, 259 n. 34
Rodríguez, Aniceto, 228
Rojas, Manuel, 260 n. 5
Rojas, Mario, 269 nn. 42 and 43
Rosenfeld, Lotty, 44, 153, 155, 254 n. 5
Rumbo al sur, deseando al norte. *See* *Heading South, Looking North* (Dorfman)

Saa, María Antonieta, 226, 256 n. 16
Sacred Cow (Eltit), 233
Salcedo, José M., 89
Saltpeter industry, 249 n. 9
Santa Cruz, Adriana, 256 n. 16
"Scents of Wood and Silence" (Barros), 132–39, 141, 143

Schild, Verónica, 227
Schneider, Cathy Lisa, 249n. 14, 257n. 22
Schneider, René, 26
Scott, James C., 79
Scraps of Life (Agosín), 86
SECh. *See* Chilean Writers' Society (SECh)
Secretaría Nacional de la Mujer. *See* National Secretariat for Women
Self-directed violence, 155–56, 160–61, 167–69, 175–76, 262n. 15
Self-financed editions, 121
Seneca, 38
SERNAM. *See* National Service for Women (SERNAM)
Serrano, Bruno, 254n. 5
Serrano, Claudia, 250n. 19
Serrano, Marcela, 266n. 13
Serrano, Pilar, 239n. 36
Servicio Nacional de la Mujer (SERNAM). *See* National Service for Women (SERNAM)
Sewing, 96, 105–15
Sexual humiliation, 52
Sexuality: and authoritarianism, 129, 132, 146, 155; body politics, 37–38, 45; and community-building, 106; and erotic desire, 45, 46, 128–47, 183–84, 215; and incest, 151, 169–92; and power, 131; and violence, 130–31, 136–39, 183–84. *See also* Gender
Sexualized slogans, 27–28
Shantytown organizations, 84, 85, 249 n. 14, 250n. 16, 256n. 17. *See also* Working class; Working-class women
Shantytown Women's Movement (MOMUPO), 256n. 17
Sharing the Table, 249n. 9
Sigmund, Paul E., 236–37n. 11
Silva, Coti, 256n. 16
Skármeta, Antonio, 32, 259n. 34
Slang, 158, 171, 180, 182
Smirnow, Gabriel, 237n. 17
Socialism, 25, 123, 195. *See also* Communist Party; Leftists
Social security, 238n. 29
Social Transformation Including Women in Africa. *See* "Stiwanism" (Social Transformation Including Women in Africa)
Sociedad de Escritores Chilenos (SECh). *See* Chilean Writer's Society (SECh)

Socioeconomic class: and disappearance, 50; and feminism, 122, 123; gender issues and, 38–39; and language, 180; and Pinochet regime, 27–28, 52; and politics, 23–34, 54; and Popular Unity, 27. *See also specific classes*
Soñé que la nieve ardía. See *I Dreamt the Snow Was Burning* (Skármeta)
Soup kitchens, 84, 154, 249n. 9
South Africa, 50, 232, 250n. 20
Spain, 265n. 3
Sportorno, Radomiro, 265n. 54
Stevens, Evelyn P., 269n. 46
"Stiwanism" (Social Transformation Including Women in Africa), 37
Straw, Jack, 221, 223–24
"Structural adjustment" packages, 9
Student organizations, 125, 127, 201
Sudacas, 186–91
Suffragists, 124
Suicide, 271n. 53
Summary of the Truth and Reconciliation Commission Report, 243n. 5
Synesthesia, 121, 137, 141, 147, 151

Taller de Investigación Teatral (TIT). *See* Investigative Theater Workshop
Talleres artesanales. *See* Artisan's workshops
Talleres literarios. *See* Literary workshops
Tax: on publications, 121; on theater tickets, 89, 251n. 23. *See also* IVA tax.
Taylor, Diana, 78, 79
Terapia. See *Blake's Therapy* (Dorfman)
Testimonios, 250nn. 18 and 19
Theweleit, Klaus, 32, 60–61, 70
Tierney-Tello, Mary Beth, 155
Time, 62
TIT. *See* Investigative Theater Workshop (TIT)
Todaro, Rosalba, 255–56n. 15
tono menor del deseo, El (Barros), 232
Torture: and body metaphor, 34–35; and economic shock, 83; and National Intelligence Directorate (DINA), 206–9, 242n. 2; and Pinochet regime, 9, 26, 50; and sexual humiliation, 52; of women, 139–43, 202–10. *See also* Violence
"Tower of silence," 25, 85, 92, 146
Town Hall (theater collective), 251n. 26

trabajadores de la muerte, Los (Eltit), 233
Traslaviña, Hugo, 248 n. 8
"Tree, The" (Bombal), 132
Treichler, Paula A., 23
Tres Marías y una Rosa (Benavente and Investigative Theater Workshop): and attendance at, 88, 250 n. 23; and community-based activism, 96–115; and displacement, 93, 97, 118–19; and domestic violence, 98–99, 105–9; and feminine values, 143; and feminism, 110–11; and gender boundaries, 98–99; humor in, 100, 101, 110; and hunger, 45, 82, 96–115; and importance of work, 96–97; and *memorias*, 91–92; and neoliberalism, 102–4; and social justice, 122; women as protagonists in, 87, 88, 117; and women's bodies, 96–99, 107, 110, 113; and working-class women, 96–115, 110, 260 n. 5. See also *Arpilleras*; Hunger; Unemployment
Triángulo Abierto. See Open Triangle
Truth and Reconciliation Commission. See Committee for Truth and Reconciliation

Ulibarri, Luisa, 258 n. 34
última canción de Manuel Sendero, La. See *Last Song of Manuel Sandero* (Dorfman)
última niebla, La. See *House of Mist* (Bombal)
Unemployment, 84, 87, 238 n. 28, 248 n. 8, 250 n. 21, 257 n. 23. See also Labor
Unidad Popular. See Popular Unity coalition
Union of Young Writers, 33
United Nations, 122, 228, 243 n. 3, 255 n. 15
United Nations Decade for Women, 122, 255 n. 15
United States, 265 n. 3
University Cultural Association, 33, 244 n. 9
Upper-class women, and Pinochet regime, 27–28
Uruguay, 240 n. 44, 245 n. 18, 250 n. 20
U.S. Immigration and Naturalization Service, 232

Vaca sagrada. See *Sacred Cow* (Eltit)
Vadell, Jaime, 89
Valdés, Adriana, 259 n. 35

Valdés, Gabriel, 230
Valdés, Teresa, 227, 250 n. 19
Valdivieso, Mercedes, 31, 259 n. 34
Valente, Ignacio, 184, 260 n. 7, 264 nn. 48 and 50
Valenzuela, Loreto, 95
Valenzuela, María Elena, 28, 237 n. 23, 238 n. 29
Venezuela, 228–29
Verdugo, Patricia, 52, 270 n. 49
Vial, Gonzalo, 229–30
Vicariate of Solidarity, 84–85, 91–93, 97, 213, 243 n. 4, 249 nn. 9 and 11
Vicuña, Cecilia, 32, 259 n. 34
Vidal, Hernán, 39–43, 44–45, 51, 91, 217, 270 n. 49, 270–71 n. 52
Video, 155, 158, 166, 167–69, 263 n. 32
vigilantes, Los (Eltit), 233, 260 n. 3
Violence: and *Astride* (Barros), 121, 130, 133, 136–43; and body metaphor, 40; and breast-feeding, 143–45; covert violence, 195; and death, 28, 50, 242 n. 2, 263–64 n. 42; and democracy, 223; denial of, 214–18; domestic violence, 98–99, 105; economic violence, 45, 83–84; effects of, 223; and erotic desire, 45, 116–47, 215–16; and gender, 98–99, 105, 120, 125, 130–31, 136–43, 206–9; and identity negotiation, 208; incest as, 171–72; interpersonal violence, 121; and language, 129–31; of mothers, 143–45; and narrative power, 161; and National Protests and Strikes, 258 n. 29; and neoliberalism, 203; and numbness, 202; pardon for, 22; and reconciliation, 184; and self-definition, 173–75; self-directed violence, 155–56, 160–61, 167–69, 175–76, 262 n. 15; in sexuality, 130–31, 136–39, 183–84; and social structuring, 60; as unacknowledged, 45; and women, 98–99, 105, 120, 125, 130–31, 136–43, 206–9. See also Torture
Visual language, 86–87
Viudas. See *Widows* (Dorfman)
Volunteerism, 256 n. 15
Voting, 124, 194

Wages, 257 n. 23
Warnken, Cristián, 253 n. 53

Wealth, 194
Weinstein, Marisa, 227
Widows (Dorfman): and alliance of feminine values and motherhood, 143; and authoritarianism, 83; and childbirth metaphor, 70–81, 178, 245n. 21; and disappearance, 44–45, 55–60, 116, 143, 212; and displacement, 55–60, 118–19, 245nn. 20 and 21; and female superiority, 211; and gender boundaries, 63–64, 73–74, 98; and motherhood, 77–81, 171; narrative distance of, 100; publication of, 55–56, 117, 245n. 20; and social representation, 54, 122; and solidarity, 77, 183; and storytelling, 110
Williams, Raymond L., 236n. 7, 265n. 52
Winn, Peter, 225–26
Wolff, Egon, 195, 196
Women: and bonding, 106–10, 126; and childbirth metaphor, 70–81; and complicity with military regime, 27–28, 237n. 23; and disappearance narratives, 55–60, 60–70; embodiment of, 46–47; feminine values, 28, 60–70; and gender scripts, 28–30, 45, 46, 65, 134–40, 207, 228, 234; in government cabinet, 226–27; and history, 58; and imprisonment, 53; "invisible" activism of, 50–52; and material human rights, 47; and misogyny, 60, 65, 74, 78, 124–25; Muslim women, 50; and passivity, 215–16; political organization of, 143, 213, 225–26, 255–56n. 15; as "servants to Fatherland," 256; and sexual humiliation, 52; and social representation, 129; and spiritual/moral superiority, 51, 65, 237n. 20, 269–70n. 46; stereotypes of, 88; and torture, 139–42, 202–10; and violence, 98–99, 105, 120, 125, 130–31, 136–43, 206–9; women writers, 52–53, 127, 213, 244n. 15. *See also* Feminism; Gender; Motherhood; Working-class women; *and specific women and women's organizations*
Women for Life, 126, 154, 211
Women of Chile (MUDECHI), 256n. 17
Women's Department of the Coordinadora Nacional Sindical (CNS), 256n. 17
Women's movement. *See* Feminism
Women's Section of Chilean Human Rights Commission, 256n. 17
Working class: and alternative theater, 87–89, 93–94; and feminine values, 29; invisibility of, 145; and magic, 198; and poverty, 257n. 23; and religion, 107; and *Tres Marías y una Rosa*, 96–115; and unemployment, 84
Working-class women: and alternative theater, 87–89, 94; and *arpilleras*, 85–89, 90, 97, 100–106; and democracy, 225; and disappeared bodies, 97–98, 103; and domestic violence, 98–99; and feminism, 256n. 17; and human rights, 10, 29; and neoliberalism, 102–3; philosophical contradictions of, 102–5; and protest movements, 29, 42, 122, 213, 224–25; and social relocation, 84; and unemployment, 84. *See also Tres Marías y una Rosa* (Benavente and Investigative Theater Workshop)
World Bank, 9, 248n. 4
World Conference on Women in Beijing (Fourth), 228, 229
"Writing as an Act of Hope" (Allende), 197, 218

Year of Human Rights in Chile, 270n. 49
Young Writers' Collective, 33

Zerán, Faride, 255n. 11
Zúñiga, Gerardo, 273n. 47
Zurita, Raúl, 44, 78, 152, 153, 246n. 28, 254n. 5, 260n. 7, 262nn. 22 and 25